MW00893902

Beverley Sutherland Smith

the seasonal kitchen

Beverley Sutherland Smith

the seasonal kitchen

Hardie Grant Books

To my children, Joanne, David, Suzanne and Scott,

who share my love for the 'Edible Garden'.

First published in 2001
by Hardie Grant Books
12 Claremont Street
South Yarra, Victoria 3141
www.hardiegrant.com.au

National Library of Australia
Cataloguing-in-Publication Data:

Sutherland Smith, Beverley.
The Seasonal Kitchen.

Includes index.
ISBN 1 876719 90 7

1. Cookery (Vegetables).
2. Vegetable gardening.
3. Herb Gardening. I. Title

643.65

Cover, text design and layout by
Hamish Freeman and Klarissa Pfisterer

Edited by Clare Coney

Printed in China through Phoenix Offset

contents

Sutherland Smith

A few years after we were married we bought a large block covered with small trees, a short distance from the city. We built a house and occasionally ran a lawnmower over the weedy front yard. We noticed gratefully that the dogs chasing each other prevented much grass growing, while children and their friends flattened the rest of the ground.

In all too short a time the children grew up and departed, the animals had become old. Meanwhile the cute little Christmas trees had developed into monsters that spread pine needles over the roof and into spoutings, while their twisted roots hunted relentlessly underground for drains and water pipes. Tall gums randomly dropped branches and the bottle brushes and wattles were diseased and woody.

Suddenly I hated it. I wanted to be surrounded by a beautiful, magical garden filled with colour and full of scent. By the time the tree loppers had removed most of the old trees and cared for those worth keeping there was almost no budget left. Being naive, I thought it would be quite easy to do it all myself. However, trucks of soil had to be moved by hand down to each section, giant rocks rolled into place and, when I needed expertise, people contracted to lay a path or put up a wall. It has been six years since then, but there is no sense that this is a new garden; on the contrary, it is a well-established one.

Being a passionate cook it never occurred to me when I planted the first vegetables for my kitchen that I should keep them tucked out of sight. Little feathery lettuces or tall cos are just as pretty in a border as a small plant, while carrots have interesting tops that, if I didn't pull them, would form big white clumps I could pick and put into a big jug on the table. The early dusk light glancing off the reddish leaves of the ballerina crab apples made everyone stop, and something as common as dill had seedheads that gave beds a soft, golden yellow in late summer.

Across the back I created a 'potager' garden – the term often used to describe an ornamental kitchen garden, although its name is derived from its role in supplying the 'pot herbs' for soup, or *potage*. The central round bed is filled with white and pastel roses surrounded by a tiny box hedge; the same white standard roses have been planted at the end of every vegetable bed, so there is a second circle with paths between. Here vegetables mingle with herbs and edible flowers used for salads, the occasional small blueberry bush or low-growing strawberry, so it has different textures and tones yet is essentially productive. There is an underlying and necessary symmetry from the paths and box borders, contrasting with the slightly untidy air of a garden that is constantly picked rather than just being decorative.

Not all is perfect, because my potager garden receives too much shade from huge trees in a reserve at the back and the possums assume is it their personal larder. Like most gardeners I have great success stories and failures: my cabbages are always wonderful yet I have trouble with brussels sprouts; onions and leeks have been a great disappointment but lettuces grow so easily that I rarely, if ever, buy one. Beetroot in many colours thrives, as does colourful chard. Big bundles of constantly seeding parsley are offered to any friends that call in.

The decorative herbs and flowers provide a purpose, interplanting helps prevent the build-up of pests and diseases, the massed planting keeps down weeds and keeping it healthy means it is almost possible to avoid using chemicals. Flowers such as marigolds, and herbs such as garlic, deters bugs as well as introducing colour and encouraging bees, while birds are attracted by the nectar in the garden and swoop on bothersome insects. I allow some things to run to seed, so perpetuating many vegetables, and these flowers and seeds provide even more food for bees and birds.

I have changed the way I cook by living with the seasons, creating zucchini dishes as the plants scramble to overtake the garden, making tomato pickles, relishes and sauces when the bushes grow too many to eat raw, picking beans like tiny green twigs for summer salads and planting vegetables not available in the shops.

I still cannot decide if vegetables that are grown at home taste so much better than anything you can buy, even at the best markets, because they are different varieties, or because they are just so fresh. They do taste wonderful, sweet and intense; perhaps they don't look as perfect, but I believe that natural flavour is the most important ingredient for anyone who loves food.

author's note and conversion charts

Temperature Conversion Chart

Centigrade (°C)	Fahrenheit (°F)
120	250
150	300
160–170	325
180	350
190	375
200	400
210–220	425
230	450

Weight Conversion Chart (approx.)

Metric	Imperial
15 g	½ oz
30 g	1 oz
60 g	2 oz
90 g	3 oz
125 g	4 oz
150 g	5 oz
180 g	6 oz
200 g	6½ oz
225 g	7 oz
250 g	8 oz
375 g	12 oz
500 g	1 lb
750 g	1½ lb
1 kg	2 lb

Liquid Conversion Chart

Metric	Imperial	US cups
15 ml	½ fl oz	1 tablespoon
30 ml	1 fl oz	2 tablespoons
60 ml	2 fl oz	¼ cup
90 ml	3 fl oz	⅓ cup
125 ml	4 fl oz	½ cup
150 ml	5 fl oz	⅔ cup
175 ml	6 fl oz	¾ cup
250 ml	8 fl oz	1 cup (½ pint)
300 ml	10 fl oz (½ pint)	1¼ cups
375 ml	12 fl oz	1½ cups
500 ml	16 fl oz	2 cups (1 pint)
600 ml	1 pint	2½ cups
1.25 litres	2 pints	1 quart

Standard measures

1 level teaspoon = 5 fl oz	
1 level tablespoon = 15 fl oz	
1 UK pint = 20 fl oz	
but 1 US pint = 16 fl oz	

In the recipes that follow, quantities have been given in both metric and imperial amounts, and temperatures in Centigrade and Fahrenheit. Very often the equivalent weight is not exact, for instance 500 g is not exactly 1 lb, but the recipes will work with these approximate conversions. Ingredients may also not be exactly the same in different countries, although I have given alternative names for ingredients where necessary.

Cream varies widely in fat content and consistency. Where I use the ingredient 'cream' in a recipe I am referring to a pouring cream of about 35% fat content, which can be whipped. If cream of a thicker consistency (double cream) is to be used, this is indicated in the list of ingredients.

Cynara scolymus

artichoke globe

I don't grow globe artichokes although they are very tall, big, bold and attractive, thistle-like plants, which can be a feature in a garden. They can be grown in the vegetable garden or used in flower gardens, where the soft grey of their foliage harmonizes gently with other plants. Most people tend to have a love or hate relationship with globe artichokes. I adore them and order by the plateful if they are in season when I travel in Italy and parts of Europe, where they grow some of the best varieties. It is a joy also to sit down to a plate of artichokes prepared by someone else. Frankly, they are a bother to prepare as we can't buy them already trimmed and peeled, as Italians can, and often I find the final result disappointing for all the work involved. One reason is their freshness; they really must be eaten quickly after picking, and this is the biggest advantage in having a few plants growing in your own garden. Because they are tender and dislike really cold weather and damp spots be careful when you place them.

planting

Not good raised from seed, as they are unreliable. You need to plant rooted offsets or suckers from a good nursery or from a kind friend and allow space, put them in about a metre/yard apart. The soil must be well drained and rich, although too much nitrogen and they won't flower. Site them in full sun. Globe artichokes are perennials; you need to replace after about four years unless the plant is very vigorous. Fertilize in mid season and keep the soil lightly moistened. In a cold area where the ground freezes you have to cut back the plant in winter, cover the stem base with a basket and scatter thickly with mulch, so the temperature won't affect the roots.

planting guide

Temperature Zone	Plant
Tropical	Not suitable
Subtropical	Spring
Temperate	Late winter, once over 13°C at night
Cool	Mid winter to late winter

varieties

- Violet Star
- Violetta – a small artichoke
- Green Globe Improved
- Large Purple and Large Green – big varieties, as the name suggests

diseases and pests

Aphids like them; hose or spray these off if you have a serious infestation. In wet soil the crowns may rot. Any infected plants should be removed instantly and destroyed.

harvesting

Pick early while the bracts are tightly closed and cut away leaving a short piece of stem attached. If you forget to keep an eye on them they will mature and, as they become larger, burst into purple flowers which look very pretty in the garden – but of course you then have a totally inedible artichoke for all your work. The first year they bear lightly, the second crop is much better.

buying and storage

The leaves must be firmly closed, the stem firm and if the leaves are beginning to open don't bother buying them as it indicates they are old. Baby artichokes are a bit harder to select as they can have a slightly more open leaf, yet can still be fresh. The artichokes should be firm to touch, taut and if you pull back a leaf – which will not impress the greengrocer, however – it should make a little squeak of protest. You can keep for a couple of days in a vegetable storage bag but it is preferable to use almost immediately.

nutrition

Globe artichokes have small amounts of protein and carbohydrate and are a good source of folate and other B-complex vitamins.

cooking

Be ruthless with them. You need to trim and trim and have some lemon nearby so you can rub or squeeze some over the cut sections. Pull away the first few leaves from the stalk, then cut off the tough top about a third down. Leave on most of the stalk, this is delicious to eat but makes it a bit more awkward for serving so you can cut these through before you take the artichokes to the table. Next pull away more leaves until they have changed to a pale greeny-yellow colour. Rub with lemon. Drop into boiling water which has some salt and a dash of lemon added and put a plate on top to keep them under the water as they float. Cook approximately 25–30 minutes, depending on size. Test by putting a skewer through the centre, you need to lift up the plate cautiously and then check them. They should be soft, any resistant sections in the centre and you need to cook a bit longer. Drain. The hairy choke is not eaten and you can either remove for your guests by scooping it out or just let them take it out as they are eating the artichoke.

globe artichokes with a tomato dressing

A plain oil and vinegar dressing is very good with cooked artichokes but this tomato and balsamic sauce is even more interesting. The artichokes are cooked first, arranged on plates and the dressing served alongside. It will be a much nicer dish if you serve them warm or at room temperature rather than chilled.

Cook artichokes until tender following instructions for Braised Artichokes, below, then set aside. Put tomatoes into a bowl with all the remaining ingredients. Stir and let it stand for several hours so the juices come out of the tomato. Stir again just before serving beside the artichokes.

Serves 6 as a light first course

6 artichokes, well trimmed

3 small tomatoes, peeled and finely chopped

1 clove garlic, crushed

1 tablespoon balsamic vinegar

6 tablespoons olive oil

1 tablespoon lemon juice

1 teaspoon brown sugar

salt and pepper

globe artichokes go with

breadcrumbs

butter

olive oil

garlic

lemon

onion

Parmesan cheese

ham

fish

pine nuts

artichokes with garlic and lemon crumb topping

There is a good contrast of soft artichokes and scented garlic and lemon topping in this dish. It has quite a different flavour to a casserole of artichoke that has been baked with crumbs on top in the oven. This is lighter and crisper.

Cook artichokes until tender following instructions for Braised Artichokes, below.

Prepare the crumbs by putting into a frying pan with oil. Keep stirring until you have a dry, crisp, golden mixture. If they are too dry and this can happen if you have very dried out crumbs, just add a dash more oil. When ready mix in salt and pepper, garlic, lemon and parsley and transfer to a plate.

Preheat oven to 180°C/350°F. Cook the onion in a small saucepan with extra oil until soft and golden. Scatter over the base of a shallow ovenproof dish about 20 cm/8 in diameter. Cut the artichokes into halves, place into the dish cut side down on top of the onion, brush with oil and bake in oven for about 20 minutes or until hot. Scatter the crumb mixture over and serve, spooning out 3 halves per person with the crumbs scattered on the plate. Some crumbs will fall into the casserole and into the juices but just scoop them up.

Serves 6

9 small artichokes, well trimmed

1 cup/4 oz breadcrumbs, made from stale white bread

1/4 cup/2 fl oz light olive oil

1/2 teaspoon salt and pepper

2 cloves garlic, finely chopped

1/2 teaspoon finely grated lemon zest

2 tablespoons finely chopped parsley

1 large onion, finely chopped

extra 3 tablespoons olive oil

hints

Water will collect in artichokes if they are boiled so drain well and then squeeze gently with some kitchen paper towel in your hand to get rid of the excess.

Aluminium causes globe artichokes to discolour, so cook in stainless steel or enamel.

easy ideas *Braised Artichokes*

Globe artichokes do not lend themselves particularly well to fast cooking but the best way is to stew them cut into smaller pieces. Trim very well, cutting into quarters or even 6 sections and then put into a frying pan with 1/2 cup/4 fl oz water, 1/2 cup/4 fl oz olive oil, plenty of pepper and a couple of cloves of garlic, left in their skin.

Cook over a medium heat, turning them over until they are almost tender. They take approximately 15 minutes. Put a lid on top and let them sit for about 5 minutes, squeeze some lemon over the top, add a little finely chopped parsley and some Parmesan cheese once they are on the plate.

artichoke jerusalem

Helianthus tuberosus

Jerusalem artichokes have absolutely no connection with Jerusalem at all, nor are they really artichokes. How they came by their name is not clear, although a number of stories circulate about them being 'roots with the flavour of artichokes' or that perhaps 'Jerusalem' is a corruption of 'girasole', which is the Italian for sunflower. Jerusalem artichokes are a native American plant and grew wild in North America. Explorers thought they were quite a novelty and took them back to Europe in the seventeenth century, where they became popular. Their flavour is earthy, sweet and a little nutty. They don't have any starch in them, so can be eaten by diabetics and hypoglycaemics. The carbohydrate they contain in the place of starch, inulin, is not broken down by any of the enzymes in our body, and is indigestible, hence the jokes about them.

For some – but not all – people they can therefore cause an embarrassing amount of wind and if you eat too many at one meal you will never need a laxative. Enjoy them occasionally but it is sensible not to eat a huge amount at one sitting.

planting

Just plant a few tubers in spring or autumn – or in frost-free areas any time of the year. Push them down about 15 cm/6 in into the ground and approximately 23 cm/9 in apart. Any patch of ground will do but they die down during winter leaving a barren spot for a short time, so it is best to put them at the back of the garden against a fence. They form big tall clumps and the pretty flowers in summer are like tiny golden sunflowers, which you can use as cut flowers. Jerusalem artichokes respond to heavy feeding.

I was given a couple of tubers many years ago and these have formed the base of my artichoke patch. They are virtually indestructible, growing in a very barren area at the back of the garden, spreading with abandon unless checked every year or so, and as they create too much shade for flowers or other crops if left to run wild you need to keep them in check. Once you have a planting of artichokes, they attach themselves to you for life, as the tiniest pieces left behind after you dig them up will produce new plants.

planting guide

Temperature Zone	Plant
Jerusalem artichokes are best grown in areas with cold winters.	
Tropical	Not suitable
Subtropical	Not suitable
Temperate	Spring
Cool	Spring
First picking	*Late summer*

varieties

I grow the old-fashioned type of artichoke which is quite knobby but I am told you can buy smoother varieties now for planting which make peeling easier and wastage less. Just pick up a few from a greengrocer's when they are in season and plant them. If you have any friends who grow Jerusalem artichokes they are usually delighted to share some tubers.

diseases and pests

Jerusalam artichokes seem to be impervious to any pests or diseases and I have never bothered with companion planting for this reason, although aphids seem to be attracted to them.

harvesting

They should be harvested when the plants have flowered and the dry stalks have begun to die down. By this time they look untidy but you can tie the stems up together in a bundle to keep them from lolling around all over the other plants in the garden.

The tubers keep best of all left in the ground so only dig what you need at one time. Do this carefully so you don't chop through the artichokes with the spade.

nutrition

Jerusalem artichokes have a high potassium content, and they also contain calcium and some B vitamins.

buying and storage

Choose big tubers rather than small so there is not as much wastage when you prepare them. Bought artichokes will be washed and may not keep quite as long as home-grown. Don't buy or use any squishy ones, or those that have become soft. Don't wash tubers from the garden, just shake or brush off any excess dirt and put them in a perforated plastic bag in the refrigerator, where they will keep for about 10 days.

cooking

I always peel Jerusalem artichokes, although some people say it doesn't matter. However, I find the finished dish is not nearly as good in flavour or texture if the skin has been left on. Peeling is easier, of course, if you pick out the least bumpy tubers to prepare. If you have very uneven ones, just slice off the worst bumps first to make it quicker to peel them.

jerusalem artichoke and root vegetable soup

jerusalem artichokes go with

most other root vegetables

butter

cheese

nutmeg

garlic

onions

shallots

tomatoes

chives

parsley

bacon and ham

chicken

rabbit

One of the best ways to enjoy Jerusalem artichokes is in soup, for just a few lend a nutty, sweet flavour. Cooked this way I also find them more digestible. The exact weight of the other root vegetables in the dish is not really important but they should all be about the same proportion; of course, if you would like one to feature more than another in the soup, just choose a larger vegetable. The topping of nuts creates some texture and blends well with the slight sweetness of the root vegetables.

Melt the butter in a large saucepan and let the onion, garlic and celery cook gently until softened. Add the remaining vegetables, cover the pan and let them stew gently for about 15 minutes, giving the pan an occasional shake, then pour in the stock. Cover again and simmer until the vegetables are very soft. Process to taste, either until a purée or for a shorter time to retain a little bit of grainy texture. Return to the saucepan and add a bit more stock if the texture is too thick, checking the seasoning. Stir in the cream, parsley and nuts and reheat.

Serves about 6

45 g/1 ½ oz butter

1 onion, finely chopped

2 cloves garlic, finely chopped

1 stalk celery, thinly sliced

250 g/8 oz peeled Jerusalem artichokes

1 medium-sized potato

1 medium-sized carrot

1 medium-sized sweet potato

3 cups/1 ½ pints light chicken stock

salt and pepper

½ cup/4 fl oz cream

some finely chopped parsley

¼ cup/1 oz finely chopped toasted almonds or hazelnuts

sautéed jerusalem artichokes

hint

As artichokes discolour quickly once peeled, drop them into water that has had a little lemon juice or vinegar added if you are not using them immediately.

This is an excellent method for cooking Jerusalem artichokes as it emphasizes their wonderful flavour. Their insides will be creamy while the outsides form a golden crust. It is much easier to make this dish if you have a non-stick pan.

Peel the artichokes, trimming large pieces so that they are as close as possible to the size of the smaller ones. Heat the butter and oil together in a non-stick pan until sizzling and add the artichokes. Partially cover pan with a lid but just tilt it a little so some steam can escape. Cook for about 10 minutes, turning artichokes over once. Then remove the lid and let them cook until they are soft, for about 15 minutes, turning them every so often to ensure they get a good crust on all sides – this is a bit tedious but well worth it. Should any squash up don't be concerned, as they will still taste delicious. When they are tender scatter on salt and pepper and serve.

Serves 4–6

about 1 kg/2 lb Jerusalem artichokes

60 g/2 oz butter

3 tablespoons olive oil

salt and pepper

easy ideas *Jerusalem Artichokes in Stock*

Peel about 500 g/1 lb artichokes and cut into even pieces. Cover with vegetable or chicken stock and simmer very gently for about 30 minutes, until tender. There should not be much liquid left, if there is just boil rapidly to cook most away. Add plenty of black pepper and a squeeze of lemon juice.

purée of potato and jerusalem artichoke

The Jerusalem artichoke adds interest to potato and lessens the strength of the artichoke for those who may prefer a lighter flavour. Use this purée as a side vegetable with any meat. I have had great success with it as a topping for a shepherd's pie, which I make not only out of minced beef but occasionally with minced duck or chicken.

Boil the potato and artichokes separately in salted water until soft. Drain both and purée together in a food processor with butter, salt and pepper – the artichoke prevents the potato becoming 'gluey', as it would do if put into a food processor on its own. Transfer to a bowl. Heat the cream and add to the purée, stirring or whisking as you go, and then mix in a little milk as needed (it is best to warm the milk first if more than ¼ cup/2 fl oz is added). You should finish up with a light, fluffy, creamy-coloured purée with a nutty, sweet taste. This can be reheated later by warming in a microwave or putting it into a basin over a pan of hot water.

Serves 4

500 g/1 lb potatoes
500 g/1 lb Jerusalem artichokes, peeled
45 g/1½ oz butter
salt and pepper
¼ cup/2 fl oz cream plus a little milk if needed

easy ideas

Jerusalem Artichoke Chips

These are great deep-fried but to cook successfully you need large pieces, so instead of traditional wedges cut them into wide circles or chunks. Don't cut them too thinly or you will have too much crisp skin and not enough soft, sweet flesh. Deep fry in oil in the same way you would make chips or fries, then drain on kitchen paper towel and season with some salt and pepper.

jerusalem artichokes with chicken

The artichokes are a sweet and interesting substitute for potato. I am not a fan of chicken breast in dishes like this as it tends to become dry, particularly if cooked in advance and reheated. Leg portions are far better. The recipe can also be made with rabbit.

Cook the bacon with onion, garlic, carrot and oil in a large, wide saucepan until the vegetables are tinged with gold and wilted. Remove to a plate. Add the butter and brown the chicken on all sides. Remove. Add the wine and stir to get up all the brown bits in the dish, then return the vegetables and chicken and pour on stock, tucking the sprig of thyme into the pan. Check seasoning and cover the pan, cook gently for about 25 minutes until the chicken is partly tender. Add the artichokes and continue cooking until both chicken and artichokes are very tender. Knead butter and flour together to a paste, then add small bits this to the pan, shaking the pan or stirring carefully to dissolve the paste until the liquid gradually thickens to a glossy sauce around the vegetables and chicken. Scatter on lots of parsley and thyme just before serving – the heat of the sauce will bring out the flavour of the herbs.

Serves 4–6

2 rashers bacon, cut into strips
1 large onion, finely chopped
4 cloves garlic, finely chopped
1 small carrot, finely chopped
2 tablespoons oil
45 g/1½ oz butter
6 chicken portions, preferably on the bone
1 cup/8 fl oz dry white wine
1 cup/8 fl oz chicken stock
sprig of thyme
salt and pepper
750 g/1½ lb Jerusalem artichokes, peeled and cut into similar-sized pieces
45 g/1½ oz soft butter
1½ tablespoons plain/all-purpose flour
3–4 tablespoons finely chopped parsley
1 tablespoon finely chopped thyme leaves

pickled jerusalem artichokes

hint

Simmer unpeeled Jerusalem artichokes for 5 minutes so the outside only is cooked and drain. Then you can peel away the skin easily and you will have less wastage. Continue cooking in whatever way you want for the recipe.

These stay quite crisp, rather like water chestnuts, and can accompany any meat in the same way you would use a relish or another pickle. There is little artichoke taste in the finished pickle and its attraction is due more to the interesting texture rather than flavour. It is a most attractive pickle in appearance. The turmeric gives a golden tinge to the slices of artichoke and the red and green peppers provide touches of bright colour. You can open the jar after about 4 days although it does mellow if kept longer and it will keep 12 months in a cool cupboard. You need a lot of liquid when making the pickle but, when I serve it, I usually drain some away.

This recipe makes a generous quantity but if you grow Jerusalem artichokes you will have vast quantities of them as they multiply so fast.

Peel the artichokes and cut into thin slices. If there is a great deal of wastage you will need to start with more than 1 kg/2 lb, as it is difficult to be exact with this vegetable. Put the slices into a bowl. Add water to just cover the artichokes, measuring liquid as you go. For every cup/8 fl oz water, add 1 tablespoon kitchen salt. Put a plate on top to keep them under the liquid. Leave the artichokes in this brine for 24 hours at room temperature.

Next day drain well and rinse with fresh cold water. Put the artichoke slices into a saucepan with red and green capsicum/bell pepper, onion and add the 1 cup/8 fl oz water, white wine vinegar, cider vinegar, sugar, celery seeds, turmeric, mustard seeds and chilli. Bring slowly to the boil, stirring, and cook for about 5 minutes. Remove from heat and bottle in hot, dry, sterilized jars.

Makes about 7 x 250 ml/8 fl oz jars

1 kg/2 lb Jerusalem artichokes salt

1 large red capsicum/ bell pepper, finely diced

1 large green capsicum/ bell pepper, finely diced

2 medium-sized white onions, finely diced

1 cup/8 fl oz water

1 cup/8 fl oz white wine vinegar

3 cups/1½ pints cider vinegar

2½ cups/1¼ lb sugar

1 teaspoon celery seeds

2 teaspoons ground turmeric

1 tablespoon mustard seeds

1 hot chilli, finely chopped (or some dried chillies)

easy ideas *Baked Jerusalem Artichokes with Herbs*

Peel 1 kg/2 lb of good-sized artichokes; cut into approximately the same size so they will be cooked at the same time. Line a baking tin with non-stick baking paper/parchment. Roll artichoke pieces in oil and bake in a moderate oven (180°C/350°F) for about 35 minutes or until tender and caramelised on the outside. Meanwhile, have some finely chopped parsley ready mixed with pepper, salt and 2 teaspoons lemon juice, toss this with the artichokes and serve immediately, while still crisp, with any roasted meat. Especially delicious with lamb or chicken.

Brassica sp.
Amaranthus sp.
Chrysanthemum sp.

asian greens

This chapter covers many of the greens that are grown in Asia. They often have names that are not familiar but don't be put off by this, for most can be just stir-fried — or used in some cases in salads. Even in China, where these greens are a major part of the diet, familiar names can vary from one area to another. Outside China many Asian greens are often referred to as 'cabbages', although many are not actually members of the cabbage family. As most Asian greens grow more easily when sown directly in the vegetable bed than if transplanted as seedlings — which they do not take kindly to — it is best to hunt around for packets of seeds. I find there is only a fairly small range of Asian greens sold for the home gardener compared to other vegetables, but no doubt this will improve as time goes by.

In my experience, many of these bolt quickly in hot weather so plant during a cooler period with enough time for them to grow before a really hot summer.

These are the kinds of greens that have been grown for centuries: bright, tender-leafed vegetables which form the basis of many Asian diets and which go so well with flavourings of sweet and sour, gentle and sharp, spicy and fragrant.

Chinese white cabbage
bok choy (also pak choy, baak choy)
Brassica chinensis

Bok choy has been grown in China since the fifth century AD and the name simply means 'white vegetable'. There are several basic kinds: bok choy has white stems while pak choy (Shanghai bok choy) stems are slightly green and Canton bok choy is squat and small – baby bok choy, really. Bok choy and its relatives can be identified by the stem colour and the leaf, which is always broad and green. When tiny they are very sweet and tender. Whether you buy a large bunch or tiny one depends on usage.

Chinese cabbage
siu choy, shao cai, huang ya bai
Brassica pekinensis

Chinese cabbage has many Asian names, and to make it even more confusing shops tend to sell it under the name of Peking cabbage. It is shaped like a barrel and has a lovely pale-green, slightly ruffled leaf. It may have an elongated shape or can be squat.

Flowering cabbage
choy sum
Brassica chinensis var. *parachinensis*

This can be recognized by the small grooves on its green stem and

characteristic tiny yellow flowers, which emerge above the leaves. The stems are the best part, but the leaves are eaten too.

Flat cabbage
tatsoi
Brassica chinensis var. *rosularis*

Flat cabbage is like a flat plate. It is a cousin of bok choy, it is often called rosette bok choy. The leaves are quite dark and it grows very close to the ground, with white stems. It makes a very good salad when tiny or can be cooked. Tatsoi is also available in some nurseries as part of a punnet of mixed seedlings sold as 'Asian lettuce'.

Oil seed rape
yau choy
Brassica rapa var. *chinensis*

This plant is best known for the seed, from which rape seed oil is extracted, but both leaves and stalks are edible and the tiny central flowering stalk is especially succulent. It is sweeter than broccoli rape and has a leaf which appears glazed.

Chinese broccoli
gai larn, gai lum
Brassica oleracea var. *alboglabra*

Also known as Chinese kale, Chinese broccoli was possibly introduced to China by the Portuguese as it is similar to the Portuguese cabbage and has small white buds and flowers with a blue–green leaf and light broccoli flavour. You do eat the flowers but, unlike regular broccoli, the stalks and leaves are more important.

Mizuna
siu cai
Brassica rapa var. *nipponinicais*

Mizuna is quite easily recognized by its feathery look and rough-edged leaves. Its flavour is similar to rocket, often known as arugula. It is juicy with small,

thin white stalks. Mizuna may appear in shops in a mix of greens for lettuce. The smaller and lighter its colour, the better will be its texture. Larger leaves are best cooked.

Mustard cabbage
dai gai choy
Brassica juncea

This is often known as large-leafed mustard green and looks like a large, loose-headed green cabbage. As indicated by the name, the flavour is sharp and reminiscent of mustard. Close to this in taste is Bamboo Mustard Cabbage (chuk gai choy), which is very loose-leafed – this one needs blanching first to be successful in a stir-fry.

Amaranth
en choy
Amaranthus gangeticus

Amaranth, a Chinese spinach, comes in a plain green variety and a very beautiful variegated red one which looks quite spectacular as a garnish. It is sold in bunches with the roots attached but you discard this root and the lower part of the stem. Both stems and leaves are used for cooking. Amaranth has more body than spinach and a slightly rougher texture. Look for plants with many leaves on their stalks as these usually have the sweetest flavour.

Garland chrysanthemum
tun ho, shingiku
Chrysanthemum coronarium

This is one of the most popular vegetables in Japan. It looks very similar to the leaf of the usual garden chrysanthemum but is paler and more delicate in colour. It could be tucked anywhere into the garden and should be picked young, before flowerbuds form, or the leaves will taste bitter.

If by accident it should flower you can just pick these, as they are very pretty in a vase indoors! Use the young leaves as a decoration or in soups, stir-fries or dipped into tempura batter then deep-fried. Very tiny leaves can be added to a salad.

planting

Asian greens almost all have similar needs in the garden. They love moist fertile soil and require plenty of water but can bolt to seed in hot weather so it is best to sow the seeds in autumn then make a later sowing after the worst of the summer heat. These can be put anywhere you have a space – in the front of other vegetables or in beds where you have removed summer annuals. I find it best to plant them where they will grow; moving tiny seedlings often causes them to go to seed quickly. You can thin them out if you have too many too close together. If they do go to seed then of course you should allow one set of seedpods to ripen. Leave them to dry slightly and pick so you have a good batch to plant again. They will all self-seed quite well.

- Chinese white cabbage takes about 6–8 weeks to reach a picking stage from seed.
- Chinese cabbage takes about 4–5 months.
- Flat cabbage takes about 4 weeks.
- Oil seed rape takes about 45 days.
- Chinese broccoli takes about 3 months.
- Mizuna takes only 2–3 weeks.
- Mustard cabbage takes about 4 months.
- Amaranth takes about 6 weeks.

varieties

As listed above. Just look through seed catalogues or in nurseries for the names of type of greens you want to plant.

diseases and pests

Aphids and cabbage worms will attack some Asian greens, especially the cabbages. Black rot, yellow virus or clubroot will also infect them in the garden; to prevent this be careful not to handle plants when they are wet. If any look sick pull out immediately and don't put into the compost. The best defence against disease is to keep the soil and garden healthy.

harvesting

The best time to harvest for most of these vegetables is when they are small and young, for the leaves will be tender and the stalks the same. The exceptions to this is the larger Chinese cabbage and those where you eat the flower, such as the flowering cabbage.

buying and storage

One of the problems with buying Asian greens is that they are not always labelled, so it can be a lucky dip if you do not recognize them. All greens should look bright, healthy, sparkling. The head of a Chinese cabbage should be firm when squeezed and feel comparatively heavy for its size.

Use all Asian greens as fresh as you can. Wash well, wrap in some paper or put into a vegetable bag and keep in the crisper, but don't keep longer than a day or two at the most.

nutrition

All Asian greens are an excellent source of Vitamin C and most have plenty of Vitamin A. The deeper the green, the higher the levels of antioxidant in that vegetable. All supply folate and are highly nutritious.

cooking

Most recipes stipulate the method for each particular green but you should be sure to wash them all very well first. In general they are sliced or chopped but baby leaves can be used in salads – just taste and learn by their texture which ones would appeal to your palate raw. I find most can be put into salads provided the leaves are baby ones, others can be blanched or steamed and then mixed with a dressing and served as a cold salad for a change. And, of course, most are ideal to stir fry.

stir-fried choy sum

Choy sum, flowering cabbage, is one of the most delicious of Chinese vegetables. It is bright green, resembling Chinese broccoli, but has small yellow, budlike flowers. When cooked it is very sweet. This method of stir-frying can be used to cook other types of Asian greens and I give it here as a basic method: to lend more flavour you can add a dash of soy sauce, oyster sauce or a little sweet chilli sauce.

Wash the choy sum and break off tender top portions, about 10 cm/4 in long. Set aside any large leaves and big flowers (these can be used in other dishes, such as soup, but not in a stir fry as they are not tender enough). In a large pot place the ginger, water and bicarbonate of soda/baking soda, and bring to a boil. Add the choy sum and blanch for 1–2 minutes or until bright green. Tip into a colander and run cold water over it for a minute. Leave to drain. It must be thoroughly drained before stir frying, so allow to sit for 1–1½ hours. Just before serving heat a wok over high heat. Add peanut oil and spread it with a spatula to coat the wok. Add salt and stir. When white smoke appears, add choy sum. Stir fry for 2–3 minutes or until hot and cooked crisp but tender. Place in a dish and serve immediately.

Serves 4

2 bunches choy sum

1 slice fresh ginger, about 1 cm/½ in thick

2 litres/4 pints cold water

½ teaspoon bicarbonate of soda/baking soda

2½ tablespoons peanut oil

¼ teaspoon salt

bok choy and vegetable soup

A soup based on baby bok choy and vegetables which is thick and chunky enough to be a meal. You could of course also add some fine cooked noodles. Ground cashew nuts are added for flavour and for texture at the finish. Alternatives to bok choy are either trimmed Chinese broccoli or a big bunch of watercress.

Wash the bok choy and roughly cut it across into pieces, including the stalks. Put the onion, garlic, ginger, pumpkin, potato, water or stock, salt and sugar into a saucepan and bring to a boil. Leave to cook, covered, for about 10 minutes or until the vegetables are partly tender. Add the bok choy and cook a further 10–15 minutes or until everything is quite tender. Stir in the tomatoes and continue cooking for a couple more minutes. The tomatoes should be soft but don't need to cook through the soup. While the soup is cooking, grind the nuts in a food processor or blender. Heat the oil and fry the nuts, stirring occasionally, until they are pale gold. Add to the soup last, stirring through, and taste for seasonings.

Variation
Instead of cashew nuts, a few drops of dark sesame oil can be added to each soup bowl when serving, to give a similar nutty flavour.

Serves 4

1 bunch bok choy

1 onion, finely chopped

2 cloves garlic, finely chopped

1 piece ginger, about 2 cm/1 in, peeled and shredded

250 g/8 oz pumpkin, peeled, seeded and cut into small pieces

125 g/4 oz potato, peeled and cut into small pieces

1½ litres/3 pints water or vegetable stock

1 teaspoon salt

1 teaspoon sugar

2 tomatoes, peeled and diced finely

30 g/1 oz cashew nuts (optional)

1 tablespoon oil

asian greens go with

capsicum/ bell peppers

garlic

mushrooms

onions

shallots

spring onions/ scallions

chilli

ginger

lemon grass

lime

black bean sauce

cooking sake

fish sauce

mirin

oyster sauce

satay sauce

soy sauce

chicken

fish

shellfish

oil

sesame oil

nuts

tofu

asian greens cooked in tomato sauce

easy ideas

*Salad of Baby
Asian Greens*

Mix 250 g/8 oz
leaves of baby
Asian greens
(one or more
kinds from bok
choy, tatsoi,
mizuna – the
stalks can be
used in a stir
fry or soup).
Stir together
1/3 cup/3 fl oz
light olive oil and
1 tablespoon
each of light
soy sauce,
lemon juice
and rice wine
vinegar, then add
2 teaspoons
brown sugar.
Season dressing
lightly with salt,
more generously
with pepper.
Toss through
the greens
and top with
toasted chopped
macadamia nuts.
A good base
for prawns,
poultry or fish.

Not so much a dish of Asian flavours as one that combines these greens in a fresh tomato sauce. I serve this with chicken dishes, grilled meat or occasionally with noodles for a quick and easy meal.

Cook the tomatoes with salt, pepper and sugar for about 10 minutes or until you have a nice thick juicy sauce.

Rinse the greens and cut away the stalks. Slice these into small pieces and keep them separate as they take longer to cook than the leaves. If leaves are very large chop these also, but smaller leaves are used whole.

Heat the oil in a large frying pan or wok, add onion segments and fry, stirring, for a few minutes then add garlic and stir fry for about 30 seconds. Tip in the cooked tomato pulp with the water and add the stems of the greens first; toss or stir them gently in the tomato mixture for about 3–5 minutes or until almost soft. Add the leaves and cook until they are softened. If the liquid is cooking away too quickly before the greens are tender just add a bit more water, trickling a little down the sides of the frying pan or wok. Scatter pine nuts on top before serving.

Serves 4

500 g/1 lb ripe tomatoes,
peeled and roughly chopped

salt and pepper

1 teaspoon sugar

500 g/1 lb greens, such as Chinese broccoli, bok choy, spinach, etc.

2 tablespoons oil

2 medium-sized onions,
peeled and cut into segments

3 cloves garlic, crushed

1/2 cup/4 fl oz hot water

4 tablespoons pine nuts,
cooked until golden in some oil

stir-fried and simmered greens

This is a great basic way of cooking Asian greens as it combines a stir-fry method with adding stock so even very firm stalks will become tender. You could use any green you like in this recipe – just judge the tenderness by tasting. You will have lots of liquid and can spoon this, along with the greens, over some rice or, as a variation, use double the stock, add a handful of fresh egg noodles to the dish and you have a quick, nourishing soup.

For convenience a carton of packaged stock can be used, but as this is highly seasoned you should then use a low-salt soy in the recipe or you will end up with an over-salty dish.

Heat the oil in a wok or big saucepan and fry the garlic, ginger and onion for a few minutes, stirring so they don't darken too much. Add the greens, stalks first if they are big; toss and fry for a few minutes, then add the leaves and stock. Simmer gently for about 4 minutes or until tender. Mix soy sauce with sweet chilli sauce, add to the dish and serve.

Serves 3–4

2 tablespoons oil

2 cloves garlic, finely chopped

1 tablespoon finely
chopped ginger

1 small onion, finely chopped

1 bunch Asian greens, chopped

1 cup/8 fl oz chicken
or vegetable stock

1 tablespoon soy sauce

1 tablespoon sweet chilli sauce

chicken cakes with asian greens

In the same way that grated carrot or potato can be used to make meat patties light and moist, Asian greens can be used. They give a speckled green appearance to these chicken patties, while the stalks of the Asian greens add texture and the peanuts a rich nutty flavour. Serve them with some rice or just plain with a bowl of interesting shreds of stir-fried vegetables. They are nice cold as a picnic dish and you can take along a sauce for dipping, such as a sweet chilli sauce.

Heat 2 tablespoons oil in a saucepan and fry onion, carrot and garlic until beginning to soften, then reduce heat, cover and cook until soft. Season with ginger and salt, put in the Asian greens and the chopped stalks, cook stirring for 1 minute, remove the pan from heat but continue to stir the greens in the hot pan or wok until they have wilted. Remove all the vegetables to a bowl and let them cool. Add sweet chilli sauce and stir well.

Process the peanuts until a finely minced texture; add these to vegetables with breadcrumbs and minced chicken. Stir in cream, mixing very well with your hands, add eggs and mix again until all holds together well. At this point you can leave the mixture, chilled in the refrigerator, for up to 8 hours.

To cook, using damp hands so the mixture won't stick form into rounds and then flatten to form patties. Dip the patties into a little cornflour/cornstarch so they have a light coating. Fry gently in oil until golden on one side, turn over and cook again – they must be cooked through to the centre, so check with a fine skewer that the juices are clear as they run out. However, be careful not to overcook these or the cakes can be dry. Depending on their thickness, they should take about 3 minutes the first side, 2 minutes the second side.

Serves 4

2 tablespoons oil

1 onion, finely chopped

1 carrot, finely chopped

2 cloves garlic, finely chopped

1 tablespoon grated ginger

1 teaspoon salt

2 cups/8 oz finely chopped leaves of Asian greens, such as bok choy, broccoli, cabbage, etc.

1/2 cup/2 oz very finely chopped stalks of Asian greens

1 tablespoon sweet chilli sauce

1/4 cup/1 oz dry roasted peanuts

1/2 cup/2 oz breadcrumbs, made from stale bread

500 g/1 lb finely minced chicken

1/4 cup cream

2 eggs, lightly beaten

cornflour/cornstarch

extra oil

easy ideas

Nutty Greens

Cook a large, finely sliced onion in oil in a wok or large frying pan until softened. Add a clove of chopped garlic and a chopped bunch (about 250 g/ 8 oz) of Asian greens such as baby bok choy, Chinese broccoli or tatsoi. Stir fry for a few minutes, season with salt and pepper. Tip 1/4 cup/ 2 fl oz water around the sides of the pan and cover with lid. Cook a couple of minutes until tender but still crisp. Toss with 2 teaspoons sesame oil and scatter some toasted sesame seeds on each serving.

easy ideas *Marinated Carrot on Wilted Asian Greens*

Coarsely grated or cut 1 large carrot into very fine matchstick shreds and marinate in 1/4 cup/2 fl oz rice vinegar, 1/4 cup/2 oz sugar, 1 teaspoon salt and 1/2 teaspoon lemon rind for about 30 minutes. Chop about 250 g/8 oz Asian greens – you can use stalks and leaves of bok choy, Chinese broccoli, mizuna, tatsoi, etc. – and then blanch. When just tender and bright green drain well and cool. Mix 2 tablespoons oil with 2 tablespoons of the marinade liquid from the carrots and toss into greens. Serve topped with drained carrot shreds and some toasted sesame seeds.

fish mousse in bok choy leaves

easy ideas

Ginger Juice

Grate very fresh ginger finely into a bowl. The amount needed depends on the freshness of the ginger. Squeeze pulp with your hand until a milky liquid appears: this is strongly flavoured pure ginger juice. Discard the fibrous pulp. Juice can be stored for 24 hours, refrigerated. Use in dressings, sauces, marinades or any dishes that would be improved by pure ginger flavour without any fibrous texture.

We think of spinach as a wrapping for fillings but bok choy (Chinese cabbage) leaves are another option: pale in colour, soft and sweet, they make a very good wrapping leaf. Obviously you don't want to use ones which are too tiny or there will be a problem when you try to fill them. It does take a while to roll and prepare the leaves but you can do it hours in advance and keep them refrigerated until you are ready to cook.

Rinse the bok choy leaves well and cut out the stem. Slice stems into fine sticks, for the base of the casserole. Cook bok choy leaves in boiling water for 4 minutes or until limp. Drain and spread them out on some kitchen paper towel.

Process the fish, prawns, spring onion, ginger, lemon rind and juice, and soy sauce with salt and pepper, until smooth. Add the egg whites and mix again. Chill for 20 minutes so the mixture will be easy to handle.

Preheat oven to 180°C/350°F. Put a bok choy leaf onto a bench. Put a spoonful of the mousse onto the leaf and fold over like a package; repeat until they are all filled. Put the stems into a shallow ovenproof casserole. Season them with salt, pepper and a little squeeze of lemon juice.

Put the filled leaves on top, seam side down, and dot with a little unsalted butter – you can have several layers of parcels on top of each other. Cover very tightly with foil or tight-fitting lid so it is sealed. Bake for about 15–20 minutes or until the fish filling is cooked. To serve, spread a thin layer of ginger sauce (see next recipe) on a plate, then arrange the parcels on top.

Serves 6

about 30 bok choy leaves

250 g/8 oz fresh white, boneless fish

500 g/1 lb raw shelled prawns

2 tablespoons finely chopped spring onion/scallion

2 teaspoons grated fresh ginger

½ teaspoon grated lemon rind

1 tablespoon lemon juice

1 teaspoon soy sauce

½ teaspoon salt and some black pepper

2 egg whites

extra salt, pepper and a squeeze of lemon juice

unsalted butter

ginger sauce

Heat the stock with all the ingredients except cornflour/cornstarch and cook for 1 minute. Add the cornflour and mix again, heating until lightly thickened.

Makes about 1 cup/8 fl oz

1 cup/8 fl oz chicken stock

1 tablespoon thinly sliced ginger

1 small clove garlic, finely chopped

1 small chilli, finely shredded (optional)

2 tablespoons brown sugar

2 tablespoons white vinegar

1 tablespoon soy sauce

2 teaspoons cornflour/cornstarch mixed with a little cold water

peking cabbage in mustard sauce

easy ideas

*Chinese Cabbage
with Mixed Greens*

Chop half a
Chinese cabbage
into bite-sized
pieces and trim
strings from
125 g/4 oz snow
or sugar peas
(mange tout).
Chop a bunch
of spring onion
roughly into
chunky strips. Fry
the cabbage in a
little oil in a wok
or large frying
pan, when hot
add peas and
spring onion and
stir fry a few
minutes until
wilted. Season
with salt and
pepper and add
a few spoonfuls
of water if the
pan becomes dry.
When ready, mix
1 tablespoon
light soy sauce
with 1 table-
spoon ginger
juice (see page
16) and 1 tea-
spoon sugar and
mix this through
greens. Serve
dish on its
own or with
pork, lamb or
chicken dishes.

I love to eat this as a hot dish but it is also excellent cold, in which case the mustard sauce can be even hotter, or you could add a pinch of cayenne or chilli powder. Cold, it makes a lovely accompaniment to a big bowl of barbecued spicy sausages, or as a bed for a hamburger that has been flavoured with some soy, garlic and ginger.

To make mustard sauce, mix all ingredients together.

Cut the cabbage into strips about 2 cm/1 in wide. Heat the oil in a wok with the garlic and then remove clove. Add the cabbage and stir fry quickly. Scatter with salt and chilli powder, then add water around the sides of the pan. Cover and cook for 2 minutes, or until just tender. Remove the lid (if there is a lot of liquid reduce it quickly) and toss the mustard sauce with the cabbage. Add cornflour/cornstarch mixture and stir until dish has lightly thickened.

Serve immediately or spoon onto a platter, cover with foil and let it cool, then eat as a salad.

Serves 3–4

1 small Peking cabbage or
½ large one

2 tablespoons oil

1 clove garlic, peeled
and left whole

salt

pinch of chilli powder

½ cup/4 fl oz water

2 teaspoons cornflour/
cornstarch mixed with
1 tablespoon cold water

Mustard Sauce

1 tablespoon hot
English-style mustard

1 tablespoon soy sauce

some ground black pepper

2 teaspoons sugar

1 tablespoon rice wine vinegar

⅓ cup/3 fl oz water

vegetarian pasta goreng

Although the ingredients mention using the stalk of bok choy, the stalk of any tender Asian green can be added to this vegetarian dish.

Cook the pasta in boiling water until almost tender. Drain, then let cool and mix through a little vegetable oil so that it will not stick together.

Heat a wok or a large frying pan until very, very hot. (If you think the heat on your stove is not strong enough, divide the mixture and cook in two portions as dish must fry, not stew.) Add oil and fry the onions, stirring for a minute, add bok choy and cook until wilted. Add pasta, bean shoots, soy sauce, tomato sauce and chilli sauce and fry, stirring, for a couple of minutes or until heated through. Finally, add tomatoes and stir quickly through until just warm.

Remove from the heat and serve on warm platters. Garnish with shredded lettuce, if you wish, or some coriander/cilantro sprigs.

Serves 4

250 g/8 oz small pasta

½ cup/4 fl oz peanut oil

1 onion, peeled and sliced

6 small bok choy or 3 large,
washed and cut into
5 cm/2 in pieces

125 g/4 oz bean shoots

4 tablespoons light soy sauce

½ cup/4 fl oz fresh tomato sauce

1–2 tablespoons sweet
chilli sauce, to taste

2 tomatoes, peeled and
finely chopped

minced chicken and asian green soup

Fragrant with lemon grass and hot with chilli, this soup has everything delicious and yet nourishing you need in one bowl to make a meal for lunch or a light dinner. It is more interesting if you use two different kinds of Asian greens, perhaps a bunch of baby bok choy and some mustard cabbage, or Chinese broccoli and Chinese spinach (amaranth).

Heat a large saucepan and fry the lemon grass, chilli, onion and garlic until aromatic. Add the capsicum/bell pepper and toss for a minute, then add chicken. Stir so you break up the minced chicken into tiny little pieces or it will form large lumps. Mix through the stalks of the Asian greens and leave to cook on low heat, covered, for a couple of minutes in the juices from the chicken. Mix in the leaves of the Asian vegetables, add stock and cook, covered, for 5 minutes. Add the noodles and cook until they are tender – which should only be another couple of minutes. Stir in lemon juice and serve.

Serves 4–6

2 tablespoons finely chopped lemon grass

I chilli, finely chopped

I small onion, finely chopped

2 cloves garlic, finely chopped

I red capsicum/bell pepper, finely chopped or cut into strips

500 g/1 lb minced chicken

2 bunches Asian greens, stalks cut into small pieces, leaves kept separate

1½ litres/3 pints chicken or vegetable stock

90 g/3 oz egg noodles

2 tablespoons lemon juice

bok choy with mushroom sauce

Whole baby bok choy are coated with a light, fragrant mushroom sauce, which has some chilli to spice it up. You can use a variety of mushrooms; for example, oyster mushrooms will lend a richer Asian flavour than plain cultivated mushrooms. I like this just with a bowl of steamed rice but it does team well with fish or chicken dishes – if they are rather plainly cooked. I am not so keen on the dish made using large bok choy. If, however, this is the only kind you can buy, cut it lengthwise into halves – or even into big sections crosswise – after cooking, before reheating in the sauce.

Heat a large pot of water, with garlic, ginger and salt added, until boiling. Add the bok choy and cook about 4 minutes, or until tender. Drain well. Put on a plate with another plate on top to keep it warm while making the sauce.

For sauce, heat the oil in a wok or frying pan and cook the onion, garlic and ginger until aromatic, add chilli and mushrooms and fry quickly, tossing in the pan. Pour in the stock, soy sauce and sugar and leave this to simmer for about 5 minutes. Mix the cornflour with water to a paste and add to the pan. Stir until it has thickened.

Carefully slide the bok choy one at a time on to the side of the pan and push each one across so they sit in the sauce. Spoon a bit of sauce over the top of each and cook just a minute or two longer until they have heated through again.

Serves 4

8 baby bok choy

3 cloves garlic, halved

3 slices fresh ginger

I teaspoon salt

Mushroom Sauce

2 tablespoons oil

I onion, finely chopped

I clove garlic, finely chopped

I tablespoon shredded ginger

I small chilli, deseeded and finely chopped

250 g/8 oz thinly sliced fresh shiitake mushrooms

I cup/8 fl oz chicken or vegetable stock

I tablespoon soy sauce

I teaspoon sugar

I tablespoon cornflour/cornstarch mixed with ¼ cup/2 fl oz cold water

hints

Sesame Oil

Toasted sesame oil is extracted from toasted sesame seeds. It is strong, pungent and dark in colour and should be used sparingly. Japanese brands are especially consistent in quality.

Hoi Sin Sauce

Once opened hoi sin sauce is best kept refrigerated.

Ginger

Ginger should feel heavy and firm, smooth and glossy. Shrivelled ginger is lighter and woody and can have an acrid taste, especially if used as an ingredient in a marinade.

Soy Sauce

Soy sauces vary from dark and thick to light and thin. Dark soy is usually less salty but gives a very deep colour to a dish. Light soy is more commonly used, it is paler in colour, clear and salty.

asparagus

Asparagus officinalis

The first crop of asparagus is one of the most important signs of spring, along with fragile blossoms and baby-new, pale green leaves softly curling forth from the branches. Asparagus is treasured by keen cooks who savour food at its best. Once I would have said it was truly seasonal, but now it seems to be available for much of the year; however, the flavour of spring asparagus is without equal. Asparagus is a member of the Liliaceae family, the lilies, and is believed to have originated in Asia Minor or the eastern Mediterranean.

American author Richard Olney in his *Simple French Food* writes:

the head of each stalk delicately limp but firmly intact, warm but not boiling hot, well drained and accompanied by olive oil, vinegar, salt and pepper – and good sweet butter to be eaten in chunks on rough country bread.

Eat it cold … toss it in butter, throw it into a salad or an omelette, cover it with bechamel and buttered breadcrumbs and gratinée it, purée the stems and mix with the tips into a souffle batter …

It takes patience to establish an asparagus bed and I regret that for years I didn't bother. It seemed too long to wait for the plants to mature before the first little shoots could be cut. Eventually, finding some of the more unusual purple asparagus, I was tempted to plant a few clumps, then some green clumps and now it is a precious moment, worth all the waiting, when the first little asparagus shoots break through the ground.

planting

You need to take time to prepare an asparagus bed in advance as its position can't be changed and so will be there for years. Asparagus needs well-drained soil and likes a very cold winter, so cold the earth on top is almost frozen, giving the asparagus a dormant period which it needs to regain its strength. I have cheated on this and planted a few crowns here and there in the flower garden and under the trees, where they don't get as much sun but still produce lots of cheeky spears and have a pretty ferny top that stays quite bright green in summer when other plants are suffering from the heat.

Dig the soil over well, work in some rich compost or fertilizer – asparagus grows best in neutral earth so make sure you don't have acid soil. Buy root divisions which are two years old and put them into the soil in a small trench, about 45 cm/20 in apart, leaving 30–45 cm/1–1½ feet between the rows. Spread the roots out and cover with a little more soil, then as they begin to grow top with more soil until the bed is well built up. Or buy seedlings, for they are quite hardy and grow well.

Restrain yourself, admire them and don't harvest too soon, they are supposed to be two to three years old before first picking, and then don't take them all, you may kill the plants. Just remember that asparagus are hungry plants and need lots of nourishment. Feed twice a year to build strong ferns in autumn and big fat spears in spring. If you don't bother to feed them well the crop will gradually decrease.

Temperature Zone	Sow or Plant
Asparagus is a perennial. Plant where it can remain permanently.	
All climates	Early spring for seeds, late winter–spring for crowns
First picking	*At least a year, up to 3 years, depending on the age of the crowns. Leave a few to build up plant reserves.*

varieties

Dutch Purple, Connover's Colossal, Mary Washington and Martha Washington are my favourites.

diseases and pests

There is an asparagus beetle but it is more usually found in commercial plantings of asparagus than in a home garden. Just pick any beetles off if they come to visit. Generally asaparagus is a very healthy plant.

harvesting

Cut asparagus spears or break them gently at the soil level, moving the soil aside so you don't cut any spears that are about to appear at the surface. Once the spears begin to get very thin it is time to leave the bed to rest. Water and feed with some fertilizer to give the asparagus strength for the next year.

nutrition

Asparagus is one of the best sources of folate and it is also a source of Vitamin E, as well as dietary fibre.

buying and storage

I like big fat spears but this is personal – some people prefer skinny ones – but whichever you choose they should have tight unblemished tips, clean smooth stems and a deep colour with a slight tinge of purple. It is sensible to get all spears about the same diameter so the cooking time will be easy to regulate. You can occasionally buy white asparagus, which is quite expensive and prized in Europe, and a lovely purple variety that changes colour to green when cooked. It does, however, have a different flavour.

I am not keen on asparagus bunches sold in tight rubber bands, which can damage it, preferring to pick the spears loose from a box.

To store, if you are not using asparagus the day you buy it, put the stalks into a tiny bit of water standing upright in a jug, the same way you would store cut flowers. Refrigerate. The spears remain crisp and fresh for double the time.

cooking

Trim any tough ends; if you exert gentle pressure on the bottom of each spear it will snap. If the end is thick you can peel a little of its skin away so every scrap can be eaten. White asparagus has tough skin so peel this completely up to the tip. I cook mine in a frying pan in plenty of water; this is very successful, as it is easy then to drain it and test, much easier than if cooked in a deep saucepan. Just be sure the water is lightly salted and keeps boiling and you need a fairly deep frying pan so the water won't evaporate before the asparagus is cooked. How crisp or how soft is personal. I don't like asparagus too hard, just cooked until tender, but not like a stir-fry crunchy vegetable. Drain. Forget about rinsing under cold water if you care about the flavour because rinsing dilutes it. Just put spears aside on a tea towel or cloth for a minute and then serve hot, or let cool and use later.

asparagus with a lid

asparagus goes with

butter

olive oil

white wine

vinegar

cream

eggs

crispy bread-crumbs

bacon

beef

chicken

ham

smoked salmon

cheese, especially Parmesan

pasta

orange

lemon

garlic

light soy sauce

pine nuts

walnuts

The 'lid' in this dish is a puffy egg and herb topping that will rise to a golden dome and completely cover the asparagus. It is rather like a soufflé in that shortly after being removed from the oven it falls to a lower, flatter covering. It still tastes great but it not as dramatic.

Preheat oven to 180°C/350°F. Trim the asparagus and cook until just tender. Drain very well. Cut spears in half and arrange in a well-buttered 23-cm/9-in diameter ovenproof dish. When arranging in the base of the dish, it is best to alternate tips and stalks so each serve will have an equal amount of both. Melt the butter in a saucepan, add the flour and cook for a few minutes, then add milk and stir constantly until the mixture has thickened. Season with mustards and salt and pepper. Cool for 5 minutes. Mix in the herbs. Add the yolks one at a time and stir well. Beat the whites until they hold stiff peaks and fold a third into the yolk mixture to lighten it, before folding in the remainder. Spoon this over the asparagus. You can leave the top plain or scatter with Parmesan cheese. Bake for 15–20 minutes or until lid is puffed and well-risen but be careful not to let the top become dry.

I find it best to use a fork to break open the top and then a big spoon to lift some of the lid on to plates, serving the asparagus alongside. This recipe can, of course, be made in individual dishes, but you may have to cut the asparagus into little pieces so they fit in the base of the cooking containers.

Serve 4 as a first course, 2 as a main dish

750 g/1 ½ lb asparagus

45 g/1 ½ oz butter

1 tablespoon flour

²⁄₃ cup/5 fl oz milk

½ teaspoon dry English mustard

1 teaspoon French mustard

salt and pepper

2 teaspoons finely chopped fresh thyme

2 teaspoons finely chopped fresh marjoram

2 tablespoons finely chopped parsley

2 egg yolks

3 egg whites

2 tablespoons grated Parmesan cheese (optional)

asparagus savoury custard

*This lovely, light, baked asparagus custard doesn't need any last-minute atten-
tion so it is easy to cook for friends. Use as a first course and be careful not
to overcook, as egg dishes such as this become too firm and it will end up dry.*

Preheat oven to 180°C/350°F. Trim the asparagus and cook until just tender.
Drain well and then cut into pieces about 4 cm/1½ in long. Melt butter and
cook the onion gently until pale golden, add the ham and cook for a minute.
Transfer to a bowl and add the asparagus. In a separate bowl, beat the cream
with the eggs, milk, salt, pepper and cheese. Gently stir in the asparagus,
onion and ham. Butter a shallow, 5-cup/2-pint ovenproof dish, pour in
custard and bake for about 25 minutes, or until it is just set on the edges.
The centre should still be a little creamy. Remove from oven and leave the
dish to sit for 10 minutes to settle. Serve with toast fingers. You can of course
make individual servings for everyone, using little soufflé dishes or ramekins.
These take less time to cook, about 15 minutes, but rely on checking by
giving the dishes a little gentle shake. The centre should be creamy but
not wobbly and the outside set.

Serves 4 as a first course, 2 as a main dish

500 g/1 lb asparagus

45 g/1½ oz butter

1 onion, finely diced

4 tablespoons
very finely diced ham

1 cup/8 fl oz cream

3 eggs

¼ cup/2 fl oz milk

salt and pepper

¼ cup/1 oz grated Jarlsburg
or Swiss-style melting cheese

hint

Asparagus's
colour fades
when in contact
with acid so
don't cover with
a vinaigrette
dressing too
far in advance
or instead of
bright green
the asparagus
will be dull.

hungarian asparagus

*This recipe is typical of Hungarian or Russian dishes, which rely on sour
cream to create a sauce or topping. A layer of this covers the asparagus,
adding a creamy coating in the same manner we would use a white sauce,
but it is much quicker to make.*

*This dish is quite rich so I would only serve it before or with a very light
main course, such as a grilled chicken or plain grilled fish. You can buy
light sour cream if you are diet-conscious instead of the creamier version –
it won't separate as the egg and flour stabilize it.*

Preheat oven to 200°C/400°F. Place the asparagus in a shallow ovenproof
dish into which they will fit in a double layer. Put the sour cream, paprika,
egg, seasonings and flour into a bowl and stir well with a fork. Just before
you are ready to bake asparagus spoon sauce over it, then scatter on the
crumbs and drizzle with the melted butter. Bake for about 15 minutes or
until the cream is bubbling and the dish is very hot. If you want a really
deep golden-brown colour on the top, slide the dish under a preheated
griller/broiler for a few minutes before taking it to the table.

Serves 4

1 kg/2 lb medium-sized asparagus,
trimmed and cooked

⅓ cup/3 fl oz sour cream

1 teaspoon paprika

1 egg

salt and pepper

¼ teaspoon sugar

2 teaspoons flour

4 tablespoons breadcrumbs,
made from stale bread

30 g/1 oz butter, melted

asparagus with sun-dried tomato mayonnaise

hint

The long, straight or twisted sexy asparagus spears are considered by many, including the famous seventeenth-century English herbalist Nicholas Culpeper, to be an aphrodisiac.

The slightly sharp, acid flavour of sun-dried tomatoes goes well with asparagus. It is best to use semi-dried tomatoes to ensure they are not too tough and chewy in the final dish.

Prepare asparagus: discard woody ends and, depending on the thickness of each spear (thin pieces should be left unpeeled) peel and cut to 12.5 cm/ 5 in long. Cook in boiling salted water or steam. Drain then wrap in kitchen paper towel and refrigerate.

Make mayonnaise: blend egg yolks, mustards and sugar in food processor or whisk by hand. Pour in oil very slowly, a few drops at a time. When about three-quarters of the oil is incorporated, blend in vinegar, then remaining oil. Add the sun-dried tomatoes and process or mix. Transfer to a bowl and fold in cream. Adjust seasoning and refrigerate until ready to serve. Then put the asparagus spears on a platter and drizzle mayonnaise over them. You can garnish with a few bits of extra sun-dried tomato which will stand out brightly against the green stalks of the asparagus.

Serves 6

36 asparagus spears

Mayonnaise
2 egg yolks
I teaspoon French mustard
½ teaspoon dry English mustard
¼ teaspoon sugar
¾ cup/6 fl oz light olive oil
1½ tablespoons white wine vinegar
2 tablespoons sun-dried or semi-dried tomatoes, finely chopped
¼ cup/2 fl oz cream, lightly whipped
salt and freshly ground black pepper

a stir fry of asparagus stalks, with onion, mushroom and ginger shreds

A dish to make when you have some asparagus stalks left over from another recipe. This can be served on its own, when it is enough for two people, or it makes four small servings as an accompanying vegetable. It goes well with chicken or lamb and although you may not have a choice, is best of all made with lovely fat spears.

Peel the asparagus and cut it into thin slices on a slant. Cut the onions into halves and then slice thinly. Slice the mushrooms thickly. Heat the oil in a frying pan, add the onions and fry for a minute, then add the mushrooms and sauté for another minute over high heat until both they and the onions are beginning to wilt. Add the asparagus pieces and ginger, season with salt and pepper, and toss for 30 seconds. Add water or stock and cook for a couple of minutes longer or until the asparagus is just barely tender. Serve with a little of the juice; most of it will have cooked away.

Serves 2 as a main dish, 4 as a side dish

500 g/I lb asparagus
2 medium-sized white onions
10 medium-sized mushrooms
2 tablespoons vegetable oil
2 teaspoons julienned fresh ginger
salt and pepper
¼ cup/2 fl oz water or chicken stock

baked asparagus mould

Here is a more elaborate treatment for asparagus, which I have adapted from Italian recipes for vegetable moulds that use carrots, fennel or artichokes as their base. Rather than just being an accompaniment this dish can be served as a light lunch or as a first course before the main one. It can be cooked either in one large mould, in which case you should unmould to serve, or in individual smaller moulds that can be taken directly to the table. Remember that it will stick, so the container in which it is cooked should be lined with buttered foil or non-stick baking paper/parchment.

Remove tough ends of asparagus and peel the stalks. Cut into small pieces, leaving the tips whole. Bring a pot of salted water to the boil and add the asparagus. Cook for a couple of minutes and drain well. Melt half the butter. Add the asparagus and cook gently, tossing until it is tender (the asparagus must be quite soft) then set aside in its pan.

Melt the remaining butter in another saucepan. Add the flour and heat, stirring, until pale golden in colour. Add the milk and cook, stirring constantly, until you have a thick sauce. Simmer gently for a couple of minutes. Leave to cool until tepid. Beat the eggs and yolks in a basin and mix in the white sauce. Season well, stir in the cheese, asparagus and its juices. You can complete all preparation to this point hours in advance.

When ready to cook preheat oven to 180°C/350°F. Butter a loaf tin about 20 cm long by 10 cm wide (8 x 4 in). If you wish to unmould, first line with buttered foil or paper; scatter crumbs over the base and sides. Pour the asparagus mixture into the mould and scatter a few more crumbs on top. Bake for about 45 minutes or until set to touch. Allow to rest for at least 10 minutes, then serve or unmould on to a plate.

Serves 6

750 g/1½ lb asparagus

60 g/3 oz butter

3 tablespoons flour

1½ cups/12 fl oz milk

2 large eggs

3 egg yolks

salt and pepper

⅓ cup/1 oz grated Parmesan cheese

4 tablespoons breadcrumbs, made from stale white or brown bread

easy ideas *Asparagus with Orange Mayonnaise*

Cook enough asparagus for 2 people, drain well and then chill, covered. Grate a teaspoon of orange rind – being careful not to take any white pith when you grate or it will be bitter – and mix into ½ cup/4 fl oz of good mayonnaise along with a tablespoon of orange juice. Spoon some over asparagus or use as a dipping sauce. If you can get a blood orange this is even better but they have only a short season and timing it with asparagus is not easy.

asparagus and parmesan

Delicate asparagus and slightly salty Parmesan cheese make a wonderful combination that I love as a first course. Not only is it so easy but it has a beautifully clean, natural taste which comes when there is not too much tampering with the best raw ingredients.

Trim the asparagus and cut the stalks level. Heat water in a frying pan. Put the asparagus into this and cook until it is just tender. Remove and drain on some kitchen paper towel. When it is dry roll in olive oil and season well with salt and pepper. When ready to cook preheat oven to 180°C/350°F and put the asparagus into a shallow ovenproof dish, or use individual ones. Bake for about 10 minutes or until very hot and bubbling. Cover quite generously with shavings of cheese. Return to the oven for about 2 minutes or until the cheese has melted. Scatter with the herbs and serve immediately.

Serves 4

1.5 kg/3 lb asparagus

salt and pepper

olive oil

very fresh Italian Parmesan cheese shavings

2 tablespoons finely chopped parsley

1 teaspoon finely chopped thyme

1 teaspoon finely chopped marjoram

asparagus with ginger dressing

For this dish the asparagus is best crunchy so cook until tender but leave with a little bite. I usually serve the spears whole but another way is to cut each one diagonally into about three pieces, then toss them with the dressing – rather like a tossed salad – and pile them up on the plates.

Trim and cook the asparagus. While it is cooking prepare the dressing: whisk the lemon juice with oil and season with salt and pepper. Peel the ginger and grate into a bowl then squeeze pulp with your hand so that the juice runs through back into the bowl. Discard pulp. You need about a good tablespoon of juice but taste dressing as you add it to suit your own palate – it should give a gentle flavour and not dominate. Add the sesame oil. When asparagus is cooked, drain very well. The asparagus should still be warm when you pour the dressing over it. Leave to marinate for 30 minutes but no longer or the acid in the lemon will fade the green of the asparagus to a pale colour. Stir the sesame seeds in a warm, dry frying pan until they are golden brown. Cool. To serve, scatter the seeds over the asparagus.

Serves 4

1 kg/2 lb asparagus

1 tablespoon lemon juice

1/2 cup/4 fl oz oil

1/2 teaspoon salt and some pepper

piece of fresh ginger, about 5 cm/2 in long

1/2 teaspoon sesame oil

1 tablespoon sesame seeds

asparagus with egg and herb sauce, french style

easy ideas

Baked Asparagus

Trim the asparagus and roll the spears in a little olive oil. Put onto a large piece of foil. Scatter with salt and pepper, a squeeze of lemon juice and knob of butter and close the foil at the top and sides as if wrapping a parcel. Bake on a tray in a moderate oven (180°C/350°F) for about 25 minutes. Divide asparagus between plates and tip the scented juices over the top.

Warm asparagus and boiled or scrambled eggs go well together and this is a similar theme but with a cold accompaniment. The asparagus is coated with an oil and vinegar dressing and the addition of hard-boiled egg both gives the dish more substance and thickens the dressing.

Here are some pointers to ensure this French dish is at its very best:
- *The asparagus should be cooked as close to serving as possible so that it is cool but not cold and does not require refrigeration.*
- *Put the sauce over the top only at serving time because it changes the colour of the vegetable and the asparagus will lose some of the fresh green look if dressed for too long.*

Peel the asparagus and cook until tender but not soft. Drain and set aside. To make the dressing, mash one of the hard-boiled eggs well and mix with mustard. Whisk the oil and vinegar together and add gradually to this egg. Finally, stir in parsley, chives and spring onion and season. To serve, chop the remaining egg finely. Arrange the asparagus on individual plates. Spoon some of the dressing across the centre of the spears, but keep some aside so it can be placed in a bowl on the table. Scatter a little of the diced egg over the strip of dressing.

Serves 4

1 kg/2 lb asparagus

2 hard-boiled eggs

1 teaspoon French mustard

3/4 cup light olive oil or peanut oil

2 tablespoons white wine vinegar

2 tablespoons finely chopped parsley

3 teaspoons finely chopped chives

1 tablespoon finely chopped spring onion/scallion

salt and pepper

asparagus with beef and onions, chinese style

A good family stir fry, not too much bother and nor does it need a big store cupboard of Asian ingredients. It is quick to make, with fresh light flavours. Just serve with some steamed rice.

Cut away the thick ends of the asparagus. Peel the bottom of the stalks and cut the asparagus into lengths of about 5 cm/2 in. Cook for 1 minute in boiling water and drain. Remove any fat from the steak if using rump. Cut into thin strips and put in a bowl with the soy, sugar and dry sherry. Let marinate for 30 minutes.

Heat the oil in a wok or large frying pan. Add the onion slices and cook, tossing constantly until slightly softened. Remove from the pan and add the beef. Stir fry until it has changed colour. Return onion and add asparagus. Toss well until asparagus is hot and flavours have mingled, then trickle half the water down the side. Toss. Mix the remaining water with cornflour/cornstarch, add to wok and stir until lightly thickened – this should take only a few seconds. Serve immediately with rice or plain noodles.

Serves 4

500 g/1 lb asparagus

375 g/12 oz rump or fillet steak

1 tablespoon light soy sauce

1 teaspoon sugar

1 teaspoon dry sherry

2 tablespoons vegetable oil

1 large onion, halved and then thinly sliced

4 tablespoons water

2 teaspoons cornflour/cornstarch

asparagus in an egg-lemon sauce, italian style

This asparagus dish is one of Giuliano Bugialli's, which he says comes from the older Jewish communities who have lived in Italy since Roman times. He claims that it is not a Greek sauce, although it could be as it has all the characteristics of the fresh, slightly tart classic Greek egg and lemon – avgolemono – sauces.

Cut any tough ends of the asparagus away but don't peel the rest of the stalks. Put asparagus into a large bowl of cold water and leave about 30 minutes. Drain and cut into 3.5 cm/1½ in pieces and let them soak again in cold water for another 5 minutes. Heat the oil in a flameproof casserole, preferably terracotta. When it is hot, add the whole garlic clove. Sauté for about 1 minute. Drain asparagus and add to the casserole. Season with salt and pepper, mix well and sauté for about 2 minutes. Remove the garlic. Add the lemon juice and mix well. Cover the casserole and cook for about 15 minutes over the lowest heat. The asparagus should be cooked through but firm with a fresh, tart flavour (and you need to keep the asparagus warm while preparing the sauce so it is important it is not overcooked at this stage).

Beat the eggs with a pinch of salt. Slowly mix in the flour, being careful to prevent lumps forming. Use a slotted spoon to transfer the asparagus from the casserole to a serving platter. Mix the beaten eggs into the juices in the casserole and stir slowly until thickened. Pour sauce over the top of asparagus and serve immediately.

Serves 4

1 kg/2 lb medium-sized asparagus
½ cup/4 fl oz olive oil
1 large clove garlic, peeled
salt and pepper
juice of 2 lemons
2 large eggs
pinch of salt
1 teaspoon flour

basil

Ocimum basilicum

Basil is simply one of the most fragrant and best-tasting herbs around and has become famous as the much-loved partner of tomato. Not only do they complement each other by bringing out the best flavours, and do well as companions in the vegetable garden, but the colours – brightest green and vivid red – together on a plate are startling. This is true whether the basil be whole leaves or a spoonful of brilliant green pesto. Basil loves warmth but hates heat in the kitchen so the best flavour and aroma comes when it is just added to dishes at the last minute, and the fresher the better. Basil fits effortlessly into both European and Asian cooking.

thai chicken and basil (recipe page 33) ▶

planting

Basil is an annual that does not cope well with frost. It should therefore be planted mid–late spring. In general basil is transplanted as seedlings, although you can buy packets of seeds, which may be the only way you will be able to grow some of the more unusual varieties.

Basil needs fertile soil, lots of sunshine and plenty of food and water and then grows well, with big, fat, healthy leaves. Plant basil around and between every tomato plant, or if you love making pesto to keep during winter tuck plants anywhere in the garden so you can make up jars to store in the freezer or refrigerator. This is a very attractive plant, so there is no need to hide it in the vegetable garden.

Basil is happy in a pot but make sure the potting soil is kept moist and fed too.

varieties

There are masses of basil varieties, from sweet Genovese-type basil, the most popular one for cooking, to ornamental basil with ruffled leaves of green and purple. Try bush basil with tiny leaves, as this is hardier than the Genovese basil, and so will be in the garden when you need it most of the year.

You can get all manner of flavours in different varieties of this herb: lemon, lime, anise, cinnamon … Sacred basil has a peppery flavour, as does Thai (holy) basil.

harvesting

Never take more than half a plant's leaves at once or it will suffer shock. Pick off developing flower heads to keep it growing. The more you pinch out tops and pick leaves the more basil branches out and becomes a bigger bush. When you pick lots, reward the plant with some food.

buying and storage

Home-grown plants seem to have a more intense flavour than bunches of shop-bought basil. However, if you are buying basil, look for bunches stored in water, and ensure the leaves are not wilted.

I just leave home-grown basil in a container with some water and it keeps fresh and green for several days. I don't find the commercial basil keeps as long or as well and this is best stored in a vegetable bag in the refrigerator crisper.

basil and mint poached apples

hint

Be careful when frying basil leaves in oil. They must be very dry but can still spit in the oil so add only a few at a time and use tongs to place them in the oil. As they cool they will become almost like green glass.

A new angle for basil – in a dessert! It is lovely and fragrant with fruit in syrup combined with mint. To extend the basil theme you can also crush up a few leaves with 4 sugar cubes using a pestle and mortar until you have a bright green paste and stir this into a bowl of whipped cream.

Heat the water and apple juice with mint, spices and sugar, stirring until sugar has dissolved. Simmer about 5 minutes. Add half the basil sprigs and all the lemon shreds. Put apple in the syrup and cook gently until tender. Remove fruit to a bowl and then pour the syrup through a sieve over the top. Add the remaining basil sprigs to the apples, pushing them under the liquid, and refrigerate until very cold. Before serving remove the basil.

Serves 6

1 cup/8 fl oz water

1 cup/8 fl oz apple juice or cider

4 sprigs mint

cinnamon stick

8 cardamom pods, lightly crushed

½ cup/4 oz sugar

8 big sprigs basil

shreds of peel from ½ a lemon

6 cooking apples, peeled, cored and quartered

goat's cheese and sun-dried tomato pâté

This spread is not too strong but has the particular fresh flavour of goat's cheese and can be used for biscuits and is very good for a snack or cocktail savoury. It can be spread onto hot toast and put under the griller for a minute or two until glazed and golden. I prefer to use a creamy fresh goat's cheese rather than a hard, drier one that will be saltier and make the pâté more crumbly. This keeps well for about 10 days, refrigerated.

Put cream cheese and butter into a food processor and process until creamy, scraping down the sides. Add the goat's cheese and mix well. Transfer to a basin and mix in the tomatoes, basil and pepper. Fill a crock and smooth the top. Seal with some foil or, for longer keeping, pour a thin film of melted butter over the spread.

Makes 1½ cups/12 fl oz

125 g/4 oz cream cheese, diced

125 g/4 oz unsalted butter, diced

200 g/6 oz goat's cheese

3 tablespoons finely chopped semi-dried tomatoes

2 tablespoons finely chopped basil

¼ teaspoon ground black pepper

uses

Basil stimulates the appetite, helps with digestion, acts as a mild sedative and has been used in cough medicines and for kidney trouble. It is supposed to be a good fly or mosquito repellent but you need to rub quite a bit on your skin for it to be effective and you will smell a bit strange.

thai chicken and basil

Basil is served in two ways in this dish: fresh leaves are added to the light sauce for the chicken and then more leaves are quickly fried until papery crisp and scattered on top.

Fry the basil leaves first so they will be ready when the chicken is cooked. Heat some oil, add a few leaves at a time and cook only for seconds or until crisp. Don't let them brown or they will taste bitter. Drain on kitchen paper towel.

Gently fry the garlic, chilli and ginger in the 3 tablespoons oil until aromatic. Add the chicken and toss until it changes colour. Add basil, cover the pan, turn the heat low and cook for 2 minutes. Mix the fish sauce with sugar, lemon juice and water and pour around the edges, tossing for a minute until the chicken is cooked. Scatter the prepared crispy basil leaves over the chicken and accompany with rice.

Serves 4

about 18 large basil leaves, for garnish

oil

3 cloves garlic, finely chopped

1 chilli, deseeded and chopped

1 tablespoon finely shredded ginger

3 tablespoons oil

4 small or 3 large boned chicken breasts, skinned and cut into fine strips

½ cup/½ oz basil leaves

1 tablespoon fish sauce

1 tablespoon sugar

1 tablespoon lemon juice

¼ cup/2 fl oz water

basil pesto

basil goes with

tomato and

olive oil

anchovies

garlic

mozzarella,
especially
bocconcini

eggplant/
aubergine

onions

squash

zucchini/
courgette

fish

lamb

Everyone probably has a favourite recipe for basil pesto and the truly important thing is to get the most fragrant green basil you can as the base. Pesto has an affinity with pasta, the starch in the pasta being the perfect vehicle to display the powerful flavours of the basil, oil, cheese and nuts. You can keep pesto refrigerated for up to 3 months – or frozen for longer – but it loses its bright, fresh colour; be sure to keep it covered with oil and well sealed.

It is worth making plenty of pesto as it has so many uses in the kitchen. Put a spoonful over tiny boiled potatoes or add to the top of any vegetable soup. Dab a bit on top of a baked or grilled tomato, spread a teaspoon over barbecued lamb pieces so it melts on top or toss with a mix of halved baby bocconcini and halved cherry tomatoes and serve on a bed of fresh basil leaves as a first course.

Put the basil and salt into a food processor and chop the leaves, then add garlic, nuts and gradually pour in the oil while the machine is on. It should not be too thick at this stage. Tip into a bowl and mix in the cheese. Pack into sterilized glass jars and spread a thin layer of oil on top. When using, take out as much as you need, then level the top and cover again with more oil.

If mixing with pasta, only lightly drain the latter as you need to leave a little of the pasta water to meld with the pesto, so the sauce is not too thick and heavy.

Makes about 2 cups/1 pint

2 cups/2 oz firmly packed basil leaves

1 teaspoon sea salt

3 cloves garlic, finely chopped

1/2 cup/2 oz walnuts or pine nuts

3/4–1 cup/6–8 fl oz olive oil

1/2 cup/2 oz finely grated Italian Parmesan cheese

Laurus nobilis

I planted my bay tree in a big pot after watching a friend struggle to get a few leaves off an overgrown tree in her garden which grew so high as if deliberately to deny anyone its leaves. It is one of the problems of the bay tree. You need to have access to it for the kitchen and potting will restrict its growth and height but not its flavour. Fresh bay leaves have a different taste to dried leaves. They send out gentle messages in casseroles, hinting at warm savoury tastes, which should be only part of the picture, rather than dominating it. Just be sure you buy the right one: the bay tree for cooking is a sweet bay tree, not a laurel, which is poisonous. Bay is a noble herb and was once twined into crowns that were worn by the victorious. If you are concerned about them, it is said

that a bay tree growing near your house will keep away witches and evil happenings, along with thunder and lightning.

In the kitchen bay can be included in all those lovely long-cooked dishes that have multi-layered flavours. It's also good to use in marinades, and of course is essential in a bouquet garni – although not too many people seem to bother putting these into dishes anymore.

planting

Get a straight little tree. You can buy bay in pots any time of the year: plant it in the garden if you prefer or use a very large pot. Bay needs sunshine constantly, likes water often and some fertilizer occasionally. It is relatively hardy, but may lose leaves in heavy frosts.

It looks attractive to have a pair of trees in two identical pots, you can then sit them beside the back or front door, where bay is supposed to bring you and your home good luck.

buying and storage

Sometimes you can buy fresh bay leaves and although there is no reason fresh cannot be available all year you may have to rely on dried if you don't have your own tree. Be sure dried leaves are not too brown or too broken in the packets. If they don't have a strong flavour when you open them, just use double the amount in the dish.

Dry your own leaves if you wish: pick a branch, let it dry hanging in a cool place and store leaves in a glass jar. Don't let it hang for too long, it may look romantic and rustic but just gets dirty and dusty.

potatoes studded with bay leaves

Push a fresh bay leaf into the centre of each potato for an interesting light bay flavour. The effect is pretty, the dark roasted bay leaves contrasting with golden potatoes. You can serve this with almost any kind of meat dish or barbecued food.

12 small potatoes
12 bay leaves
olive oil
salt and pepper

Preheat oven to 180°C/350°F. Cut a deep slash into the side of each potato and poke a bay leaf well in so it won't come out during cooking. Roll the potatoes in olive oil and then season well and bake for about 45 minutes or until they are soft inside and crispy on the outside. Just serve as they are.

Serves 6

bay leaf custard

In the same way that bay gives a gentle, barely noticeable flavour to a meat dish, bay can do the same for sweet custard. Serve with any kind of warm fruity pudding or leave to cool and then chill. Or even fold a little lightly whipped cream through the custard, topping with some finely chopped glacé fruits. If eaten hot, the custard will taste sweeter than when allowed to cool, so if planning a chilled custard you may wish to increase the sugar.

1 litre/2 pints milk
1/3 cup/3 oz castor/superfine sugar
6 fresh bay leaves
1/4 vanilla bean, halved lengthwise
4 egg yolks
1 tablespoon cornflour/cornstarch

Heat the milk with sugar, bay leaves and vanilla. When it is almost bubbling on the edges turn off the heat and leave for several hours. Beat the yolks with cornflour/cornstarch and strain the milk into yolks through a sieve. Return to the saucepan and cook again, stirring constantly until custard has lightly thickened and coats the back of a spoon. Serve warm or cool, stirring occasionally so it doesn't get a skin on top.

Serves 6

uses

As well as for flavouring, bay leaves have been used for preserving and marinating. They also stimulate the appetite, relieve indigestion and are recommended as a sedative. Bay is good for nausea and nervous headaches.

Tuck some bay leaves into your cupboards to deter silverfish (although you need lots to be effective) and in the pantry to discourage weevils.

beans

Phaseolus spp.

The genus name means a small, swift, sailing boat and the pod supposedly represents that by its shape (broad beans are quite different, see page 49). These beans were introduced to Europe by Christopher Columbus and Jane Grigson called them 'one of our greatest blessings from the New World ...'. The French have perfected the growing of beans, and their fine tiny green beans (*Phaseolus vulgaris*), also known as snap beans, are almost like matchsticks, and one of the great vegetables of France. I can remember when all beans had strings and a daily chore for most housewives was stringing the sides and then cutting the beans into fine diagonal strips. It must have seemed like a dream when the first French stringless beans came into the shops, requiring only to be cooked quickly in boiling water and then tossed in butter. Baby beans are exquisite if picked young, just tossed in a little butter after they have been boiled quickly and served on their own so nothing else detracts from their flavour. Occasionally now you can buy these baby beans, but they are very expensive, which is understandable, as it takes much more time to pull the babies from the bushes than more mature beans, and the farmer is losing a crop that would have yielded treble the weight if the beans had been left to mature. If I don't have enough from my garden I cheerfully pay for the top-quality beans, preferring to eat less of them – or eat them less often – rather than settle for large ones.

Runner beans are also a *Phaseolus* species, *P. coccineus*, but are distinct from French or snap beans in that they are much larger with flattened pods and rough-textured skins. They usually have purple beans within the pods, unlike French beans, which are pale green or white inside. These are native to South America.

You may come across one further type of bean, often used in Asian cooking: snake, or yardlong, beans. These are not related to the *Phaseolus* beans, being *Vigna unguiculata* subsp. *sesquipedalis*. They are pencil-thin, very long pods and only grow well in hot conditions.

Beans are tender annuals. You can buy dwarf or climbing varieties, which you prefer really depends on your space. I find that the climbing types give larger crops but you need to erect a trellis or put them against a wall.

planting

Wait until the frosts are over before planting seeds as they need warm soil to germinate. Select a bed in full sunlight and mix in a fertilizer or compost but not one high in nitrogen as that will result in lots of leaves but not so many beans. If planting dwarf beans sow seeds about 5 cm/2 in apart but space climbers 40 cm/18 in apart. Once shoots appear thin them out so you have beans only every 10 cm/4 in, but don't pull the unwanted seedlings from the ground as this can disturb the others, just cut off at ground level. Beans are friendly vegetables and don't mind being close and touchy as they help support each other. Fertilize again when the plants are half grown, before they have beans on them. The soil should be moist but too much water on the flowers may cause them to fall off.

Once the beans are established put some mulch up to the bottom leaves so root growth along the stem is promoted.

Temperature Zone	Sow
Tropical, subtropical	Summer–late spring
Temperate	Spring–summer
Cool	Late spring–mid summer
First picking	10–12 weeks

varieties

There are numerous varieties, and here is a selection:

French dwarf

- Dragon's Tongue – a Dutch heirloom variety with yellow waxy fat pods streaked purple; stringless
- Italian Romano – wide flat beans (these can be dried for soups)
- Windsor Long Pod – stringless only if picked early
- Stringless Pioneer – resistant to bean rust.

Climbers

- Blue Lake – has a crease in the back
- Epicure – a stringless type with well-shaped pods

- Lazy Housewife's Bean – believed to be the first stringless
- Purple King – purple flowers and pods.

Runner beans also come in many types:

- Scarlet Runner – lovely bright scarlet flowers and a tasty bean
- Painted Lady – dark brown, almost chocolate, markings on the seeds.

diseases and pests

Aphids like them and bean beetles, leafhoppers and mites can attack them. If you don't want to spray they will survive but the crop will be reduced. Plant disease-resistant varieties and should a plant become infected with blight take it out so it doesn't spread any disease to the rest of the garden.

harvesting

When green beans are babies, pick and keep picking, as the plant will keep producing. If you forget to harvest them the plant can die once the seeds mature and large beans form. Don't be rough as you pick for the stems of baby beans are fragile, just give a gentle twist rather than pulling firmly. Once the pods are full of swollen seeds bulging out, they are not as nice to eat. If this happens let the pods dry and uproot the plants. Put some newspaper on the ground near a wall and hit the plants against it so the beans fall from the stalks onto the paper. Dry them and store away from light.

Runner beans, although bigger than green beans, should not be too large either, so pick before you see the outline of the beans inside the pod.

buying and storage

Fresh and crisp, pods should snap when you bend them, although this kind of test is not one that impresses the greengrocer. Swollen pods are over-mature beans. There shouldn't be any damp or brown patches, indicating long or poor storage.

Use garden beans straight away. After all, that is why you planted them and the fresher they are the sweeter the beans. Shop beans which have travelled a distance should be eaten quickly but you can keep beans in a vegetable storage bag in the crisper of the refrigerator for a couple of days. French stringless beans keep a little better than runner beans, which do not store well.

nutrition

Beans are excellent nutritionally: they provide protein and fibre, and are low in fat. They also contain Vitamin C, plus minerals such as folic acid, iron, potassium and zinc. Additionally, their skins contain anti-oxidants.

cooking

Just cut off the little ends where the beans were attached to the bush, no need to cut the other, tail, end. Use plenty of salted water to cook as the chlorophyll in green beans reacts with acids in the cooking water but the more water you have, the less these acids affect the bean. Drop the beans into boiling water and cook uncovered until they are just tender. Test by removing one and checking by taste. I don't like them either too hard or too soft. The cooking time can vary not only with the size but also with the freshness of the beans. Drain well but don't run cold water over them, as is often advised 'to keep the green colour'; they will stay green for the time it takes to serve them and cold water just dilutes the beautiful green bean taste.

Runner beans need to be topped and tailed and if you find threads on the side they need stringing. Then cut into slices with a very sharp knife and boil gently.

tossed noodles with green beans

The flavours in this are quite simple and pure – green beans and fresh noodles surrounded by a flavoursome stock.

Toast the sesame seeds in a frying pan until golden, stirring. Leave aside to cool. Cook the noodles in a pot of boiling water until just tender. Drain and rinse quickly in hot water to separate them and remove the starch. If beans are large, cut each one into about three pieces, or if tiny into halves (cut snake beans into small pieces). Cook beans in boiling salted water for about 3 minutes (the timing varies: taste as they cook as they should remain firm). Drain well. Heat the stock and add the beans, cook until just tender, possibly a further 3 minutes. Add the hoi sin and soy sauces, sesame oil and sugar; remove the pot from the heat.

Heat the oil in a wok. Fry garlic and ginger until aromatic and add the noodles, beans and the flavoured stock from around the beans. Heat through, stirring so the noodles are well coated with liquid. If the dish is not very moist, add a little more hot stock as it should be quite a wet dish. Finally, scatter on the sesame seeds and serve with some extra soy on the table if you wish.

Serves 4 as a light meal, 6–8 as a side dish

1 tablespoon sesame seeds

250 g/8 oz Chinese wheat flour noodles

200 g/6 oz young green beans or snake beans, trimmed

3/4 cup/6 fl oz chicken or vegetable stock

2 tablespoons hoi sin sauce

1 tablespoon soy sauce

1 teaspoon sesame oil

1 teaspoon brown sugar

1 tablespoon oil

2 cloves garlic, finely chopped

1 tablespoon finely shredded ginger

a little extra soy sauce, if necessary

spicy green beans

easy ideas

Beans with Bacon

Cook enough beans for 2 people. While they are cooking fry several rashers of finely chopped bacon in a pan with a tablespoon of olive oil. When crispy add a clove of crushed garlic. Drain the beans and toss in the bacon pan so they are lightly coated with bacon fat and garlic. Serve immediately.

These are cooked in a spicy sauce, fragrant with garlic, ginger and ground spices. Typical of Indian dishes, the beans are well cooked, so don't use the very baby beans. Larger ones can cope with the long cooking. The beans don't remain bright green and end up a rather dull colour because the spices are meant to flavour the beans throughout and so need long, slow cooking. Like a curry, this is a recipe that can be prepared in advance and then reheated. You can use as a side dish with some plainly cooked meat or serve spoonfuls of these beans over rice. Make the beans as fiery hot or as gently mellow as your taste dictates.

Cut the ends from the beans and, if large, chop them into about three pieces. Put the ginger with garlic and water into a blender and process to a paste. Heat the oil in a saucepan and add the ginger and garlic paste and fry, stirring for a minute or two or until most of the water has cooked away. Add the beans to the pot with the turmeric. Fry another minute and then add the remaining ingredients. Cook over low heat, covered, for about 45 minutes. As the pan becomes dry, add 1–2 tablespoons water, to ensure the beans don't stick or burn and there are a few spoonfuls of juice around them as they must not be dry.

Serves 4

500 g/1 lb green stringless beans

6 slices fresh ginger

2 cloves garlic, peeled

1/3 cup/3 fl oz water

2 tablespoons vegetable oil

1 teaspoon ground turmeric

1/2 teaspoon chilli paste or chopped chilli

1 teaspoon ground coriander/cilantro

1/2 teaspoon ground cumin

1/2 teaspoon salt

2 teaspoons lemon juice

1 teaspoon garam masala

bean and potato salad

easy ideas

Warm Bean Salad

Cook enough baby beans for 4 people. Mix 4 tablespoons olive oil with 1 tablespoon white vinegar, salt, pepper, a finely chopped skinned tomato and a clove of finely chopped garlic. When the beans are ready, drain, toss with the dressing, tomato etc., season well and serve tepid.

Tiny waxy potatoes with papery skins and baby green stringless beans make an exquisite salad. I can't bear to serve this with any other dish – except perhaps some baby racks of lamb that have been roasted and cut into chops. It should be made on the day it is to be served so you don't have to refrigerate the salad, as chilling dulls the flavours.

Cut the potatoes into thick slices and mix with the beans in a bowl. Shake all dressing ingredients in a jar, and pour over the vegetables and gently toss. Just before serving fry the bacon until crisp in a frying pan and scatter on top. Grate the egg over the top so it falls in a light pattern and then scatter parsley over. Give the salad a toss when it goes to the table.

Serves 4–6

500 g/1 lb tiny potatoes, boiled until tender

500 g/1 lb small green stringless beans, cooked until tender

2 rashers bacon, diced

2 eggs, hard-boiled

4 tablespoons finely chopped parsley

Dressing

8 tablespoons olive oil

1 tablespoon lemon juice

1 tablespoon white wine vinegar

1 clove garlic, finely chopped

2 teaspoons French mustard

1/2 teaspoon sugar

salt and pepper

beans in a creamy sauce

I use either green or yellow (butter/wax) stringless beans in this dish. They are coated with a light sauce so the sauce soaks into the beans a little and then baked long enough for a nice golden-brown speckled crust to form on top. It goes with just about any meat dish and is very good just with crusty bread as a light meal.

Preheat oven to 180°C/350°F. Cook the beans in salted water until just tender, drain well. Melt the butter and cook the onion until soft and golden. Scatter flour on top – if the pan is dry you may need to add a bit more butter. Stir for a few minutes, pour in the milk and cook, stirring constantly, until it has come to a boil and lightly thickened (this sauce is meant to be on the runny side). Cook for a few minutes and mix into the beans. Transfer to a shallow, small ovenproof dish. Scatter the bacon on top and bake in oven for about 25 minutes, until the top has formed a crust.

Serves 4–6

375 g/12 oz young beans

30 g/1 oz butter

1 onion, finely chopped

1 tablespoon plain/all-purpose flour

1½ cups/12 fl oz milk

1 rasher bacon, cut into tiny pieces (optional)

beans in a savoury custard

Not the kind of dish that you usually associate with beans, but have an open mind as it is very interesting and different. It is the mix of garlic and butter, onion and cheese that makes it so good. You can use any kind of young bean. This goes well with chicken and a fresh tomato sauce over both.

Preheat oven to 180°C/350°F. Cook the beans in water until just tender. Drain well and chop into pieces. Mix while warm with butter, garlic, parsley, pepper and spring onions. Beat the eggs in a bowl with the milk, add the beans and cheese and mix. Put into a buttered small casserole and bake, standing in a dish of boiling water that comes halfway up casserole, and covered, until just set. Timing will depend on the dish you use but allow approximately 20–30 minutes. Let rest for 5 minutes before serving.

Serves 4 as a main course, 6 as a side dish

375 g/12 oz beans

30 g/1 oz butter

1 clove garlic, crushed

1 tablespoon finely chopped parsley

some black pepper

4 spring onions/scallions, chopped

3 eggs

½ cup/4 fl oz milk

2 tablespoons grated Parmesan cheese

beans go with

butter

oil

basil

chives

parsley

curry powder

lemon

mustard

carrots

chilli

corn

mushrooms

onion

potatoes

tomato

tuna

bacon

ham

cheese, especially Parmesan

almonds

pine nuts

walnuts

noodles

rice

chicken stock

beetroot
beets

Beta vulgaris

Jane Grigson describes beetroot as a 'bossy vegetable'. You could only characterize it as such because of its colour – it does leak all over every dish in which it is included, so the food ends up a lurid purple. But the flavour is quite gentle and sweet, by no means dominating other ingredients. Mrs Grigson clearly indicated she was not a fan of beetroot as she mentioned in the same paragraph that she had never heard anyone say it was their favourite vegetable. Early experiences of beetroot, sodden with a harsh vinegar solution, would have put many people off beetroot and in the past it rarely appeared except as an addition to add colour to a salad. It is only recently that chefs have become inspired by beetroot and given it a touch of class. Charlie Trotter, the darling of the Chicago food scene, seems to feel quite differently. For example, he has seven entries for beetroot dishes in his famous *Vegetables* book. He uses beetroot in a ragout and makes an oil from it, puts it into a terrine, makes a flourless chocolate cake with beetroot, and generally treats it as a sophisticated, exotic creature. It is interesting that this vegetable can attract such opposing viewpoints.

What we know as beetroot is just a small part of a family that also includes Swiss chard (silverbeet) and other foliage beets. It is not common to eat the leaves of beetroot – we mainly use them for the root – but the baby leaves are delicious in a salad and when a little larger they can be chopped and cooked like any green vegetables. In Boston one of the traditional ways of preparing them in the days when not a scrap of food was wasted was to cook both root and leaves separately, then combine cubes of the beetroot with the green stewed leaves. The Romans knew the leaves were good for they only ate the tops. We do tend to forget that this whole plant is edible, not just the root.

planting

Make sure the soil is well broken up, stones or bumps may cause malformed roots on the beetroot. They can cope with shade or sun but dislike acid soil, so work in a bit of potassium if your soil is not balanced and mix in some well-balanced fertilizer a week before planting.

If sowing seed put the little clusters about 2.5 cm/1 in deep and the same distance apart in rows, which should be 20–30 cm/8–12 in apart. I usually plant beetroot as borders around the edges of the vegetable garden and find this most successful. As a number of seedlings emerge from each cluster you must thin the plants out; you can use these tiny leaves in salads.

Seedlings are easy but handle carefully in the punnets and don't disturb the roots too much, as beetroot does not transplant well.

Fertilize when the plants are about half grown and water regularly, for beetroot are thirsty vegetables, not enough moisture and they will spite you by becoming tough. Weed by hand, as a fork or spade easily dislodges their shallow roots.

Temperature Zone	Plant or Sow
Tropical	Any time
Subtropical	All year round in frost-free areas
Temperate	Spring–late summer
Cool	Mid spring–mid summer
First picking	2½–3 months

varieties

The common red ones are not usually identified by name in the shops or nurseries. Detroit Dark Red and Darwin Globe are well known and available as seedlings. Try some of the more unusual varieties for a wonderful effect in salads: with colours of gold, Golden Beetroot; Italian Chioggia, rings of pink with white flesh; Albina Vereduna, which has sweet roots that don't bleed; or grow the mini gourmet beetroot favoured by restaurants. Most of the more unusual varieties need to be grown from seeds.

diseases and pests

Hardy vegetables, beetroot have no serious pest problems or diseases.

harvesting

Just when you want them, as you can see how large the root is from above the ground. You can harvest them small when it is baby beetroot you need or you can leave them until fat round roots

for pickling. For leaves in salads only use the very young or baby shoots. They don't all grow at the same rate so there will be plenty of variety in the garden.

buying and storage

In hot weather faded beetroot may have been subjected to high temperature. Don't worry if the leaves are limp but they should still be dark and intact. Avoid any root that has split and discard any that have the stems cut too close to the root, as they will bleed during cooking.

Beetroot keep well for weeks in the refrigerator. The leaves keep about the same time as spinach or lettuce if stored in a plastic bag.

nutrition

A medium-sized beetroot (around 130 g/4 oz) has virtually no fat, 11 g of carbohydrate, 4 g of dietary fibre and 225 kJ. The leaves are rich in beta-carotene, which the body converts to Vitamin A, and also supply Vitamin C, calcium, potassium, magnesium and iron. A cup of raw leaves has no fat, contains 1.5 g of dietary fibre and 30 kJ.

cooking

Rinse the beetroot and never, ever cut away the root or all the colour will bleed during cooking. Leave on the stem end and boil gently in plenty of salted water until tender. This can take from 30 minutes for tiny beetroot to well over an hour for large ones. For a richer flavour you can bake them in oiled foil – it is sensible to do this for some dishes or if you have the oven on, but it may seem a bother otherwise as they do take longer to bake than boil. Check for tenderness with a fine skewer, as they must be properly cooked through.

pickled beetroot

**beetroot
goes with**

butter

cream,
especially
sour cream

oil

yoghurt

chives

dill

parsley

chilli

apples

greens,
particularly
its own tops

cucumber

horseradish

lemon

onion

orange

potatoes

red and white
wine vinegar

herrings

beef and
corned beef

game

hare

pork

Everybody used to make their own jars of pickled beetroot once, but now it is so easy to buy a can in a supermarket it is rather a lost art. Home-made is simple and much nicer than any commercial beetroot. This pickle stores well, refrigerated, for about a month and you will always have some on hand for salads or sandwiches in the summer.

Leave on root and some stalks and place the beetroot in a saucepan, cover with water, add a little salt and cook gently, covered, until tender. Cool a little and when you can handle them remove from the liquid – but keep it – and rub away the skin. When the beetroot are cool slice them.

Put all remaining ingredients into a saucepan, cover and simmer for 5 minutes. Add a cup of the beetroot cooking liquid to your pickle base and heat again until it comes to a boil. Put the beetroot slices in a big, sterilized jar or container and pour the liquid from the saucepan over the slices while it is still very hot. Beetroot must be completely covered. Seal when cold.

2 bunches (about 1 kg/2 lb) beetroot

2 cups/1 pint white malt vinegar

1½ cups/12 oz sugar

1 teaspoon crushed cardamom pods

12 peppercorns

12 allspice

beetroot and onion salad

I love this with a steak; the beetroot is mixed with soft, sweet caramelized onions and scattered on a bed of greens.

Cook the onions in the oil in a saucepan until they are wilted and softened, stirring every so often. Then cover and cook until quite tender. Take off the lid, turn up the heat and add sugar, cook until onion has lots of light gold-brown edges. Remove to a plate. At dinner time mix up the dressing and add the onions to it. Put lettuce into a salad bowl, top with beetroot and tip the dressing and onions over this.

Serves 4

2 onions, halved and then sliced

3 tablespoons olive oil

1 teaspoon sugar

2 medium-sized beetroot, cooked and cubed

mixed greens

Dressing

4 tablespoons olive oil

1 tablespoon red wine vinegar

½ teaspoon brown sugar

½ teaspoon dry English mustard

salt and pepper

baked beetroot with citrus cream

Lemon and orange go well with the sweetness of beetroot and although this sauce includes cream it is not a lot per serving. The sauce is best made at the last minute but can be kept warm for a short time. Use this as a side dish with pork, game or chicken.

Cook the beetroot either by boiling or baking. Cool and peel. (You can do this in advance and then warm later by either putting them in a covered container in a microwave or steaming to heat through.) Cut into thick slices. For sauce, melt the butter and cook the onion gently in it until soft. Add lemon and orange juices, orange rind and season. Pour on cream and leave to warm through, then cook a few minutes until lightly thickened. Put beetroot slices onto each serving plate and lightly coat with sauce. Don't mix the beetroot into the sauce or it will become quite lurid in colour.

Serves 4

12 baby beetroot

Sauce
30 g/1 oz butter
1 small onion, finely chopped
1 tablespoon lemon juice
¼ cup/2 fl oz orange juice
½ teaspoon orange rind, grated
salt and pepper
½ cup sour cream

hint

When peeling beetroot after it has been cooked, do so while it is warm or it be comes quite difficult to re- move the skin. Your hands will become stained; if this worries you put on a pair of rubber gloves. Never peel un- cooked beetroot except when you need it for colour in a dish, such as soup, or you are making a raw salad.

beetroot caviar

Although the word 'caviar' is used, it does not mean this recipe is a substitute for the real thing. Beetroot caviar is – or was – eaten by Russian peasants and has no pretensions of grand dining; the description 'caviar' only relates to the fine texture of the dish. It was usually made from vegetables and in this case the unusual choice is beetroot, a vegetable that appears frequently in Russian cooking.

This beetroot caviar is served on some pumpernickel bread, or on pieces of buttered wholemeal toast, and it is very good as a base for a piece of pickled herring.

Cook the beetroot, either by boiling in salted water or by baking it wrapped in foil in the oven. When tender, cool slightly and rub away the skin. Grate the beetroot finely. Mix in all the remaining ingredients and place in a saucepan. Cook gently, giving it an occasional stir, until you have a moist but not wet mixture. Remove from heat, cool and taste for the balance of salt, pepper, lemon, etc., adjusting as necessary. Make sure it is quite highly seasoned. Pack into a small crock and press down. Chill for at least 4 hours before use. It can be kept for about 4 days.

1 large or 2 medium-sized beetroot
2 teaspoons sugar
rind of 1 small lemon
1 tablespoon lemon juice
¼ teaspoon salt
2 tablespoons light olive oil

easy ideas

Beetroot Sandwich

Grate a beetroot, a carrot and a large apple and mix with a chopped stalk of celery and small, finely chopped onion. Season well; moisten with mayonnaise and pile between lettuce in a sandwich. Tasty and healthy with lots of anti-oxidants.

beetroot salad

hint

Never leave
the stove when
frying mustard
seeds as they
burn quickly.
When very hot
and ready to
remove from the
pan, some will
begin to 'jump'.

This is not a pickled beetroot dish but rather a salad that goes very well with barbecued meats or other salads in the summer. It has only a light dressing and keeps, refrigerated, for a couple of days.

Wrap each beetroot in foil and bake in the middle of a moderate oven (180°C/350°F) for about an hour, or until tender when pierced with a fine skewer. Leave to cool until tepid. Once you can handle them, rub away the outer skin with your fingers. Cut each beetroot into half, then into very thin slices and arrange in a bowl. Whisk the oil with vinegar and capers and pour over the top. Season well with some pepper and a little salt. Put the mustard seeds into a dry frying pan and cook until they have begun to change colour. Remove immediately to a bowl and when cool scatter over the beetroot. Last, scatter the chives on top. If preparing in advance keep the mustard seeds and chives aside until close to serving time.

Serves 6

3 medium-sized beetroot

4 tablespoons light olive oil

1 tablespoon white wine vinegar

1 tablespoon chopped capers

salt and pepper

2 tablespoons mustard seeds

2 tablespoons finely chopped chives

easy ideas

Sautéed Beetroot

Grate 3 small
beetroot, enough
for 2–3 people.
Melt about 45 g/
1 ½ oz butter and
add the beetroot,
season well, toss
and mix in a
couple of table-
spoons of either
lemon or orange
juice. Cook,
stirring, for a few
minutes until limp,
add 3 tablespoons
water and cook
about another
10 minutes, until
tender. Season
with more lemon
and a pinch of
brown sugar and
serve with a
pork chop or
fillet of pork.

beetroot timbale

Many varieties of vegetables can be used to make a timbale – carrot, mixed root vegetables, asparagus ... It is more unusual to make one with a beetroot base but this makes quite a delicate, smooth, creamy dish. It would be best as a first course where its colours and flavours can be really appreciated.

To make sauce, melt butter and cook the shallots a minute, add wine and boil for a minute, season and pour in stock. Reduce until about half original volume, then add the mustard, cayenne and cream. Simmer for a minute. This can all be done in advance. Set aside.

Cook the beetroot until tender in salted water and drain. Peel, dice and then purée in a food processor. You should have about 2 cups/1 pint purée. Place in a saucepan and cook, stirring, to dry it out a little. Add cream and let cool.

Preheat oven to 180°C/350°F. Beat the eggs with a fork in a bowl, add the beetroot purée and season well. Spoon into individual buttered moulds. Place in a baking tin and add hot water until it comes about halfway up the sides of the moulds. Bake until timbales are set – test by touch. Timing depends on the kind of dishes you use, the depth of the water, etc., but begin checking them after 20 minutes. Stand for 5 minutes before serving. You can invert them onto a plate or serve in the moulds. To finish sauce, heat the mustard seeds in a dry pan until they begin to pop. Add to the sauce along with some chives. To serve, trickle a tiny bit of the spicy sauce around each timbale.

Makes about 6–8 small moulds

500 g/1 lb beetroot

½ cup/4 fl oz thick/double cream

3 large eggs

salt and pepper

Spicy Sauce

30 g/1 oz butter

1 shallot, finely chopped

¼ cup/2 fl oz dry white wine

salt and pepper

½ cup/4 fl oz vegetable or chicken stock

2 teaspoons French mustard

good dash of cayenne pepper

½ cup/4 fl oz cream

1 tablespoon mustard seeds

finely chopped chives

Vicia faba

Broad beans ranked with tripe, liver and olives as loathsome food when I was growing up, yet these are all things which I adore now, especially broad beans, which have risen through the ranks over the past few years to become one of the fashionable vegetables. They are truly seasonal, you cannot buy them fresh except in late winter, through spring to early summer. Perhaps this is one reason they are treasured. Traces of broad beans have been found in the tombs of Egyptian pharaohs. It is the only bean native to Europe; all others came from the New World, being introduced by Christopher Columbus. Mostly they are known as fava beans, occasionally shell beans, Australia is one of the few places where they are always sold as 'broad beans'. They are tall and very pretty plants, in early spring producing white flowers which have a dark throat, then tiny little pods sprout from between the leaves.

planting

Plant in mid to late autumn for beans in spring, or late winter and early spring if you live in an area with cool early summers. Broad beans need cool weather to set their pods. They love full sun. Put them in 2.5–5 cm/1–2 in deep, in well-drained soil high in organic matter. The ground should be moist but not too wet and work in a bit of fertilizer the week beforehand, they prefer an alkaline soil. I plant the seeds in rows quite close, thinning out the weaker members of the group when they all come through, but I leave them a bit crowded as they seem a friendly vegetable, using each other for support. Once well through the ground, I spread a layer of lucerne carefully around each plant. I stake around the bed and link the stakes with twine to make a little fence around them, which contains the stalks as they grow. Broad beans become quite untidy and flop all over the place and onto the paths otherwise.

From start to finish they need about 4½ months to mature so are not for impatient gardeners. About halfway through the season when the plants are quite high and producing the first flowers pour a little liquid fertilizer around them, otherwise they manage very well on their own.

Temperature Zone	Sow
Tropical	Not suitable
Subtropical	Not suitable
Temperate	Mid–late autumn
Cool	Autumn–early spring
First picking	4–5 months

varieties

• Longpod or Roma – for an early crop
• Acquadulce – prolific
• Dwarf – a small growing bean for a tiny garden.

harvesting

Broad beans can be harvested when they are quite small: if the pods are tiny they can be cooked and eaten whole. As they grow bigger they are shelled, and just the beans are eaten. Do not let pods grow so large that you can see individual beans swelling against the pods, as they will no longer be really sweet and tender. Remove the pods gently, taking care not to tear the stems as you do so. Keep picking, as this will stimulate the plant to produce more flowers.

disease and pests

I have never sprayed and don't have a major problem with bugs but know that aphids, bean beetles, mites, and leafhoppers attack them so it may be best to choose disease-resistant varieties. Rust can also be a problem as the season progresses.

buying and storage

The fresher they are the sweeter and more delicate will be the flavour and the pods need to look moist. Hold up a bean from the batch in the shop, when lifted, if it falls over and bends, these flabby beans will have a strong and slightly bitter taste. Don't worry if the skin is a bit speckled, but choose small pods, which don't have the indent of large distinct beans showing through them.

They are best eaten as fresh as possible but if you need to, store refrigerated in a container for a couple of days.

nutrition

A good source of vitamins A, B1 and B2. High in protein and carbohydrates, they also provide potassium, iron and other minerals.

cooking

Shell just before using. Cook in lots of boiling water for about 4–6 minutes, depending on how tiny they are. Drain. If skinning beans tip them into a bowl of cold water so you can handle them quickly, as they are easier to skin if still a little warm. Pinch a bit from the end skin and the beans will pop out easily, revealing a lovely bright apple green inner bean. If picking baby home-grown beans you may not bother with this, as the skin is tender, especially early in the season. Either serve immediately or warm later in a knob of butter or olive oil or put back into boiling water for a minute.

Broad beans are eaten raw in many parts of Europe, being shelled at the table and dipped in salt and pepper or accompanied with cheese. Some people have an inherited allergy to toxins found in raw broad beans, most notably those with Greek or Armenian ancestry, so bear this in mind if serving raw beans - although I have never personally encountered anyone allergic to them. This toxin is harmless once the beans are cooked.

caramelised onion with broad bean bruschetta

Not a true bruschetta although it looks like one. Instead of the bread being toasted and the topping spread over it, the onion and broad bean mix is put onto sliced bread which is then baked until warm, so it is much easier for the cook to prepare. Wonderful colours of burgundy onion and bright green beans make this a startling first course or savoury.

Cook the onions in oil and butter until softened and pale gold; add red wine and sugar, season and keep cooking until very soft and almost all the wine has cooked away. Season with salt and pepper. It should have a balance of sweet and slightly sharp flavours. Remove and cool.

Cook the beans, drain, rinse and remove the skins. Mash about a quarter of the beans, the best way is to put them onto a flat plate and use a fork. Mix into onion along with whole beans, this can be done hours in advance.

When assembling put the onion and bean mix onto the bread, top each with a shaving of cheese. Bake in a moderate oven (180°C/350°F) for about 6–8 minutes or until warm and the cheese has melted.

Makes 20 slices

2 onions, finely chopped

2 tablespoons oil

30 g/1 oz butter

½ cup/4 fl oz red wine

1 tablespoon sugar

salt and pepper

a little water

250 g/8 oz broad beans, shelled

some shavings of Parmesan cheese

20 thin slices of breadstick/baguette

hints

Broad bean skin is slightly bitter, which is often the reason some people dislike them; there is no bitterness once they are skinned.

You will lose at least half your quantity of beans if skinned so allow for this when calculating amounts.

Young beans can be eaten fresh in any way but old, late-season beans, which become mealy, should be kept for dips or spreads.

a purée of broad beans

A delicate pale green with a creamy texture, this purée is wonderful as a side dish with baby lamb or grilled chicken. In Turkey, it is served cold as an appetizer with some flat bread that has been slightly warmed. It can also become a filling in mushrooms, being topped with crumbs and baked, or in cooked tomato halves with crispy bacon scattered over it. Broad beans don't go very far once peeled and puréed, so you need a fair amount to make it worthwhile.

Shell the beans and cook in some salted water until just tender. Drain well and leave until cool enough to handle. Peel, put into a food processor with some pepper and the butter and process. Add the cream to the purée when you reheat, stirring gently in a basin that sits over a pot of boiling water. It can also be reheated in a microwave, in which case it is best to warm the purée first then add cream, as you may not need all of it. Check for seasoning again before serving.

Serves 4

2 kg/4 lb broad beans

salt and pepper

75 g/3 oz butter, cut into small pieces

3 tablespoons thick/double cream

potato and spring vegetable salad

easy ideas

*Sautéed
Broad Beans*

Warm a little
oil with some
chopped garlic
and onion and
add very baby
beans. Stir over
a low heat about
3 minutes, add
about 3 table-
spoons of water,
a little thyme
and season well,
cook gently until
beans are tender
and liquid has
reduced away.
If you cook these
on high heat —
as I did the first
time I made this
dish — I found
the oil fried
the outside skin
and they tasted
tough, so be
sure to use
a gentle heat.

I love this salad, not just for the flavours but for the lovely colours of pale to emerald green contrasting with the creaminess of baby waxy potatoes. This goes really well with food such as ham, hot chicken, lamb, cold or hot beef and fish. I like to use kipfler potatoes if I can get them or any tiny new potato that still has a papery fragile baby skin.

Cook the potatoes until tender. Drain and peel them if you don't like the skin left on. Cut into thick slices or quarters. Cook the peas, drain and cover with cold water so they don't wrinkle. Cook the broad beans until tender. Snap the ends of the asparagus, then peel the stalks to within the second tip and cut into large diagonal chunks. Cook until just tender in salted water and drain. Drain the peas just before you are ready to mix up the salad, then put all vegetables in a serving bowl. Whisk oil and vinegar, season dressing well and pour on top. Toss everything gently and leave to mellow for an hour. Spoon mayonnaise on top and toss again. Scatter on herbs and serve.

Serves 6

1 kg/2 lb waxy potatoes

250 g/8 oz peas, shelled

500 g/1 lb broad beans, shelled

500 g/1 lb asparagus

1 small red onion, finely chopped

8 tablespoons olive oil

2 tablespoons wine vinegar

salt and pepper

½ cup/4 fl oz mayonnaise

2 tablespoons finely chopped parsley

2 tablespoons finely chopped other fresh herbs, such as chives, marjoram, oregano

country broad beans

No need to serve anything with this dish as it combines both meat and vegetables; it can be a course on its own for a casual meal. This is great with some pasta on the side to mop up the sauce.

Cook the beans until tender, drain and remove their skins. Heat the oil and fry the onion until wilted, add the lettuce and garlic and fry for a few minutes, add ham and stock. Cover and cook gently for 5 minutes, check seasoning and add sugar. Add the beans and mix through, being careful not to break them up. Cook again for a few minutes, then at the finish mix in the butter and let it melt. There should just be a little sauce around the beans.

Serves 2 as a main course, 4 as a side dish

500 g/1 lb broad beans, shelled

3 tablespoons olive oil

1 small onion, finely chopped

1 soft-leafed lettuce, cut into rough pieces

1 clove garlic, finely chopped

150 g/5 oz thickly sliced ham, cut into chunky dice

¾ cup/6 oz vegetable stock

salt and pepper if needed

½ teaspoon sugar

30 g/1 oz butter

broad bean sauce for pasta

Best if there is as much broad bean and sauce as there is pasta for this. The beans are the stars and combine with smoky bacon and mustard to make a rich sauce. Easy and quick to make – apart from shelling the broad beans, which is important for the dish, both for colour and flavour.

Cook the beans in plenty of water and drain (being sure to reserve ½ cup/ 4 fl oz of the liquid), shell the beans and leave aside. This can be done hours in advance.

Heat the butter with oil in a medium saucepan, add bacon, shallots and cook gently until the bacon has given out some fat, then add garlic. Stir for half a minute, mix in stock and the liquid from the beans and simmer for 5 minutes to reduce it slightly and bring out the bacon flavour. Mix cream with mustard and sugar, stir through and heat again, check for seasonings. Bring to a boil, then add the beans and warm them through gently.

Cook the pasta until tender, drain well, mix in the broad bean sauce and stir through. Serve in little bowls with shavings of cheese on top.

Note
If you forget to save the sauce from cooking the beans – which I do occasionally – just use a bit more stock to make up the amount of liquid.

Serves 4 as a first course, 2 as a main course

I kg/2 lb broad beans
30 g/1 oz butter
1 tablespoon olive oil
2 rashers bacon, cut into thick strips
1 shallot, roughly chopped
2 cloves garlic, finely chopped
1 cup/8 fl oz chicken stock
½ cup/4 fl oz cooking liquid from beans
¼ cup/2 fl oz cream
1 teaspoon French mustard
1 teaspoon brown sugar
salt and pepper
150 g/5 oz small pasta
some shavings of Parmesan cheese

broad beans go with

olive oil and butter

cheese

garlic

onions

tomatoes

creamy sauces

prosciutto, bacon and ham

parsley, chives, oregano and thyme

cumin, paprika and chilli

almonds

easy ideas *Broad Beans with Couscous*

Shell 500 g/1 lb broad beans and cook until tender, drain and skin. Prepare a cup of couscous according to the packet directions. Mix with some virgin olive oil, a little lemon juice, a clove of crushed garlic and the broad beans. Toss with two forks. Should the beans have become cold while preparing the couscous, pour some boiling water from the kettle over them and leave for a minute, letting them heat through without over cooking. This goes well with lamb dishes.

granny's gratin of broad beans

hint

Any kind of cheese will become tough if overcooked, so if you are reheating a dish with a cheese topping, it is a good idea to scatter with the cheese only when reheating.

Except she didn't call it by such an extravagant name as a 'gratin', for to granny this was just plain old beans in white sauce, popped into the oven to keep hot while everyone washed their hands after work. While it continued cooking, the top formed a golden crisp crust under a creamy, rich sauce. On washday nights it was eaten with toast fingers, when there was a bit more time she served it with a big portion of roasted chicken.

Put the beans into a shallow ovenproof casserole about 20 cm/8 in diameter. Put the onion, bacon and butter into a saucepan and cook gently until the onion has softened. Scatter the flour on top and stir, there should be enough moisture to absorb it, if not add a bit more butter. Pour in milk and stir constantly until it is boiling and thickened – but this should be a thinnish sauce at this stage. Cook gently for a few minutes to allow it to reduce slightly, season well and pour over the beans. Leave for 30 minutes so the sauce sets a little on top. Mix cheese and crumbs and scatter on top. Dish can be prepared hours in advance to this stage.

Preheat oven to 180°C/350°F. Bake for about 30 minutes, until bubbling on the edges and the top has crisped to a golden crust. You can grill for extra colour if a crust has not formed.

Serves 4

I kg/2 lb broad beans, cooked until just tender and skins left on

I large onion, finely chopped

2 rashers bacon, cut into small strips

30 g/I oz butter

2 tablespoons plain/ all-purpose flour

2 cups/I pint milk

salt and pepper

½ cup/2 oz grated tasty/ cheddar cheese

I cup/4 oz breadcrumbs, made from stale white bread

Brassica oleracea var. italica

broccoli

Broccoli is a member of the cauliflower and cabbage family. It was cultivated by the Venetians in the sixteenth century but has been a part of the Italian table for much longer: it was served frequently at Roman dinners when the chefs of the day, as was the custom for vegetables, just boiled it in a huge pot. They then 'bruised' the broccoli in the way that Apicius prescribed, which meant covering the top with a mixture of '... cumin and coriander seeds, chopped onion plus a few drops of oil and sun made wine ...'. Broccoli was known to the Romans as the 'five green fingers of Jupiter' because of its branches which hold the green flowerets. Home-grown broccoli does taste wonderful. There is a distinct difference, a sweeter, fresher taste, you get from picking your own and cooking it

varieties

immediately as compared to even the best supermarket counterpart. It is easy to grow and a very attractive plant, with lovely dark bluey-green leaves and then fat heads that stand up straight from the centre. Indeed, broccoli is so attractive there is no reason it cannot be a pot plant, you can use it for decoration, allow one plant per pot, making sure there is quite rich soil underneath it (and when the head is mature just cut and eat as you would from the garden bed).

planting

Broccoli can cope with a tiny bit of shade if being grown in a hot area but likes well-drained soil. It is a heavy feeder so the soil must be fertile: prepare the bed by digging in a nitrogen fertilizer or a mix of compost and cow manure. Broccoli can be planted most of the year in a temperate zone but if too hot it can bolt to seed before it forms a head. Again, too much cold and it will do the same, so I begin planting in early autumn and then keep up successive sowings except during summer. It is quite a good idea to get the seeds started in little pots rather than directly into the ground. When they are 5 cm/2in high and have 4–5 true leaves transplant into the garden. They should be about 45 cm/18 in apart, with 60 cm/2 ft between the rows. Plant quite deeply, up to the first leaves, so they will grow up straight and strong. Fertilize before planting and again when they are half grown.

Temperature Zone	Plant or Sow
Tropical	Not suitable
Subtropical	Summer
Temperate	Summer–early autumn
Cool	Summer–early autumn
First picking	3½–4 months

varieties

- Green Sprouting – has a smallish head but good side shoots
- Premium Crop F1 – large heads and is a good heat-tolerant broccoli
- Purple Sprouting – tinged with purple Skiff and Green Duke Hybrid – good for very cold areas
- Romanesco – the 'minaret' version; it is quite beautiful, with a pale green colour and a spiralled head; it is less likely to develop side shoots than some other varieties.

diseases and pests

Same as the cabbage family, caterpillars and cutworms, all of which can be controlled with an organic product. A very healthy garden helps most of all and if you get any mildewed plants, pull them out immediately so it doesn't spread to the healthy plants and don't put these diseased plants into the compost.

harvesting

Broccoli are ready to harvest about 3½ months from planting the seeds, but the harvest then extends over quite a long time. At first plants form a central, firm, blue-green budded head that you take out using a sharp knife and severing cleanly from the main stem. Next side buds appear where the leaves meet the stem and although they are much smaller than the head on the central stalk, they are just as flavoursome and you should carefully cut these out too. As a broccoli head becomes mature its colour develops a yellow tinge and the top separates, indicating the flowerets are becoming too mature; at this stage it will taste very strong so it not worth picking.

buying and storage

Heads must be compact, should smell sweet and be blue-green in colour. It keeps quite well: store in crisper bags in the refrigerator for up to 3 days or stand in a jug with a little water in the base so it can drink it. This way it may keep longer.

nutrition

Broccoli is incredibly good for you – but then so are lots of other things which taste horrible, while broccoli is crunchy, bright green and fresh; if it were a bit more expensive, it would be treasured as a luxury vegetable. It contains more protein and calcium than nearly any other vegetable, plus more Vitamin C than oranges, and as you are munching away you can happily note that it is reputed to be a cancer preventative, one of the best of all the greens for our bodies.

cooking

Tiny bugs and caterpillars love to hide in its stems and swirls and so you need to wash it well before use; leave it in a bowl of water for a short time. Separate the stalks from the heads. The stalk needs peeling but never waste it, as the flavour is great and texture tender. Always boil in a very large pot of water without a lid as the chlorophyll reacts with acids in the water changing the broccoli's colour. The more water used, the more chance of retaining the bright green colour.

Cook in salted water for about 4 minutes or until tender but a little firm. If you steam broccoli it will take longer to cook. Drain well and toss with a little olive oil or butter to serve.

broccoli mousse

This light, pale green mousse can be eaten from the little dishes you cook it in, or line them with some non-stick baking paper/parchment and turn each one out. The mousse can be eaten on its own or with a sauce, such as one made from fresh tomatoes, a light creamy, chicken sauce or a lemon-flavoured one.

Preheat oven to 180°C/350°F. Trim the tops of the broccoli and peel the stalks, chopping them roughly. Bring a pot of water to the boil and salt lightly. Add the broccoli and cook for about 3 minutes or until slightly softened. Drain, chop with a knife into small pieces, put into a bowl and add the butter, tossing so it melts over the broccoli. Heat the cream. Add the broccoli. Put the mixture into a food processor or blender and purée.

Transfer to a bowl. Add eggs, yolk, salt, pepper and cheese and mix well. Put into 8 small soufflé dishes or ramekins, ones that will hold about ¾ cup/6 fl oz, leaving room at the top. Stand the dishes in a baking tin and add boiling water to about halfway up. Cover baking pan loosely with a sheet of foil. Bake in oven for about 18–20 minutes or until just set. Before inverting the moulds, allow to stand for a couple of minutes then run a knife around the edge of the moulds, tap them gently to loosen, then turn on to plates.

Serves 8 as a first course

500 g/1 lb broccoli
30 g/1 oz butter
½ cup/4 fl oz cream
3 large eggs
1 egg yolk
½ teaspoon salt
white pepper
¼ cup/1 oz grated Jarlsburg cheese

hints

The stalks and tops take different times to cook, so for perfect texture you would put them into two different saucepans but this can be a nuisance. It is more sensible just to put the stalks in boiling water a minute before you add the tops.

When soaking broccoli from the garden, add a little salt to the water, which will draw the bugs out more quickly.

broccoli with salmon

This is one of those marvellous dishes which looks and tastes interesting and can be made in just a few minutes.

Trim the broccoli into flowerets. Peel the thick pieces of stalk and slice the stalk up. Put both heads and stalks into a pot of boiling salted water and cook for 5–6 minutes or until just tender. Drain.

Melt the butter in a frying pan; add curry powder and heat for about 30 seconds or until aromatic. Add the broccoli and toss or turn over so it is lightly coated with the mixture. Put into a buttered shallow casserole or small pie dish (a good size is about 20 cm/8 in square). It will only be a flat layer, but this is better than using a deep dish in which not all the salmon and broccoli would be covered by sauce. Remove any bones from the salmon but keep the liquid. Break up the fish and scatter over the top of the broccoli. Season with a little pepper.

Mix the cream with mustard, mayonnaise, salt and chutney. Spread a layer over the fish so that it is lightly coated. Refrigerate if not cooking within 30 minutes, covering the top of the dish with some plastic wrap.

When ready to cook preheat oven to 180°C/350°F and bake for 20–25 minutes or until the sauce has melted and the salmon and broccoli are hot. As you serve you may find some juices in the base, just spoon these over the top of each plate as they have a lovely flavour.

Serves 3–4 as a main dish

250 g/8 oz broccoli heads
30 g/1 oz butter
2 teaspoons mild Madras curry powder
1 x 220 g/7 oz can red salmon
black pepper
½ cup/4 fl oz thick/double cream
1 teaspoon French mustard
2 tablespoons mayonnaise
¼ teaspoon salt
1 tablespoon medium–hot mango chutney

broccoli with a ginger and garlic sauce

In this simple dish the broccoli is coated with a glaze and it has sufficient spice to enable it to be just served with some fluffy rice, for an easy vegetable meal. Cut the broccoli into tiny flowerets for this dish, peeling the stem of each one if you suspect it will be coarse. The flowerets should only be about 3 cm/1¼ in long. Any bits of big stem from the centre stalk can be peeled, cut into julienne strips and added.

Heat the oil and fry the ginger and garlic for a couple of seconds in a wok or large frying pan, add the broccoli and toss for 30 seconds, then add the stock or water. When it has come to a boil cover the pan and leave over medium heat for a couple of minutes or until the broccoli is tender. Meanwhile mix the cornflour/cornstarch with all the remaining ingredients in a small bowl. Pour over the broccoli and stir so it is coated with glaze and lightly thickened.

Serves 4

4 tablespoons oil

2 tablespoons julienned ginger

4 cloves garlic, finely chopped

500 g/1 lb broccoli

½ cup/4 fl oz seasoned vegetable stock or lightly salted water

2 teaspoons cornflour/cornstarch

1 tablespoon soy sauce

1 tablespoon Chinese rice wine

1 teaspoon sesame oil

¼ cup/2 fl oz vegetable stock or water

broccoli cheese with mustard sauce

hint

More mustard has probably been thrown out than is eaten and it is impossible to put out the right amount each time. If you make your own from dry English mustard powder, store any leftover in a tiny jar and put a teaspoon of oil on top. This can then be used in any cooked dishes and keeps very well.

Don't use a Philadelphia-style cream cheese for this dish, as it results in a rather sticky, heavy mousse. Buy some fresh ricotta, a cottage cheese that comes either in small containers in the supermarkets or in bulk at delicatessens. Butter the sides and base of a container (or individual moulds) and line the base with non-stick baking paper/parchment so it will be easy and quick to unmould the mousse.

Preheat oven to 180°C/350°F.

Cut the flowerets from the broccoli and peel the heavy stalks, then slice them. You should have 375 g/12 oz of prepared broccoli. Cook in salted water for about 6 minutes or until tender. Drain well and process until roughly chopped. Add the ricotta or cream cheese, salt and pepper and process to a coarse purée. Remove to a bowl and add the yolks one at a time, along with Parmesan. Beat the egg whites until they hold stiff peaks. Add a third of this at a time to the broccoli mix, folding in carefully with a metal spatula or metal tablespoon.

Spoon or pour the mousse into prepared ramekins or a loaf tin, and place in a baking dish. Pour sufficient boiling water around so that it comes halfway up the sides. Baking in oven for about 20 minutes for small dishes, 30 minutes for a loaf tin, but check mousse is firm to touch. Leave to rest for 5 minutes before inverting on to plates.

Make up the sauce while the mousse is cooking: melt butter in a medium-sized saucepan, add the flour and fry until it is grainy. Pour in the milk and stock, stir until it comes to a boil and thickens. Turn the heat low and let cook for about 3 minutes. Add the mustards, lemon juice, salt and pepper, horseradish and cream. Keep warm and when the mousse is ready to serve, trickle the sauce over the top.

Serves 4

500 g/1 lb broccoli

90 g/3 oz ricotta or cream cheese

½ teaspoon salt

¼ teaspoon ground white pepper

2 large eggs, separated

¼ cup/1 oz grated Parmesan cheese

Mustard Sauce

45 g/1½ oz butter

1½ tablespoon plain/all-purpose flour

1 cup/8 fl oz milk

½ cup/4 fl oz vegetable stock

1 tablespoon French mustard

1 teaspoon dry English mustard

1 teaspoon lemon juice

salt and pepper to taste

1 teaspoon horseradish sauce

1 tablespoon cream

broccoli and potato frittata

easy ideas

Broccoli Pesto

Boil or steam about 250 g/ 8 oz sliced broccoli heads for 3 minutes, it should be a little crisp still. Drain well and put into a food processor with 3 cloves chopped garlic, I small chilli, handful of pecan nuts, salt, pepper, 1/3 cup grated Parmesan cheese and 1/2 cup basil leaves. Process, then gradually add enough oil to make a thinnish purée. This keeps in a jar, refrigerated, for several days. Serve tossed through freshly cooked pasta.

In a Spanish tortilla onions and potatoes are cooked in a large amount of oil which becomes absorbed into the potato as it becomes tender, while the added onion gives a sweet taste. This is a similar idea but broccoli is included as well. The dish is quite substantial and I like to take it to the table in the big pan in which it was cooked, so it has a really casual feel. I serve it either hot or cold because these kinds of egg dishes are just as nice at room temperature. As the frittata requires quite a lot of oil you should use a good olive oil to ensure the finished dish has a fruity character.

Put the potatoes into a non-stick saucepan with the oil and onion and heat gently, stirring occasionally, until potatoes have softened. You will hardly have any oil left and don't be fussed if there are bits of broken potato, you really won't notice at all in the finished dish. Tip into a basin. This can be done hours in advance.

When ready to proceed, cook the broccoli until tender in boiling salted water. If any bits of the broccoli are large you need to chop them up so the frittata will have an even layer throughout. Drain and add to the potato and onion along with remaining ingredients. Heat a pan about 23 cm/9 in diameter and add oil to cover the base. When it is very hot, almost smoking, tip in the frittata mixture: this should sizzle and set instantly. Turn the heat down and cook gently until frittata is cooked a bit more than half way through. Preheat griller/broiler and put pan under this so the top cooks. When frittata is golden on top, remove from heat, cover with some foil or a big lid and let sit for about 15 minutes while the frittata releases a little steam and softens on top.

Serves 6

500 g/1 lb potatoes, peeled and sliced

1/2 cup/4 fl oz olive oil

I onion, finely chopped

500 g/1 lb broccoli broken into small flowerets

2 cloves garlic, finely chopped

1/2 cup/2 oz grated Parmesan cheese

6 eggs, lightly beaten

stir-fried broccoli

Broccoli is a symbol of jade to the Chinese and jade is a symbol of youth and good health. This recipe is very quick and relies only on a little fresh ginger and salt to add some spice to the broccoli. Serve with almost any meat or chicken or over some noodles for a quick meal.

Cut away most of the stalk and reserve for another use, then cut the broccoli flowerets into very thin slices. Heat the oil in a wok or large frying pan and add the ginger, cook 30 seconds, add broccoli and scatter salt on top. Stir-fry quickly for 2 minutes. Pour water around the edges of the pan and toss. As soon as the broccoli has become bright green it is ready. Should the broccoli remain too firm, add a little more water but again tip it around the edges not over the top, so it creates steam.

Serves 4

375 g/12 oz broccoli

2 tablespoons oil

2 slices fresh ginger

1/2 teaspoon salt

3 tablespoons water

pasta with broccoli and tomato

Oriecchette is very specialized pasta made in the south of Italy. You can buy it commercially but it costs far more than the usual pasta. It is quite dense and the pasta is moulded so a 'thumbprint' in the centre forms a little ear. Vegetable sauces feature strongly in this area and among the most popular is one made of broccoli and nuts, the sauce being trapped in the hollows of the oriecchette. Any pasta that has a similar feature will also catch the sauce, so you can use small penne or shells instead. The tomato part of the dish can be made in advance but the broccoli needs to be cooked at the last minute. It is traditional to use the pasta water to cook the broccoli. The topping of crumbs – instead of cheese – lends an interesting crunch to the soft sauce.

Put the crumbs and oil in a frying pan over a high heat and stir until the crumbs are a deep gold–light brown colour and very crisp. Transfer to a plate. Gently cook the tomatoes with garlic in the pan for about 10 minutes until softened. Add the anchovy and chilli and season well.

Cook the pasta in a large saucepan with plenty of salted boiling water. Separate the broccoli flowerets and peel and slice the stalks thinly. When the pasta is almost ready add the broccoli to the water and cook for about 4 minutes, or until just tender. Drain both pasta and broccoli in a colander, leaving a little moisture on the pasta. Warm the tomato again and toss through the pasta so it is well coated. Spoon into bowls or on to a platter and at the last minute toss on the crumbs (if you do this too soon they will soften and you lose the contrast of textures).

Serves 2 as a main dish, 4 as a first course

½ cup/1½ oz fresh brown breadcrumbs

about 3 tablespoons olive oil

4 large ripe tomatoes, peeled and roughly diced

2 cloves garlic, finely chopped

4 anchovy fillets, roughly chopped

1 small chilli, deseeded and finely chopped

salt and pepper

300 g/10 oz pasta

500 g/1 lb broccoli

venetian broccoli purée

This is a light purée which can be served in the same way you would a spinach purée or similar, with meats that don't have too much sauce. The broccoli must be fairly well cooked but watch and snatch it from the heat before it overcooks or you will have a strong purée instead of a light, delicate, velvety one. The recipe is not exactly slimming but as it is an old dish this would have been of no concern to the Italian ladies with voluptuous curves who originally ate it – nor to the men who liked them that way.

Gently cook prosciutto in the butter for about 5 minutes, stirring until you have plenty of fat in the pan. Add the broccoli and toss, then pour on chicken stock and cook until it is almost tender and the stock has reduced a little. Add the cream and boil over high heat for a few minutes. You should end up with about a cup of liquid. Purée, check seasonings and then serve warmed again or leave to cool and reheat later.

Serves 6

2 slices prosciutto, cut into small pieces

45 g/1½ oz butter

750 g/1½ lb broccoli, separated into flowerets

1½ cups/12 fl oz chicken stock

½ cup/4 fl oz cream

salt and pepper

broccoli goes with

olive oil

butter

capsicum/ bell pepper

garlic

onion

tomato

chilli

lemon

pasta

chicken

bacon and prosciutto

ham

salmon

almonds

pine nuts

pecan nuts

Parmesan, melting and light blue cheeses

ricotta

creamy sauces

basil

oregano

spiced beef and broccoli

easy ideas

Broccoli Stalks with Parmesan

Take about 375 g/ 12 oz stalks, peel-ed and cook for a few minutes, until just tender, in boil-ing salted water. Drain well. Cut into strips. Toss with a tablespoon of olive oil and several table-spoons of finely grated Parmesan, which will stick to the broccoli. Serve immediately with steak or chicken.

To the Chinese eye a floweret atop a longish stalk is very beautiful, so for this dish cut the broccoli head into slices that look like tiny trees. Some bits from the top won't have any stalk and if you have very wide broccoli it is best to cut each broccoli head into halves first. Of course the stalks must be peeled first. The beef can be marinated a day in advance and the final cooking takes only about 6–7 minutes. This dish goes equally well resting on a bed of slippery, silky noodles or over some steaming hot rice.

Put the fillet steak into a basin, add the sugar, light soy, peanut oil and cornflour/cornstarch and stir with your hands until each piece of beef is coated. Cover and refrigerate overnight. Take it out of the fridge half an hour before the dish is to be finished so it is not too cold and separate the pieces of beef. Heat 3 tablespoons of the oil and add the broccoli, stir-fry so it is coated with oil then scatter with salt and sugar and toss. Add rice wine, then tip the water around the edges and cook until green. Remove to a bowl, covering with a plate to keep it warm. Add remaining oil and mix in chilli and ginger and toss, add the beef and toss well, ensuring beef doesn't stick together as it cooks. When beef has changed colour on the outside, mix in the broccoli again, stir to combine and serve.

Serves 3–4

375 g/12 oz fillet steak, cut into very thin slices across the grain

1 teaspoon brown sugar

2 tablespoons light soy sauce

1 teaspoon peanut oil

2 teaspoons cornflour/cornstarch

5 tablespoons oil

500 g/1 lb broccoli, sliced

1 teaspoon salt

1 teaspoon sugar

1 tablespoon Chinese rice wine

1/4 cup/2 fl oz water

1 small chilli, deseeded and finely chopped

2 teaspoons grated fresh ginger

broccoli with blue cheese

The best kind of blue cheese for this is a creamy one that will melt smoothly and give a tart, rich taste without being so strong it overwhelms the broccoli. I like this on its own, it is luxurious enough it doesn't need to be teamed with any other dish.

Boil the broccoli until just tender and drain well. Put into the base of a shallow ovenproof dish. Cook the onion in oil until soft then add butter. When it has melted mix in the flour and cook a few minutes then tip in the milk. Stir until it comes to the boil and cook a minute. Add the cheese, take off the heat and stir until the cheese has melted into the sauce. Taste now and season: different cheeses vary in their saltiness so it is best to wait until cheese has been added before seasoning. Spoon sauce over the broccoli, then scatter on crumbs and nuts. The dish can be completed to this stage hours in advance.

When ready to cook, bake in a preheated moderate oven (180°C/350°F) for about 25 minutes or until the dish is bubbling at the edges and the top has coloured a little.

Serves 4

500 g/1 lb broccoli

1 onion, finely chopped

2 tablespoons oil

30 g/1 oz butter

2 tablespoons flour

1 3/4 cups/14 fl oz milk

100 g/3 oz creamy blue cheese

salt and pepper

breadcrumbs made from stale bread

1/3 cup/1 1/2 oz roughly chopped walnuts

Brassica oleracea var. gemmifera

Brussels sprouts are so much prettier growing in the garden than you could ever imagine from the loose ones you find in the shops. The plants look like tiny trees covered with small round balls sprouting from a big main stem, the sprouts nestling in the large green leaves which act as an umbrella, guarding the rosettes. The Germans call them *rosenkohl* – rose cabbages – which is a descriptive name. The time to pick them is when they are sweet and tender, and you have control over this when you grow them yourself. So often they are too large in the shops, becoming strong tasting and a bit coarse. I find they are rarely listed as a favourite vegetable for most people but often this is the result of bad cooking. Traditionally in Britain the Christmas turkey is served with Brussels sprouts and embellished with chestnuts, which make a contrast in colour and texture. In Australia, however, chestnuts are not in season when sprouts are at their best so if you like this combination you will need to use frozen chestnuts.

As is obvious from their name, sprouts originated from Brussels; there is a reference to them from that country in 1213. They are again mentioned in the 1500s, yet appear rarely in historical notes throughout Europe so obviously were not popular. It seems that the first person in England to mention them, and even create a recipe, was the writer Eliza Acton.

I think they are best treated quite simply. Just steamed and then dressed with some butter or perhaps a little olive oil. They can be covered with a creamy sauce and baked like a gratin but this needs to be made and then heated quickly in the oven or the flavour is strong. You can make soup but take care it doesn't taste like cabbage soup. For soup the sprouts should only be just cooked with onion in stock and then puréed in a processor. Nice with a bit of cream added but this is not a soup that reheats well.

planting

Of all the members of the cabbage family sprouts are the most frost tolerant and do best in a cool growing season. If the weather is too hot for too long – or, conversely, too cold for too long – they can become bitter tasting. Brussels sprouts are not really suitable for hot climates, as the sprouts then don't form compact heads but just make little tufts of leaves on the stalk. You must, however, plant in hot weather to ensure they will be maturing when the

weather is cooling down. The following is perhaps not altogether a perfect calculation (and how can a perfect calculation be made when our seasons can vary so much?) but they will be producing their first edible heads and need cool days approximately 12–14 weeks after planting.

Soil should be well-drained, and high in nitrogen so add some well-balanced fertilizer. If your soil is acid dig some lime or dolomite into the plot liberally prior to planting, working it in to a depth of about 15 cm/6 in.

Put in seedlings when they are four or five weeks old with 4–5 true leaves. If they are leggy or crooked plant well down and heap a little soil up to the base of the leaves to help them grow straight from the beginning. Plant 45 cm/18 in apart, keeping the rows 60 cm/2 ft apart. Seeds should be put in a fairly shallow hole 1 cm/½ in deep and transplanted when ready. Fertilize growing plants with a liquid fertilizer fairly regularly but cut down on watering as they reach maturity.

Temperature Zone	Plant or Sow
Tropical	Not suitable
Subtropical	Not suitable
Temperate	Mid summer–autumn
Cool	Spring–mid summer
First picking	16–20 weeks

varieties

- Champion Long Island
- Citadel
- Giant Prolific
- Jade Cross
- Ruby – for a decorative effect: it's an heirloom with a distinctive blue leaf and little red button sprouts, available as seed rather than seedlings.

diseases and pests

Similar to cabbages, and all the members of the cabbage family, their enemies are caterpillars, while cutworms and aphids are also serious pests. It is especially important to control pests on Brussels sprouts because once these are well tucked into the tightly curled sprouts you just can't get to them.

Check fairly regularly, use some cabbage dust and if you find the aphids you need to spray with a 'wet spray' of pyrethrum, making sure it reaches the little colony they are establishing. Dry powder can't get into the curls and bulges of the leaves so you need a liquid to wash them out before they take control.

harvesting

At approximately 4 months from planting. Sprouts mature from the base of the plant up and should be picked this way until all are gone. Then the top can be removed and steamed or used as a green vegetable.

nutrition

Brussels sprouts contain lower levels of minerals than broccoli but they make up for it with higher levels of vitamins and a high content of sulphur compounds, which have anti-cancer properties. They are a good source of dietary fibre and folate, as well as vitamins B and C.

buying and storage

Sprouts must be bright green, very firm looking and without a trace of yellow. If the outside leaves are loose and look a bit floppy they have been picked a little too late. It is important that sprouts smell quite sweet and fresh, as if they have a 'cabbage' smell in their raw state they will be horrible and strong when cooked. Keep them in a vegetable storage bag in the crisper in the refrigerator but use within a couple of days, for the longer they are kept the stronger their flavour will be when cooked.

cooking

Like cabbage it is important they are not overcooked. First take away any loose outer leaves. Wash them, although because of the way they grow they rarely have dirt in the leaves; however, if they are from the garden get rid of any aphids by soaking in salted tepid water for 15 minutes. Trim the stem at the base but make sure you leave the little sprouts intact, so don't cut too short or they will break apart.

To retain a bright colour cook in lots of boiling water as the chlorophyll in them reacts with acids in the cooking water and they turn a drab green. Tiny ones should only take about 8 minutes, slightly larger ones about 10 minutes.

If you have picked the babies from the garden they may only need 5 minutes. I often cut sprouts into half so they will cook very quickly; this keeps them brighter in colour and fresher tasting.

brussels sprouts with egg and crisp crumbs

This garnish can be used with other vegetables, such as asparagus, beans and broccoli. It adds a contrasting texture and colour to the sprouts without dominating them.

Put the crumbs into a frying pan with half the butter and toss crumbs around using a fork until they are quite crisp. Transfer to a plate. Crumbs can be prepared hours in advance. When ready to cook, boil the sprouts in plenty of salted water and drain well. Heat the remaining butter, add the sprouts and toss until the outside is well coated with butter, season and add the lemon. Tip them into a bowl and grate the egg over the top, using the coarse part of your grater, then tip the crumbs over. If you are serving individual plates put a few sprouts onto each plate and scatter with egg and crumbs.

Serves 4–6

½ cup/1½ oz breadcrumbs made from stale bread

90 g/3 oz butter

500 g/1 lb Brussels sprouts

salt and pepper

juice of ½ lemon

2 hard-boiled eggs

brussels sprouts go with

butter

oil

chilli

garlic

ginger

onion

lemon

cheese

creamy sauces

eggs

bacon and ham

breadcrumbs

nuts, especially chestnuts

curry

brussels sprouts with bacon and onion

easy ideas

Buttered Sprouts

Cook for about
4 minutes in
plenty of salted
boiling water and
drain well. Cut
into thin slices
and drain again
to get rid of any
water. Put into a
pan with a big
knob of butter,
salt and pepper
and toss for a
few minutes until
they are soft and
buttery with just
a little juice
around them.

The bacon fat gives a lovely flavour to the sprouts while the onion adds sweetness. This is good with chicken, quail or duck.

Put bacon and onion into a saucepan with the oil and cook gently until the bacon has given out some fat, cover and let the mixture cook until you have very soft, tender onion. Meanwhile quickly steam or cook the Brussels sprouts until just tender. Drain them. Cut into halves or quarters and add to the pan with bacon and onion. Reheat, tossing and stirring gently. Sprouts will break up a bit but gain more flavour. Season. When they are well coated serve.

Serves 4-6

3 rashers bacon, cut into strips

1 large onion, finely chopped

2 tablespoons olive oil

500 g/1 lb Brussels sprouts

salt and pepper

lightly curried brussels sprouts

You don't need much curry to give a spicy flavour; it should just coat the sprouts with a speckled glacé without being too strong.

Cook the sprouts by steaming or boiling in salted water until just tender. Drain. Melt the butter in a pan, add the curry and almonds and cook gently until the almonds are slightly toasted. Add the sprouts and reheat them, shaking the pan so they are coated with curry butter. Season with a salt and pepper to taste.

Serves 4

500 g/1 lb Brussels sprouts

45 g/1½ oz butter

3 teaspoons curry powder

2 tablespoons almond slivers

salt and pepper

hint

Many people find
that cutting a
small cross in
the base of the
stalk helps the
Brussels sprouts
to cook more
evenly. Others
totally disagree
with this, claiming
that it leads to a
loss of shape and
flavour. So just
please yourself as
to whether you
do this or not.
It may be worth
trying if you are
preparing large
Brussels sprouts.

crushed brussels sprouts

This is not meant to be a purée, but neither should the dish include large pieces of sprouts. The idea is to have a crumbly, soft mix of sprouts with plenty of creamy butter around them. A good side dish with pork or duck.

Steam or boil the Brussels sprouts until they are just soft (if you boil them be sure to drain them well or the mixture will be too wet). Put them into a bowl and add the nutmeg and some salt and pepper. Heat the butter with milk until almost boiling. Using a potato masher, smash down firmly onto the sprouts, crushing them, at the same time adding bits of hot milk and butter. The liquid should be absorbed into the green mix, making it very soft but not watery. If you need to you can reheat this – but not for long or it will lose its lovely pale green colour.

Serves 4

500 g/1 lb Brussels sprouts

pinch of nutmeg

salt and pepper

45 g/1½ oz butter

½ cup/4 fl oz milk

Brassica oleracea var. capitata

cabbage

Cabbages, with their overlapping leaves and big fat heart which sits in the centre like a giant green flower, are a very attractive vegetable in the garden and the flavour of home-grown cabbages is sweet and fresh. Even when they go to seed these enormous blossom heads are as pretty as any flower and they are one of my favourites in the decorative garden. Early cabbages were not as chubby and round as the ones we know now, growing straight upwards. The modern, hearted variety was developed from the earlier thick-stalked variety in Germany in the twelfth century. Cabbages are one of the most versatile of vegetables, being crunchy and delicious in a green salad, soft and tender in cooked dishes. In Asian dishes cabbage can be stir fried in a spicy mix, while in European traditions it is salted and fermented, braised gently with aromatics or left quite simple, being steamed and served with a butter sauce. Added in shreds to the top of vegetable soup for the last few minutes of cooking it lends a fresh green crunchy taste, quite different to soup that has cabbage added early in the cooking, where it braises and softens.

planting

Cabbages are easy to grow and very rewarding for the amount you get from just one big cabbage bed. They like well-drained and fertile soil which is not too acid. Work a well-balanced fertilizer into the ground before planting. The nitrogen content should be quite high and the healthier the soil the more diseases will be discouraged.

Sow the right variety for the time of year. Seeds should be about 1 cm/½ in deep and about 7 cm/3 in apart. Plants will need thinning when they are big enough to lift and should then be placed 60 cm/2 ft apart so the leaves don't overlap. Seedlings need to be planted the same distance, 60 cm/2 ft apart, and in rows about 70 cm/2½ ft apart. If they have crooked stems or look leggy, plant well into the soil and heap a little earth around up to the bottom leaf, firming it up to keep the stalks straight in the early stages.

Cabbages need plenty of water early in their growing stages and one of the secrets is to maintain steady growth. They are gross feeders so every couple of weeks give them a little liquid fertilizer. When the heads are formed slow down the watering as once the heads are maturing they may split open and go to seed quickly – I must add this can vary according to the variety you plant.

Temperature Zone	Plant or Sow
Tropical	Not suitable
Subtropical	Autumn–winter
Temperate	Summer, autumn and spring
Cool	Summer, autumn and spring
First picking	*4–5 months from sowing*

varieties

The first three are heirloom varieties, so are likely only to be found as seeds from specialized growers.
- January King – a blue semi-Savoy type that stores well
- Mini (Emerald Acre) – matures about a month ahead of other cabbages
- Red Drum Head – has red medium-sized heads with blue leaves, looks lovely and holds well for 30 days.

Early season varieties

- Earlibau
- First Early Improved
- Sugarloaf – a pretty little cone-shaped cabbage
- Headstart – grows quickly and makes a small solid heart quite early
- Supercite
- Savoy King – for warmer areas.

Late season varieties

- Drumhead
- Greengold Hybrid
- Savoy
- Succession.

diseases and pests

They have a few enemies, mainly cabbage white butterfly, caterpillars, cutworms and cabbage loopers, but these can be controlled with an organic spray, while derris powder is also effective against cabbage

white caterpillars and aphids. Black rot and clubroot fungus can attack cabbages but be sure to plant disease-resistant varieties and if you do get any infected cabbages just pull them out. Don't put into the compost. Having a healthy garden increases the chances of fewer problems. When you plant the seedlings you can put a cut-down soft-drink bottle over the top of each one, which will help protect them from snails and caterpillars until they are established.

harvesting

About 4–4½ months from planting but picking times vary according to the variety of cabbage. Thankfully even if you plant half a dozen at a time they all seem to mature at slightly different stages, but try to stagger the plantings. As soon as the head is firm you can pick it, cutting away so the outer leaves are left. I find if I don't harvest when they are ready they do begin to split so I don't leave them too long in the garden. It is better to pick them and store in the refrigerator – and become imaginative with cabbage dishes while they are at their peak.

nutrition

A good source of dietary fibre. All cabbages are a great source of Vitamin C and provide folate. It is interesting that the Savoy cabbages contain double the folate of other varieties and also the highest levels of Vitamin C, potassium, iron and beta-carotene.

buying and storage

If you can, avoid cabbages that have been cut and wrapped in plastic film as you don't really know how long the vegetable has been suffocating in this package. In a vegetable storage bag cabbages should keep for a week but the tight variety keep a little better and longer than loose-leafed cabbage.

Tight cabbage varieties

Look for the firmest, tightest, heaviest head, one that is smooth and bright green, almost squeaky to touch. Cabbages may smell a bit in cooking but should never smell anything but sweet when raw, if they have a strong scent it means they are ageing and will taste stronger when cooked.

Loose-leafed cabbage varieties

These should be crisp and bright, with lively looking leaves that spring out from each other. Skip over any droopy cabbages and again check they smell fresh.

cooking

It is best to cut cabbages before washing them, as it is difficult for the water to penetrate to the centre leaves of whole cabbages, so you are just really rinsing the outside. This is even more important for home-grown cabbages, as all kinds of little members of the garden community can be found lurking inside to surprise you.

That dreadful smell of cooking cabbage, the joke of many a boarding-house story, comes from overcooking it until the cabbage has become a sulphurous, watery flabby object, and even draining well won't get rid of the liquid in overcooked vegetables. The longer you boil cabbage (and other brassicas) the stronger the smell will be. Yet there are many wonderful European dishes where the cabbage is gently cooked in a very slow oven for hours and it ends up smelling delicious and tasting soft and sweet, which may seem a contradiction.

cabbage salad with spicy tomato dressing

This unusual salad needs the hot bite of chilli or it would be too sweet. I like to leave it for several hours so the flavours all blend. Although the recipe may seem to include a lot of sugar, most tomatoes have enough acid to balance this. Perhaps in the heart of summer, when the tomatoes are sweeter, you may cut down on the sugar just a tiny bit. It is a simple and interesting dish, which is worth building into your repertoire as a base for barbecued meat or grilled chicken.

Heat the oil in a saucepan, add the onion and cook gently, stirring occasionally until it has softened slightly. Add tomatoes and cook for a few minutes. Season with salt and pepper, add chilli and cook covered until a thick sauce. Push mixture through a sieve or mouli into a bowl. Add the sugar, oil and vinegar. Shred the cabbage finely and mix with the warm sauce. Toss so the cabbage strands are covered. Every so often until you serve it, give the salad another toss.

Variation
For a simple and very inexpensive meal, mix salad with some cooked, cooled fine egg noodles. After noodles are drained toss them with a bit of oil to keep them separate so they don't become sticky and then mix into the cabbage.

Serves 4

1 teaspoon vegetable oil

1 large onion, finely diced

2 ripe tomatoes, cut into chunks

salt and pepper

1 hot chilli, deseeded and finely chopped

1/4 cup/2 oz sugar

1/4 cup/2 fl oz vegetable oil

1/4 cup/2 fl oz white wine vinegar

1/2 small, or 1/4 large, cabbage

hint

For softer cabbage salads mix the dressing, including salt, and stir it into the cabbage well in advance. The salt, vinegar or lemon will break down the vegetable fibres and even quite tough leaves become soft after a couple of hours.

asian cabbage and chicken salad

easy ideas

*Steamed Balsamic
and Buttered
Cabbage*

Cut half a
small cabbage
into thinnish
wedges. Steam
these over water
until just tender.
While they are
cooking melt
about 60 g/
2 oz butter, add
salt and pepper
and mix in
3 teaspoons
balsamic vinegar
and I teaspoon
brown sugar.
Drain the
cabbage for a
minute, chop
roughly and
toss with the
buttery mix.
Great with
sausages or
pork. Provide
a little pot of
spicy mustard
on the table.

A light meal, or make without the chicken as an accompaniment to fish, beef or almost any roasted meat. This particular salad gets lots of liquid around it with storage but I quite like it soft, and when you serve just drain some of the juices away if too much has formed. Serve within 20 minutes of preparation for a crisp salad or leave overnight if a 'soft salad' is preferred. You can cheat if you are in a hurry and buy a portion of barbecued chicken from a good poultry shop – one where they don't cook it until it is dry – discard the skin and pull the chicken flesh into shreds before adding to salad.

To make sauce, heat the oil and fry the chilli for a minute, stirring. Remove and add the remaining ingredients. (If a large cabbage is being used, double the dressing.)

Mix together all the ingredients for the salad. Add the sauce and toss well. Cover and refrigerate for the flavours to blend, for at least 20 minutes but salad can be left for several hours. Serve scattered with a few extra mint and basil leaves over the top.

Serves 4 as a main course, 6 or more as a side dish

½ small cabbage, finely shredded

I medium-sized carrot, grated

I small red onion, finely chopped

10 mint leaves, chopped

10 basil leaves, roughly broken

½ medium-sized
cooked chicken, shredded

½ cup/3 oz dry roasted
peanuts, roughly chopped

Sauce

3 tablespoons light olive oil

I hot chilli, deseeded and
cut into slices

2 tablespoons fish sauce

3 tablespoons lemon juice

2 tablespoons brown sugar

2 cloves garlic, crushed

I teaspoon salt

ham and coleslaw salad

An easy picnic salad or one you could pile into pita bread for lunch. The combination of cabbage, ham and cheese is quite sustaining and nourishing and sunflower seeds give it an interesting, nutty flavour. It can be made hours in advance – and then stored in the refrigerator – and can even be left overnight, in which case I usually add the apple in the morning so that it retains its freshness. The salad is best served as a main course for a meal rather than an accompaniment.

Mix all the salad ingredients except sunflower seeds together. Stir the lemon into the olive oil and add mayonnaise. Stir through the salad and season with salt and pepper. Put the sunflower seeds into a dry frying pan and roast them until they are tinged with gold. Keep stirring them so they colour evenly. Add to the salad and stir through.

Serves 4

¼ cabbage, finely shredded
(about 4 cups)

I small carrot, finely grated

I medium-sized apple,
peeled and grated coarsely

125 g/4 oz ham, cut into fine
strips

½ cup/4 oz grated tasty/
cheddar cheese

¼ cup/good handful
sunflower seeds

Dressing

juice of I lemon

2 tablespoons light olive oil

2 tablespoons mayonnaise
(or enough to moisten)

salt and pepper

coleslaw with asian flavours

Have the cabbage really finely shredded for this dish as the dressing's flavours thus have more impact and also wilt the cabbage nicely as they soak into the strands. It is interesting as a change with some grilled or pan-fried fish, and of course goes nicely with chicken.

Mix all the salad ingredients together in a bowl and toss well. Chill if you are not ready to add the dressing.

When dressing the salad, the soy should not be too dominant, so buy a sauce that is light in flavour and colour. If you have one that is dark and intense, it can be diluted with water. Put soy sauce, garlic and ginger in a saucepan and warm gently. Add the vinegar, sugar and chilli and let cool. Heat again and pour through a sieve over the salad to remove the bits of ginger and chilli. Toss well and marinate salad for several hours before serving.

Serves 6

3 cups/10 oz finely shredded cabbage

1 cup/4 oz grated carrot

1 cup/2½ oz bean shoots

6 spring onions/scallions, finely chopped

Dressing

½ cup/4 fl oz light soy sauce

1 clove garlic, crushed

1 teaspoon grated ginger

1 tablespoon white wine vinegar

1 tablespoon sugar

1 small chilli, deseeded and finely chopped (optional)

vietnamese-style cabbage salad

One of the Vietnamese salads I love is a mixture of pork, prawns, sometimes crunchy and translucent jellyfish, and cabbage. The fish sauce dressing, with sugar, provides the sweetness and salt. The heat comes from the chilli, the fresh taste from lemon, thus balancing and completing the flavours.

Bring some lightly salted water to a boil in a medium-sized saucepan. Add the pork fillet. Cover and cook on a very low heat until the pork is cooked through. Timing depends on the thickness of the meat but it mustn't be dry. Remove to a large bowl, put a few spoonfuls of liquid on top to keep pork moist and cover with a plate. Add the chicken to the same water, cover and cook gently for about 5–6 minutes. Remove and add to the bowl with the pork. Be sure there is enough liquid, otherwise pour on a bit more. Both meats can be cooked a day in advance. Refrigerate, covered.

Cut the pork into slices and then into strips. Pull the chicken into fine shreds. Shell the prawns and cut into chunky pieces. Cut the onion into quarters and then thin slices and place into a bowl with vinegar and sugar. Stand for 30 minutes, drain well. Mix the meats with onion, cucumber, cabbage and carrot. To make the dressing stir everything together; pour over the salad and toss. Top with peanuts and mint leaves.

Serves 4

200 g/6 oz pork fillet, trimmed of any sinew

250 g/8 oz boned and skinned chicken breast

375 g/12 oz cooked prawns in the shell

1 medium-sized mild white onion

1 tablespoon white wine vinegar

1 teaspoon sugar

1 medium-sized cucumber, peeled, cut into halves lengthwise and then finely sliced

3 cups/10 oz very finely shredded cabbage

1 cup/4 oz grated carrot

⅓ cup/2 oz dry roasted peanuts, roughly chopped

mint leaves for garnishing

Dressing

2 tablespoons Vietnamese or Thai fish sauce

4 tablespoons water

2 large cloves garlic, crushed

1 small hot chilli, deseeded and chopped

2 tablespoons lemon juice

1 tablespoon sugar

easy ideas

Braised Cabbage

Shred half a cabbage coarsely and toss in a knob of butter or some olive oil. Add a couple of cloves of chopped garlic, some pepper and a cup of seasoned chicken or vegetable stock. Cover and cook gently until just tender and serve with some of the stock juices around it under a piece of roasted chicken or pork. Also good with sausages and mustard.

cabbage with noodles

This very tasty, spiced cabbage can be a main course if you heap it over some egg noodles or serve it with rice. It is quite hot but of course you can cut down the spices if you are not keen on very hot food. However, don't delete them to the extent that the dish loses its balance and character.

Use a wide shallow saucepan for this dish or a wok with a lid. Wash cabbage well and leave in a colander to drain while preparing the base. There should just be a little moisture on the cabbage shreds by the time you add them to the saucepan.

Heat the oil and gently fry the capsicum/bell pepper, onion, carrot and garlic until the vegetables have wilted. Turn up the heat and add the ginger, curry powder, pepper and chilli and keep cooking until the spices are aromatic and the vegetables well coated. Mix in the tomatoes and cook for 1 minute, then add the cabbage with water and salt. Stir so that the cabbage is coated with all the spices, and cook for about 5 minutes with a lid on top, occasionally stirring. Then take off the lid and cook until the cabbage is tender. You should have plenty of spicy vegetable juices to spoon over cooked noodles or rice. If there is too much liquid, boil very rapidly for a minute or two to reduce it. Just be careful the pan doesn't become dry at any stage while the cabbage is cooking; if it does add a couple of spoonfuls of water. When serving sprinkle roasted peanuts over the cabbage.

Serves 6

½ small cabbage, finely shredded

⅓ cup/3 fl oz light olive oil

1 red capsicum/bell pepper, chopped into small pieces

1 large onion, finely chopped

1 medium-sized carrot, grated

2 large cloves garlic, finely chopped

2 teaspoons grated ginger

1 teaspoon curry powder

1 teaspoon coarsely ground black pepper

1 small chilli, deseeded and chopped small, or a little Tabasco sauce

2 tomatoes, deseeded and cut into pieces

⅓ cup/3 fl oz water

½ teaspoon salt or to taste

250 g/8 oz fine egg noodles

⅓ cup/2 oz roasted peanuts, roughly chopped

cabbage goes with

butter

oil

cheese, all kinds

cream

milk

apples

ginger

sesame seeds

carrots

garlic

onions

potatoes

chestnuts

lentils

caraway seeds

paprika

nutmeg

curry

juniper berries

bacon

corned beef

ham

most kinds of sausages, incluing frankfurts

chicken

duck

game

lamb or mutton

pork

wine

puff pastry and filo

rice

mince east-west

This combines some of the flavours of the Orient with a Western taste – a base of beef mince. It is a quickly made dish that goes well with rice or noodles, to make an inexpensive main course.

Heat the oil in a very large frying pan or a wok. Add the onion and red capsicum/bell pepper and toss over high heat until just slightly softened. Add garlic and shredded cabbage and cook for a couple of minutes or until the cabbage has wilted – but be sure it still has a crisp texture. Add the bean shoots, stir for a few seconds and remove the vegetables to a bowl. Add beef to the pan. If it is dry, you can moisten it with a little more oil. Fry, stirring to break up the meat so it becomes crumbly, and let it cook gently for a few minutes. Mix all the remaining ingredients in a small bowl and pour over the beef. Liquid will lightly thicken. Return the vegetables to pan and stir them only until they are heated through again.

If you want to do some preparation in advance, you can cook the vegetables but keep them a bit underdone, cook the beef and then warm it again without the sauce, adding this at the finish with the vegetables. This way it will retain a fresher taste.

Serves 6

2 tablespoons vegetable oil

2 medium-sized white onions, halved and then thinly sliced

1 medium-sized red capsicum/ bell pepper, cut into strips

1 large clove garlic, finely chopped

2 cups shredded cabbage

1 cup/2½ oz bean shoots

500 g/1 lb finely minced lean beef

¼ cup/2 fl oz water

2 tablespoons soy sauce

1 teaspoon grated fresh ginger

¼ teaspoon chilli sauce

2 teaspoons sugar

3 teaspoons cornflour/cornstarch

red braised cabbage

hint

If you chop cabbage using a food processor you'll find most machines bruise the cabbage as it is cut and result in little scrappy bits among the shreds. When processed cabbage is cooked or mixed into salad it quickly develops an unpleasant flavour. So always cut by hand using a very sharp knife. It is worth the bother to get sweet-tasting cabbage.

There are many versions of this type of slow-cooked cabbage. It is perfect with any kind of game, with sausages, and most kinds of pork or rabbit. There should still be an indication of the apple slices in the finished dish but the cabbage will be melting and soft. Use eating apples in this recipe, as they are more likely to retain their shape rather than a tart apple such as Granny Smith. This is one of the few cabbage dishes that is even better reheated next day – and the day after that – so you can afford to make a bit extra.

Put the cabbage into a big saucepan with the butter and onion and sauté, stirring frequently, for about 10 minutes. Add red wine, sugar and salt and mix well. Cover and cook very, very gently for about 30 minutes or until partly tender. Add apple and continue cooking about another 20 minutes. Then mix in vinegar and the additional butter and cook another 10 minutes. It will look quite shiny and be very soft and tender with purple juices around the cabbage.

½ large or I small red cabbage, finely shredded

45 g/1½ oz butter

I onion, finely chopped

I cup/8 fl oz red wine

2 tablespoons brown sugar

pinch of salt

2 apples, peeled, cored and sliced

2 teaspoons red wine vinegar

extra 30 g/I oz butter

cabbage meatballs

Finely chopped cabbage is added raw to the meat base. It will cook through and soften in the mixture, adding moisture and speckles of pale green. These are nice little patties for a casual lunch and you can barbecue them so they have a lovely brown crust. Just add a tossed salad and some golden sautéed potatoes or a bowl of potato salad for a great meal. I sometimes make these in tiny little balls and serve them with pre-dinner drinks. Because they are quite light you can serve them cold.

Put all the ingredients into a bowl and mix well with your hands; leave for an hour, refrigerated, to blend all the flavours. Then using damp hands, form into small balls and flatten. Dust the outside with some plain flour. (You can do all this hours in advance – and in fact this is recommended, as then fragments of dry flour don't come away in the oil, making it splatter.)

For tiny cocktail-sized balls deep-fry for a couple of minutes in oil. For larger meatballs, heat some oil in a frying pan, only enough to film the base, as a certain amount of moisture will come from the patties. Cook over a moderate flame until golden on one side, then turn over and cook on the second side – about 3 minutes each side but of course it will depend on their thickness. Drain very well and serve with a little dab of spicy tomato chutney on top and a basil leaf or a sprig of coriander/cilantro in the chutney.

Makes 12 large patties, 24 small ones

500 g/I lb finely minced pork

2 cloves garlic, crushed

2 tablespoons ginger juice, extracted from grated ginger

I egg

I cup/3 oz breadcrumbs, made from stale bread

salt and pepper

I tablespoon lemon juice

I tablespoon sweet Thai chilli sauce

2 cups/7 oz very finely chopped cabbage

60 g/2 oz fine egg noodles, cooked until tender and cut into little pieces

Lycopersicon esculetum

This vegetable is very confusing. One minute you will read about peppers, the next reference calls them capsicums, although these are the same. The chilli is closely related. The capsicum was another of Columbus's discoveries – except he was also confused, as he had really been searching for a relative of the highly prized *Piper nigrum*, the black peppercorn. It mattered little when he returned with a shipload of capsicum, because Europeans adored them. The sweet capsicums were immediately grown in the royal Spanish gardens and soon became known as 'Spanish peppers'. A brisk trade commenced, with these sweet peppers becoming a major ingredient in the food of Southern Europe. Botanically both the sweet and hot peppers are part of the *Capsicum* genus, which in turn is a member of the solanaceous family that includes

▲ rustic capsicum medley (recipe page 81)

eggplant, potatoes and tomatoes. They all team well together.

Capsicums, or bell peppers, have thicker flesh than the chillies and are usually larger – although there are no hard and fast rules for this family. The flavour of capsicum does become more pronounced once it is cooked.

Everything about capsicums is colourful: their flavours are a reminder of sunny climates, they are happy vegetables and it is difficult to imagine summer food without their brightness on a table. All of them begin life as a green baby, changing to other colours as they ripen, ending up bright red and yellow, even orange or purple. Once cooked the colours may not be as vibrant and some revert to green, although the red holds its colour the best.

planting

Capsicum peppers are grown as annuals, although I have a couple of plants in a sheltered spot that grew for much longer but this is rare. They are very decorative plants so you can use them in a flower border or put them into a pot. The leaves are bright and very green, their creamy flowers are almost concealed underneath. Later the capsicum peppers dangle like coloured bells. If the crop is large stake the plants as they can tilt over with the weight of a good crop.

Seedlings are easy for the gardener to find. Plant in soil high in organic matter and add a little lime to lower the soil acidity. Put them in a place that is moist but not too wet – they love full sun. Feed them but not overly, or you get masses of green leaves with fewer fruits.

Temperature Zone	Plant
Tropical	Not suitable
Subtropical	Spring–autumn
Temperate	Spring
Cool	Spring
First picking	*12–20 weeks from planting*

varieties

There are just so many but I think the red are probably the best for cooking and roasting.

- Californian Wonder – comes in green and yellow
- Bell Boy Hybrid
- Long Sweet Yellow
- Chinese Giant – the sweetest of the reds Seven Colour Mix – a seed mix with a range of colours and has some of the best eating and most colorful varieties, in all sizes
- Marconi Purple – a long capsicum with a purple colour and big fruit
- Mini Sweet – bite-sized and can be tossed in salads like tomatoes.

diseases and pests

Aphids like them and cutworms too. Just hose off the aphids. You can discourage cutworms by putting a little collar around each seedling when you plant them or spray carbaryl around to the base of the plant. Put in disease-resistant seedlings as they can get mildew or the occasional bacterial spot, although I have never had a problem with any of these. I do change their position in the garden around from one area to another each year and the result is they are one of my healthiest plants.

harvesting

From 2–4 months, depending on the variety. Pick capsicum peppers by cutting them from the plant; don't pull

as you can tear lots of stalk and leaves away with the fruit. If you want them green wait until they are a good size and the skin becomes very fleshy; left longer and you end up with red capsicum.

nutrition

Red capsicum peppers contain double the Vitamin C of green ones and are a good source of beta-carotene. All capsicums are highly nutritious, with small quantities of vitamins and minerals.

buying and storage

Choose crisp capsicum peppers, almost bursting with freshness. Never buy one with wrinkled skin, as they won't be as sweet. When you cut a capsicum it should make a crisp crack as it is pierced. The skin should be shiny and quite taut.

Capsicum peppers should be stored in the refrigerator but avoid plastic, which makes them sweat and they will go soft and rotten within a few days. Very fresh capsicum should keep about a week.

cooking

There are no hard and fast rules. Capsicum peppers are delicious raw, thinly sliced, or can be grilled, sautéed, roasted ... it depends on the final taste you want to attain in the dish. Remove skin for a sweeter flavour – it is then more digestible.

Grilled capsicum has a smokey flavour, baked a roasted taste and sautéed it is mild and sweet.

Put in oil when roasting so they don't wrinkle. Cooked, it can be refrigerated for 4 days.

bruschetta with marinated capsicums

Bruschetta deservedly has become well known as a snack or pre-dinner dish and it is wonderful food for serving with a glass of wine outdoors. There are many things you can put on top of bruschetta but none nicer than this mix of smoky capsicum and salty anchovies. The topping can be made in advance and refrigerated, but remove it several hours before using so it is at room temperature.

Cut capsicums/bell peppers into halves and remove seeds. Flatten slightly and grill/broil until blistered and dark under a preheated griller/broiler. Remove and place in a paper bag. When cool, peel away the papery skin and cut capsicum/bell pepper into thick strips. Season with salt and pepper.

Heat about 3 tablespoons oil in a large frying pan, cook the onion until it is golden and soft, then add the anchovies, crushing them in the oil. Put in capsicum/bell pepper and turn until well coated with anchovy and onion. Remove and set aside to cool.

Toast the bread; rub with garlic and drizzle with oil. Pile on the capsicum and scatter a few capers on top.

Makes topping for 4 large or about 8 small pieces of bruschetta

2 red capsicums/bell peppers

1 yellow capsicum/bell pepper

1 green capsicum/bell pepper

salt and pepper

3 tablespoons olive oil

1 onion, roughly chopped

4 anchovies, roughly chopped

4 slices bread

1 clove garlic

a little extra olive oil

a few capers, rinsed and dried

capsicum roasted with honeyed tomatoes

These can be served either cold or warm but you can reheat gently if you want to cook them earlier in the day. The tomatoes should be red, ripe and juicy so as they heat through in the capsicum and give out juices, which mingle with the honey to lend a deep colour. For an even brighter effect scatter on some shreds of basil or put one whole fat basil leaf on top when serving. This is a brilliant first course simply served with bread to mop up the juices.

Preheat oven to 200°C/400°F. Halve the capsicums/peppers and carefully take out the seeds and pithy section. The end result looks nicer, though, if you leave on the stalk. Put them onto a piece of non-stick baking paper/ parchment so they won't leave a sticky mess on the tray to clean. Cut the tomatoes up roughly. Mix some salt and pepper with olive oil, honey and balsamic vinegar (if the honey is too thick you can warm slightly). Tip the tomatoes into this and stir so they are coated and divide between the capsicum/pepper halves. Bake in oven until the capsicum/pepper has wilted and the top is sizzling – about 40 minutes. If the capsicum/pepper is getting too dark turn the oven down. Let rest for 10 minutes at least before serving if you are using as a warm dish, so the juices settle.

Serves 4

4 smallish red capsicums/bell peppers

6 ripe tomatoes, peeled

salt and pepper

2 tablespoons olive oil

1 tablespoon honey

2 teaspoons balsamic vinegar

spanish salad

easy ideas

*Quick Anchovy
Capsicum*

Cut 2 red capsicum/
bell peppers into
fine strips and pour
over boiling water,
stand for a few
minutes and drain.
Mash a couple of
anchovy fillets with
4 tablespoons oil
and 1 of vinegar,
add a crushed clove
of garlic and mix
with the capsicum.
Toss with some
mixed greens and
pine nuts eat for a
summer lunch
or in flat bread.

In Spain this style of salad would use all kinds of mushrooms, such as cepes, boletus, puffballs, etc. You can use a range of wild or cultivated mushrooms, but not Asian ones as their flavours conflict with the capsicum. It makes a very good quick salad for the summer lunch table. Serve on its own or along with barbecued meats.

Halve the capsicums/bell peppers; grill/broil the tops until they are blistered and dark. Put into a paper bag and leave to cool. Peel away the skin and cut the capsicum/pepper into strips. Cut the mushroom stalks level with their caps.

Heat some oil in a large frying pan. Add the mushrooms a few at a time and cook for 30 seconds or until the outside is just sealed – they don't have to be soft as they will soften later. Remove to a bowl and while hot add the cumin, lemon juice, salt and pepper. Mix in the capsicum/pepper. Stir together all the dressing ingredients and add to the salad. Marinate at room temperature for about an hour; you will find some smoky juices form around the mushrooms. Garnish at the last minute with plenty of parsley to give a fresh flavour and bright colour.

Serves 4

3 capsicums/bell peppers,
red or yellow

500 g/1 lb mushrooms,
left whole unless very large

olive oil

scant teaspoon ground cumin

squeeze of lemon juice

salt and pepper

finely chopped parsley

capsicum sautéed in tomato (peperonata)

The capsicum peppers are simmered in tomatoes, cooked just long enough to retain some of their crispness and yet keep the sweet, light quality of the tomatoes – without the acidity that results if cooked for too long. The large number of Mediterranean dishes that combine capsicum with tomatoes suggests the affinity between these two ingredients. You will find this dish may be served either warm or cold in Florence and you can enjoy it as an appetizer, alongside barbecued meats, or just piled on crusty bread.

Remove stems and seeds from the capsicums/bell peppers and cut into pieces about 5 cm/2 in square. Chop onion and garlic into small pieces; skin the tomatoes and remove some of their seeds. Heat the oil in a saucepan or large casserole. Add onion and garlic and sauté gently for about 4 minutes or until they are a bit limp. Add the capsicum and put tomatoes on top. Don't mix them together at this stage. Season with salt and pepper. Cover the saucepan or casserole and cook for 15–20 minutes so the onion and capsicum fry gently on the base with the juices from the tomato falling on top. Then mix the ingredients with a wooden spoon. Taste for salt and pepper and cook uncovered for a further 15 minutes or until the capsicum pepper is soft and you have a lovely thick mixture. Remove from the heat and transfer to a serving dish or let it cool. This is best served at room temperature so if you chill it then be sure to remove from fridge an hour before you want to serve.

Serves 4

6 capsicums/bell peppers –
yellow, orange, red or green
(use a variety if available)

1 medium-sized onion

2 large cloves garlic

8 ripe tomatoes

1 tablespoon virgin olive oil

salt and freshly ground pepper
to taste

polenta crêpes with a mediterranean filling

Only a small amount of polenta is added to the batter for the crêpes, not so much that it becomes heavy, rather just enough to give a corn texture. These are quite different to the usual fine flour crêpes and make a substantial lunch or light dinner. No reason you can't fill them with all manner of stuffings but they are especially good with ingredients which are highly flavoured and brightly coloured.

Mix all crêpe ingredients in a bowl and leave to stand for 1 hour. Stir again: if mixture seems too thick you will need to add some more milk. If not sure make a very little crêpe first to check consistency, as you don't want them too solid. Butter a small pan (15 cm/ 6 in) and make crêpes, turning them over so both sides are golden.

Preheat oven to 180°C/350°F. For filling, cut unpeeled onions into quarters but leave joined at the base. Cut capsicum/bell pepper in half and remove seeds. Pierce the eggplant/aubergine in several places. Trickle oil on all vegetables and toss lightly to coat. Put all onto some non-stick baking paper/parchment in a baking tin and cook in the oven for about 1 hour or everything is quite soft. The onions usually take longer than the other vegetables and if the tomatoes are cooked first, remove these.

Peel onions and chop roughly, chop capsicum/pepper roughly. Cut eggplant/ aubergine in half and scoop out the seeds, mix flesh with onions, capsicum/ pepper, tomatoes, garlic, parsley, salt, pepper and Tabasco, mixing it all together and seasoning very well. Roll up each polenta crêpe with some of the filling inside – these can be prepared some hours in advance.

Reheat in the oven (180°C/350°F) to serve. Brush each crêpe with butter first and place them close together in a buttered, shallow, ovenproof dish. Scatter a little cheese on top. Timing depends on how long beforehand they were made but they take approximately 15–20 minutes to reheat.

Serves 4–6

2 eggs

½ cup/4 fl oz milk

2 tablespoons polenta/cornmeal

⅓ cup/1½ oz plain/ all-purpose flour

pinch of salt

1 tablespoon melted butter

a little grated Parmesan cheese

Filling

2 onions

2 capsicums/bell peppers

1 eggplant/aubergine, about 375 g/12 oz

a little olive oil

6 tomatoes, halved and cut sides scattered with sugar, salt and pepper

2 cloves garlic, finely chopped

2 tablespoons parsley

lots of salt and pepper

dash of Tabasco, chilli sauce or cayenne pepper

hint

Buy the best Italian Parmesan you can find. It will have a nutty, rich flavour, and you don't need as much for this to permeate the dish as you would if using a cheese which is an imitation. I use Parmigiano Reggiano in all my dishes – this is not a kind of Parmesan, as often thought, but the *only* Parmesan cheese.

capsicum, tomato and parsley butter

This butter can be used in many ways and is a good standby to keep in the freezer. Put a spoonful on top of a baked potato – making a slash so it will melt inside – dab a little bit on top of some warm cooked chicken or a piece of lamb or spread inside a cut breadstick for a change from garlic flavours. Bake the bread in a moderately hot oven just until the butter melts and the bread becomes crisp on the outside. You can make this butter up to 4 days in advance and refrigerate or freeze it for a month.

Put the butter into a processor and process until soft, add the capsicum, tomatoes, parsley and black pepper, process, then add olive oil and process again.

Makes about ⅔ cup

90 g/3 oz butter, cut into small pieces

1 grilled capsicum/bell pepper, chopped small

6 semi-dried tomatoes

4 tablespoons finely chopped parsley

½ teaspoon ground black pepper

1 tablespoon olive oil

roasted eggplant compote

The word 'compote' is usually associated with poached fruits, but the French make a savoury compote, a delicious smoky flavoured, brightly coloured mix of capsicum, herbs and anchovy. Piled into a bowl, small spoonfuls can be served on circles of French bread, toast or, even better, thin slices of French breadstick/baguette baked in the oven to a crispy, light brown.

Cut each capsicum/bell pepper in half lengthways and remove the seeds. Press down on the capsicums to flatten a little; don't be concerned if they split. Put the capsicums/peppers on to a griller/broiler tray (I put some foil underneath as the juices are very sticky to clean away). Grill/broil until quite black, then transfer to a paper bag and allow to become cold. Peel away the dark skin.

Put the garlic, thyme and oil in a saucepan and heat until the garlic is aromatic. Tip into a bowl. Cut capsicums/peppers into long thin strips and add to the flavoured oil. Season with pepper and lemon juice and stir gently. Leave to marinate overnight, chilled and well covered, as the marinade is quite strong and will 'perfume' the refrigerator. You can prepare the dish to this stage about 2 days in advance.

Put anchovy fillets into a saucer and cover with milk. Stand for 30 minutes, drain away the milk and chop the anchovies. Pour some of the oily liquid from the capsicum over the anchovy and crush them so they almost make a paste. Mix with the capsicum and stir again. Turn into a brightly coloured bowl and drain a little if you feel the mixture is too wet. Scatter on basil. Keep the liquid, as it is delicious if a little is added to a French dressing for a green salad.

Serves 6

6 fleshy red capsicums/bell peppers

3 cloves garlic, finely chopped

1 teaspoon finely chopped thyme leaves

3 tablespoons virgin olive oil

pepper

2 teaspoons lemon juice

45 g/1 1/2 oz anchovy fillets

milk

12 basil leaves

bacon, capsicum and herb loaf

This easy, yeastless bread not only tastes very moist and fresh the day it is made, but even a couple of days later you will find it quite fresh enough to slice and eat without heating again. I like to serve it with a salad in the summer or soup in the winter, or just put it out on a picnic along with some cheese and a green salad.

Preheat oven to 180°C/350°F. Cut capsicum/bell pepper in half and remove seeds. Grill/broil, skin side uppermost, until it is blackened, then put into a paper bag. When cool, remove the skin and dice. Fry the bacon until it is slightly crisp, add the garlic, herbs and pepper and mix with the capsicum.

Sift dry ingredients into a large bowl. In a separate bowl, beat the eggs and mix with melted butter and milk. With a wooden spoon, stir egg mixture into the dry ingredients, then add the capsicum/pepper, herbs, and so on. Mix well. Butter a log tin about 30 × 11 cm (12 × 4 in). Line the base with non-stick baking paper/parchment and spoon in the mixture. Level the top and bake for about 30 minutes or until firm to touch on top. Leave in the tin for 10 minutes then invert on to a cake rack and let cool.

1 red capsicum/bell pepper

2 rashers bacon

2 cloves garlic, crushed

1/4 cup/1/4 oz parsley, finely chopped

2 teaspoons fresh thyme, finely chopped

1 teaspoon cracked black pepper

2 cups/8 oz plain/all-purpose flour

1 teaspoon baking powder

1/2 teaspoon bicarbonate of soda/baking soda

1 teaspoon salt

2 teaspoons castor sugar

2 eggs

30 g/1 oz butter, melted

1 cup/8 fl oz milk

tomato and capsicum sauce for pasta

Combining grilled capsicums with tomatoes gives an intensely rich sauce, having a lovely smoky flavour, and the sauce develops a vibrant, intense colour. Pasta really doesn't need anything else with this sauce, barring some freshly grated Parmesan cheese on top, but to ring some changes you could scatter on shreds of basil if you wish or some finely chopped bacon, cooked until it is crunchy, or small black olives. This recipe makes sufficient for 250–375 g/8–12 oz dried pasta, but that depends on whether you like your pasta just lightly coated with sauce or with lots.

Halve the capsicums/bell peppers, remove seeds and flatten them slightly. Grill/broil until blackened and the skin has blistered. Remove and put into a paper bag until they are quite cool. Put the tomatoes into a saucepan with the remaining ingredients and cook until you have a thickish sauce. Peel away the papery skin on the capsicums/peppers, roughly chop them and put into a food processor. Add the tomato and process together until you have a sauce that is blended but not too smooth. Some texture is nice in the dish.

When pasta is ready, reheat the sauce, check seasoning, and mix into the pasta, tossing lightly so each strand is coated.

Serves 3–4

2 red capsicums/bell peppers

500 g/1 lb ripe tomatoes, peeled and roughly chopped

salt and pepper

2 cloves garlic, roughly chopped

3 tablespoons virgin olive oil

rustic capsicum medley

A dish to enjoy in autumn or late summer when there are really colourful capsicums/bell peppers around and very red, ripe tomatoes. It is a bright dish with intense flavours and I usually serve it for lunch on toast or as an antipasto. There are times when I have poached some eggs and drained them carefully before sliding one on top of each serving of the medley. If lightly cooked the yolk will break when you cut it, releasing its soft contents to mix into the capsicum.

Cook onion and capsicum/bell pepper on quite a high heat in the oil until softening, being sure to stir frequently. Add the garlic, turn the heat down and cook until quite soft. Put the tomatoes into a separate saucepan and simmer until you have a thick sauce. When the onion and capsicum are ready, sieve the tomato over the top. Season with salt, pepper and sugar. This can be done up to 48 hours in advance.

On the day you want to serve this dish fry the pancetta until crisp. Drain and crumble into little pieces. Scatter pancetta on top of vegetables and, if you wish, add a few chopped herbs on top. Serve immediately.

Serves 4

2 onions, halved then sliced

2 red capsicums/bell peppers, cut into small pieces

2 yellow capsicums/bell peppers, cut into small pieces

5 tablespoons olive oil

4 cloves garlic, finely chopped

4 tomatoes, roughly chopped

salt and pepper

1 teaspoon sugar

4 slices pancetta or bacon, finely chopped

chopped chives, basil or parsley (optional)

capsicum goes with

eggplant/ aubergine

garlic

greens for salads

onions

potatoes

tomatoes

lime

lemon

anchovies

pasta

noodles

rice

goat's cheese

Parmesan

pine nuts

oil

butter

parsley

thyme

rosemary

coriander/ cilantro

eggs

palm sugar

fish sauce

fish and shellfish

beef

chicken

lamb

pork

carrots

Daucus carota

The carrot has a collection of relatives that include parsley, parsnip, celery, chervil, caraway and anise. The plant has a white flower, which is similar to the delicate, feminine Queen Anne's lace, also a member of the carrot family, the Umbelliferae. Carrots that we might recognise were first grown in Afghanistan at the beginning of the seventh century AD but these early carrots were not the bright orange roots we now love, instead they were a purple colour. The carrot spread through Europe via Spain and then Holland – the Dutch produced carrots of the now-familiar orange variety around the fourteenth century, but surprisingly these were not treasured for the table but fed to cows so they would produce bright yellow, rich butter. From Holland carrots reached France and finally England, and became a common standby in the kitchen.

The ancient Greeks, who ate a type of yellow carrot, believed that they were an aphrodisiac – whether because of their flavour or their shape is not recorded. When I was small I can always remember being told that if you ate enough carrots it would help you see in the dark and British fighter pilots were fed big plates of carrots when they went on missions during World War II. None of this may be true but they are very good for you so eat them for whatever reason you like.

Probably the best carrot of all is the one you pick from the garden, scrub under very cold water and then munch immediately, using the green top as a handle. Carrots from the garden, whether raw or cooked, have a flavour and sweetness that is so much more intense than a shop-bought carrot, which may have been stored for some time.

Carrots contain more natural sugar than any other vegetable aside from sugar beet and it is this sweetness which flavours stocks, casseroles, salads and vegetarian dishes. As well as all the savoury dishes, cooks in Italy, France and England were making some lovely sweet tarts and cakes from carrots years ago. The use of carrot in dessert dishes was largely ignored in Australia, but over recent years carrot has become accepted as making a moist and colourful addition to the dessert part of the meal, mainly in cakes.

Carrots are wonderful for any odd patches in the garden you need to fill with some greenery. Use them as borders at the front of the vegetable garden, where they will form a soft loose pattern. Be patient with their growth, especially if you plant seeds before the ground begins to warm up. Carrot tops are quite lovely; fern-like with fronds, which will eventually turn into white flowers for picking if you forget to dig up the last of the crop. These were considered so beautiful that they were worn as a decoration on the splendid hats of Stuart England in much the same way as people wore feathery plumage.

We may not wear carrot leaves on our hats today, but it is impossible to imagine a kitchen without them. There are hundreds and hundreds of ways of preparing them and they seem to fit into any sort of menu.

planting

Just keep up continuous sowings and you will have your own carrots for most of the year, although some gardeners say that if you just sow once and keep thinning there is no need to do this. They are a cool-weather crop but the seeds don't germinate in very cold weather. You can tuck them into ground that gets some shade or leave them grow in full sun. Before planting work a little low-nitrogen fertilizer into the soil. Turn it over well as lumpy bits of soil or rocks result in split or strange-shaped carrots, which kids think funny but are not great for the cook.

The kind of soil you have may determine the sort of carrot you can grow. Heavy soil is best planted with little fat short carrots, lighter soil will take the long carrots and, for those without much of a garden, carrots can also be grown in containers. Little carrots do really well if planted in pots about 30 cm/12 in across and with the same depth whereas long carrots need to have a deeper pot.

Pull a stick along the soil to make a row and scatter in seeds. Carrots are not easy to plant well as the seeds are quite tiny and clump together. A little sand mixed in with them helps; tea leaves are also good (the tea leaves help discourage ants). In theory you should plant in rows about 30 cm/12 in apart to get a really good yield from a small area but as I like them in all sizes I don't do this. I plant quite close, then as soon as they have formed baby roots begin thinning them out. These tiny little carrots are exquisite in stews or with a sauce for spring pasta and this essential thinning then allows space for the remainder to grow. The seeds should just have about 2 cm/¾ in of soil on top and be sure to keep the ground moist. They need plenty of water to get them growing quickly; this is about all the attention they need apart from thinning. Water a little less when they are fully mature.

Weed by hand, especially when they are very young, or the weeds will take over quickly and stifle their growth.

Temperature Zone	Sow
Tropical and subtropical	Spring–early autumn
Temperate	Spring–early autumn
Cool	Early spring–late summer
First picking	3–4½ months

varieties

There are lots of different types you can plant as carrots come in all shapes, sizes and colours. Here is a very small selection.
• For early planting – Chantenay, Osborn Park, Guerande, St Valery
• Topweight – a long, red-cored, virus-resistant, early variety
• All Seasons Topweight – as Topweight but you can plant all year except autumn
• Market King – also virus-resistant
• Early Horn – a stump-rooted carrot

- Intermediate – a large long-rooted carrot
- Mini Round (Paris Market) – good for pots and heavy soil and can be sown twice as thickly as common varieties
- Heirloom Mixed – packaged mix of interesting old types, which have a rainbow of colours from orange to yellow and white, producing medium roots.

diseases and pests

Carrots can get a virus disease from aphids, the leaves turn yellow and wilt and the roots are stunted. Spray with malathion, which will also stop carrot weevil. If you suspect any carrots are diseased destroy the plants and don't plant carrots again in that spot – or any other kind of root vegetable – until you have fumigated the ground.

harvesting

From 60 days for tiny carrots to 126 days for some varieties. Harvest any time you can find a little carrot, one that is about 1 cm/½ in thick where the leaves meet the root. My rule is to harvest when they are just the size I want for a particular dish! As you will need to thin carrots out if you have sown the seeds extravagantly you must pull some early. Water first if the ground is dry as the leaves may break off if you pull them from hard ground. Twist gently, don't yank or you will be left just with a bunch of greenery in your hand. If this happens don't fuss as tiny leaves

can make another appearance in the salad bowl, where they will lend a spicy taste. When you have long large roots of a meaty orange-red colour you may need to dig carefully and loosen the ground a good distance away from the roots, then gently pull them out of the loose soil.

nutrition

Carrots are a good source of beta-carotene and alpha-carotene. Very red carrots have some lycopene, which is a carotenoid that may reduce the risk of prostate cancer. They supply Vitamin C and small amounts of other vitamins and minerals.

buying and storage

Inspect critically when you are buying bunches. Carrots should have fresh sprightly tops and be firm, crisp and sweet-smelling. As so many are sold in plastic packets now it is harder to judge. Large carrots rarely have their tops on in the shops, but check the roots are not splitting. If a carrot is too big you may find the centre has become woody.

Bought carrots should only be kept for about 5 days. Baby ones should have their tops are removed, as if you leave the green on the carrots will wilt as the root keeps feeding the leaves. Home-grown carrots store really well and are an easy vegetable to keep. Put them into a vegetable bag in the refrigerator for a month or more, or store wrapped in newspaper in a very cool place. Don't

store near melon, bananas or apples, as the ethylene gas these fruits produce increase the bitter-tasting compounds in carrots.

cooking

Little ones need only scrubbing as their skins are as tender as the flesh and most of the goodness is in the skin. You can leave on the tiniest bit of stalk as this looks attractive when they are served. It is best to peel large carrots, as the skin can taste bitter. If you do have some carrots in the garden that have gone to seed don't waste them. Peel and use the outer part of the carrot. Grate it or cut alongside the hard part and make little sticks of carrot. Then just discard the woody centre.

You can steam, boil, sauté, stir fry carrots … just about any method of cooking is satisfactory. The time will depend on the carrot: its size, type and also how long it was in the shops. I find my carrots from the garden cook much faster than bought carrots. Carrots can be crunchy in a stir fry but for most dishes need cooking until they are just tender.

Boil them in a little salted water, just add a pinch and only enough water to come close to the top of the carrots. I usually add a small piece of butter and a pinch of sugar and cook quickly so the liquid has almost evaporated by the time the carrot is cooked. This little bit of rich carrot juice can be served over them.

carrot and ginger soup

This creamy soup has a mix of some Asian flavours, ginger and coriander, combined with more traditional ingredients of potato and cream. Make ginger juice by finely grating very fresh, juicy ginger into a bowl. Squeeze with your hand firmly into another bowl, a milky liquid will result, with a very fresh ginger flavour. Discard all the woody fibrous gratings.

Heat 30 g/1 oz butter and the oil in a large saucepan and fry the onion for about 5 minutes until wilted, add the carrot and potato and fry, stirring. Mix in ginger juice and stock, bring to the boil and simmer, covered, until the vegetables are tender. While this is cooking fry the ground coriander in the remaining butter until aromatic, stirring so it does not burn. Add to the soup. Mix in cream and coriander/cilantro leaves and process in a food processor until a purée. Heat again. Add the lemon juice and serve with a sprig of coriander/cilantro to decorate each bowl.

Serves 4

45 g/1 ½ oz butter

2 tablespoons oil

1 onion, finely chopped

500 g/1 lb carrots, sliced

1 medium-sized potato, peeled and roughly chopped

2 tablespoons ginger juice

4 cups/2 pints chicken or vegetable stock

½ teaspoon ground coriander

½ cup/4 fl oz cream

salt and pepper

4 tablespoons coriander/ cilantro leaves

1 tablespoon lemon juice

hint

If you don't want to use cream, mix the same quantity of low-fat milk with 2 teaspoons plain/all purpose flour. Put the flour into a small bowl and gradually add the milk, stirring so you don't have any lumps. Mix into the soup and stir intil it heats through.

carrot and artichoke soup

As both carrots and artichokes have a sweet flavour, this soup has a natural sweetness which is lovely. Although it has some milk added the texture is light. Jerusalem artichokes give some people indigestion, but mixed with carrots and puréed in soup their effect is mild. Parsnip is a good alternative, however, if you would prefer not to use artichokes.

Melt the butter and heat the oil together in a medium saucepan. Add onion and carrot. Leave to cook over a fairly gentle heat until the onion has softened and the carrot is limp. Don't let the mixture colour or become dark, as you want a sweet flavour. You can use the time while the vegetables are cooking to trim the artichokes. Peel them, cutting off the knobbly bits as you go. There is always a fair bit of wastage with artichokes, so you will end up with less than the original weight. Slice them into chunky pieces. Add with the garlic and cook for 30 seconds, then add stock. Stir once or twice until the mixture comes to a boil to make sure nothing sticks to the pan. Cover and cook gently over low heat until the vegetables are quite soft. Then allow to cool slightly before putting into a food processor and puréeing.

If you are serving the soup immediately, return to the saucepan and add the milk. Heat until it is piping hot, but do not let it boil as the flavour is not as nice. Check seasoning.

If not serving immediately it is best to cool the soup and store refrigerated without adding the milk. It can be kept 2 days, but cover as it may leave a strong aroma in the refrigerator. If it thickens with storage a bit more than you like, add some more milk to dilute it. Don't do this however until it is reheated, as the chilled consistency can be deceptive.

Serves 4–6

30 g/1 oz butter

1 tablespoon vegetable or peanut oil

1 medium-sized onion, finely diced

2 medium-sized carrots, peeled and roughly diced or sliced

500 g/1 lb Jerusalem artichokes

1 small clove garlic

3 cups/1 ½ pints chicken or vegetable stock

1 cup/8 fl oz milk

salt and pepper to taste

baked carrot custard

I first ate this style of dish in Provence: a creamy soft-set custard of carrot, which was eaten as a side dish to some herby roasted chicken. The idea could be used for any cooked vegetable but I think it is particularly successful with carrot owing to the lovely colour and sweet flavours it adds to the custard. Not for those obsessed with weight, as you can't leave out the cream or substitute it with milk successfully, but this recipe does make enough for eight people so don't feel too guilty. That is only a couple of tablespoons of cream at the most per serve. You can ring some changes by mixing in lots of freshly chopped herbs, adding a little grated cheese to the custard or diced onion that has first been gently cooked in butter.

Heat the carrots, stirring, with butter, orange juice, salt, pepper and sugar for about 5 minutes, until they are a little bit fried. Add water and cover. Cook very gently for about 25 minutes or until quite soft. Take off the lid and cook until most of the liquid has reduced away to syrup, being careful it doesn't begin to burn on the bottom. Mash lightly with a potato masher or a fork so you have little chunks of carrot. Cool. Mix the cream, eggs and yolk together and stir into the carrot. You can prepare custard to this stage the night beforehand.

Preheat oven to 180°C/350°F. Spoon custard into a 20 cm/8 in diameter shallow ovenproof dish that has been quite generously smeared with soft butter. Bake for about 30 minutes until it is firm on the edges but a little bit creamy in the centre. Let custard rest for 10 minutes before you serve it, giving everyone big spoonfuls of the mixture.

Serves 8

1 kg/2 lb carrots, peeled and chopped

45 g/1 ½ oz butter

2 tablespoons fresh orange juice

1 teaspoon salt and some pepper

1 teaspoon sugar

1 cup/8 fl oz water

1 cup/8 fl oz cream

3 eggs plus 1 egg yolk

carrot and noodle salad

An Asian-flavoured salad with sprightly colours and a fresh taste of grated carrot, mint and basil. Make it as an interesting accompaniment for barbecued meats, roasted chicken or pork. I also use it as a base for cooked prawns or shredded cooked chicken in the summer.

Mix the carrots with vermicelli and herbs. Then make dressing by heating the chilli in a small saucepan with lemon grass and oil and, when sizzling, add water. Remove from the heat and add remaining ingredients. Pour over the carrot and vermicelli and toss. Serve garnished with more sprigs of mint and basil. You can scatter on some chopped peanuts or cashew nuts if you like. Sometimes I chop up the vermicelli a bit to make it less awkward to dish up at the table.

Serves 4

2 large carrots, grated

250 g/8 oz vermicelli, cooked and drained

4 tablespoons mint leaves

2 cups/2 oz basil leaves

¼ cup/¼ oz small parsley sprigs

Dressing

1 hot chilli

3 teaspoons finely chopped lemon grass

3 tablespoons oil

3 tablespoons water

3 tablespoons lemon juice

2 tablespoons sugar

1 teaspoon salt

cold chinese carrot and cucumber salad

easy ideas

Carrots with Orange

Put a bunch of baby carrots into a saucepan, add 1/3 cup/3 fl oz water, a knob of butter, strip of orange peel and 1/2 cup/4 fl oz orange juice. Season with a pinch of salt and teaspoon of sugar and cook rapidly without a lid until the carrots are tender and the sauce is syrupy. If the liquid cooks away too quickly before the carrots are tender add a little bit extra water. A teaspoon of honey could be added to the carrots instead of sugar, giving a more aromatic finish.

The light, sesame oil-based vinaigrette in this northern Chinese salad provides a piquant contrast to the fresh vegetables, sliced shrimp and roasted peanut topping. Sometimes I substitute shredded chicken or pork for the prawns. In a cold salad such as this, it is traditional – and considered more refined – to trim the ends of the bean shoots, but this is optional and depends on whether you have nothing better to do with your time. The salad, all beautifully arranged, should be taken to the table and the dressing poured on top there, then it should be tossed in front of everyone – or else let everybody join in and help toss, for good luck.

Combine the cucumber with two-thirds of the carrot. Put the mixture in the centre of a large platter, and scatter the remaining carrot around the edge. Put the bean shoots around the cucumber–carrot mixture. Holding a cleaver or a large knife parallel to the cutting surface, slice the prawns in half lengthwise. Arrange the prawns, pink uncut side up, on top of the bean shoots. Scatter with finely chopped peanuts.

Mix all the dressing ingredients in a bowl and stir thoroughly to blend. To serve, take salad to table then pour the Chinese vinaigrette dressing over the salad and toss.

Serves 4

2 cups coarsely grated continental cucumber, seeds discarded

2 medium-sized carrots, coarsely grated

375 g/12 oz bean shoots

8–12 small cooked prawns, peeled

1/2 cup/3 oz finely chopped dry-roasted peanuts

Dressing

1/4 cup/2 fl oz light soy sauce

1/4 teaspoon salt

1 tablespoon light brown sugar

1 tablespoon sesame oil

3 tablespoons Chinese rice vinegar

1 tablespoon rice wine

2 tablespoons oil

quick family pasta dish

A really easy vegetable sauce that makes sufficient coating for about 300 g/ 10 oz of uncooked pasta – depending on whether you like it a bit sloppy with sauce or drier. I like my pasta quite wet so I always making plenty of sauce. You can use spaghetti or shell macaroni or a flat pasta such as tagliatelle. For really busy mums, just buy a bottle of one of the best commercial tomato sauces from a supermarket. Don't get one that has all kinds of extra flavours such as garlic, herbs, and so on – go for a perfectly plain tomato variety.

Bring a large pot filled with water to the boil before beginning to make the sauce. By the time the sauce is ready the pasta will be ready too.

Put the bacon and onion in a saucepan and let it cook gently until the onion has softened (there should be sufficient fat in the bacon to fry onion but if it is lean, add a tablespoon of olive oil). Toss in the garlic and cook a minute, then mix in the grated carrot and zucchini/courgette, stir and put a lid on the pan so the vegetables will soften nicely. Stir occasionally, but do not season at this stage. It is best to do this after adding the tomato sauce. Add the sauce, cream and basil, stir and simmer gently for a couple of minutes. Season. If the sauce is ready before the pasta it can be kept warm or else reheated later. Toss cheese over the top for serving.

Serves 3–4

2 rashers bacon, cut into strips

1 large onion, diced

1 clove garlic, diced finely

2 medium-sized carrots, grated

2 medium-sized zucchini/courgettes, grated

1 cup/8 fl oz fresh tomato sauce (see 'easy ideas' on page 350 or 358)

1/2 cup/4 fl oz thick/double cream

6 basil leaves

salt and pepper

some finely grated Parmesan cheese

carrot meatballs

In Scandinavian countries grated carrot or cooked beetroot is sometimes added to meatballs. Usually the base is minced veal or a mix of veal and pork, but I don't find veal has enough flavour and prefer to make these meatballs with minced chicken or minced pork. Traditionally these are cooked and served in a sauce with some stock and sour cream but they are just as nice served plain. I find them very popular served with drinks, as they are so light they sop up the pre-dinner alcohol but are not too filling before dinner. Cold they make great picnic food.

Put the crumbs and stock into a basin and stir, leave for 5 minutes, then add all the ingredients except butter. Chill for 30 minutes, covered, so mixture firms. Using damp hands roll into small balls about the size of a large walnut and cook a few – you can't crowd them at this stage or the meatballs are hard to turn over – in melted butter in a frying pan until brown all over. Shake gently so they roll around or turn over using a spoon and fork. Meatballs should keep a fairly even shape, although a few bumpy ones don't matter. Transfer to a plate and add a little bit more butter or oil as needed to the pan and keep cooking. When last batch is done, return all to the frying pan, add a tablespoon of water to the pan and put a lid on top. Cook gently for about 5 minutes so meatballs are cooked right through to the centre. Serve straight away or reheat. Even when cold you will find they are quite moist and light.

Serves 4

⅔ cup/1½ oz breadcrumbs, made from stale wholemeal/ wholewheat bread

½ cup/4 fl oz chicken stock

500 g/1 lb minced chicken or pork

1 medium-sized carrot, finely grated

1 egg

1 teaspoon salt

½ teaspoon pepper

1 small onion, finely chopped

¼ teaspoon freshly grated nutmeg

some butter or oil

carrot pilaf with nuts

In some exotic countries like Morocco rice dishes can be scattered with scented rose water, or dressed with fine pieces of gold or silver leaf, but this pilaf doesn't need any such gilding to make it taste better. The carrot melds with the rice and the pilaf has a lovely pinky-salmon colour when cooked. It could be eaten on its own but is also very good with just about any kind of plain meat dish and very good with barbecues.

Heat oil and butter in a heavy-based saucepan and add the onion. Cook gently for about 10 minutes, giving an occasional stir until onion has softened and is pale gold. Add rice and stir so it is coated with oil and butter. Mix in carrot, cinnamon, cardamom, ginger and lemon and pour over the white wine. Cook rapidly for a couple of minutes, then add the stock and bring to a boil. Cover the pan tightly. Cook over low heat for 20 minutes. Take off the heat and set aside but don't lift the lid for 10 more minutes. Then fluff rice up with 2 forks, adding the nuts and cheese as you do this. Or you can heap rice up lightly onto a platter and scatter the nuts on top.

Serves 4 as a main course, 6 as a side dish

2 tablespoons olive oil

30 g/1 oz butter

1 large onion, finely chopped

1½ cups/12 oz long-grain rice

2 medium-sized carrots, grated (to make about 2 cups)

1 cinnamon stick

8 cardamom pods

1 tablespoon shredded ginger

2 strips lemon peel

½ cup/4 fl oz dry white wine or stock

2½ cups/1 pint well-seasoned vegetable or chicken stock

½ cup/2 oz almond slivers, browned, or whole blanched almonds

¼ cup/1 oz shelled pistachio nuts

⅓ cup/1 oz grated Parmesan cheese

easy ideas
Carrot Spaghetti

Shred 2 large carrots using a vegetable peeler so you have long thin strands. Don't attempt to use the centre core, it will be tough and it is far too difficult to slice this successfully with the vegetable peeler. Cook for a few minutes in plenty of boiling salted water. Strands must be soft. Drain and mix with 45g/ 1½ oz butter and 2 tablespoons finely chopped parsley, lots of pepper and salt and scatter on some grated Parmesan cheese. You can also shred a long zucchini the same way, then cook and mix its strands with the carrot.

almond carrot torte

This is nothing like the healthy but very heavy wholemeal or wholewheat carrot cakes you get served in many cafés, which are like a meal. Serve this light and luscious cake for dessert or at a special tea party. I love it and think it is one of the best carrot cake recipes I know. It keeps well, is very moist and contains no flour. You can serve it absolutely plain or with a bowl of vanilla-flavoured, fluffy whipped cream alongside. Bake the torte in a springform tin, first buttering the base and sides well, as it is quite fragile to turn out.

Preheat oven to 180°C/350°F. Mix ground almonds with grated carrot in a large bowl. Add the breadcrumbs, lemon rind, nutmeg and baking powder. Stir well so all the ingredients are fairly well mixed together. Place the egg yolks and sugar in another bowl and beat until thick, and then stir into the carrot and almond mixture. Beat the egg whites until they hold stiff peaks. Add a third to the carrot mixture to lighten it, then fold in another third; finally add the rest. Fold gently, but thoroughly.

Place the cake in the prepared springform tin, about 23 cm/9 in diameter, and bake for about 30 minutes. Then turn the oven down to 160°C/325°F and bake for another 30 minutes or until the cake is firm to touch on top. If it is colouring too much you can rest a piece of foil lightly on top of the tin for the last 10 minutes or so of baking. Remove, but leave to cool for 5 minutes in the tin. Then carefully loosen the sides of the springform and leave the cake sitting on the base of the tin until cold.

To make the icing, mash the butter and add the icing/confectioners' sugar. Add sufficient lemon juice to make a creamy icing. Spread over the top of the cooled carrot cake and decorate with some raspberries or a scatter of glacéd lemon peel.

185 g/6 oz ground almonds

1 cup/4 oz firmly packed grated carrot

¾ cup/1½ oz breadcrumbs, made from stale white bread

grated rind of 1 lemon

½ teaspoon nutmeg

1 teaspoon baking powder

6 eggs, separated

1¼ cups/10 oz castor sugar

Icing

30 g/1 oz unsalted butter

1 cup/8 oz icing/confectioners' sugar

lemon juice

carrot gingerbread

A lovely sticky, spicy gingerbread which stays moist for a long time. If you have any sort of love for ginger you will think this cake is heaven. I find it much lighter than many of the English gingerbread cakes.

Preheat oven to 180°C/350°F. Warm butter with golden syrup and sugar until melted. Beat the eggs in a bowl, tip in the melted mixture and then add all the remaining ingredients and stir well. If too dry mix in a little milk, but consistency should be a batter that just falls from a spoon. Bake in a 20 cm/8 in diameter cake tin that has been well buttered and the base lined with some baking paper/parchment for about an hour or until the centre is firm to touch.

Note
Self-raising flour can be made by adding 1½ teaspoons baking powder and ½ teaspoon salt to each cup/4 oz all-purpose flour.

125 g/4 oz butter

1 tablespoon golden syrup/light treacle

100 g/3 oz brown sugar

2 eggs

1 cup/4 oz self-raising flour (see Note)

1 teaspoon ground ginger

1 cup/4 oz grated carrot

4 tablespoons breadcrumbs, made from stale white bread

2 tablespoons chopped crystallized ginger

¼ cup/1 oz roughly chopped pecan nuts

carrot salad with a blue cheese sauce

easy ideas

Carrots in Foil

Enclosed tightly in a foil package, carrots steam in their own juices. Unless you use baby carrots you will need to cut large ones into sticks or little chunks. Pile a bundle, enough for 2, onto each sheet of foil. Put a knob of butter on top, a clove of unpeeled garlic, a few sprigs of herbs such as parsley, thyme and mint, salt, pepper and a scatter of sugar and wrap up the package very well so no juices can escape. Stick on a rack anywhere in the oven when you are roasting some meat and leave them just cook through. They take about 25–30 minutes and are best soft rather than crunchy. Spoon all the herb juice over the top for serving.

This may sound a strange recipe but it is really nice, as the crisp freshness of the carrots contrasts with the well-seasoned dressing mixed with a blue cheese. It is rich in flavour so I usually find this amount will easily serve up to eight people. Blue cheese goes well with a steak so you could put a spoonful of this dressing as a sauce alongside some barbecued steak or even hamburgers. As blue cheese can vary considerably, from creamy and soft to salty and strong, the type you include will of course make a big difference to the salad. Just choose the kind you like, adding more if it is a light soft cheese as against a rich one.

Put the carrot and celery in a bowl. Season lightly with salt, more generously with pepper. Mash the cheese with the olive oil and then gradually add the cream. Once it is smooth, crumble in the additional tablespoon of blue cheese, so it remains in little pieces through the dressing to give some texture. Add a squeeze of lemon juice to freshen the flavours and taste for salt before you add any more, as some of these blue cheese varieties are quite high in salt. Season with pepper and mix through the carrot. Leave to mellow for about 30 minutes. This salad need to be eaten fairly soon after it is made.

Serves 6-8

250 g/8 oz carrots, peeled and grated

1 stalk celery, finely chopped

salt and pepper

Dressing

45 g/1½ oz blue cheese

1 tablespoon light olive oil

½ cup/4 fl oz thick/double cream

extra 1 tablespoon blue cheese

a little lemon juice

salt and pepper

pickled baby carrots

I usually keep a jar of these pickled carrots in the refrigerator, they look interesting and have an attractive colour on a platter. Use to accompany a terrine in much the same way you would use small pickled French gherkins, or the carrots can be sliced as a garnish on savouries. They have a place in an antipasto alongside some sliced meats, especially ham, or cheese. The secret to their charm is to use tiny carrots, leaving on a little bit of the green top for appearance. Let them marinate for at least 3 days so the flavours mellow. They can be kept for about 2 months but are best stored refrigerated. However, as they are so easy to pickle, when one batch is partly used you can make a second batch.

Peel the carrots and cut the stalks near to the top of the carrots. Warm the vinegar with sugar, bay leaves, mustard seeds, dill and salt. When the sugar has dissolved add the carrots and cook for about 3–4 minutes – timing depends on their size but you don't want them soft. Strain the liquid through a colander into a bowl and then pack the carrots into warm, sterilized glass jars. Pour the vinegar mixture over the top so carrots are completely covered and leave to cool before sealing.

2 bunches of baby carrots

4 cups/2 pints cider vinegar

2 cups/1 lb sugar

several large bay leaves

1 tablespoon mustard seeds

½ teaspoon dill seeds

1 teaspoon salt

carrot pudding

This makes a wonderful winter pudding, moist and sweet, with many ingredients from the garden forming a base. Apples are blended with carrots and potatoes and mixed with sweet sultanas and crunchy walnuts.

Smear a 2-litre/4-pint pudding basin liberally with soft butter and put a little piece of non-stick baking paper/parchment on the base. Cream the butter, sugar and citrus rind until creamy. Add egg and beat until light and fluffy. Stir in the carrots, potatoes, apple, raisins and nuts. Sift the dry ingredients over and fold them through the mixture until well combined. Spoon into the pudding basin. Cover the top with greased baking paper and two thicknesses of greaseproof paper or foil. Tie firmly with string. Set on a plate or a small rack in a large deep saucepan containing hot water. Bring to a boil and steam, covered, for 2 hours 45 minutes. Check to see that there is enough water from time to time, add a bit more boiling water if necessary. Remove pudding and leave to rest for 5 minutes, then run a knife carefully around to loosen sides and unmould on to a platter.

You can make this pudding several days in advance, then reheat in the basin again in boiling water for 1 hour. Serve with a runny vanilla custard or a bowl of vanilla-flavoured whipped cream.

Serves 8

125 g/4 oz butter

250 g/8 oz sugar

finely grated rind of
$\frac{1}{2}$ a lemon and $\frac{1}{2}$ an orange

1 egg, well beaten

100 g/3 oz raw carrot, grated

150 g/5 oz raw potato, grated

125 g/4 oz tart apple, grated

150 g/5 oz seedless raisins
or sultanas

125 g/4 oz chopped walnuts
or pecans

$\frac{3}{4}$ cup/3 oz plain/all-purpose flour

1 teaspoon bicarbonate of
soda/baking soda

1 teaspoon cinnamon

$\frac{1}{2}$ teaspoon each allspice
and nutmeg

pinch of cloves

carrot bread

This is a good use for cooked carrots. Just add a few extra carrots to the pot when you are steaming or boiling carrots and make this bread. However, you don't want to cook them with lots of salt or the bread will taste quite strange. The cooked carrots can be mashed with a fork - this ensures the bread has a bit of texture through it. Although I call it a 'bread' in fact this is an oil-based cake, so can be quickly and easily mixed and you don't have to spend precious time creaming butter and sugar.

Preheat oven to 180°C/350°F. Beat the eggs in a bowl and add the sugar, lemon rind, carrots, oil and lemon juice. Sift the flour, bicarbonate of soda/baking soda, baking powder and cinnamon over the top. Mix in currants and pecan nuts and stir briskly with a spoon for 30 seconds. Spoon into a buttered loaf tin, about 20 x 8 cm (8 x 3 in). Bake for about an hour or until cake has shrunk a bit from the sides and bounces back when you touch it. Leave in the tin to cool for 10 minutes before inverting onto a rack. You can eat this sliced plain or with some butter spread on top when it is a few days old, or you can ice it with a runny lemon- or orange-flavoured icing.

2 eggs

$\frac{3}{4}$ cup/6 oz sugar

1 teaspoon grated lemon rind

2 medium-sized carrots, cooked
and mashed (to make 1 cup)

$\frac{1}{2}$ cup/4 fl oz light olive oil

2 tablespoons lemon juice

$1\frac{1}{2}$ cups/6 oz plain/
all-purpose flour

1 teaspoon bicarbonate of
soda/baking soda

1 teaspoon baking powder

$\frac{1}{2}$ teaspoon cinnamon

$\frac{1}{2}$ cup/$2\frac{1}{2}$ oz currants

$\frac{1}{2}$ cup/2 oz chopped pecan nuts

cauliflower

Brassica oleracea var. botrytis

It wasn't until I grew cauliflower that I realized how beautiful they are in the garden, long leaves which curl around the central white heart, protecting it from the sun and weather until the last moment when it is ready to make its debut. The leaves begin to open and tucked protectively inside is the snowy white, little head made of tight curds. Home-grown are sweet, delicate and when cooked soon after they are picked are a great delicacy. If you don't want to be bothered cooking them, just eat raw. These garden-fresh white flowerets are sweet and crisp like little apples. Cauliflower is a member of the cabbage family and with a similar structure to broccoli, to which it is closely related. It is another vegetable that was carried from the Arab world to Europe by the Moors. Initially it was judged to be ornamental rather than edible, and sometimes a small, perfect cauliflower was tucked into the décolletage of a Spanish maiden so her suitors became aware of her natural endowments.

Cauliflower need much the same conditions for growth as their brassica relations and do like to have some cool weather. Cauliflower grown in constant heat will be stronger tasting. Once it was necessary to blanch cauliflower as it grew by wrapping the outer leaves around the head like a small pouch. Tied in place, the leaves then protected the cauliflower from the sun so it remained pure white. New breeding has changed this by developing some self-blanching cauliflowers, whose leaves take longer to open out. Check when you buy seeds or seedlings so you know whether you have to protect the hearts or not.

planting

Put into fertile, rich soil and plant in stages so you will have cauliflower over a good period of time. Seeds should be about 1 cm/½ in deep, 7 cm/3 in apart, and when they have 5 good leaves, carefully lift them up and transplant, putting them into the ground up to the first leaves. I prefer seedlings, which are easier, but you won't find as much variety in the nurseries. If seedlings look leggy, plant them deeply so they grow into sturdy plants. Don't let the ground dry out and keep feeding every month as if cauliflowers' growth is interrupted by heat, lack of water or cold they don't get a good head. Keep weeded by hand and do this gently so you don't interfere with the roots. Baby-sized heads can be produced by planting quite close together, and you will then have some mini cauliflowers for individual dishes. The same conditions for planting and harvesting apply if you are putting in some of the other interesting varieties

such as the lime-green cauli, a purple variety or even a chartreuse one.

Temperature Zone	Sow or Plant
Needs 2 cool months in which to mature so is restricted to cooler areas	
Tropical	Unsuitable
Subtropical	Autumn
Temperate	Summer–autumn
Cool	Late spring–early autumn
First picking	4–5 months

varieties

- Phenomenal Early – can be planted first
- Phenomenal Maincrop, Perfected Deepheart – for later in the season
- Macerata Green – lime green and a vigorous grower
- Chartreuse 11 – also greenish
- Orange Bouquet – for a different colour
- Violet Sicilian – a reddish cauli which has a slightly different flavour
- Mini Cauliflower – can be sown summer to autumn for a constant supply.

diseases and pests

Cutworms, caterpillars, cabbage worms may want to visit cauliflower, so you may need to spray and watch for bugs. If any cauliflower get yellow leaves it may be from root rot; pull it out immediately so this doesn't spread to any others and don't put the plant into the compost.

harvesting

About 4–5 months from seedlings. You will know when it is time to harvest when the white head forms. Its curds should be very compact, the head a minimum of 15 cm/6 in diameter. Pick it before it opens any further. Just cut off firmly and cleanly from the main stem.

nutrition

A good source of Vitamin C, folate and Vitamin K, with small quantities of other vitamins.

buying and storage

Smell them. Use your nose when buying cauliflower as well as your eyes as a strong cauli smell when raw will be even worse when it is cooked. There should be a fresh, slight, cabbage scent and the curds should be crisp, not crumbly. The colour should be white, the head tightly packed and the leaves crisply curling around the centre. Size has no relation to quality and avoid any yellowing heads or open swirls, this indicates the cauliflower was left too long in the ground.

Remove the big outside leaves and put into a container in the crisper. Use within a few days.

cooking

It is sensible to wash cauliflower well, especially ones from the garden as little insects can linger inside all the tiny flowerets. Soak the cauliflower in a little lightly salted water. You can break the head into flowerets first to make this quicker.

Don't boil cauliflower in aluminum, as cauliflower reacts with the chemical make-up of this metal and the head changes from white to yellow. I just cook it in lightly salted water with the stalks down and the heads up until it is tender. Times vary, depending on so many things, such as how big the pieces of cauliflower were, how fresh, etc. Just use common sense and stick a skewer into a piece to test. In most cases cauliflower should be tender, not too soft so it is breaking up but not crisp or hard either.

cauliflower in tempura

cauliflower goes with

cheese

cream and milk

butter

olive oil

lemon juice

chilli

garlic

ginger

potatoes

tomatoes

ham and bacon

chicken stock

anchovies

All kinds of vegetables are delicious dipped into a light, crisp Japanese batter and cauliflower is particularly good. These kinds of batter dishes are a bit of a bother for serving to guests as you have to dip, cook and serve at the last minute, but if you have dinner in the kitchen so everyone is part of the fun it is well worth considering.

Cut the cauliflower into little flowerets (use the stalk for another recipe). Cook flowerets in boiling salted water for 2 minutes, drain and run cold water over the top, then drain again on kitchen paper towel. This is better done hours in advance so the vegetable is quite dry for the next stage.

Mix flour with salt in a bowl. Add egg yolks and water and stir until smooth. Mix in oil and set batter aside.

When you are ready to cook, beat the egg whites until they hold stiff peaks and fold a little at a time into the batter. Have the oil hot (190°C/375°F). Dip cauliflower into the batter and hold for a moment to let the excess drip away. Deep fry for a few minutes or until the batter has formed a golden puffed coat around cauliflower. Put onto paper-lined plates and keep warm in the oven with the door ajar while cooking the rest. Pile them on individual plates and serve with chopsticks, accompanied by soy sauce, lemon and coriander, or nibble as finger food with a dish of soy mixed with a little grated ginger some ginger juice.

Serves 4

1 small, firm cauliflower

1 cup/4 oz plain/all-purpose flour

good pinch of salt

2 eggs, separated

¾ cup/6 fl oz iced water

1 tablespoon light oil

plenty of oil to deep-fry

soy sauce, lemon wedges and coriander/cilantro sprigs

cauliflower cream

A very light purée of cauliflower, thickened with some potato, is a fluffy dish that can be served alongside a firm piece of meat which needs something soft and sensuous as its partner. This purée can be reheated but be cautious and don't warm again for too long or it can develop a strong, overcooked taste.

Cook the cauliflower in salted water or simmer in a pot of half milk and half water until it is tender – it should be soft. Cook the potato separately until tender. Drain both and process with nutmeg, butter and cream until a light mixture. Add Tabasco and taste for salt and pepper. Warm the whole thing through again to serve, or leave and reheat in a basin over boiling water.

Serves 4

½ large or 1 small cauliflower, cut into flowerets

250 g/8 oz potato, peeled and cut into pieces

½ teaspoon nutmeg

60 g/2 oz butter

⅓ cup/3 fl oz cream or milk

dash of Tabasco sauce

salt and pepper

spiced cauliflower soup

Cauliflower lends itself well to spicy flavourings, whether in a curry, sautéed or a salad, and there is no better way to display this than in soup.

Heat the vegetable oil in a saucepan and add the strips of capsicum/pepper. Cook, giving a stir every so often, until strips are softened. Remove to a bowl and leave aside – this is the garnish for the soup.

Leave the oil in the saucepan, add the butter and onion and cook over gentle heat until the onion has softened and is a very pale golden colour. Add the curry powder and cook for a few seconds or until you can smell the spices.

You can prepare the cauliflower while the onion is sautéing. Remove the flowerets from the stalks, cut the stalks into several pieces if they are very large, and put flowerets and stalks into a basin and cover with water. Leave in the water for about a minute, then drain in a colander. Add the cauliflower and ginger to the curried onion and stir to coat. Cook for a minute, then add the stock. Bring to a boil, place a lid on the saucepan, reduce heat and leave to cook gently for about 20 minutes or until the cauliflower has softened. Careful you don't overcook or it will become stronger in flavour. Process the soup until smooth, it will be rather thick. If you are not serving immediately, put into the refrigerator, but cover well as it will have a fairly pungent smell. The red capsicum can either be added to the soup base, or you can keep it separate.

When ready to serve add 1 cup/8 fl oz milk to the base and heat through. Once hot check the texture, pour in more milk to reach the consistency you would like. When you serve the soup be sure to ladle it out so that a little of the red capsicum is in each bowl. Or scatter on top.

Serves 4

1 tablespoon vegetable oil

1 medium-sized red capsicum/ bell pepper, deseeded and cut into fine strips

30 g/1 oz butter

1 medium-sized onion, finely chopped

1 teaspoon medium to mild curry powder

1/2 teaspoon grated fresh ginger

1/2 medium-sized cauliflower

3 cups/1 1/2 pints chicken stock

1–1 1/2 cups/8–12 fl oz milk

easy ideas

Cauli in Spicy Tomato Sauce

Roughly process 450 g/1 lb canned tomatoes with 1 hot chilli, 2 cloves garlic, 2 teaspoons sugar and 1/4 cup/ 2 fl oz olive oil. Separate flowerets of a medium-sized cauliflower, and slice the stalks into bite-sized pieces. Cook cauliflower in plenty of salted boiling water until tender, then drain. Heat tomato sauce in the pan in which cauliflower was cooked and when bubbling return cauliflower to pan, stir gently to coat and reheat. Good with lamb, chicken or over rice.

cauliflower with ham and tomato topping

Moving right away from the creamy sauces, this is a spicy pink topping that converts cauliflower into a new range of colour and flavour. The dish can be baked like a gratin, but if everything is piping hot you can serve it as soon as you add the topping.

Cook the cauliflower until tender in salted water and drain. Heat the oil and butter and fry the onion gently until softened, add ham and tomatoes, chilli and sugar and let the whole thing simmer away while the cauliflower is cooking until you have a pot of a good, rich pink, thickish sauce. When ready season to taste with salt and pepper.

Cook the crumbs in a frying pan in the oil, stirring so they colour to a crisp golden crumb and remove to a plate. Add the cheese and leave them aside.

Put the cauliflower into a dish with the ham and tomato sauce on top, spreading it out evenly. Then top with the crispy crumb and cheese topping and serve or reheat later in a moderate (180°C/350°F) oven until bubbling hot.

Serves 4

1 small cauliflower
2 tablespoons oil
30 g/1 oz butter
1 onion, finely chopped
125 g/4 oz ham, finely chopped
500 g/1 lb tomatoes, peeled and roughly chopped
1 small chilli, deseeded and finely chopped
1 teaspoon sugar
salt and pepper
1 cup/3 oz breadcrumbs, made from stale bread
1/4 cup/2 fl oz olive oil
1/2 cup/2 oz grated Parmesan cheese

cauliflower with chermoula

The spices and herbs in this recipe give a very different flavour and character to cauliflower. This is quite a self-contained dish, to be eaten on its own, but if you want to serve it with a meat I like it best with pieces of lamb or rather simply cooked chicken. Although I haven't found broccoli used in Moroccan cooking, I see no reason why you couldn't adapt this dish using it.

Cut the cauliflower stalks into thick slices, removing flowerets and leaving them whole. Put the onion, garlic, ginger, chilli, pepper, cumin, salt, olive oil, water and lemon juice into a medium-sized saucepan with a lid. Heat, then add the cauliflower and stir so it is well coated with the spicy mixture. Keep the heat fairly low under the saucepan so liquid is just gently simmering and cook, covered, for about 25 minutes, or until the cauliflower is tender. Stir the coriander and parsley into the sauce and serve.

Variation

You can also make Zucchini with Chermoula: use small zucchini/courgettes and make a few slashes down each one lengthwise to allow the chermoula to seep into the flesh. Zucchini/courgette will take a little less time to cook than cauliflower but the end result is meant to be squishy soft, not crisp.

Serves 4 as a main dish, 6 as a side dish

1 small whole or 1/2 large cauliflower
1 small onion, very finely chopped
2 fat cloves garlic, crushed
1/2 teaspoon grated fresh ginger
1/2 chilli, finely chopped
1/2 teaspoon ground black pepper
1/2 teaspoon ground cumin
1/4 teaspoon salt
4 tablespoons olive oil
1/2 cup/4 fl oz water
1 tablespoon lemon juice
2 tablespoons finely chopped coriander/cilantro
2 tablespoons finely chopped parsley

ginger-laced cauliflower

easy ideas

Creamy Cauli Cheese Bake

Separate 1 small cauliflower into flowerets, and cook in salted water until tender. Dice 2 medium-sized potatoes and cook in another pan until tender. Drain and purée cauliflower and potato together with 30 g/1 oz butter, 1/3 cup/ 3 fl oz thick cream and 1 egg. Season and spread in a buttered shallow overproof dish, about 20 cm/ 8 in diameter. Top with plenty of melted butter and about 1/2 cup/ 1 1/2 oz white breadcrumbs and 1/2 cup/2 oz grated melting cheese such as Jarlsberg, Gruyère or Mozz-arella. Bake in a moderate oven (180°C/350°F) until hot and the top is a melted, golden layer. Serve with any kind of meat.

This recipe is based on Indian dishes, which combine hot spices with cauliflower – cauliflower being one of the most popular vegetables in India. It can either be very hot or mellow according to how much chilli is added. Serve with some rice, pappadams and a dish of meat curry if you wish.

Cut the cauliflower into small flowerets and rinse well. Don't drain too much, as you want a bit of water around them. Heat the oil in a saucepan and add the cauliflower, scatter on the ginger, chilli, turmeric, coriander, cumin and salt and keep turning flowerets over until they are well coated with the spices. Add water, cover the pan and cook very gently until cauliflower is almost tender. Remove lid and continue cooking until most of the liquid has cooked away, turning the cauliflower over in the spiced sauce until it is quite tender and there is just a bit of spicy glaze around it. Serve scattered with the spring onions/scallions.

Serves 4

1 medium-sized cauliflower

3 tablespoons light-flavoured oil

1 tablespoon shredded fresh ginger

1 small chilli, deseeded and chopped

1 teaspoon ground turmeric

3 teaspoons ground coriander

1 teaspoon ground cumin

1 teaspoon salt

1/2 cup/4 fl oz warm water

4 tablespoons finely chopped spring onions/scallions

golden gingered cauliflower and peas

It was not until I began to use them in a number of dishes I realised how well cauliflower goes with baby peas and the combination is very successful mixed with spicy shreds of ginger, a little garlic and chilli. Good with roasted chicken or lamb or pile over a spoonful of fluffy long grain rice in a big soup bowl and serve as a vegetable main course.

Heat the oil in a wide saucepan, add ginger, garlic and chilli and fry for a minute, stirring. Add the onion and lettuce and cook over medium heart until wilted. Add the tumeric, stir in cauliflower and peas and keep stirring until coated with spices. Add water, season with salt, pepper and sugar and bring to the boil. Cover, cook over a low heat for about 20 minutes or until the vegetables are tender. You should only have about three-quarters a cup of liquid left, if too much, cook uncovered over a high heat so it reduces.

Serves 4 as a main course, 6 as an accompaniment

4 tablespoons oil

1 piece of ginger, 2.5 cm/1 in, cut into fine shreds

2 cloves of garlic, finely chopped

1 small chilli, finely chopped and seeds discarded

1 onion, cut into halves and thin slices

1/2 soft green lettuce such as cos or butter lettuce, roughly shredded

2 teaspoons tumeric

1 small cauliflower, broken into florets

500 g/1lb peas, shelled

1 1/2 cups/12 oz water

salt and pepper

1 teaspoon sugar

cauliflower and vegetable gratin

I love gratins of all kinds; it is their combination of a creamy sauce and a crispy, sticky golden crust on top that makes them so appealing. The best known are made from potato but almost any vegetable can be covered with a white sauce and baked in the oven. Not only are they delicious but they are a very forgiving kind of food, one which you can prepare well beforehand and just pop into the oven about 30 minutes before dinner – so good for parties! One of the secrets of a good gratin is that you mustn't be stingy with the sauce, it is meant to coat and seep through the vegetables so they keep very moist. This particular gratin – a mix of vegetables topped with cauliflower – is meant to be a main course. If you feel compelled to serve meat, make it something simple like chicken or a grilled chop.

Put the cauliflower into salted water and cook gently until tender. Drain.

Put the onion and pepper into a saucepan with oil or butter, cook gently, stirring occasionally until soft. Add mushrooms, turn up the heat and cook until this has become limp – it should take only a few minutes. Season with salt and pepper and add the parsley. Remove from heat and put the vegetables into a gratin dish, about 20 cm/8 in square or an oblong one of about the same volume. Cut the stalk from the cooked cauliflower and slice thickly. Put on top of the vegetables and then add the rest of the flowerets from the cauliflower so the top is covered evenly.

To make the sauce melt the butter and add flour, cook a few minutes, stirring. Add the milk and bring to a boil, stirring constantly. Turn the heat to low and let simmer for about 5 minutes. Mix the mustards together – if the mixture is too stiff add a few spoonfuls of the sauce to thin them. Add to the sauce and season with salt and pepper. Mix both kinds of cheese together. Remove the pan from the heat; stir in two-thirds of the cheese. Spoon sauce over the top of the vegetables to cover them. Scatter the rest of the cheese on top and refrigerate if you are keeping the dish for more than 2 hours.

Preheat oven to 180°C/350°F. If you want to cook gratin immediately it is prepared, bake for about 20 minutes. The edges should be bubbling and the top golden. If you have made this dish in advance and refrigerated it, allow an extra 10 minutes for cooking. It has a better appearance if put under a griller/broiler for a couple of minutes before taking to the table, so the top is a deep golden brown.

Serves 4 as a main course, 6 as a side dish

½ cauliflower

1 large onion, roughly diced

2 red capsicums/bell peppers, deseeded and cut into strips

1 tablespoon olive oil or 30 g/1 oz butter

125 g/4 oz mushrooms, thickly sliced

salt and pepper

2 tablespoons finely chopped parsley

White Sauce

45 g/1½ oz butter

2 tablespoons plain/all-purpose flour

2 cups/1 pint milk

1 teaspoon dry English mustard

2 teaspoons French mustard

salt and pepper

½ cup/3 oz grated melting cheese, such as Jarlsburg or Gruyère

¼ cup/1 oz grated Parmesan cheese

easy ideas

Cauliflower Salad

Cook half a cauliflower until tender but not soft and drain. When cool cut into thin slices. Gradually mix 6 tablespoons olive oil into a mashed hard-boiled egg; add a tablespoon French mustard, a tablespoon of lemon juice and one of balsamic vinegar, a teaspoon of honey and plenty of salt and pepper. Mix into the cauliflower so it is well coated and top with toasted pine nuts.

cauliflower with a green sauce

I adore cauliflower with plain cheese sauce and this uses that basic recipe with a different theme. You cook young peas and purée them into a sauce, pouring it over the cooked cauliflower, to give a more unusual dish with a soft spring green colour and sweet flavour. It is wonderful with lamb, any young spring meat or chicken.

Preheat oven to 180°C/350°F. Stand cauliflower in a large pot of water with the stalk in the water and the head above, cover and cook until tender. Drain and cut into flowerets. Put these into a shallow ovenproof dish. Cook the peas until tender in a pan of water with salt, pepper and sugar. Drain and purée them, adding a tablespoon of the cooking water if they are difficult to purée. Melt the butter, add flour and cook a few minutes, stirring. Add milk and stir constantly until it comes to a boil and is lightly thickened. Cook a couple of minutes and then mix in the pea purée and parsley. Sauce should just coat a spoon, if a bit runny leave for a few minutes over the heat. Coat the cauliflower. Scatter with cheese and crumbs and bake in the oven until the topping is golden – 15–25 minutes. Timing depends on whether the dish is hot when put into the oven, or if it has been prepared in advance and is cool.

Serves 4–6

1 smallish cauliflower

500 g/1 lb peas, shelled

salt and pepper

a little sugar

45 g/1 ½ oz butter

2 tablespoons plain/ all-purpose flour

2 cups/1 pint milk

2 tablespoons finely chopped parsley

¼ cup/1 oz grated Parmesan cheese

¼ cup/1 oz breadcrumbs, made from stale bread

old-fashioned vegetable pickle

This has the typical golden colour associated with old-fashioned pickles but it is a little more colourful than usual, with its pieces of capsicum and beans. A great picnic relish with small cold meat pies, it is also very good in sandwiches with cold meats.

Bring the vinegar and sugar to a boil. Add all the vegetables except the beans and cook for about 10 minutes. Meantime, boil the beans for 3–5 minutes, or until just tender. Drain very well, then add to the vinegar with the rest of the vegetables. Cook a further 5 minutes. Mix the mustard with turmeric and cornflour/cornstarch, add enough cold vinegar to mix to a thin paste and add to the pan with the vegetables. Heat until pickle is bubbling and lightly thickened. Spoon into warm, sterilized jars and seal. The pickle will have plenty of golden, thickened juices around the vegetables.

Makes about 6–7 jars

2½ cups/1 pint white wine vinegar

2 cups/1 lb sugar

1 cup/8 oz brown sugar

1 teaspoon salt

2 onions, roughly chopped

1 large red capsicum/bell pepper, chopped into pieces about 1 cm/½ in long

3 cloves garlic, roughly chopped

½ cauliflower, broken into flowerets (about 2 cups)

250 g/8 oz green beans, in 5 cm/2 in long pieces

1 teaspoon dry English mustard

2 teaspoons ground turmeric

2 tablespoons cornflour/ cornstarch

extra white wine vinegar

old-fashioned cauliflower gratin

You never find dishes such as this in the books of the smart young chefs of London or Los Angeles, or in most restaurants, but everyone loves a soft, creamy cauliflower gratin. One day, like bread and butter pudding, mashed potato or rice, it will probably become famous as some of the new breed discover how great it can be alongside some roasted chicken, with a thick piece of beef or just on its own in a little gratin dish. I am already encouraged when English writer Nigel Slater says in his acclaimed book Appetites '... there are few more suitable ends for a cauliflower than to find itself boiled, drained and coated in a properly made cheese sauce ...'. One of the secrets of a good gratin is to keep the cauliflower in a single layer so each little bit has it own generous coating of sauce. Another is not to have the vegetable crispy, it should be soothingly soft.

Preheat oven to 200°C/400°F. Cook cauliflower in a pan of salted water until tender, or steam it. Drain and put into a shallow ovenproof dish about 18 cm/7 in square or round. In a separate pan melt butter and add flour, cook for a few minutes until bubbling, then pour in the milk. Stir constantly until sauce comes to a boil and season with salt, pepper and nutmeg. Take the pan off the heat and mix in the melting cheese. Spoon over the cauliflower so every little swirl and ridge is nicely coated. Mix the Parmesan cheese and crumbs and scatter on top, put into hot oven and bake for about 12 minutes or until the cheese on top has melted and crumbs are crisp. Or put aside until later and then heat for about 25 minutes, so it is hot all the way through.

Variation

Should your taste run to salty, pungent blue cheese flavours you can add some blue instead of the melting cheese. Try Gorgonzola, Roquefort, or a Danish-blue style, but just be careful not to leave the dish too long in the oven as when blue cheeses are overcooked they can go a bit oily.

Serves 4-6

1 cauliflower, separated into flowerets

60 g/2 oz butter

2 tablespoons plain/all-purpose flour

1 1/2 cups/12 fl oz milk

salt and pepper

pinch of nutmeg

1/2 cup/3 oz melting cheese, such as Gruyère

1/4 cup/1 oz grated Parmesan cheese

1/2 cup/3 oz breadcrumbs, made from stale bread

easy ideas

Cauliflower and Dips

Cook little flowerets, cut so there is a tiny bit of stalk on each one, for a few minutes in water – they should be crisp. Drain well. Chill them. Buy some dips such as Anchovy, Eggplant (Aubergine) or Hummus and serve the cauliflower arranged around them.

celery

Apium graveolens var. dulce

Celery is a member of the parsley family and most likely was first grown in Mediterranean countries. Its original use was not in the kitchen but instead was mainly for medicinal purposes – it was quite a bitter-tasting plant. We always had masses of celery in the house when I was growing up. It was the base for vegetable soups that were made every week, the outside tough stalks being cut into thin slices and cooked with other vegetables and a lamb shank, the softer white heart being served as a vegetable with a cream sauce or spooned into tiny tarts for special occasions. Now we rely on celery more for crunchiness in salads; occasionally it is made into soup but it is more likely to be eaten raw. Curiously, although the stalk is mainly eaten the pale green tops are delicious when finely chopped and added to dishes such as stews, potato salad, green salads or as a topping for puréed vegetable soup.

planting

Celery is not the easiest plant for the home gardener and I have only had moderate success growing it. It likes cool weather but too cold and growth is inhibited. Seeds are difficult to grow so buy seedlings. You can plant in light shade. Celery must have good drainage and soil that has a low sodium content, because salt prevents plants absorbing moisture. It is a greedy feeder so work in some fertilizer in advance. Plant seedlings about 7 cm/2½ in deep, 20 cm/8 in apart, in spring through to midsummer. Feed about every 10 days with something like a seaweed spray or liquid fertilizer. Weed carefully by hand so you don't damage the roots, which are very close to the surface.

Temperature Zone	Plant
Tropical	Unsuitable
Subtropical	Spring–summer
Temperate	Spring–mid summer
Cool	Spring–mid summer
First picking	about 5 months

special handling

To get the lovely white colour and stop the stalks being bitter you need to blanch them. Mound soil around them about 3 weeks before picking – but not for too long or they will rot. Using soil to blanch means you have to wash celery really well before cooking, but paper can also be used: wrap a number of layers of paper around the stalks, tying it with string.

varieties

• Stringless – a new strain with a big stalk and nutty flavour
• Crisp Salad
• White Plume.

diseases and pests

If brown fungal bits get on the outside leaves pull them off and don't put them into the compost.

harvesting

When you have healthy heads and the stalks are about 5–6 cm/2–2½ in diameter at the base. Cut just below the soil level with a sharp knife so you don't disturb the soil and loosen nearby celery plants.

nutrition

Celery has small amounts of vitamins and minerals, in particular Vitamin C and potassium.

buying and storage

Celery is now often sold halved. Check it was not cut days ago and left in the plastic wrap, it is then better to buy a whole bunch because this is a very cheap vegetable. Avoid any celery with cracks in the outside stalks. It should have crisp lively leaves. Store in a vegetable bag in the crisper for up to 4 days.

cooking

Use outside stalks for soup but string them first if you have the variety of celery with strings. To string, make a tiny slit at the wide end and gently pull the strings down and away from the stalk with a knife. If serving raw put pieces of celery into a jug of cold water and refrigerate so it becomes very crunchy. The cooking method will depend on what you are making but if serving it as a vegetable it is best braised rather than boiled. Wash and cut into pieces and boil for a few minutes in water. Drain. Put back into the pan and add vegetable stock and cover. Let simmer very gently until tender. The stock can be used in a soup or casserole again.

italian potato and celery salad

celery goes with

carrots

garlic

onions

oil

butter

lemon

mustard

bay leaves

parsley

tarragon

bacon

stock

cream

cheese, especially Parmesan or goat's cheese

fresh and salted fish

chicken

mayonnaise

pecan nuts

walnuts

Italians use both the tops and stalks of celery in their potato salad and each lend a different taste and texture. An interesting salad, this goes with just about anything that potato salad teams well with, from barbecued food to roasted meats. The topping of celery is quite pretty, being a pale fragile green against the creamy mayonnaise. This salad is always popular and people are a bit greedy around good potato salads so I always allow extra.

Cook the potatoes until tender in salted water and either peel or leave on the skins. Cut into big dice or slices and season well. Mix celery stalks with all the other ingredients except capsicum/bell pepper, mayonnaise and celery leaves and stir into the warm potato. Let cool. Halve the capsicum/bell pepper and remove the seeds. Grill skin-side up until blackened and put into a paper bag. Cool and then take off the papery skin and roughly chop the flesh (this can be done days beforehand and the capsicum/bell pepper then stored, refrigerated). Some juices will form around the capsicum/bell pepper, you can add these to the salad as they give it an interesting, smoky flavour.

Before serving mix in the capsicum/bell pepper pieces and half the mayonnaise. Spoon salad into a serving bowl, top with the rest of the mayonnaise and scatter on the celery leaves.

Serves 4–6

1.5 kg/3 lb waxy potatoes

salt and pepper

2 stalks celery, finely sliced

1 tablespoon balsamic vinegar

3 tablespoons olive oil

1 teaspoon brown sugar

2 teaspoons lemon juice

1 teaspoon hot mustard

2 red capsicums/bell peppers

1 cup/8 fl oz mayonnaise

1 cup finely shredded celery leaves (use the pale yellow ones from the centre)

stir-fried celery with prosciutto

This is good with chicken or grilled steak. Sometimes I just spoon it over a little cooked rice. You can use some bacon if prosciutto or pancetta are not easily available. Be sure to peel away any strings on the celery or you will find the stalks quite tough and unpleasant in this dish.

Heat the oil in a wok or large frying pan. Add the prosciutto and toss, stir in onions, garlic and celery and toss over the heat until vegetables are just cooked but still crunchy. Season well with salt and pepper. Add a few spoonfuls of water, tipping it in around the edge, and let the vegetables steam for a minute or two.

Serves 4 as a side dish

1 tablespoon light olive oil

4 slices prosciutto or spicy pancetta, cut into strips

2 onions, halved and thinly sliced

1 clove garlic, thinly sliced

6 stalks celery, cut into chunks about 2 cm/1 in long

salt and pepper

water

chicken waldorf salad

This is a variation of the original Waldorf salad, a simple salad that included apples, nuts and celery in a creamy mayonnaise. It is suitable as a buffet dish and amounts can be doubled or trebled for a large number. It makes a lovely spring lunch dish.

Sauté the chicken in oil until outside has changed colour. Season lightly with salt and pepper. Add 2 tablespoons of water and put a lid on top. Leave to cook over lowest heat for about 5 minutes, then remove from the heat and let the chicken sit in the pan for 10 minutes. Remove and pull into strips or cut into pieces.

Place the celery and apple in a bowl, add lemon and stir to coat the apple. Mix in chicken, sultanas, mayonnaise and stir well. If the mayonnaise is thick, it can be thinned with a couple of spoonfuls of the liquid in which you cooked the chicken – this light chicken stock will also add some flavour. Close to serving time, mix through the walnuts.

The salad is not so nice if chilled as it makes the chicken firm. If you need to prepare in advance, make the dish without chicken, cook it only an hour or so beforehand and add then.

Serves 4

2 chicken breasts, boned and skinned

2 teaspoons oil

salt and pepper

water

4 stalks celery, cut into pieces about 1.5 cm/½ in long

2 large apples, peeled, cored and diced

1 tablespoon lemon juice

¼ cup/1½ oz sultanas

½ cup/4 fl oz mayonnaise

½ cup/3 oz large pieces of walnut

easy ideas

Celery Sandwich Filling

Thinly slice 1 stalk celery, mix in ½ a grated apple, small can of tuna or salmon and enough mayonnaise to moisten. Season and flavour with a dash of lemon juice and fill into pita/flat bread or between brown sliced bread.

stir-fried celery with chicken

Celery is an ideal vegetable in stir-fries, remaining crisp, and is a good foil for the tenderness of chicken. In the recipe either use the white inner stalk or be sure to peel away any strings if you use the tougher outside pieces. This dish can be cooked quickly and should be served immediately while the celery is still crisp.

Cut the celery into pieces about 5 cm/2 in long, then slice these into thick matchstick pieces. Cut the onion into halves and then fine segments. Put the almond slithers in a pan with 1 tablespoon of oil and toast them, stirring, until they have browned. Remove and leave to drain on some kitchen paper towel. Cut the chicken breast into long strips. All this preparation can be done in advance.

Heat remaining oil in a wok or large frying pan. Add the celery, onion and garlic and fry quickly, tossing. After a couple of minutes, push to the side or remove. Add the chicken strips and fry, tossing so that they separate. Tip the stock around the edge of the pan, cook the chicken for a couple of minutes and then return the vegetables. Mix the soy with sugar, salt, pepper and water. Mix in cornflour/cornstarch. Add to the chicken, stir and toss until you have a light sauce on the dish. Serve with almonds scattered on top.

Serves 4

4 stalks celery

1 onion

¼ cup/1 oz almond slithers

4 tablespoons oil

1 clove garlic, chopped

3 chicken breasts

½ cup/4 fl oz chicken stock

1 tablespoon soy sauce

1 teaspoon sugar

salt and pepper

about ⅓ cup/3 fl oz cold water

1 tablespoon cornflour/cornstarch

braised celery

I like to braise celery with chicken stock, but if you're serving this dish to a vegetarian, use a vegetable stock. Prepared this way, the celery will have lots of flavour and can be used as a side dish for most meats. In San Francisco there was a restaurant that became famous for their first course of celery. Very young celery sections from the base were left joined in a section, braised until quite soft in stock, then drained and when cold coated with a vinaigrette of olive oil and vinegar. I have a vague recollection of a smattering of parsley on top or on the side to brighten up the pale dish and some bread to mop up the celery flavoured juices. You could try it if you have any celery left over from braising some time.

Trim any strings from the celery. Melt the butter in a casserole and, when hot, add the celery. Toss occasionally until it is well glazed. Add the sugar and cook a few minutes longer. Tip in the chicken stock, add the garlic, pepper and salt if the stock is not salted. Cover the casserole and leave to simmer gently until the celery is tender. Add a squeeze of lemon juice to taste. Serve plain with a spoonful of stock on top and scatter with a little parsley.

Serves 4

12 pieces celery, about 10 cm/3 in long

45 g/1 ½ oz butter

½ teaspoon sugar

¾ cup/6 fl oz chicken stock

1 slice garlic

black pepper and salt

lemon juice

some finely chopped parsley

celery and cheese muffins

Although delicious plain, I have often put a small slice of ham in the centre of each muffin when buttering them. They are very light, moist and have a gorgeous rich cheese finish.

Preheat oven to 200°C/400°F. Melt butter in a small saucepan and add the celery. Cook for about 10 minutes or until slightly softened, place a lid on top and leave over low heat to 'sweat' until it is quite soft. Remove, season and let cool. Sift the dry ingredients into a bowl and add the cheese. Mix the egg with the milk and melted butter and pour into the flour. Add the celery and mix until the flour is just moist. The batter will look a bit lumpy, don't overmix. Spoon into 12 well-buttered muffin moulds, filling each one about two-thirds full. Bake for about 20–25 minutes or until golden brown and well risen. These muffins won't be smooth on top – the end results are rather uneven. Turn them out on to a cake rack and eat while warm.

Makes 12 muffins

30 g/1 oz butter

1 large stalk celery, very finely sliced

salt and pepper

2 cups/8 oz plain/all-purpose flour

1 tablespoon baking powder

¼ cup/1 oz grated Parmesan cheese

¼ cup/1 oz grated tasty/ cheddar cheese

1 egg, lightly beaten

1 ¼ cups/10 fl oz milk

extra 60 g/2 oz butter, melted

celery and cheese scones

easy ideas

*Cheese Filling
for Celery*

Once popular at
cocktail parties,
this is still a great
snack. Mash equal
quantities of soft
butter and a
creamy white or
blue cheese and
season with
plenty of pepper.
Fill the centre of
inner stalks of
celery. Scatter
thickly with
finely chopped
pecan nuts and
cut into small
bite-sized pieces
for serving.
Keep chilled.

Like baking bread – recommended by some real estate agents during inspections as a way to sell your house – cheese scones give a delicious aroma to the kitchen. Scones (known as biscuits in the USA) are not so much bother as bread but fewer people make scones for afternoon tea than once did. Scones are more likely to appear as a side dish for soup in winter or perhaps served with pre-dinner drinks for fun on a wintry night. Warm and buttered, these particular scones are very good, with a crisp biscuity top from the cheese and moist crumb from the buttery cooked celery. A bit of grain mustard could be mashed into the butter you use to spread on the scone, or fill them with finely diced ham to make them more substantial.

Preheat oven to 200°C/400°F. Put the celery, salt and half the butter into a small saucepan and cook gently until the celery is well coated. Pour the milk over the top and leave to simmer very gently until the celery is tender. This will take about 10 minutes. Most of the milk cooks away. If the mix becomes too dry, add a little extra or even a few spoonfuls of water – don't worry if it looks a bit curdled. When the celery is tender, drain and keep the liquid.

Sift the flour into a bowl; add remaining butter in tiny pieces, the cheese and cayenne pepper. Make a well, add the milk in which the celery was cooked and mix to a soft dough, adding more milk as necessary until you have a moist scone mix. Knead lightly and pat out to a layer about 2.5 cm/1 in thick. Cut into rounds using a scone cutter or into small triangles. Place on a buttered tray and brush the tops lightly with milk. Bake for about 20 minutes for large scones, 15 minutes for the babies, or until they are well risen and browned on top.

Makes 12–24, depending on size

2 stalks celery,
very finely sliced

60 g/2 oz butter

pinch of salt

3/4 cup/6 fl oz milk

2 cups/8 oz self-raising flour
or 2 cups/8 oz all-purpose flour
plus 3 teaspoons baking powder
and 1 teaspoon salt

3/4 cup/3 oz grated tasty/
cheddar cheese

pinch of cayenne pepper

chervil

Anthriscus cerefolium

In French cooking chervil is an essential herb, more so than parsley – which it often replaces. It originated in ancient Rome and has a delicate lacy appearance, which is equalled by the delicacy of its light, slightly sweet, aniseed flavour. Team with food with a light taste or it will be overwhelmed. Grow chervil not only for its flavour but for the soft pretty effect it gives to the garden. It is not frequently used today but is still very popular in France, being an important part of fine herbes, a mix of chervil, parsley, tarragon and chives. It seems to be a perfect combination. I find that I make the most use of it as a garnish over dishes, where it not only looks pretty but also adds to the final flavour.

planting

Chervil hates heat so can be difficult to grow over a hot summer, when the plants get tinged with red, then some wither. It can die easily. Treat as an annual and plant well before summer so you have a good crop before the worst heat. You can plant in autumn for an early crop the following spring. Put into a protected area with some shade and water well but not too much, as it hates to be drowned. You can use lots in dishes so don't stint on growing plenty. Scatter seed lightly on top of the soil, then press it in a little.

You will see little green tops in a few weeks. It can be grown in pots and then of course could be moved into a shady area, or even indoors, to keep it growing longer in summer.

harvesting

Pick green leaves, as any reddish parts mean the plant has been affected by heat and these leaves are not so tender or delicate. Avoid brown or red leaves when buying and choose green bunches. Chervil is seasonal, whether you grow it or rely on buying, and it is not one of the herbs kept by small shops. There is no real substitute but if necessary you can use parsley, some chives or a little tarragon.

Chervil gets gritty and the fine leaves need to be washed carefully. Float the chervil in a large bowl and lift out of the water onto a piece of kitchen paper towel. Chop or take the tiny little bits from the branches for garnishing. Don't wash if you are storing it as after washing it does not keep. Store dry chervil in a container or paper-lined plastic bag in the refrigerator.

salmon with chervil mayonnaise

Try chervil instead of dill with fish and, when you chop it, leave little triangular pieces of the herb so it has a more interesting look than if it is chopped to a fine green mass. In this recipe, as the fish is not actually cooked but is cured instead, it is important that the salmon is really fresh.

Cut the salmon into diagonal slices as thinly as you can, taking them from the skin (this is made easier if you first chill the fish, even almost freeze it, so the flesh is very firm). Put onto a plate and brush each piece with lemon juice, scatter with salt and grind on some pepper and leave to stand refrigerated for about 30 minutes. The salmon will change colour, becoming paler. Mix the mayonnaise and herbs. Drain the salmon and arrange slices on chilled plates and top with a little spoonful of the chervil mayonnaise.

Serves 4

1 tail-end piece salmon, about 750 g/1½ lb

¼ cup/2 fl oz lemon juice

salt and pepper

½ cup/4 fl oz mayonnaise

1 tablespoon finely chopped chives

2 tablespoons chopped chervil

chervil goes with

other herbs

eggs and omelettes

salmon

other fish

baby vegetables

potatoes

green salads

eggs with chervil

A very pretty dish but one which you have to do at the last minute so it's not sensible to tackle it for more than four people. It is one of those lovely delicate dishes to use as a first course or for a brunch, and goes particularly well with a glass of something bubbly.

Beat the eggs with salt, pepper and cream. Heat the butter in a pan, add the egg and stir around, it will set quite quickly and it must be creamy so snatch it from the heat long before it firms to hard curds. Add the mayonnaise and chervil, stir through gently. Spoon onto toast and decorate with some salmon roe, or smoked salmon and a leaf of chervil.

Serves 4

8 eggs

salt and pepper

½ cup/4 fl oz cream

60 g/2 oz butter

1 tablespoon mayonnaise

2 tablespoons finely chopped chervil

4 slices brown toast, buttered

a little salmon roe or some smoked salmon

uses

Chervil stimulates all functions of the metabolism and, if finely chopped and slightly warmed, can be used as a poultice on painful joints.

chilli

Capsicum frutescens

Sweet capsicum peppers are popular but it is their close relative, the chilli, that is the most widely used seasoning in the world. The general rule with chillies is the smaller the hotter – although be careful, this can be misleading: there are so many varieties and shapes you need to be cautious if you are not certain of the scale of heat. Mexican and some American recipes are very specific as to which kind of chilli should be used. More than one variety may be used in a particular dish, as each can offer a different heat or flavour. It takes quite a lot of experience to understand the differences between types of chillies. Although chilli was only introduced around the world after Columbus's day, Asian cuisines have embraced it, and use chilli widely.

The fiery heat of small chillies is due to a chemical called capsaicin that is found in their tiny seeds, in the pale innocent spines and the thin skin. The chillies make capsaicin to discourage insects attacking them while they are growing.

planting

Chilli plants can vary from tiny to very tall and large, so you will have to look at the variety of the seedlings to see how much space to give them. These are even more interesting than capsicum to look at, first being masses of green, then red chillies cover the plants – or in some cases you will have bright orange balls or multi-coloured little chillies all over them.

Temperature Zone	Plant
Tropical	Not suitable
Subtropical	Spring–autumn
Temperate	Spring–early summer
Cool	Spring–early summer
First picking	*12–20 weeks from planting*

varieties

The varieties can be tricky, for while some are mildly hot, others will leave your mouth on fire for a long time.

• Habanero – a 10 out of 10 for heat, so treat very carefully and with respect
• Medium–mild types include Jalapeño, Numex Big Jim, Black Mulato
• small fine cayenne chillies are also available.

diseases and pests

As for Capsicum, see page 76.

harvesting

From 50–110 days, depending on the variety. Chillies can be harvested while green, but if you let them hang on the bushes for longer they turn red.

nutrition

Chillies are a very rich source of Vitamin C; if you eat just one red chilli you will have eaten your whole day's supply.

buying and storage

Chillies can be fresh and firm but will wrinkle and dry and yet still give the right heat for your dish. Don't buy any soft ones, they go mouldy quickly. I put chillies in a dry place or hang them so they dry naturally. When I have masses on the bushes I spread them out on some kitchen paper towel for days until quite dry and crisp and then store in an open container. They keep for about 9 months – or until the next season. Drying intensifies their heat.

If you are unable to buy fresh chillies in markets there are many imported dried chillies, which have good directions on their packets.

cooking

If you are not sure what heat is in the chilli you have on hand, cut a tiny slice from the tip, rest the little cut bit on the end of your tongue and you will quickly have an instant gauge. It won't burn too much as you are not eating the chilli, just finding out how much heat resides in it. Be careful when handling chillies. Treat them with caution and whatever you do don't rub your eyes or touch your face after chopping them, as the residue left on your fingers can burn sensitive skin for a long time. Be sure to scrub the chopping board afterwards to get rid of the heat, along with the knives and anything else that may have touched the chilli. Many recipes recommend removing the seeds, which are the hottest part, before adding chillies to a dish and you can do this if you wish. In some dishes the seeds are left in – I like to leave them in Tomato Chilli Jam or when I slice some thinly to put into small dishes for an accompaniment to spicy Asian food, so those people who have cast-iron tongues can really heat up their portions.

If you are not sure of what heat you should be aiming at in a recipe you have read there is one good rule to follow. If it uses lots of chillies, they are unlikely to be a blazing hot kind but more likely a sweeter, milder variety. When you see only one chilli in the ingredients you can assume this is meant to be quite a hot type. However, it is sensible to err on the cautious side if you are not sure whether your guests can cope with too much heat at a dinner.

cucumber and peanut salad with rose petals

easy ideas

Chilli and Mushroom Salad

Finely chop 1 hot chilli and mix with a clove of crushed garlic, 2 table-spoons lemon juice and 1/3 cup/ 3 fl oz light olive oil. Taste this dres-sing: if it is too sharp add 1–2 tea-spoons sugar. Set aside. Thinly slice 500 g/1 lb very fresh button mushrooms. Toss dressing through mushrooms with lots of salt and pepper. At first this may look dry but after an hour the mushrooms will soften and you will have lots of juice. Add either some finely chopped parsley or finely chopped coriander and serve as a side dish with chicken or as a first course. If there is too much liquid drain some away before serving.

A spicy side dish for fish, cold meals such as a plain roasted chicken or beef salad. The rose petals at the finish add a pretty and fragrant touch. If there is too much liquid around the cucumber you can strain most away before scattering on the petals.

Crisply fried shallots can be bought in packets at Asian grocers or you can make your own at home. Thinly slice small Asian red shallots lengthwise, deep-fry them in medium-hot oil until golden, then drain. These are easy to overcook, so watch them carefully.

Halve the cucumbers lengthwise, remove the seeds and cut into thin slices. Place in a bowl. Warm the rice wine vinegar with palm sugar, roots, ginger, chilli and garlic in a small saucepan, stirring, until the sugar has dissolved. Pour over the cucumbers and leave to marinate for 1 hour.

Just before serving, stir in the peanuts, coriander/cilantro leaves and shallots. Scatter the rose petals over the salad.

Serves 6–8 as a side dish

2 continental cucumbers

100 ml/3 fl oz rice wine vinegar

50 g/2 oz palm sugar

6 coriander/cilantro roots, finely chopped

1 teaspoon grated ginger

1 red banana chilli

1 clove garlic, peeled and chopped

100 g/3½ oz roasted peanuts

12 coriander/cilantro leaves

100 g/3½ oz crispy fried shallots

petals from 1 dark red rose, torn into a few strips

chilli dressing

A spicy dressing for cold noodles, fine pasta, salads or even just lettuce salad which has had some cooked, shredded, fine noodles and cucumber strips added.

Blend the oil and coriander in a food processor until green and thick. Add the remaining dressing ingredients and process again. Taste – the dressing should be a combination of fresh, tart flavours. Add a little more lemon juice if you think it is needed. Mix the dressing through salad or cold, drained, thin noodles or hot pasta and stir lightly but thoroughly.

½ cup/4 fl oz vegetable or light olive oil

¾ cup/¾ oz coriander/ cilantro sprigs

1/3 cup/1 oz walnuts

1 small chilli, deseeded and chopped

1 clove garlic, roughly chopped

2 teaspoons brown sugar

2 tablespoons lemon juice

nonya lemon chicken

A dish of great flavour which is typical of the nonya *style of cooking, a mix of the Chinese and Malay influence. The dish was given to me by the late Mama Lee, the mother of the Prime Minister of Malaysia at the time, who dedicated the last part of her life to ensuring that these traditional dishes were not lost, recording them in writing for future generations.*

Pat the chicken dry. Heat the oil in a wide-based saucepan and gently fry the onions and chilli for about 5 minutes until soft, then turn up the heat and fry until golden. Remove. Cook the chicken drumsticks in the same pan, turning them over until they have changed colour. You may have to do these in two batches. Put the onions back into the pan. Mix sugar, soy and stock and pour over the top. Cover and cook for about 10–15 minutes or until partly cooked. Then remove the lid and continue cooking, stirring every so often, until the chicken is cooked through. There will only be a little bit of sauce around them but it should be quite rich and concentrated. Add the lemon juice and shake through and then serve immediately with some additional lemon wedges on the table.

Serves 4–6

12 chicken drumsticks, skin left on

4 tablespoons oil

3 onions, halved and very thinly sliced

1–2 chillies, deseeded and finely chopped

1½ tablespoons brown sugar

3 tablespoons soy sauce

1 cup/8 fl oz chicken stock

2 tablespoons lemon juice

baked spicy fish

An easy fish dish for entertaining as it is cooked in the oven rather than a pan and relies only on good timing. Any sort of medium-fleshed fish is ideal, such as snapper, dory or flathead. However, this recipe is not suitable for fine-fleshed fish such as whiting.

Rinse and dry fish. In a bowl mix all topping ingredients. Cook sesame seeds in a small dry saucepan or frying pan until golden, stirring so they don't burn and then grind and add to spicy topping mixture. Dab the top of each fillet with the spices (or coat whole fish inside and out) and put them on an oiled piece of baking paper/parchment. The fish can be baked or grilled/broiled. Depending on the thickness of the fish they will take approximately 8–12 minutes in a moderate oven (180°C/350°F) and a little less under a preheated griller.

Serves 6

6 fillets fish, about 185 g/6 oz each or 6 small whole fish

1 tablespoon sesame seeds

extra 1 tablespoon oil

Topping

1 tablespoon soy sauce

2 teaspoons sugar

2 teaspoons sesame oil

1 large clove garlic, crushed

½ teaspoon grated ginger

1 chilli, finely chopped

1 teaspoon sugar

chillies go with

Asian greens

eggplant/aubergine

garlic

greens for salads

potatoes

onions

tomatoes

lime

lemon

anchovies

pasta

noodles

rice

goat's cheese

Parmesan

pine nuts

oil

butter

coriander/cilantro

parsley

rosemary

thyme

eggs

fish sauce

coconut milk

galangal

ginger

lemon grass

palm sugar

tamarind

chicken

lamb

pork

beef

fish and shellfish

curry spices

tomato and chilli jam

hint

I use hot chilli in a spray to deter pests that eat leaves and suck sap. Just soak chillies for about 4 days in vinegar to cover, then mix 1 part of this very hot vinegar with 5 parts water and a bit of detergent to make it stick to the leaves. You need to spray every few days but I find that once pests have had a taste of it on a precious rose bush they tend to let it alone for some time. Hot vinegar will keep for several months and only repels, does not kill any pests.

Known as 'jam', this is a tomato-flavoured spicy relish, which on first taste may appear to be far too sweet, then its heat sneaks up and leaves a wonderful rich chilli flavour. It has a brilliant colour and even rather ordinary tomatoes will look bright and taste marvellous in this jam. You should include the seeds of the chillies in this recipe. Serve a small spoonful with any kind of cold meat or add it to dishes to give the same result as using a sweet Thai chilli sauce. You can mix some into a meatloaf, put a little in vinaigrette for a vegetable salad or use in a chicken salad. Leave a week before opening; I find it keeps well for 12 months.

Put tomatoes and sugar into a bowl. Leave to marinate overnight, at least 12 hours, with a plate on top. Next day put into a heavy-based saucepan, scraping up all the sugar which will have sunk to the bottom, add remaining ingredients and cook until lightly thickened, stirring from time to time (as it thickens it may begin to stick to the bottom and catch, so stir it more then). Timing depends on the juice in the tomatoes but I mostly find about 45 minutes is enough. It will thicken more as it cools, rather like a jam. Pour into hot, sterilized jars and leave to cool. Seal when cold.

Makes about 3–4 jars

750 g/1 ½ lb tomatoes, peeled and roughly chopped

500 g/1 lb sugar

3 tablespoons lemon juice

⅓ cup/2 ½ fl oz white wine vinegar

4–6 hot chillies, thinly sliced

2 teaspoons salt

cucumber and pineapple sambal

You would serve this kind of relish on the table in conjunction with other dishes, for instance chicken wings and rice, and it goes well as a side dish with any type of chicken, pork or beef. It is quite spicy and yet fresh at the same time.

Cut pineapple into neat sections (you can do several slices at a time). Place in a bowl with cucumber, chilli and onion. Mix the salt with sugar and lemon juice and pour over the top, tossing very gently so the pieces are all coated. Leave to marinate refrigerated for 30 minutes but no longer than 2 hours, or the mixture becomes very wet.

½ small, sweet pineapple, peeled, cored and thinly sliced

1 small cucumber (or ½ continental cucumber), peeled and diced

1 chilli, deseeded and finely chopped

½ red onion, finely chopped

½ teaspoon salt

2 tablespoons sugar

3 tablespoons lemon juice or 2 tablespoons lime juice

tiny chickens in tandoori

easy ideas

Chef's Pasta

A dish that an Italian chef told me he makes after finishing work in the kitchen on nights when he needs a quick meal with a real bite to give some energy.

Cook about 100 g/3½ oz dried fine spaghetti per person. While it is cooking fry several halved chillies in ¼ cup/ 2 fl oz oil for each serve of pasta. Remove chillies and when pasta is ready, drain, toss pasta with hot spicy oil and then mix through lots of freshly grated Parmesan and a bit of finely chopped parsley.

The rice for the stuffing should be cooked the day beforehand so it is cold. To do this soak ½ cup/¼ lb long-grain rice, preferably basmati. Rinse and put into a saucepan with water to cover by 2 cm/1 in. Bring to a boil, put on the lid. Cook over low heat for 20 minutes. Turn off the heat but don't lift the lid for a further 20 minutes. Then fluff up the rice and spread out on a tray to dry – you'll end up with about 2 cups cooked rice. This recipe makes sufficient tandoori marinade for 4 chickens, and you should allow half a chicken per person. You can buy tandoori marinade in shops and it usually very good but you can also make your own, which I prefer. Here is my recipe for a home-made one.

For marinade, put the cumin seeds into a dry frying pan until they smell aromatic then process in food processor with the lemon juice, oil, yoghurt, garlic, chilli, garam masala, curry powder, tomato and tandoori paste. Add remaining marinade ingredients – only add part of the milk to begin as you may not need it all – and process again. The mixture should be like a thick cream. Refrigerate.

Rinse chickens. Put into a very large non-metallic bowl, pour over sufficient marinade to cover (you will need about half) and leave for 24–48 hours. Remove. Mix the rice with some of the marinade to flavour it. Push into the centre of the chickens and skewer the tails. Tie up the legs. Preheat oven to 180°C/350°F. Put birds onto a tray lined with foil and spoon a little more marinade on top. Roast chickens for 45 minutes or until cooked.

Mix the honey and Worcestershire sauce to make a glaze. Brush on top of the chickens. Return to the oven for about 8–10 minutes or until glazed. Remove chickens and cut carefully into halves. Serve with some lemon wedges and garnished with coriander/cilantro.

Serves 8

4 very small chickens
(about 750 g/1½ lb each)
2 cups cooked rice

Marinade
1 teaspoon cumin seeds
2 tablespoons lemon juice
2 tablespoons oil
½ cup/4 fl oz plain yoghurt
2 garlic cloves, finely chopped
1 fresh chilli, deseeded
and finely chopped
1 teaspoon garam masala
1 teaspoon curry powder
1 tablespoon tomato paste
1 tablespoon red tandoori paste
½ teaspoon salt
2 tablespoons chopped
fresh coriander/cilantro
½ cup/4 fl oz milk

Glaze
2 tablespoons honey
1 tablespoon Worcestershire
sauce

corn and chilli loaf

Yellow from the polenta/cornmeal and slightly crunchy in texture, this spicy loaf is good both with creamy soups and with chicken dishes. It is best eaten warm or freshly made, as it becomes heavy if left to go completely cold. However, it can be reheated in a 170°C/325°F oven for about 12 minutes, or in a microwave on high for about 30 seconds.

Preheat oven to 220°C/425°F. Heat the oil in a small saucepan and add the garlic and chilli. Fry for a minute then transfer to a bowl. Strip the leaves and silk from the corn and finely grate kernels into the garlic and chilli, with all the juice.

Sift the flour and cornmeal with salt and pepper into a large bowl. Mix the egg, sugar and milk into the bowl with the vegetables and incorporate liquid into the flour. The mixture should be moist. If too wet – this varies according to the juiciness of the corn – add a couple of extra spoonfuls of flour. Finally, add coriander/cilantro.

Butter the base and sides of a 30 cm/12 in long log tin or a square 23 cm/9 in cake tin. Line the base with non-stick baking paper/parchment and spoon in mixture. Cook loaf for 10 minutes, then turn down to 200°C/400°F and cook for a further 30–35 minutes or until it is well risen and golden on top. Test by touching the centre. It should spring back. Serve in slices or cut into squares

2 tablespoons olive oil

2 cloves garlic, finely chopped

I chilli, finely chopped

I corn cob

I cup/4 oz self-raising flour or all-purpose flour plus I ½ teaspoons baking powder and ½ teaspoon salt added

I cup/4 oz polenta/cornmeal

I teaspoon salt

½ teaspoon white pepper

I egg

2 teaspoons sugar

I ¼ cups/10 fl oz milk

3 tablespoons finely chopped fresh coriander/cilantro leaves

easy ideas

Chilli and Orange Mushrooms

Remove stalks from 8 plump, big mushrooms. Mix ¼ cup/2 fl oz oil and ½ cup/ 4 fl oz orange juice with I diced chilli and ½ teaspoon cumin. Put mushrooms in a single layer in a shallow, ovenproof casserole and cover with orange mixture, then bake at 180°C/350°F for about 20 minutes or until soft. Eat with hot toast and spoon juices over the top.

easy ideas *Chilli Tomato Sauce*

Deseed and dice 3 chillies and mix with 3 cloves chopped garlic, I tablespoon fresh ginger shreds and I teaspoon finely chopped lemon rind. Fry gently in ¼ cup/2 fl oz olive oil and add I kg/2 lb ripe diced tomatoes. Add 2 teaspoons sugar and simmer gently for 30 minutes, covered, then put through a moulin. Sauce should be a hot, spicy, thick purée. It will keep for 5 days if refrigerated. Eat with pasta, meats or mix through rice.

Allium schoenoprasum

chives

Chives are a very old herb, going back to the days of the ancient Chinese and being introduced into England by the Romans. They look like a clump of thick grass and are a well-known member of the onion family. They have a delicate onion flavour and scent, and are useful in cold dishes where you want this flavour without the strength of raw onion. Garlic chives (*A. tuberosum*) are also available and impart a light garlic flavour in the same manner. They have flat blades whereas chives have round ones and I find they seem to survive the first cold weather and frost better than onion chives. The flower of the garlic chive is white and, like the chive, is also suitable for garnishing or using in dishes. Garlic chives are used frequently in Asian dishes where they are known as *gau choi*.

chive and bacon potato cakes (recipe page 124) ►

planting

Chives can be planted as seeds or seedlings, in spring to early summer. They are hardy and will grow in just about any garden soil. Keep moist in very hot weather but they are quite strong and resilient. Chives die down in the winter but reappear by spring. Each year a clump of chives will become thicker and stronger so after a couple of years separate it and plant some more divisions. The mauve pompom flowers are pretty but should be cut or the plant dies down quickly. The flowers can be scattered on top of salads or used as a garnish.

Chives grow well in pots but feed them; when you see any yellow tops the plant is pleading for some nourishment.

harvesting

Snip chives from the ground, don't pull or the roots come up and don't pick the whole clump at one time or it will need lots of feeding as it tries to replenish all the stalks at once. Use as soon as you can after picking, for they become slimy when stored. In fact, much of the joy of chives is the springy freshness they have when just picked.

buying and storage

Buy chives which look straight and smell fresh and are not wilting or bending over. If they are sitting in water in the shop check they are not slimy at the base. You can store them for a day wrapped in damp kitchen paper in the refrigerator crisper. Chives are best snipped with scissors into fine pieces rather than chopped on a board.

chive and bacon potato cakes

**chives
go with**

cucumber

lettuce salads

potatoes

pumpkin

omelettes

scrambled egg

fish

This is the sort of potato cake, crisp on the outside and creamy inside, which seems to just about go with anything. It could of course have other herbs added instead of chives.

Boil the potatoes in plenty of salted water until soft. Drain well and mash or put them through a sieve or moulin. Add butter, salt and pepper and cool a little, then add the egg and yolk. Cook the bacon in a pan until crisp and add to potato along with chives. Cover and chill the mixture. Form into patties and dust the outside with crumbs. Refrigerate until you are ready to cook, but they should be used the day they are made.

Heat enough oil to lightly cover the base of a frying pan and add a knob of butter. When it has melted and is foaming carefully slide in the potato cakes and cook until golden brown, turn over and cook on the second side. I find it best not to crowd the pan or it is difficult to turn cakes without breaking the edges of other ones.

hint

Cook bacon slowly so it will crisp well as it releases the fat.

Serves 4

500 g/1 lb floury potatoes

45 g/1½ oz butter

salt and pepper

1 egg and 1 egg yolk

2 rashers bacon, cut into strips

2 tablespoons freshly snipped chives

some breadcrumbs made from stale white bread

a little oil and butter

Coriandrum sativum

coriander
cilantro

Coriander's name in Australia and the UK (in the USA it is known as cilantro) comes from the Greek word *koris*, which means a bug. Whether or not it smells like a squashed bug is debatable. It has such a distinctive flavour and aroma you just can't ignore it: people often hate-it-with-a-vengeance initially, love-it-to-death eventually. Coriander has become one of the most popular herbs over the last ten years and although it is often referred to as Chinese parsley it has no resemblance at all to parsley. Coriander's leaves, seeds and root all have different uses and tastes. If using the root (an ingredient of Thai curry sauces) scrape away any hairs and chop. The seeds can be crushed and are often toasted through so they have more flavour before using in dishes.

planting

Coriander is an annual, and dislikes heavy frost. It helps to have well-aerated soil. Coriander likes the sun but goes to seed quickly in summer so to keep a supply going you need to scatter new seed around every few weeks. Sow from early spring onwards and at the end of summer for a further crop. I usually plant seeds but you can buy small pots of coriander instead. It is a good idea to allow one plant to eventually go to seed and collect these for planting another time. Seeds must be dried before planting or storing.

harvesting

Leaves should be picked for cooking while the plant is young or they are tough and once the seeds form the plant develops a strong flavour and aroma. The best way to collect seeds is to tie a brown paper bag around the plant and they will fall into this. You can harvest seeds after they have turned grey.

buying and storage

Bought coriander must look fresh and smell sweet and not be limp. It does collapse quite quickly if kept out of water. Wash well, for it traps dirt in the leaves; drop leaves into a bowl of water and lift out onto absorbent paper towel.

mussel tagine

Moroccan tagines are usually dishes of meat or poultry which are slowly cooked for hours in the tagine pot, so all the flavours develop gently over time. Mussels are treated in a similar manner to a meat tagine but of course you don't need to cook them for nearly as long. Serve with lots of crusty bread for mopping up the fragrant juices.

Scrub mussels and debeard. Place into a pot with 1 cup/8 fl oz water, cover and heat quickly, shaking until the shells open. Remove the mussels and strain the mussel liquid from the pot – you will need ¾ cup/6 fl oz reserved – being sure there is no grit or sand in it. Put mussel liquid into a blender with the garlic, herbs, cumin, paprika and cayenne and liquidize. Remove to a saucepan and add tomato paste, olive oil, vinegar and at this stage the juice of ½ a lemon. Take mussels out of their shells, add to sauce, bring gently to a boil and put a lid on top. Let them sit in the liquid over a low heat for about 30 minutes. The mussels should be very tender, if not then leave a little longer. Taste liquid, which will have become a sauce, and add more lemon juice if not very fresh. You can either serve musssels in tiny bowls with some sauce or you can put each mussel back into a half shell and coat with a teaspoon of sauce.

Serves 4

4 dozen mussels

3 cloves garlic, roughly chopped

½ cup/½ oz fresh parsley

1 cup/2 oz fresh coriander/cilantro leaves

½ teaspoon ground cumin

1 teaspoon paprika

generous dash cayenne pepper or chilli powder

scant tablespoon tomato paste

⅓ cup/3 fl oz olive oil

2 teaspoons white wine vinegar

juice of 1 lemon

chicken strips with chermoula

The first time I tasted Moroccan food I was surprised to find one of the major flavourings in their classic chermoula was coriander. These marinated strips of chicken can be served as a meal but are also good as a nibble with drinks, as the meat remains firm and is quite easy to handle in fingers. You can wrap the ends in some little serviettes for finger food or a bit of foil so no one burns themselves. The chicken needs to be fresh and piping hot from the pan for the best taste and texture.

Cut the chicken into strips about 1.25 cm/½ in wide. Put all marinade ingredients into a bowl and mix well. Add the chicken and stir around so it is completely coated, cover and refrigerate for at least 2 hours but no longer than 4 hours. When ready to cook, remove the chicken and shake off excess liquid. There is not need to dry it. Dredge the chicken in some flour and shake off any excess. In a very large frying pan heat sufficient oil to just cover the chicken strips. When it is very hot, add the chicken, just a few strips at a time so the temperature is not lowered quickly. Fry over a moderate heat for about 4 minutes, or until it is very crisp on the outside and the inside is cooked. It should be light golden colour. Transfer to a dish and scatter with fresh coriander.

Serves 3–4

2 chicken breasts, boned and skinned

plain/all-purpose flour

olive oil

extra chopped coriander/cilantro

Marinade

1 tablespoon sweet paprika

1 teaspoon ground cumin

3 tablespoons water

1 tablespoon white vinegar

1 tablespoon lemon juice

½ small onion, very finely chopped

1 small clove garlic, finely crushed

3 tablespoons very finely chopped coriander/cilantro

coriander goes with

garlic

Asian dishes

chicken

mussels

prawns

scallops

pork

fish sauce

chillies

lemon grass

mint

coconut

spicy indian potatoes in coriander

These potatoes can be eaten as part of a vegetarian meal with hot chapatis and a salad but I love them with any simple roasted poultry or meat dish. Just add a few more potatoes if you have more than three people for dinner.

Rinse the potatoes, leaving on their skins and place in a bowl of cold water. Process or blend the ginger, turmeric and water until smooth. Heat the oil in a heavy based, wide saucepan and add the whole cumin seeds. When they change colour, after about 10 seconds, add the ginger paste. Cook for a minute, stirring. Add the chilli and cook a further 30 seconds. Drain the potatoes, add and fry for about 5 minutes, tossing or stirring and scraping the base of the pan as you cook them so the bits of spices don't burn. Add the coriander/cilantro, lower the heat and fry for a further couple of minutes, stirring occasionally. Add salt, garam masala, ground coriander, lemon juice and about 3 tablespoons of warm water. Stir, scraping the bottom well of any bits which may have stuck, cover and cook over lowest heat for about 20 minutes. As the water evaporates, stir every so often, because the potatoes have a tendency to stick.

Lift out the potatoes carefully and serve in a warm, shallow dish. Spoon the dark bits of herbs and spices left in the saucepan over the top, then freshen the flavour with more coriander/cilantro sprigs.

Serves 3

500 g/1 lb tiny potatoes

3.5 cm/1½ in knob of fresh ginger, peeled and coarsely chopped

½ teaspoon ground turmeric

3 tablespoons water

4 tablespoons vegetable oil

¼ teaspoon cumin seeds

½ fresh chilli, finely sliced, or some cayenne pepper

1 cup/2 oz chopped coriander/cilantro

1 teaspoon salt

1 teaspoon garam masala

1 tablespoon ground coriander

1 tablespoon lemon juice, or to taste

extra 3 tablespoons water

some fresh coriander/cilantro sprigs

coriander chicken salad with greens

A mustard-spiced sauce with lots of chopped coriander gives a sparkle to even the most boring and bland piece of chicken. The 'greens' in this recipe can be any green vegetable you like: snow peas, spring onions, or some spinach leaves, for instance. Allow about a handful of greens for each serving and the more variety you have the more exciting textures and tastes will come into the dish.

I usually roast the chicken so it is warm when I mix it into the dressing, but you can buy a ready-cooked chicken and then proceed in exactly the same way if you are desperately short of time.

Preheat oven to 180°C/350°F. Season the chicken inside and out with some salt and pepper and rub the skin with oil. Bake in a moderate oven, basting several times, for about 1¼ hours or until cooked. Remove and immediately wrap in foil for 15 minutes.

Prepare the dressing by mixing the coriander with oil, soy, lemon juice or vinegar, sugar and hot mustard. Taste and, if not fresh tasting, add a little more lemon or vinegar. Check for salt and pepper. Reserve a ¼ cup/2 fl oz of this dressing for the greens.

Remove chicken from foil. Cut into bite-sized pieces and toss with the dressing. Cover and refrigerate but not for longer than a few hours or it won't taste as fresh. Blanch hard vegetables (for instance broccoli, snow peas) for 1 minute so they are crisply tender and bright green, but leave greens like spinach raw. Toss vegetables with reserved dressing, put into a big salad bowl and scatter the chicken on top.

Serves 4

1 chicken, about 1.75 kg/4 lb

salt and pepper

some light olive oil

4 handfuls of greens
(snow peas, young green beans, small broccoli flowerets, baby spinach leaves, etc.)

Dressing

⅓ cup/¾ oz finely chopped coriander/cilantro

1 cup/8 fl oz light olive oil

1 tablespoon soy sauce

2–3 tablespoons lemon juice or white wine vinegar

3 teaspoons sugar

1 teaspoon hot mustard

uses

Coriander is only used to a small extent in medicines. It stimulates digestion and is used to flavour disagreeable medicines, as a tonic and in cough syrups. The oil in the seeds is used in perfumes, to flavour confectionery, chocolate, liqueurs and tobacco.

baked sweet potatoes with coriander and chilli butter

Although this butter is particularly good with sweet potatoes a scoop of it could be tucked into the top of a baked or steamed potato, allowed to melt into a dish of pasta or spread over some grilled meat. The butter can be made well in advance and refrigerated or frozen.

Scrub the sweet potatoes well. Push a skewer into each end to make a slight hole. Preheat oven to 200°C/400°F. Bake potatoes for about 45 minutes, depending on their size until quite crisp on the outside and soft inside.

Mix the chilli with coriander. Mash or process the butter. Then using a fork dipped in hot water mash in the chilli and coriander mixture. Season with salt if needed. Cut or pull away some of the top skin of each potato and split through the centre to make an opening, pressing the ends a little to open it up. Put a dob of the butter onto this and allow it to melt into a little pink pool.

Serves 4, generously, or 8 small serves

8 medium-sized sweet potatoes

1 chilli, very finely chopped

2 tablespoons finely chopped coriander/cilantro leaves

60 g/2 oz butter, in small pieces

salt (optional)

spiced fish in paper parcels

Tuck food into a package and it cooks through with all the flavours trapped inside, releasing them only at the dinner table. This is one such dish where the fish is first marinated, then cooked and the parcel is opened at the table, so you have lots of juice around the fish, which breaks into lovely chunks as it is eaten with a fork. It is such an easy dish because there is no last-minute cooking – a deterrence to people when they think of serving a fish dinner to friends.

Every fish takes a different time to cook. It is difficult to make any hard and fast rules when cooking time is determined by the variety of fish you buy and the thickness of the fillets. Use your own judgement and, if you are uncertain, cheat a bit: open one package and put a fork into the fish to check it is ready and flaking.

Fry the cumin seeds for a minute until fragrant, remove. Heat oil and fry the onions gently until soft, add garlic, ginger, salt, cayenne, ground cumin, turmeric and remove from the heat. Add the cumin seeds and mix with parsley and coriander/cilantro. Cool slightly. Moisten with lemon juice. Spread mixture over the fillets and refrigerate them for an hour.

Preheat oven to 200°C/400°F. Put 6 pieces of foil on a bench, each more than double the size of a fillet. Put a fish fillet with some marinade onto foil and seal the edges firmly so none of the juices can escape. Bake for about 15–20 minutes – but timing really does depend on the thickness of the fish. Remove from oven, use scissors to snip open the top of the packages and put them straight onto plates. It is then quite easy for people to open them at the table.

Serves 6

2 teaspoons cumin seed

4 tablespoons olive oil

2 onions, finely chopped

3 cloves garlic, finely chopped

2 tablespoons grated ginger

good dash of salt and cayenne pepper

$^1\!/_2$ teaspoon ground cumin

2 teaspoons ground turmeric

3 tablespoons finely chopped parsley

$^1\!/_4$ cup/$^1\!/_2$ oz roughly chopped coriander/cilantro

2 tablespoons lemon juice

6 fish fillets of your choice

---

mexican chilli bread

An interesting butter, much spicier than the garlic butter often put into breadsticks, and a great dish to serve outdoors while watching a barbecue or to nibble with a drink.

Put the garlic, coriander/cilantro, chilli, spring onion and butter into a food processor, process and then add the oil. Add sufficient cayenne to give the butter a bit of a zing, and process once more to mix. Check for seasoning. Cut the bread into halves, lengthwise. Spread the top of each half with the butter. Top with grated Parmesan cheese. You can freeze bread at this stage or refrigerate, covered, for up to 12 hours.

Preheat oven to 200°C/400°F. Bake bread (in separate pieces, you don't put halves together again) on a tray for about 8–10 minutes or until the edges are crispy and the top speckled with colour. Cut into chunky pieces and serve warm.

I long breadstick/baguette

Chilli Butter

4 cloves garlic, finely chopped

3 tablespoons chopped coriander/cilantro

I spring onion/scallion, finely chopped

125 g/4 oz soft butter, cut into rough pieces

I tablespoon virgin olive oil

a little cayenne pepper

$^3\!/_4$ cup/3 oz grated Parmesan cheese

---

easy ideas

Green Oysters

In a bowl mix 2 tablespoons lemon juice, 3 tablespoons light olive oil, dash of chilli sauce or Tabasco, I clove crushed garlic and I teaspoon sugar. Season with salt and stir in $^1\!/_3$ cup/$^3\!/_4$ oz chopped coriander. Spoon a little over oysters in their half-shell. Quantity should be enough to coat about 2 dozen oysters. To vary this, mash half a ripe avocado into sauce, and then either coat oysters, or place sauce under them on the shell.

cannellini patties with coriander

I am not the greatest fan of bean dishes except in the heart of a chilly winter but these patties are a different matter. As they cook, the coriander flavours the beans and the mixture of sautéed onion and zucchini keeps them very moist. The result is a mealy but nutty flavoured croquette. I like to make a sauce to go with them, generally from lots of diced tomatoes cooked in a little olive oil or butter and well seasoned with salt, pepper and a dash of Tabasco, spooning this bright red mixture around the creamy patties. I think this is one time you shouldn't feel the need to serve any meat as, like most bean dishes, they are quite substantial.

Rinse the beans to get rid of the gluey stuff around them and leave to drain again. Heat the oil in a saucepan, add onion and cook until limp. Scatter in the curry powder, fry until aromatic and add zucchini, let it cook until soft, which should only be a couple of minutes. Transfer to a bowl.

Purée the beans roughly – you can leave a few pieces to add texture if you like – and mix this purée into the vegetables. Season well; mix in the egg, 1/2 cup crumbs and coriander/cilantro. Let mixture cool or it will be too sticky and difficult to form into rounds. Form into patties, flattening gently. If you still find the mixture hard to handle add more crumbs.

Place flour on a plate, beat the egg and have the extra crumbs on another plate. Dip each patty into flour, then egg and finally crumbs so the outside is coated. Chill patties until you are ready to cook – they can be prepared hours in advance (and kept for 24 hours at this stage) but it is best to leave refrigerated for at least an hour to set. Fry on both sides in a little light olive oil until nicely crisp and a good pale golden brown colour. Drain on some kitchen paper towel.

Makes about 12

1 x 450 g can cannellini beans, drained

2 tablespoons light olive oil

1 onion, finely diced

1 teaspoon curry powder

1 cup/4 oz grated zucchini/courgette

salt and pepper

1 large egg

1/2 cup/1 1/2 oz breadcrumbs, made from stale bread

1/3 cup/3/4 oz coriander/cilantro sprigs

plain/all-purpose flour, seasoned

extra 1 large egg

extra breadcrumbs

easy ideas

Spicy Mussels in Coriander Sauce

Rinse 1 kg/2 lb mussels and pull out beards. If very dirty scrape shells with a small knife. In a large, wide pan with a tight-fitting lid heat together 1/2 cup/4 fl oz water, 1/4 cup/ 2 fl oz Thai chilli sauce and 2 table-spoons lemon juice. When hot add mussels, stir, put on lid and cook about 3 minutes over high heat, shaking pan once or twice, until shells open. Stir in 1/2 cup/1 oz chopped coriander. Serve in big bowls, spooning a little liquid over the top.

Zea mays

corn

Corn originated in prehistoric Mexico and is the only cereal crop native to the Americas. Legend has it that a golden-haired girl appeared to a brave young warrior demanding he set the prairie alight and then drag her through the ashes by her long hair. Corn sprang up from the tufts of the golden hair that were left on the ground. For the Pueblo Indians of southwestern United States corn is an especially ancient and important food, revered for more than just its use in the kitchen, as it is associated with their religious and ceremonial life. They plant varieties in a rainbow of colours and of many kinds: some are for using fresh and some for drying. Once the dried corn would be ground to varying stages of fineness on stone metates (shallow basins in the rock). Today ground corn is used by the Pueblo alone or with wheat flour, to make fried, steamed or stove-cooked breads. Fresh corn – along with beans, pumpkin and chilli – is used to create many vegetable dishes, the strong base of their diet.

Corn is one of the most popular of American vegetables, and it is becoming ever more popular in Australia each summer and autumn, yet in most of Europe it is regarded more as a curiosity, being fed to animals. Eating plain fresh corn on the cob is considered quite an odd habit.

Corn is also known as maize in many areas of the world, and when cobs are eaten fresh they are often called sweetcorn. The reason for growing corn at home is so you can eat it almost immediately it has been picked. The less time between the corn leaving the plant and entering the water in the pot, the sweeter it will be. It begins to lose its sweetness as soon as it is stored, the sugars turning into starch, although some of the newer varieties of corn are bred to change this.

Corn is not a really sensible choice for a tiny vegetable garden as it does take up space and it only gives a small return for the area it occupies. However, what it does offer is a vegetable that is so sweet, juicy and exquisite in flavour that I keep aside one bed for it each year. I am patient when it shades the rest of the garden, rising above the standard roses, even when it rewards with only two or three cobs from each tall stalk. If careful you can get two crops: plant a second one when the first is about knee high, to stagger the corn.

planting

Corn must be in full sun and likes fertile, well-drained soil. Be sure to feed the soil a couple of weeks before planting and sow seed when the ground is warm, late spring is best I find. Put the seeds or seedlings into the ground 30 cm/12 in apart, in blocks rather than single rows as it is pollinated by the wind. Also in a single row it is more likely to be disturbed by high winds, while in blocks the corn is more protected. Corn is really a grass – you will soon see that by the shallow root system – and it can never have too much food, so feed, mulch and feed again. I always mulch around plants with plenty of straw to keep the ground damp and weed carefully by hand when the plants are babies, so as not to disturb the roots too much. When corn is well established I like to water with a light liquid seaweed mix every few weeks.

Temperature Zone	Sow or plant
Tropical	All year
Subtropical	Mid winter–late summer
Temperate	Spring–mid summer
Cool	Late spring–early summer
First picking	2½–3 months

varieties

Super sweet corn is now taking over America: these ears are twice as sweet as ordinary corn. They convert sugar to starch slowly so are relatively much sweeter 48 hours after picking than older varieties, and do keep well for much longer.

Super sweet

• Breakthrough F1
• Breakthrough Honey and Cream – yellow and white kernels on each cob.

Other varieties

• Miracle – matures in 65–80 days
• Snogold – also has white and gold kernels
• Golden Bantam – a very prolific cropper.

diseases and pests

Horrible little greedy *Heliothis* caterpillars will burrow into the ears and eat the kernels without you being aware of them, so you won't get any corn for all your hard work. Watch for their telltale sawdust-like deposits and wipe the silk with mineral oil once a week to deter them – or just squash the bugs by hand. I have never sprayed any of my corn so perhaps have been lucky that I have never had a bug on them. I know pests such as cutworms, wireworms, corn earworms and corn borers can attack them. Wireworms and cutworms can be controlled by a soil drench or get rid of corn earworms and borers with carbaryl.

harvesting

Pick corn as soon as the kernels are filled. This is indicated when the silk tassels dry off. Pull the husks back a little to check and if the kernels are round, full and lustrous, the corn is ready. Don't be greedy for bigger corn and wait longer, as young corn is the sweetest of all while older corn becomes tough. There is usually one very large corn cob on the bushes, then two smaller ones down the stalk; even with a good crop it is rare they are the same size.

buying and storage

There is a new habit of removing the husks and wrapping corn in plastic for sale. Avoid these; buy corn still left in the husk with its tassel of pale silk visible, as it will keep much better. Any yellow colour on the husk or dryness show it is old corn. Likewise, if the juice from the kernels is thick and sticky instead of pale and milky it is also old corn. Leave corn in the refrigerator still in the husk and use as soon as possible for the best flavour.

nutrition

Corn contains Vitamin C and carotenoids that function as anti-oxidants, and some folate. It is interesting that baby corn contains more nutrients than mature corn.

cooking

In his book *Greene on Greens* American chef Bert Greene says, 'you may stroll to the garden to cut the corn but you had darn well better run back to the kitchen to cook it'. It is then of course the corn dish of perfection, but this is not realistic for everyone. Just cook it as soon as you can after buying. For the simplest cooking just strip back the husk and silk. Have a pot of water ready with a teaspoon of sugar and add the corn, bring to a boil, cover and turn off the heat and leave it sit for about 10 minutes. This method of boiling and then leaving it to continue cooking gently in the heat gives very tender corn. If you have bought larger corn you may need to cook for a few minutes before turning off the heat and leaving it sit. Drain and serve. Salt only when it is being served as salting the water stops the softening of the kernels.

easy ideas

Corn and Bacon

Cut the kernels from 4 cobs. Cook 4 rashers diced bacon in a frying pan until the fat is transparent, add 30 g/1 oz butter and the corn kernels, season with pepper and cook, tossing, for a couple of minutes. Add ⅓ cup/3 fl oz water and boil rapidly until the water has cooked away. The corn should be tender by this time. Salt if you wish but the bacon will usually provide plenty.

corn moulds

Serve these little timbales of corn in the dishes in which they have been baked, or turn them out on to a plate. The mixture is light but full of flavour. You can eat these quite plain or with a fresh tomato sauce (cook three tomatoes and when they are thick, push the juices through a sieve).

This recipe is sufficient for 4 moulds, about 1 cup/8 fl oz in size. The mixture swells when cooking so only fill the moulds three-quarters of the way up.

Preheat oven to 180°C/350°F. Using a sharp knife, scrape the cobs down to remove all the pieces of corn. Don't take knife too close to the cob as these pieces are tough and won't cook through in the time the mixture takes to set. You should have about 1½ cups/12 oz fine corn pieces. Mix with all the remaining ingredients and put into 4 greased individual ramekins or soufflé dishes. Place in a baking tin to which boiling water is added to half the depth of the ramekins. Cook for 25–30 minutes in oven and check they are just set. Remove from the oven and leave in the dishes still sitting in the water bath for 10 minutes before serving.

Serves 4

4 corn cobs

3 large eggs

½ cup/1½ oz breadcrumbs made from stale bread

½ small onion, very finely diced

1 tablespoon finely chopped parsley

½ cup/2 oz grated tasty/cheddar cheese

some black pepper and a little salt

corn chowder

Sweet, juicy corn grows in abundance in America and features in dozens of ways in dishes, but particularly in their thick chowders. Corn chowder is always made with fresh corn – never canned – as part of the flavour comes from the milky residue near the cob. Chowder in America is either made with just a creamy base, or it has a mix of tomato, depending which school of thought you follow. For my taste the American creamy chowders are too thick and heavy, almost like a porridge consistency; they are fine if you want a meal of soup but not good before anything else as they are so substantial.

Remove the husks and silk from the corn. Using a sharp knife cut the kernels from the corn, but not too close to the cob. Grate the corn nearer the cob over a bowl to get all the milky part and juices. It is a messy job as the corn splashes, so do it near the sink with an apron of generous proportions wrapped around you. Mix the kernels and corn juices together. Cook the bacon in a large saucepan until the fat has become transparent. Add the capsicum/bell pepper and onions, fry gently for about 5 minutes. Add water and potatoes and bring to the boil. Cover and cook for 15 minutes or until the potatoes have softened. Mix in tomatoes, sugar, salt and pepper, stir in the corn and cover the pan. Cook 10 minutes or until all the vegetables are tender. Bring the milk and cream to a boil. Add to the chowder and heat through. Mix in the parsley and serve. If making in advance, it is a good idea to leave out the milk and cream and add these when reheating.

Serves 4–6

Variation
Add a dozen oysters to the finished soup, warm for a minute.

4 fresh corn cobs

4 rashers bacon, cut into thick strips

1 red capsicum/bell pepper, deseeded and finely chopped

1 large onion, finely diced

1 cup/8 fl oz water

375 g/12 oz potatoes, peeled and finely diced

500 g/1 lb tomatoes, peeled and chopped roughly

1 teaspoon sugar

salt and pepper

2 cups/1 pint milk

1/2 cup/4 fl oz cream

plenty of freshly chopped parsley

hint

The corn chowder has a mix of tomato and dairy products that can result in curdling, so it is important that the milk and cream are heated first until they boil, and then are added to the chowder.

spicy chicken slices with coconut corn sauce

An easy dish to make, the corn gives a sweet flavour to coconut milk but needs spice and lemon to balance the final taste. Two chicken breasts go quite a long way in this dish and with rice I find it will serve three.

Grate the corn into a basin, using a coarse grater. Mix chilli with flour and salt and rub into the chicken. Leave a few minutes, then cut chicken across into thin slices. Heat the oil with butter in a frying pan, add the chicken strips and fry quickly, turning them over until they have changed colour. Remove to a plate and put a second plate on top to keep them from drying out. Tip in the coconut milk, water, sugar and salt and boil quickly for about 5 minutes until lightly thickened. Add the grated corn and juices and heat a minute, then return the chicken and leave to cook very gently another minute so it just warms through again. Lastly add coriander or basil leaves and stir through. Taste and add lemon juice as desired.

Serves 3

2 corn cobs

1 teaspoon chilli powder

2 tablespoons plain/all-purpose flour

salt

2 chicken breasts, skinned

2 tablespoons oil

30 g/1 oz butter

1 cup/8 fl oz coconut milk

1/2 cup/4 fl oz water

1 teaspoon brown sugar

extra salt

2 tablespoons finely chopped coriander/cilantro leaves, or 12 whole basil leaves

lemon juice, to taste

herbed corn soup

hint

Croutons are
a good topping
for any soup.
Make them more
interesting by
cutting into heart
shapes, triangles
or rounds and
gently fry in a
little butter until
golden and crisp.
While still warm
roll the edges in
parsley and let
them cool.

Make this with fresh corn and fresh herbs and you will find it has a rustic, rich country flavour. Although some of the ingredients are similar to those used in the corn chowder, the finished dish has quite a different flavour.

Remove the husks and silk from the corn and carefully strip the kernels from the husks by cutting down with a sharp knife and having the corn in a basin to stop the juices being lost. Melt the butter and add onion and capsicum/pepper. Cook gently a couple of minutes until slightly limp. Add the corn, potato and stock and simmer gently about 10 minutes. Add the herbs and cook another couple of minutes. Take about 1½ cups/12 fl oz of the mixture and purée it. Return to the pan, it will slightly thicken the soup. Stir in the cream.

If you are reheating the soup don't add the cheese until dinnertime, as it can become sticky and tacky. Heat the soup again, scatter in the cheese and immediately remove from the heat and stir until the cheese has melted. Serve with a fine dusting of parsley on top, if you wish.

Serves 4

3 corn cobs

45 g/1½ oz butter

1 onion, finely chopped

1 red capsicum/bell pepper, cut into fine strips

1 medium-sized potato, peeled and neatly diced

3 cups/1½ pints chicken stock

4 tablespoons finely chopped fresh marjoram

2 leaves sage, finely chopped

2 teaspoons finely chopped thyme

¾ cup/6 fl oz cream

½ cup/2 oz grated tasty/cheddar cheese

golden corn soup with avocado

Just because avocados are around in such volume, don't take them for granted. This pale green fruit is one of the most nutritious foods in the world. It contains in its velvety texture lots of the B vitamins, and vitamins A, C and E, which act as anti-oxidants and help protect cells from damage caused by stress. If you are not impressed with that, you may like to know that the Aztecs regarded them highly because they were considered a sex stimulant which vastly improved their love life. Try this soup for either – or both – of these reasons.

Heat the oil in a large saucepan, add the onion, capsicum and garlic and cook gently for about 10 minutes or until the vegetables are wilted. Scatter with flour and stir for a few minutes. Pour in the stock and let it come to the boil, stirring until lightly thickened. Grate the corn into a deep basin. This is a messy job. Corn splashes juice as you grate it, so using a deep basin helps stop these juices from going all over the bench. Tip the grated corn and all the liquid around it into the soup and cover. Leave to cook for about 20 minutes or until the vegetables are quite tender.

When ready to serve, cook the bacon until it is crisp. Drain well. Cut the avocado into small cubes and mix with the bacon and chives. Reheat the soup and add the avocado mixture at the finish, stir and take off the heat. You mustn't let avocado cook for long or it will become bitter. Serve, ladling out some of the avocado with each portion. Or if you find it easier, serve the soup in a bowl, topping with the avocado and bacon mix.

Serves 4, generously

¼ cup/2 fl oz olive oil

1 large onion, finely diced

1 red capsicum/bell pepper, finely diced

2 large cloves garlic, finely chopped

1 tablespoon flour

4 cups/2 pints vegetable or chicken stock

3 corn cobs

2 rashers bacon, cut into fine strips

1 ripe avocado

2 tablespoons finely chopped chives or parsley

baked corn cake

corn goes with

butter

cheese

olive oil

avocado

capsicum/ bell pepper

chilli

garlic

onions

potatoes

tomatoes

zucchini/ courgette

bacon

chicken

ham

crab

prawns

milk

cream and sour cream

chives

coriander/ cilantro

parsley

A large flattish cake which is quite firm enough to cut into wedges, corn cake is a good accompaniment to rustic dishes like fat brown grilled sausages and stuffed or barbecued chicken, or you can use it for a light lunch with a spoonful of a mixed green salad.

Preheat oven to 180°C/350°F. Put the onion, capsicum and oil into a saucepan and cook for about 10 minutes or until soft. Add the chilli and garlic and cook a further minute or until the garlic smells aromatic. While the onion mixture is cooking, scrape the kernels from 4 of the cobs – don't take it too close to the centre or it will be tough. Put the kernels into the pot. Cover and cook gently for 10 minutes or until the corn is soft. Remove to a bowl.

Grate the remaining corn over the top, collecting all the juices in the bowl, and mix through. Season well with salt and pepper. Add the eggs and sour cream and beat gently. Melt the butter and stir through. Cook this in a buttered china quiche dish or use a metal container, but first line the base with buttered non-stick baking paper/parchment. Pour in the mixture and smooth the top. Bake for 20 minutes or until the centre is barely firm when touched. It will firm more as it settles.

Leave to rest for 10 minutes then either serve from the quiche dish or invert over a plate. It will be pale on the base so you may like to invert it again to show the golden-brown top. This corn cake is meant to be served just warm for the best flavour and is also very interesting cold, but not refrigerated.

Serves 8

1 large onion, finely chopped

1 red capsicum/bell pepper, finely chopped

3 tablespoons olive oil

1 chilli, deseeded and chopped

2 cloves garlic, finely chopped

6 corn cobs

1 teaspoon salt and ½ teaspoon pepper

5 eggs

2 cup/3 fl oz sour cream

60 g/2 oz butter

green and gold corn salad

On the various occasions I have eaten corn salad in America it was nearly always made with canned or frozen kernels, surprising for a country which grows so much corn. Unless sweet, juicy and fresh corn is used, the salad – to my taste – is boring and the corn texture is too soft. This version melts with sweet flavours, sparked by some chilli and onion. With diced avocado tossed through at the finish, it makes a fine bed for some roasted chicken, lamb or beef. It could also be used as an accompaniment under a simple grilled fillet of fish.

Put the corn into a saucepan and add water to come to the top, season with sugar, cover and bring to a boil. Cook 5 minutes, turn off the heat and leave to sit in the water for 20 minutes, then drain. Cut the corn off the cob and mix with all the remaining ingredients except avocado. Toss and leave to marinate for several hours. The salad keeps well for a day. Add the avocado just before serving and mix through gently so you don't break it up.

Serves 6

6 cobs corn

½ small red onion, finely chopped

1 small chilli, deseeded and finely chopped

1 tablespoon white wine vinegar

5 tablespoons olive oil

1 tablespoon lemon juice

salt and pepper

2 tablespoons finely chopped parsley

2 tablespoons finely chopped coriander/cilantro

1 large ripe avocado, peeled, stoned and cut into large dice

daufuskie quilt

The late Bert Greene, an American food writer, wrote about this rendition of a dish the locals call 'a lef'over sla' and it is an ideal salad for summer or autumn when vegetables are warm with sunny flavours. Daufuskie Island is in the Gullah country of South Carolina and the people living there have farmed the land for centuries, making famous patchwork quilts formed of the many colours that appear in this dish.

Cook the corn in boiling water for 5 minutes and drain, cut the kernels from the cob and put into a bowl with the other vegetables and garlic. Season. Add oil, vinegar and herbs. Put the cumin into a dry frying pan and heat until it smells aromatic, crush or grind in a pestle and mortar and add along with chicken to the vegetables. Leave for 5 minutes to marinate but serve once you have added the chicken, as the salad is not so good if chilled. Of course you can mix up the salad base during the day and then add the chicken at dinnertime.

Serves 3

3 corn cobs

1 baby zucchini/courgette, cut into halves lengthwise and thinly sliced

1 ripe tomato, cut into halves and thinly sliced

1 small capsicum/bell pepper, seeded and finely chopped

1/4 small red onion, finely chopped

1 clove garlic, crushed

salt and pepper

4 tablespoons olive oil

1 tablespoon red wine vinegar

1 tablespoon fresh basil

6 leaves chopped fresh thyme

1/2 teaspoon cumin seeds

1 1/2 cups/12 oz cooked chicken cubes or shredded pieces

hint

Don't cook corn in salted water as this will toughen the corn pieces. Add a little sugar to the water instead; salt the dish before serving.

easy ideas

Barbecued Corn

Carefully strip back the leaves so they don't break at the base remove silk. Fold the leaves back and tie with string. Cook the corn in water for about 10 minutes. Drain and cool. At dinnertime remove string, put onto a hot plate on a barbecue or into a very hot oven on a baking tray until corn is heated through and the leaves are slightly charred.

corn and ham puff

Not quite a soufflé but lighter than a baked dish, this is a creamy soft mix of corn and ham, designed for a first course or lunch dish. That slight saltiness of the ham contrasts perfectly with the sweetness of grated corn.

Heat the butter and oil in a saucepan, add the onion and corn and cook gently until the onion has softened. Mix in the ham, toss and scatter flour over the top. Stir to cook the flour, then pour in the milk and stir until it has come to the boil. Let it cook gently for a few minutes so it will thicken a little and the corn become creamy. Season with nutmeg, salt and pepper. Let the mixture cool for about 10 minutes, then add the yolks and stir through. You can complete dish about an hour in advance to this stage but don't refrigerate or it will be too firm.

Preheat oven to 190°C/375°F. Beat the whites until stiff and fold through a mixture a third at a time. Have a baking dish ready and buttered, about 20 cm/8 in diameter, and pour the mixture into the dish, topping with cheese. Bake in the oven for about 25 minutes until it is puffed, golden and just set to touch. This needs to be served straight away or the 'puff' will vanish.

Serves 4

45 g/1 1/2 oz butter

1 tablespoon olive oil

1 small onion, finely chopped

3 corn cobs, kernels scraped or coarsely grated from the cob

125 g/4 oz sliced ham, cut into small dice

1 tablespoon flour

1 cup/8 fl oz milk

pinch of nutmeg

salt and pepper

2 egg yolks

4 egg whites

1/4 cup/1 oz grated Parmesan cheese

Cucumis sativus

cucumber

These are rambly creatures, members of a large family that includes melons, zucchini and pumpkins, most of which have similar inclinations. Cucumbers spread over the ground and are weak-stemmed but can be encouraged to climb up a little trellis or a fence if you don't have enough room for them to spread. This also helps prevent mildew. Strangely, the expression 'as cool as a cucumber' is one that the plant does not echo. It likes warm weather but after a really cool spell it can shrivel up quickly. Cucumbers are about crunchy texture rather than lots of flavour, their taste is cool and refreshing and it is often the contrast they offer that is important in dishes. The bitterness which was often a part of cucumbers has vanished, they are now rarely bitter. This was originally part of the genetic makeup of cucumbers and almost all the research around this vegetable has been aimed at removing it. If they don't taste fresh and sweet you may be depriving them of water, which they need in generous amounts.

Once cucumbers were out of popularity, suffering from the belief that they were indigestible, that they needed to be scraped with a fork hard down the sides to make them easier to eat, had to be salted and even then made people burp. They have returned to favour, especially with their use in so many Asian dishes and salads. Asia is the largest supplier of cucumbers on the world markets.

You don't need to plant many, a couple of plants of several types will be generous in their offerings, and I usually put in varieties such as apple cucumber which are not quite as easy to find in the shops. Like zucchini they spring from small to huge quickly so you need to check them regularly.

planting

Best in the sun as cucumbers need the bees to pollinate the flowers and the bees don't visit as regularly if other vegetables heavily shade them. Only female flowers produce cucumbers. There are far more male flowers on each vine to improve their chances but you can help the bees do their job by brushing pollen from a male flower onto the female flowers.

Cucumbers love rich soil so enrich with well-rotted manure or compost and add lime or dolomite to reduce acidity. Make little mounds in the soil with a small rim around for water and so the rain won't wash the soil away from the baby cucumber plants leaving the roots exposed. You can plant seeds – but then will have too many cucumbers for most people so probably need to distribute them between gardening friends.

Put about four seeds in each circle just below the surface. After they are through – which should be 7–10 days – take out the two weakest shoots by cutting them off with scissors at root level so as not to disturb the others. Seedlings can be planted in a group of two but, again, be careful until they are established not to water hard or you may dislodge them. As they begin to grow just spread the vine branches out in several directions. Water and mulch to keep the moisture in the soil.

Cucumbers can be grown in pots, which need to be 30 cm/12 in wide and quite deep. It is sensible to give them a little trellis to hang onto which they do obligingly with their tendrils.

Temperature Zone	Sow or plant
Dislikes frost and needs full sun for bees to pollinate	
Tropical	All year
Subtropical	All year
Temperate	Mid spring–early summer
Cool	Mid spring–early summer
First picking	2½–3 months

varieties

There are so many of these I have only listed a few, just get a catalogue and have some fun choosing for yourself.

Apple cucumber

- Lemon – an heirloom cucumber with a tangy flavour and never becomes bitter.

Green–skinned cucumbers

- Burpee Hybrid
- Green Gem
- Marketer
- Long Green
- Patio Pik
- Moneymaker.

Others

- Armenian – pale green and ribbed, stores very well
- Russian – a giant pale brown one, which keeps for months
- Lebanese – a mini that can be sliced or pickled and is never bitter
- Burpless Telegraph – has a huge yield and is supposedly burpless
- Bush Cucumber – for people with smaller spaces or for a tub (this is a new bush type which grows 20 cm/ 8 in green cucumbers and twice as many plants can be grown in the same area as more sprawling varieties).

For pickling

- Heinz Pickling
- Super Pickle
- Venio Pickling.

pests and diseases

Aphids can be a pest, just hose or spray with malathion if the infestation is really severe. Cucumber beetles may find them too but just pick the beetles off if you see any.

Because cucumbers need so much water they have a tendency to powdery mildew. Mix 1 cup milk with 8 cups water to which you have added 1 teaspoon bicarbonate of soda (baking soda) and spray once or twice a week with this.

harvesting

From 50–120 days, depending on the type. The more you pick cucumbers the more they will reward with produce. Never let them become too large, they can be coarse or bitter then but it will depend on the variety of cucumber you have planted as to the size to expect. Cut carefully from the stem so you don't pull out the plant. As plants reach the end of their productive cycle they will often be struck down by downy mildew. Take out the plants and don't put into the compost.

buying and storage

Cucumbers should be firm and crisp to touch. This is hard to tell when they are often sealed tightly in plastic but you can judge by touching as far as possible. Green ones should be very green. Apple cucumbers can have a tinge of yellow, this is fine.

Cucumbers don't store for long – a week at most refrigerated – and the best flavour is from fresh cucumbers. Don't put in with fruit such as apples, melon, bananas, which give off a gas that causes cucumbers to soften. If you have a glut or find plenty cheap in the market, pickling is the ideal way to use up cucumbers.

nutrition

Not much, as cucumbers are mainly water, but they have some Vitamin C and small quantities of other vitamins and minerals. Surprisingly, the little Lebanese cucumbers have about twice the Vitamin C of other types.

cooking

It is rather rare to have cooked cucumber; the joy of them is in the fresh flavour. Peeling is an option. Sometimes if the skin is heavy for a particular dish I score the outside heavily with a fork, which gives a pretty effect when they are sliced. If you want cucumbers in a mixture where you don't need too much liquid, slice the cucumber first, season with plenty of salt and sugar and a couple of tablespoons of vinegar. Let stand for several hours. Squeeze slices firmly to get rid of the salty taste, and you will have crisp bright green to pale green cucumber that won't leak juices into a salad to the same extent.

spiced pickled cucumber slices

hint

Cucumber without the seeds has a different and firmer taste in salads. The best way to get them out is to cut lengthwise, then use a teaspoon to scrape down the seeds. Peel first if you want an even more delicate flavour.

Sometimes known as 'same-day pickles', this can be used as a side dish with meats and terrines, and it is great in sandwiches with cheese but drain it well first. I like it a bit hot and if you love spicy food just adjust the chilli accordingly. I have found the heat does dissipate a little over time when it is stored.

Wash the cucumbers well, cut into thin slices – use a food processor if you wish but try to keep the cucumbers straight so you don't have uneven pieces. Put into a bowl with the onions and salt. Add water to barely cover and stand 2 hours. Drain well.

Put all remaining ingredients into a saucepan and stir until the sugar has dissolved. Add the cucumber and onion and push into the liquid. There won't be enough to cover them at this stage. Simmer gently about 8 minutes, turning the bits from the top over to the bottom a couple of times and when the cucumber slices are almost transparent take from the heat. Put into warm, sterilized jars and seal. Leave a day before using.

Makes about 6 cups

1 kg/2 lb long green cucumbers

2 large onions, thinly sliced

2 tablespoons kitchen salt

1½ cups/12 fl oz white wine vinegar

3 red chillies, cut into quarters

6 garlic cloves, peeled and halved

4 fresh or 2 dried bay leaves

250 g/8 oz sugar

1 tablespoon dill seeds

spicy cucumber salad

In this salad, the cucumber becomes soft and highly flavoured with a mixture of garlic, spring onion, sesame and rice wine vinegar. Use one of the long, continental cucumbers, which have small seeds.

The salad can be made hours in advance, but is nicest eaten the day it is made and always add the dressing close to serving time. It is an adaptation of a Korean salad, the original being very spicy and hot, and served as a side dish with meat. In this version, I have cut out much of the chilli, but if you love very spicy foods be less cautious and add one or two more chopped chillies with the seeds removed.

Peel the cucumber and cut into very thin slices. Place in a bowl and add salt and water. Allow to stand for about 30 minutes, then drain and squeeze out the liquid. If not using for several hours, refrigerate the cucumber.

When you are ready to serve, mix all dressing ingredients in a bowl and add the cucumber, stirring so that the slices are well coated.

Note
This salad is slightly sweet. If you wish, cut the sugar to 1 teaspoon. However, the more heat you add, the more sugar it can take.

Serves 4

1 continental cucumber
2 teaspoons salt
$1/2$ cup/4 fl oz water

Dressing
1 large clove garlic, crushed
4 spring onions/scallions, very finely diced
2 teaspoons sugar
1 teaspoon dark sesame oil
1 tablespoon rice wine vinegar
generous dash of chilli sauce, Tabasco or a small chilli, deseeded and finely chopped

easy ideas

Cucumber Salad with Thai Chilli Sauce

Great as a side salad with chicken or meat. Peel cucumbers if you wish, depending on the skin, then slice very thinly and add a bit of salt, leave in a bowl for a short time, then squeeze to get rid of some moisture. Mix with a good dash of sweet Thai chilli sauce, a small handful of chopped coriander/cilantro and serve with roasted chopped peanuts on top.

cucumber and mint raita

Few things could be more soothing than a raita, used at an Indian meal to soothe the palate when eating fiery food. Try it with any spicy dish or just put on the table at a barbecue if you have some spicy sausages or some marinated meats, as its cooling freshness is good in summer.

Stir the yoghurt well with a fork so it becomes creamy and add all the remaining ingredients except for whole mint leaves. Cover and refrigerate. After a short time the cucumber will ooze juice if you make it well in advance so it is a good idea to keep the grated and squeezed cucumber refrigerated in a separate bowl. Drain it and mix with the yoghurt before serving at the table, with mint leaves scattered on top.

2 cups/1 pint thick plain yoghurt
1 small cucumber, peeled, coarsely grated and squeezed well
2 tablespoons finely chopped mint
1 teaspoon salt
$1/2$ teaspoon ground cumin
$1/2$ teaspoon ground coriander
6 fresh mint leaves to garnish

cucumber and yoghurt soup

hint

Older cucumbers can be treated so they will become crisp again. Cut into thickish slices and scatter with some salt. Put into a strainer or colander standing over a bowl and pack ice cubes over the top. Let them stand for at least an hour, then rinse and dry on paper towels.

A very refreshing, healthy soup for a summer day that leaves a light sharp flavour on your palate from the cultured yoghurt base. Serve plain or with a spoonful of salmon caviar or pink lumpfish roe on top. For a special occasion you can lightly butter some toasted light rye bread and top with smoked salmon. Serve strips of this on a plate alongside the soup.

Just mix everything together in a big bowl and chill. The cucumber will give out a bit of liquid, which is good in this case, as otherwise the soup would be too thick. Chill at least a couple of hours but for no more than 6 hours or it then gets too runny. Serve with a mint leaf on top and a cucumber slice if you like but make sure the cucumber is wafer thin.

Serves 6

3 cups/1 1/2 pints plain yoghurt

2 cloves garlic, crushed

1 large long green cucumber, grated

1 tablespoon lemon juice

2 teaspoons white wine vinegar

salt and pepper

1 tablespoon mint leaves cut into fine strips

2 tablespoons finely chopped parsley

sautéed cucumbers

We mostly think of cucumber as a salad, less frequently as a vegetable, but it is light and has a delicate crunchy taste. These go well with chicken or fish dishes and, although tender, they still have a nice crisp texture. You don't want to cook them until they are limp or they are then boring.

Peel and then cut the cucumbers down alongside the seeds so you have just long strips of cucumber flesh. Cut into sticks and discard the seeds. Put them into a colander, scatter on a little salt and let stand for about an hour. Dry on kitchen paper towel.

Cook the onion in butter until softened and golden, add the garlic and cucumber and cook for about 3 minutes gently until just tender. Toss the tomatoes into the pan, cook over high heat for a few minutes so you have a thick sauce. Add parsley and a generous grind of pepper.

Serves 6

2 long green cucumbers

salt

1 large onion, halved and thinly sliced

45 g/1 1/2 oz butter

2 cloves garlic, finely chopped

2 tomatoes, peeled and chopped

2 tablespoons finely chopped parsley

pepper

easy ideas *Cucumber Mayonnaise*

Use with quickly sautéed fish and also good with chicken. Grate half a cucumber, squeeze dry. Mix with 3/4 cup/ 6 fl oz well-flavoured mayonnaise, a good squeeze lemon juice; a spoonful of whipped cream and a scatter of chopped parsley or dill. If you have them on hand, a few pickled capers that have been rinsed improve it even more.

Cucumber Sticks with Salmon

Cut some crisp cucumber into sticks and wrap around with a piece of smoked salmon so the end of the cucumber is showing. Dunk this end into a bit of mayonnaise and then into some finely chopped parsley. Serve with drinks as a nibble.

duck and noodle cucumber salad

A stunning special-occasion dish in which the richness of duck becomes the perfect partner for the light fresh taste and crunchy texture of cucumber.

Preheat oven to 180°C/350°F. Season the duck breasts and squeeze on some lemon juice. Seal the duck in a pan until outside is brown. Transfer to the oven and leave to cook for 15 minutes. Remove and let duck rest, covered, for 15 minutes. Take the skin and any fat from the duck. Keep the skin, discarding the fat.

While duck is resting make up the lemon sauce. Mix the stock with soy, sugar, lemon juice, garlic, lemon rind and ginger juice and heat in a saucepan for 5 minutes. Add sweet Thai chilli sauce. Cut the duck into strips, strain half the sauce over the top and then refrigerate duck.

Cook the noodles until tender. Drain and rinse. Put into a bowl and rub a little oil through them to keep them separate. Refrigerate.

Peel the cucumber, cut into halves, remove the seeds and slice thinly. Season with sugar, salt and vinegar and stand for 1 hour. Squeeze out the liquid and mix with soy and mint.

Crisp the duck skin by cooking in a frying pan with oil. Drain on paper towel.

Near to serving time pour the reserved sauce into the noodles and mix with the cucumber and spring onion/scallion. Arrange on a platter and put the duck on top. Garnish with the crispy bits of duck skin and mint sprigs.

Serves 6

6 duck breasts

salt, pepper and a little lemon juice

Lemon Sauce

1 cup/8 fl oz chicken stock, skimmed of any fat

3 tablespoons soy sauce

3 tablespoons brown sugar

2/3 cup/5 fl oz lemon juice

3 cloves garlic, finely chopped

grated rind of 1 lemon

2 tablespoons ginger juice

1 tablespoon sweet Thai chilli sauce

Noodle Cucumber Base

250 g/8 oz fine egg noodles

1–2 cucumbers, depending on their size

2 tablespoons sugar

2 teaspoons salt

2 tablespoons rice wine vinegar

2 tablespoons soy sauce

2 tablespoons shredded mint

1 small bunch spring onions/scallions, cut into diagonal pieces and soaked

cucumber goes with

white or malt vinegar

rice vinegar

oil

sugar

chilli

garlic

ginger

onion

spring onions/ scallions

lemon

tomatoes

Thai chilli sauce

fish sauce

soy sauce

mustard seeds

cashew nuts

peanuts

cream

mayonnaise

sour cream

yoghurt

chives

coriander/ cilantro

dill

mint

parsley

salmon

trout

most kinds of fish

chicken

duck

cold noodles

dill

*Peucedanum graveolens or
Anethum graveolens*

Dill is a member of the parsley and carrot family and its special culinary role is with all kinds of fish, from fine white-fleshed fish to pink salmon or meatier herrings. Any other herb cannot match its delicate flavour. It is quite similar in appearance to fennel but the colour of dill is more of a blue-green. An ancient herb, it was mentioned in old Egyptian texts and used for medical purposes by Greek and Roman physicians. Dill is very decorative and I often cut the yellow flat flowers and use them inside to create a fragrant, cottage look for my vases, while the feathery strands give a soft look to garden beds. When the plant forms seeds these can also be gathered, as they are important in pickles — while some left to float to the ground will give you more plants the following year. A European friend would make up a big batch of pickled herrings annually

gravlax and scandinavian mustard sauce (recipe page 149) ▶

for summer and much of the charm of this dish was the way he ringed the platter of fish with big sprigs of his own fresh dill flowers and seeds, so you could pick off a few to nibble with the spiced herring and dark rye bread.

planting

Dill is an annual. Sow seeds or plant seedlings in spring in a sheltered position but you can grow them almost anywhere. Seeds should be sown shallow in a clump or rows. Keep the soil moist. Dill doesn't cope well with transplanting although you can buy pots of dill in the nurseries. Be careful when you transfer these to the garden that you disturb the roots as little as possible. Weed carefully by hand until they are well established. Dill has a short growing period so you need to make successive sowings or plantings to have a constant supply.

harvesting

Just cut and trim for picking, snipping off the young leaves. Put a bag over the seeds as they are drying and gather them for the kitchen – although you need lots of dill to make this worthwhile.

buying and storage

Buy very green dill, it should look sprightly. As it is stored it becomes yellow. Wrap in kitchen paper and put into a plastic bag in the refrigerator for up to 5 days.

prawns in dill butter

dill goes with

fish, all kinds

sour cream

yoghurt

mayonnaise

cucumbers

potatoes

eggs

One of those really easy dishes that taste succulent and exotic, this is a last-minute recipe but I usually make up the dill butter before hand and have everything else chopped so it can be put together quickly, without spending too much time in the kitchen.

Mash butter with lemon juice and dill – this is easiest if butter is not cold, or the lemon doesn't blend in well. Season with Tabasco. Roll butter into a thin sausage shape and chill. When cold cut into thick slices and leave ready, covered, for final cooking.

Dust prawns with flour, shaking away any excess. Heat oil in a frying pan, put in prawns and cook, turning them over until they have changed colour on the outside and are just cooked through. Add tomato and season, cook gently until you have some juices forming. Then quickly add sliced butter, heat for a moment but take pan off heat as soon as butter begins to soften as you want the butter to melt into the tomato but not to become oily. Take out prawns and put on plates, give tomato and butter a last quick stir and spoon a little on top of each prawn along with a squeeze of lemon juice, or serve with a wedge of lemon on each plate.

Serves 6 as a first course, 3 as a main dish

90 g/3 oz butter, in small pieces

1 tablespoon lemon juice

2 tablespoons finely chopped dill

a dash of Tabasco sauce

18 large, peeled green prawns/ jumbo shrimp

plain flour

$1/3$ cup/3 fl oz olive oil

4 ripe tomatoes, peeled and finely chopped

salt and pepper

lemon, to garnish

gravlax and scandinavian mustard sauce

I love gravlax and it is so easy to make at home I am surprised more people don't try it. Buy two bits of the tail section of a salmon or an ocean trout – they need to be a similar size as you put one on top of the other – and 500–750 g (1–1½ lb) each is a good weight. Tails don't have any bones so it is much easier and quicker to make gravlax with them. There is no need to use whole fish, as you would then have far too much – unless you are very greedy for salmon or having a big party. Small pieces are very successful made into gravlax. After a day or so of marinating, use your sharpest knife to cut the fish into very thin slices, cutting on a diagonal and cutting the fish from the skin as you slice it. Eat with some toast, sliced and buttered rye bread, mustard sauce and, if you like, put a little dish of capers and another of lemon wedges on the table.

Choose a shallow, glass or ceramic dish in which the fish fits neatly and scatter the bottom with a third of the dill. Mix the sugar with salt and scatter on a bit. Put one piece of fish, skin side down, onto this. Scatter more sugar and salt on the fish along with a bit more dill. Put the other portion of fish over this, skin side upwards, and scatter on the rest of the salt and sugar, rubbing it in and then the rest of the dill. Put a piece of plastic wrap over the fish, rest a plate on top and weight it down, for instance with as a couple of cans, and refrigerate for 12 hours. Turn the fish over and refrigerate again for another 12 hours.

You can keep gravlax for a short time but take it out of the mixture after 24 hours, scraping away the salty bits and dill and pat dry. Store wrapped for up to 3 days.

Serve with mustard sauce: mix the mustards together with brown sugar and vinegar. Whisk in the oil very slowly and add a bit of salt if you wish. Lastly add dill and chill.

Ample for 4–6 people as a first course

¾ small bunch dill, chopped (about ½ cup/1 oz)

3 tablespoons brown sugar

2 tablespoons rock salt or sea salt

2 pieces salmon or ocean trout, 1–1.5 kg/2–3lb in all

Mustard Sauce

2 tablespoons French mustard

2 teaspoons dry English mustard

1 tablespoon brown sugar

1 tablespoon red or white wine vinegar

4 tablespoons light olive oil

salt to taste

2 tablespoons finely chopped dill

uses

Dill makes a good seasoning for salt-free diets. It settles indigestion; helps cure stomach aches, induces sleep and stimulates appetite and milk production in nursing mothers. For these purposes, the dill leaves may be infused in water. Mothers used to rely on dill water to soothe difficult babies with indigestion problems and allow them to have a good night's sleep. It got its name from *dillian* meaning 'to lull' in the ancient Saxon language.

easy ideas *Fish with a Dill Crust*

Season 4 fish fillets (snapper, whiting or dory, for instance) with salt and pepper and squeeze some lemon juice over. Mix 1½ cups/4 oz stale white bread-crumbs with 2 tablespoons each of chopped dill and parsley. Dust the fish with flour, dip fillets in beaten egg and then the herbed crumbs, patting the crumbs down gently with your hands to ensure an even coating. Cook fish in a large frying pan in a little hot oil until crusty on both sides. Timing depends on the fish, but it is easier to make this using thin rather than thick fillets, which may brown too much before the centre is cooked through. Serve with lemon wedges and put some dill sprigs on top.

eggplant
aubergine

Solanum melongena

I think of this vegetable as eggplant, which is the common Australian and American name, but in England it is called aubergine. Either way, it is one of the delights of the Mediterranean area, yet really belongs to tropical Asia – which I find somewhat surprising as it is used more freely in Italian, French and Turkish cuisines. 'Eggplant' refers to the shape, certainly not the dark colour of the most common variety, but there is a very beautiful ivory-white one, which looks rather like an exotic china egg. I have seen eggplant varieties with striped pink and white skin, and with green, violet, creamy white and orange skins and in sizes ranging from tiny like a walnut to big fat specimens. The first eggplant were small and very delicate, the shape and colour being associated with birds' eggs. Although Asian, it was some time before it was accepted in China, where the vegetable achieved a reputation that it could be deadly in unskilled hands; it was given the name ch'ieh-pzu, meaning 'poison' or 'medicine'.

Eggplant is stunning in the garden, bold leaves with some grey shades and displaying shiny purple-black, elongated fruit which look almost ready to burst they are so taut. You can forget about salting eggplant if you pick your own, there is no bitterness in their flesh – indicating how much of this is due to them being kept in the shops too long or picked too late.

Eggplant lends depth to a casserole, has a smoky, pungent flavour when made into a dip or as part of a plate of antipasto, tastes like smooth velvet when scooped out of the skin and mashed and loves its Mediterranean partners – tomato, capsicum, garlic and olive oil – with passion. Eggplant is the most important ingredient in the Italian dish Parmigiana di melanzane, in the Greek moussaka, and in dips from the Middle East, and I love it spiced with curry sauce or covered with a soy-bean paste in a Japanese style.

It is enjoying a new vogue, being mixed into all kinds of modern dishes, along with being cooked in the old traditional ways. Its popularity has encouraged growers to develop and sell some new varieties, which are well worth trying. I have found the difference between varieties lies more than in the colour of the outside skin, the size of the eggplant being important, and is most noticeable when you cook. In general, steaming eggplant produces a soft and gentle result, grilling a crunchy dish, while baking or barbecuing produces a smoky flavour and frying results in a far richer dish than other cooking methods.

If you use tiny eggplant or Japanese ones you have a far greater proportion of skin in the dish than with a big fat eggplant, which has more flesh. Thai pea eggplant are quite different, these are tiny, and usually are not cooked to a velvety softness but left firm; they are shown at their best in the dishes from that country. In Thai dishes you also find apple eggplant: these are in fact the size of golfballs, not apples, and are generally quartered or halved in recipes.

planting

Eggplant can be grown from seed but take a long time and it is much easier to buy seedlings, but wait until the ground is warm as they won't develop in cold soil. They must be planted in full sun and like a rich soil with moisture, but it must not be too wet or they can rot. My first mistakes were in planting a bit early and I ended up with almost no eggplant on the bushes but have been much more successful since I waited patiently.

Plant seedlings about 50 cm/20 in apart. I put a fine stake next to each one as the weight of a crop of big eggplant can topple the bush over. Once they are looking sturdy, mulch generously around them to keep the roots moist. Feed them with a liquid fertilizer to keep the fruit growing.

Temperature Zone	Plant or sow
Tropical	All year
Sub tropical	All year
Temperate	Spring
Cool	Spring – but grow new fast hybrid variety
First picking	*4–4½ months*

varieties

Seedlings

• Black Beauty
• Blue King
• Market Supreme
• Moneymaker.

Seed

More unusual varieties are grown mainly from seed. You may have to get them started in a warm place – even indoors if you live in a cool area – then plant out in late spring or early summer.

• Heirloom – packet of mixed eggplant with colours of lavender, pink and white
• Long – a white-streaked variety with beautiful lavender-flecked fruit, bearing up to 35 a plant
• Long Purple Heirloom
• Turkish Orange – a mini eggplant with an orange skin
• Golden Egg – golden, egg-shaped fruit; grows in 75 days and is successful as a border or grown in a container
• Ping Tung Long – traditional Japanese variety; quite slender with a good fruit production.

diseases and pests

They can be attacked by aphids, spider mites, tomato caterpillars and cutworms. Remove beetles or hose off aphids. You may have to spray for spider mites although I have never encountered them. For the best results plant disease-resistant varieties and if you have a fungus-affected plant take it straight out and don't put into the compost.

harvesting

About 4 months after planting, depending on the size of the seedlings.

Pick eggplant when young and firm. They should be very shiny. Don't let them age too much or the flesh, instead of being white and sweet, may become loose and pithy. Cut away the eggplant with a small sharp knife, as it has quite a strong stem.

nutrition

Eggplant supplies a small amount of minerals and vitamins but is not rich in any particular nutrient. The skin does contain anti-oxidants.

buying and storage

The late French chef and American writer Dione Lucas was very definite about her produce and claimed that over-the-hill eggplant betrayed its age in precisely the same manner as over-the-hill debutantes – slack skin and puckered posteriors. It is tricky to buy eggplant without touching, as all eggplant have their skin rubbed so they will look shiny; feel is the best way to make a decision. A good eggplant should feel quite heavy for its size, have tight firm flesh when gently squeezed and if the thumb pressure causes the flesh to sink, it will be seedy and probably bitter. A damaged surface or scarring means poor handling from the garden – just check these eggplant for any little holes, as you can sometimes find worms inside. Buy large ones for stuffing and small for baking, while medium-sized are usually the best buy for general use as they will have firmer flesh. I like to keep eggplant only about 4–5 days, as the fresher it is the sweeter it will be. Store in the vegetable crisper in the refrigerator.

cooking

To salt or not, to peel or not ... these are very personal decisions and will be reflected in the finished flavour of the dish. One advantage of salting is that the eggplant then does not absorb as much oil during cooking.

I never salt garden-fresh eggplant. With bought ones I usually decide when I cut them if they need salting, by looking at the amount and size of seeds. If you do salt, slice the eggplant thickly or cut into wedges or whatever and scatter generously with kitchen salt, putting it on a tray with a plate on top. The brown juices ooze away within about an hour and you should then rinse the eggplant and pat dry.

- To roast: put in the oven on a sheet of baking paper/parchment, rubbing the outside of the cut or uncut eggplant generously with oil. Test with a skewer for softness.

- If frying, brush one side with oil and put oil-side down into a hot pan – the eggplant absorbs less oil this way than if you fill the pan with oil, as it will greedily soak it all up. Brush the second side with oil before you flip it over.

- Eggplant can be steamed if you don't want to have any oil in the dish or your diet – just put over a little water and cook until tender. The eggplant's texture will change very suddenly from hard to soft as you steam, so you need to watch it carefully.

- It is very successful grilled/broiled but you need to brush with oil and don't have pieces too close or they won't soften before becoming dark. If grilling it is a good idea to salt first and then rinse them.

- Some Middle Eastern recipes insist you must roast over a flame until skin has blackened. Don't try this over a gas jet unless you want a terrible mess all over the stove: do it on a barbecue and the resulting drips won't matter. This direct fire roasting is really the only way to get the particular smoky flavour that is so important in eggplant purée dishes from the Mediterranean, India and the Middle East.

Occasionally I peel eggplant, particularly if I am cooking a curry or a vegetable casserole or a dish where I would prefer a gentle flavour, for removing the skin reduces the strength of the eggplant taste.

eggplant and meat terrine

An unusual terrine, based on an outside layer of meat with layers of eggplant through the centre, some smoky capsicum and ham which is then baked and left to cool. It has an interesting, soft, rolled layer throughout and rich, deep flavours. It keeps for days and is a sensational picnic dish or summery lunch one.

Slice the eggplant/aubergine thinly and season with salt, stand for about 2 hours, wash, pat dry and cook until golden on both sides in oil. Set aside.

Cook the onion in oil until soft and golden. Mix the crumbs with onion, egg, milk, salt, pepper and herbs. Stir well and then add pork and beef and mix again. Spread the meat out on some plastic wrap so you have a shape like a Swiss roll, about 30 x 18 cm (12 x 7 in) (you can make two slightly smaller rolls if you prefer). Flatten roll with a damp hand so it is as level as possible. Put on top firstly a layer of eggplant/aubergine, then ham, tomatoes, capsicum, cheese and basil and roll over gently so as not to squeeze everything out. Pinch the join with wet hands and pinch together the ends of the roll.

Preheat oven to 180°C/350°F. Have ready a large buttered terrine dish – or use two if they are small. You can also make this terrine as a free-form shape on a baking tray, which makes it look more rustic. Be sure to have some baking paper/parchment on the bottom if you do so you can pick the terrine up easily afterwards and it is a good idea to put baking paper on the bottom of the terrine dish if it is not a non-stick one. With the help of the plastic wrap carefully lift and put the roll into the terrine container, remove wrap, cover with foil or put a lid on top and bake in oven for about 1¼ hours. Leave to cool in the container, refrigerated.

Serves 10

2 medium-sized or
1 large eggplant/aubergine

olive oil

2 onions, finely chopped

1 cup/3 oz breadcrumbs,
made from stale bread

3 eggs

¼ cup/2 fl oz cream or milk

2 teaspoons salt

1 teaspoon black pepper

¼ cup/½ oz mixed chopped
parsley and other fresh herbs

750 g/1½ lb finely minced pork

250 g/8 oz finely minced beef

2–3 slices ham, depending on size

about 6 semi-dried tomatoes

1 capsicum/bell pepper, peeled,
roasted or grilled cut in fine strips

½ cup/2 oz tiny cubes
of Jarlsburg

12 basil leaves

**eggplant
goes with**

olive oil

vinegar

sugar

capsicum/
bell pepper

garlic

tomatoes

zucchini/
courgette

chilli

ginger

lemon juice

pasta

noodles

rice

yoghurt

tahini

coriander/
cilantro

mint

oregano

parsley

saffron

curry

soy sauce

mirin

capers

olives

anchovies

Parmesan cheese

melting cheese

breadcrumbs

beef

lamb

eggs

turkish eggplant salad

easy ideas

*Eggplant
Coconut Curry*

Bring 1 cup/8 fl oz
coconut milk to
the boil in a wok
or deep saucepan
and add 2 table-
spoons green Thai
curry paste. Boil
quickly until a bit
oily. Add about
750 g/1 ½ lb
peeled eggplant/
aubergine, cut
into 2.5 cm/1 in
cubes and another
½ cup/4 fl oz
coconut milk, salt,
a squeeze of lemon
and 1 teaspoon
sugar. Cook until
the eggplant is
tender; if the
sauce is becoming
too thick add a
couple of spoon-
fuls of water every
so often – more
coconut milk will
make it too rich.
Mix in lots of
coriander leaves
and a dozen or so
basil leaves. Serve
with rice or under
grilled chicken.

This is typical of the first courses that appear everywhere in Turkey. The flavour of charcoal and smokiness are a distinct part of the dish, something that is achieved by cooking it on a charcoal grill or over a fire. If this is not possible you can cook the eggplant in the oven when, although still a lovely salad, the flavour will be a little different.

I have noticed, too, that on Turkish tables where their mezze includes many cold dishes, the eggplant ones had a paler and prettier colour than ours, being the palest green or with almost no colour at all. Cooked eggplant here tends to end up as a rather unattractive brown mass but you can cover this if it concerns you by garnishing with something green and fresh like parsley. In this dish the colour doesn't matter so much as there is bright tomato, capsicum, parsley and dark olives over the top. This salad keeps for at least 4–5 days so I usually do a bit extra to have some over for myself.

Pierce the eggplant/aubergine with a fine skewer or fork and place directly on an oven rack. Put a foil-covered dish underneath to catch the sticky juices that will drip and caramelize, so you don't spend the rest of the day cleaning the pan. Bake at 220ºC/425ºF until the eggplant/aubergine is very soft and the skin is dark. Remove and leave to cool. Then cut into halves and scoop out the flesh. Discard all the moisture – the best way is to put the flesh in a sieve for 5 minutes and let it drain – then mash the flesh on a plate or board with a fork. Place in a bowl, add remaining ingredients, mashing well until it a coarse purée. Don't process: you need to have some texture in it. Chill for several hours – it can be left for up to 4–5 days and keeps well if covered in the refrigerator.

To serve, put into a small bowl, decorate with tomato, capsicum, parsley and olives and serve with chunks of warm Turkish bread or some crispy heated pita/flat bread.

Serves 6

3 large eggplants/aubergines

⅓ cup/3 fl oz virgin olive oil

salt and pepper

2 large cloves garlic,
finely crushed

2–3 tablespoons lemon juice

1 cup/8 fl oz plain yoghurt

Garnish

2 ripe small tomatoes,
cut into small wedges

1 red capsicum/bell pepper,
cut into tiny dice

⅓ cup/¾ oz finely
chopped parsley

some tiny black olives

baby japanese eggplant with herb sauce

You need the small, long Japanese eggplant in this dish and will find them quite easily in autumn when they are in season, at other times more rarely. It also essential to use fresh herbs, as dried ones would be too strong and create an imbalance in the dish. If you don't have easy access to all the fresh herbs listed, just use plenty of parsley and one other herb.

Remove the stalk end from the eggplant/aubergine and, using a vegetable peeler, cut strips of skin down the length of each to produce a striped effect. Put them into a bowl, scatter with salt and leave to stand for 30 minutes. Rinse and then drain very well. Preheat oven to 180°C/350°F. Put the eggplant/aubergine into a shallow, ovenproof, china dish in which they will fit in a single layer. Mix the oil with garlic and pour over the top. Bake until soft (30–45 minutes).

For the herb sauce mix all herbs with tomato, vinegars, sugar and pepper and, when the eggplant/aubergines are cooked, tip over the top while eggplant/aubergine are still hot. Shake the pan gently so the warmth of the eggplant/aubergine allows the herbs to release their aroma. Leave to cool in the dish, then transfer to a serving plate, spooning the sauce over the top. If you want to make this in advance, dress the eggplant/aubergine, let it cool, then cover dish tightly and refrigerate for up to 12 hours – but make sure you take it out of the fridge at least an hour before serving so it is not chilled or the sauce thick.

Serves 4 as a first course, 2 as a light meal

500 g/1 lb baby Japanese eggplant/aubergine

1 teaspoon salt

1/3 cup/3 fl oz virgin olive oil

1 large clove garlic, finely chopped or crushed

Sauce

2 tablespoons finely chopped fresh parsley

1 teaspoon finely chopped fresh rosemary

2 tablespoons finely chopped fresh basil

1 teaspoon finely chopped fresh thyme

1 large tomato, peeled and finely diced

1 tablespoon white wine vinegar

2 teaspoons balsamic vinegar

1 teaspoon sugar

freshly ground black pepper

hint

Be careful when handling and cutting eggplant that the green calyx on the end does not jab you – it is quite sharp. Trim away before preparing in dishes.

baby eggplant and tomatoes in balsamic

The tiny long eggplant, often called Japanese eggplant, are perfect in this dish. You need to use quite a firm eggplant, one that will hold its shape. The balsamic vinegar gives a mellow yet sharply defined caramel richness to the dish, while the tomatoes balance the acid.

Rinse the eggplant/aubergine and dry. Cut into halves. Criss-cross the cut side lightly. Halve the tomatoes. Mix all remaining ingredients except for basil. Rub the eggplant/aubergine all over with the garlic mixture. Put some garlic mixture on top of the tomatoes and leave both marinate for at least 2 hours.

When ready to bake preheat oven to 180°C/350°F. Put eggplant/aubergine and tomatoes into a shallow tin on a sheet of non-stick baking paper/ parchment with the cut side of the eggplant/aubergine down on the paper and the cut side of the tomato upwards. Bake for about 20–30 minutes or until both are tender and soft. Serve warm on a platter with basil leaves on top.

6 baby eggplant/aubergine

4 tomatoes

4 cloves garlic, crushed

1 teaspoon salt

1 teaspoon sugar

freshly ground pepper

1/4 cup/2 fl oz olive oil

1 tablespoon balsamic vinegar

some basil leaves, to garnish

meat-stuffed eggplant

Only a small amount of meat is needed with eggplant as the flesh is quite rich and creamy. Eating one of these lovely, fat eggplant halves, with its bright-red tomato and cheese topping contrasting with the almost purple-black baked skin, in a sunny corner of the house can make you feel that you are sitting on a Mediterranean balcony.

Cut each eggplant/aubergine in half lengthwise. Cut slashes in a diamond design into the flesh, being careful not to cut into the skin. Season with salt, leave to stand for about 45 minutes (or up to 4 hours), then rinse and squeeze very firmly in your hand to get rid of the liquid from the slashes. Pat dry on top. Heat sufficient oil in a frying pan to generously coat the base, put the eggplant/aubergine cut side down into the oil. Fry over a moderate heat until golden brown, cover with a lid and cook until just softened. Remove and cool and take the centre from the eggplant/aubergine, leaving a thick enough shell so that it won't collapse. Chop flesh roughly.

Heat a little more oil and fry the onion and capsicum until soft, add the garlic and meat and fry, stirring and breaking it up with a fork or spoon so it is crumbly and brown. Add tomato paste, the little chunks from the cooked eggplant/aubergine, water or stock, then season and cook gently, covered, until the meat is tender. Add half the cheese. Pack this mixture into the eggplant/aubergine shells, making it nicely mounded. Cut the tomato into slices and arrange on top. Scatter on crumbs and the remaining cheese and trickle on just a little olive oil.

Preheat oven to 180°C/350°F. Bake for about 25 minutes or until golden brown on top and piping hot.

Serves 4

4 medium-sized or large eggplants/aubergines

salt

extra light olive oil

I large onion, finely chopped

I large red capsicum/bell pepper, finely chopped

4 cloves garlic, finely chopped

250 g/8 oz finely minced beef

I tablespoon tomato paste

¼ cup/2 fl oz water or vegetable stock

salt and pepper to taste

½ cup/2 oz grated Parmesan or tasty/cheddar cheese

3 very ripe red tomatoes

½ cup/2 oz breadcrumbs made from stale white bread

a little extra olive oil

easy ideas *Aromatic Eggplant Slices*

Thinly slice an eggplant/aubergine and brush generously on both sides with oil. Grill under a preheated griller/broiler, about 3 minutes per side, turning over until well coloured and soft. Have ready a teaspoon of balsamic vinegar mixed with a clove of crushed garlic and a teaspoon of brown sugar and brush lightly on top of each slice before serving.

eggplant with spicy sauce

Many years ago I was a judge for a food competition in Hong Kong and the Hunan Restaurant won the appetizer section with a presentation of four cold dishes: spare ribs in a vinegar sauce, butterfly-shaped fish fillets, prawns in spicy champagne sauce and chicken Hunan style. These were arranged exquisitely in little portions and the platter was decorated with an extravagant carrot carving which stood high on the plates. There was a similar theme in the sauce used on some of their dishes and I love to use this Hunan sauce with eggplant. There is no need to reserve the dish just for a Chinese dinner, you can use it as a first course at a Western dinner, or serve with rice for a casual light meal.

First make the sauce: mix all ingredients together in a bowl.

Peel eggplant/aubergine and cut into wedges like thick chips, about 4 cm/ 2 in long. Heat the oil until almost smoking and add the eggplant/aubergine, fry for about a minute or until it has softened. Remove and leave to drain in a colander. Tip out most of the oil into a heatproof bowl and return the pan to the heat with about a tablespoon left in the bottom. Put the garlic into the pan, stir until it is pale golden, then return eggplant/aubergine and pour the sauce over the top, stir constantly until the sauce has thickened and coats the wedges. Remove and serve immediately.

Note
Hunan pepper is the spicy residue in the base of a hot oil which you can buy at some Asian shops. The oil can be used flavour dishes and to add heat. The spicy flakes from the bottom are removed and used for seasoning. If you don't want to buy Hunan oil, I suggest just adding a little fresh chilli to this dish and a good grinding of black pepper.

Serves 4

500 g/1 lb eggplant/aubergine

3 cups/1$\frac{1}{2}$ pints peanut oil

1 large clove garlic,
 finely chopped or crushed

Sauce

1 tablespoon dark soy sauce

$\frac{1}{2}$ teaspoon Hunan pepper
(see note) or some chilli

2 teaspoons oyster sauce

2 teaspoons sugar

1 teaspoon rice wine vinegar
or white vinegar

pinch of salt

1 teaspoon cornflour/cornstarch

1 tablespoon cold water

1 teaspoon dry sherry
or dry vermouth

easy ideas *Eggplant and Yoghurt Dip*

Bake 2 large or 4 small eggplant/aubergines in the oven until soft and when cooked halve and scrape out the flesh. Process this with salt, a dash of cayenne, 1 tablespoon lemon juice, 1 teaspoon sugar and $\frac{1}{2}$ teaspoon ground cumin. Mix in $\frac{1}{2}$ cup/4 fl oz thick yoghurt and chill for up to 48 hours.

To serve, spoon onto a platter and top with some finely diced ripe tomato and spring onion. The dip is rather a murky colour, so a scatter of chopped parsley will brighten the picture. Eat with pita bread, flat bread or hot toast.

stuffed eggplants

It takes time to make up the stuffing for the eggplant but all the different tastes and textures combine to make a wonderful and quite substantial vegetarian dish. The positive thing about stuffed eggplant is that you don't have to bake it straight away. It quite happily waits for up to 24 hours in the refrigerator until you are ready to reheat it.

Cut each eggplant/aubergine into half lengthwise and, using a sharp knife, cut carefully around just a little inside the skin of each one. Cut diagonal slashes in the flesh, making these quite deep but being careful not to cut through the skin or it will fall to bits. Scatter lightly with table salt and leave them stand for 30 minutes. Rinse eggplant/aubergine and press the sides together to squeeze out any extra water. Leave to drain on a towel.

Heat enough oil in a big frying pan to reach a depth of about 1.5 cm/½ in. Slide the eggplant/aubergine halves into this, cut side down. Maintain the temperature so they cook gently and soften without browning too much but don't have the heat so low that they soak up the oil, which they love to do. They should sizzle on the edges slightly all the time. Turn them over so that both sides soften but be careful not to overcook so the shape is spoiled. When soft inside, remove and cool until you can handle them without scalding your hands. Scoop out all the flesh from the shell and dice it.

Discard most of the oil, or if it has gone, add a little more and gently fry the onion, garlic and capsicum/bell pepper until softened. Stir in the tomato and tomato paste and cook until you have a thick, rich-looking, chunky sauce.

Put the allspice, parsley, anchovy and crumbs into a food processor and blend them, or mash everything together well. Season with cayenne pepper. Stir the vegetable sauce into the eggplant/aubergine dice, add the crumb mixture and mix well. Pack into the eggplant/aubergine cases, smoothing over with the back of a spoon. You can prepare it to this stage 24 hours in advance of cooking.

When ready to cook preheat oven to 180°C/350°F. Cut the tomatoes into thin slices and arrange one or two slices on top of each eggplant/aubergine half's filling. Mix the crumbs with thyme and scatter on top, then dribble with a little oil. Bake in a well-oiled dish or on a sheet of baking paper/parchment for about 25 minutes or until the top is crisp and well coloured.

Serves 4

---

easy ideas

Crusted Eggplant Mountain

Peel 2 large eggplants/aubergines (about 1 kg/2 lb in weight) and dice into cubes of about 4 cm/1½ in. Roll cubes generously in oil, then bake in preheated oven at 180°C/350°F until soft, stirring a few times. Season generously with salt and pepper. Pile up in a small mound on an ovenproof plate and scatter on top some finely chopped garlic, finely chopped ripe tomato and lots of grated Parmesan cheese mixed with an equal amount of breadcrumbs made from white stale bread. Bake in oven at 180°C/350°F until the crumbs and cheese have formed a crust. If the crumbs look dry after cooking just dribble over a tiny bit of oil before serving.

---

4 medium-sized eggplants/aubergines

salt

some light olive oil

2 onions, halved and sliced

3 cloves garlic, chopped

1 red capsicum/bell pepper, cut into small dice or strips

4 tomatoes, peeled and roughly diced

1 tablespoon tomato paste

generous pinch of allspice

2 anchovy fillets

4 tablespoons parsley sprigs

½ cup/1½ oz breadcrumbs, made from stale bread

large pinch of cayenne pepper

Topping

2 tomatoes

½ cup/1½ oz breadcrumbs

2 teaspoons chopped fresh thyme leaves

virgin olive oil

crispy eggplant chips

A heaped basket of these fries can be served with drinks and should be nibbled in the fingers, with perhaps a dip of some highly seasoned salt and pepper. They need to be done at the last minute, as kept in the oven the eggplant loses its light, crunchy texture, which is the best part of the dish.

Cut eggplant/aubergine into thick slices. Then cut into strips so they are like big chips. Season with some table salt and spread out on a board and let it stand for 30 minutes to leach out any bitterness. Rinse in a colander and then spread on some kitchen paper towel to drain.

Beat the egg with oil. Dip the wedges into egg. Dip next into flour and cornmeal mixture. Heat some peanut or light olive oil in a deep fryer or saucepan and add the chips, frying until they are golden brown. Drain on kitchen paper towel and serve immediately. These are also delicious if lightly dusted with some freshly grated Parmesan cheese.

Serves 4

1 eggplant/aubergine, about 500g/1 lb

salt

1 large egg

1 teaspoon oil

½ cup/2 oz plain/all-purpose flour mixed with 1 tablespoon polenta/cornmeal

oil

the ritz's baked ratatouille

This recipe comes from the Ritz cooking school where some years ago, when I attended a class, the chef prepared ratatouille three ways, demonstrating how the same basic dish can vary widely if the ingredients were cut differently and cooked differently. Everything in this ratatouille is baked first and then mixed together afterwards and reheated. The flavours are intense, yet each blends with the next, and it is my favourite way of making ratatouille, even though it is far from the traditional method. Like most ratatouille, it goes with just about anything simple.

Preheat oven to 180ºC/350ºF. Separately put each vegetable into a bowl in turn, dash with a little oil and turn them over with your hands so they are evenly coated. Put some pieces of non-stick baking paper/parchment on a baking tray, pull up the sides a bit and transfer each vegetable to its own paper package. Season well with salt and pepper, adding sugar to the Roma tomato tops. Sprinkle on a little water, about a tablespoon per package. Put the garlic cloves into the zucchini or onion packages. Bake them all in a moderate oven until they are tender. You need to stir gently a couple of times with a fork or they don't cook evenly. Most of the vegetables take at least an hour. Remove and cut the tomatoes into quarters.

Gently toss everything together in a bowl. Add ¼ cup/2 fl oz water. Transfer all to a saucepan and reheat gently at dinner time, adding basil leaves at the finish. This keeps well for several days but only add the basil just before serving.

Serves 4–6

olive oil

2 red capsicums/bell peppers, cut in fine strips

2 yellow capsicums/bell peppers, cut in fine strips

3 onions, peeled and cut in fine strips

3 zucchini/courgettes, cut in fine strips

2 smallish eggplants/aubergines, part peeled in stripes and flesh cut into fine strips

6 long or Roma tomatoes, cut into halves

salt, pepper and sugar

12 peeled garlic cloves

basil leaves

ratatouille niçoise

Ratatouille is among the many things which still linger from the old Provençal language and the dish, composed of many colours and many flavours, should 'sing with sunshine'. This is an old and ancient dish from the south of France, yet fits well into all the flavours we love today, with olive oil and fresh and healthy vegetables. It is quite forgiving and reheats well. A bowl of ratatouille in the refrigerator can be the beginning of many a meal. Use as a base for portions of cut chicken, serve under spicy sausages, mix into eggs in an omelette, add some to a pasta sauce, fill into a crepe or just eat with crusty bread with a poached egg on top. You can serve ratatouille hot or cool, it is equally good both ways.

Put the eggplant/aubergine on to a tray or plate and scatter with salt. Leave to stand for 30 minutes and then rinse. Drain well on kitchen paper towel.

Gently heat half the oil in a large saucepan. Add the onion and cook until soft and golden. Remove the onion to a bowl. Add the remaining oil to the saucepan and turn up the heat. Cook the eggplant/aubergine, stirring, for about 5 minutes or until tinged with gold, then add the zucchini/courgette, capsicum/bell pepper, tomato and sugar. Return the onion to the saucepan. Scatter on the garlic and herbs, stir gently, check seasoning and cover the saucepan. Cook over a very low heat for about 45 minutes or until the vegetables are tender, stirring once or twice. Watch carefully – if left too long the vegetables will become soft and the dish watery. If there is too much liquid after 30 minutes, remove the lid and leave to cook uncovered. To serve, transfer to a large bowl and scatter the top with parsley.

Serves 6

2 eggplants/aubergines
(about 500 g/1 lb) cut into
1.5 cm/½ in dice

salt

½ cup/4 fl oz olive oil

2 onions, halved and thinly sliced

375 g/12 oz zucchini/courgette,
thickly sliced

1 red capsicum/bell pepper,
deseeded and cut into strips

1 green capsicum/bell pepper,
deseeded and cut into strips

600 g/1¼ lb tomatoes,
peeled and roughly chopped

1 teaspoon sugar

3 cloves garlic, roughly chopped

1 teaspoon freshly
chopped thyme

1 tablespoon freshly
chopped basil

½ teaspoon ground coriander

¼ cup/½ oz finely chopped
fresh parsley

freshly ground black pepper

extra fresh parsley, finely chopped

hint

It is rare for home-grown eggplant to need salting, as it is so fresh there is little bitterness. However, it is a good idea to salt bought eggplant, to extract any bitter juices. Slice, halve or cube according to the recipe, put onto a tray and scatter with some kitchen salt. Let stand about 30–60 minutes, until there are lots of dark juices. Rinse and then dry on some kitchen paper towel.

ratatouille with a ricotta crust

Topped with a rich, cheesy mixture, either of the previous ratatouille recipes can be used to make this more substantial dish. Instead of a large casserole you can put the ratatouille into individual dishes but, if serving it that way, only bake for 20 minutes.

Preheat oven to 180°C/350°F. Spoon the ratatouille into a shallow, ovenproof dish and level the top. In a food processor, blend the ricotta, cream and eggs. Mix the cheese through this and season with a little salt and plenty of pepper. Spoon mixture over the ratatouille. Bake for 30 minutes or until the ratatouille is piping hot and the topping set to a light creamy consistency, firmer on the edges than it is in the centre. Serve straight from the oven, accompanied by a green salad.

Serves 4

2 cups/1 pint ratatouille

250 g/8 oz ricotta

½ cup/4 fl oz cream

3 eggs

½ cup/2 oz grated tasty/
cheddar cheese or Parmesan

salt

freshly ground black pepper

Foeniculum vulgare var. dulce

fennel

Fennel is grown in the garden not just as a vegetable but for its feathery stalks and golden flowers in summer, which are delightful as a bowl of cottage flowers, and also for the seeds that can be used in cooking. Fennel is a member of the parsley family. The vegetable fennel is related to the sweet fennel that is grown as an herb; the seeds and leaves of both types can be used for flavouring. Sweet fennel grows wild anywhere and everywhere, and can be a pest, so there seems little point in planting it in the garden. After all, the bulb fennel will provide you with the same feathery leaves, the same aromatic seeds and give you the bonus of its bulb for cooking. Florence fennel is the type grown as a vegetable for the bulb. It is much loved in Italy where it is braised gently so it is soft and tender or served raw and crisp in salads. Eaten at the end of a meal it aids digestion and leaves the palate clean; nibbling the seeds has much the same effect. However, to like fennel you do have to like licorice, as it has quite a strong aniseed flavour. Many people do not particularly care for it because of this.

planting

Once you put in fennel and let it go to seed you will find little plants constantly appearing, but they are quite easy to remove if you no longer want them. Fennel likes well-drained, well-fertilized soil. You can plant seeds if you have a big family who adore aniseed-tasting food or if you want to pick lots of baby fennel – put them in ½ cm/¼ in deep and in full sun, then thin out to about 25 cm/10 in apart. Otherwise, begin small and just buy one small pot plant from a nursery. Fennel does grow quite high, so you may need to stake it if it begins to fall over the rest of the garden.

Temperature Zone	Sow or plant
Tropical	All year
Sub tropical	All year
Temperate	Early spring–early summer
Cool	Early spring–early summer
First picking	*60 days, 120 days for fat bulbs*

diseases and pests

Only the parsley caterpillar may visit, it is easy to remove by hand.

harvesting

You can harvest about 60 days from planting for the tops or baby bulbs, longer if you want big fat ones. Just pick when it is established. Use the feathery fronds in a stuffing for fish, or make a herb bed from them underneath a baking fish, or slice the bulb through when it is the size you want, cutting off just like celery below the base.

nutrition

Not much. It has a bit of Vitamin C and some folate, plus tiny amounts of other vitamins and minerals. In the main just enjoy it for the taste.

buying and storage

Fennel is available for most of the year but it is at its best in cold weather. Most bulb fennel is sold with tops on. Choose these if you can, as you will know by the tops how fresh it is. They should be very green, feathery strands that are sweet smelling. Avoid bruised or damaged fennel bulbs. Never wash, put into the refrigerator and use within 3–4 days.

cooking

As the rule the outside layer is a bit tough and stringy and sometimes a little damaged so peel this away and trim the base. Slice very thinly for raw fennel and crisp in iced water before use for at least an hour. The light feathery tops are great as a garnish or can be chopped and added to sauces in the same way that dill is. The cooked bulb may be halved for some recipes, cut into quarters or if tiny left whole, most recipes give instructions.

fennel gratin

easy ideas

Fennel Salad

Slice some fennel as wafer thin as you can and some red onion sliced equally thinly and put both into iced water for a short time. Mix up a dressing of oil and vinegar and add a good spoonful of mustard and a teaspoon of brown sugar. Drain and dry the fennel and onion, mix with the dressing and scatter over some lettuce. Toss at the table.

This delicious gratin uses fennel that is gently braised before receiving an addition of a little cream along with a topping of cheese and breadcrumbs. The dish is so good you can eat it on its own but the soft, gentle aniseed taste of fennel is also marvellous with chicken, plainly grilled or sautéed fish or any grilled meats.

Trim the outer blemished stalks from the fennel and cut away the stem. Keep just a few of the feathery leaves for a garnish. Cut each fennel into quarters if large or halves if tiny. In a heavy-based frying pan, warm sufficient oil to lightly coat the base. When it is hot, arrange the fennel pieces cut-side down (you may need to do this in batches). Scatter on just a trace of salt and let the fennel cook gently until light brown. Turn the fennel over, sprinkle with a little more salt and cook the second side until coloured. Pour the wine over the fennel and scatter on a little pepper. Cover and cook over the lowest heat until the fennel is tender, turning it over once or twice. If the liquid is evaporating, add a few spoonfuls of water.

When fennel is meltingly tender, pour the cream as evenly as you can on top. Mix the cheese with the breadcrumbs and scatter this over the cream. Have the griller/broiler hot and put the pan underneath until the top is bubbling and the cheese and crumbs have become crisp. (If the handle of the pan is not metal, transfer the fennel to a shallow casserole before adding the topping.) Serve immediately, garnished with the retained fennel leaves.

Serves 6

3 medium-sized or 6 small fennel

olive oil

salt

1 cup/8 fl oz dry white wine

freshly ground black pepper

1/2 cup/4 fl oz cream

1/4 cup/1/2 oz freshly grated Parmesan cheese

1/3 cup/1 oz breadcrumbs made from stale bread

easy ideas *Fennel Pasta Sauce*

Slice 1 bulb fennel very finely, discarding any tough outside layers. Slice about 1/4 cup/2 fl oz of the feathery tops. Chop 3 rashers bacon and fry in a large pan in some oil; when cooked add fennel and tops and season. Add enough water to almost cover and cook until fennel is very soft. Drain but keep about 1/2 cup/4 fl oz liquid aside. Purée fennel, add the reserved liquid and 1/2 cup/4 fl oz cream. Sauce should be a 'coating' consistency. Heat and serve with cooked pasta such as macaroni, adding plenty of grated Parmesan and a scatter of more green fennel tops.

Baked Fennel Cream

Slice fennel as for Fennel Pasta Sauce. Dice a large potato. Cook fennel and potato in boiling water to cover until fennel is soft. The potato will soften and may break up – that's fine. Drain and purée both together, then season very well, as it tends to be tasteless if you don't add enough salt. You can add a couple of tablespoons of cream for a richer taste. Spread this almost translucent, soft purée in a small, buttered, shallow casserole and top with a few breadcrumbs made from stale bread and if you wish a little grated tasty cheese or Parmesan. Heat in oven at 180°C/350°F until bubbling and serve with fish.

fennel marinated fish

Prepare the marinade well in advance, put under and over the fish and wrap in foil. At dinnertime just put the foil packages of fish into the oven: timing will depend on their size. Let each person open their package so everyone gets all the aroma of the fennel and spices.

For marinade, chop the fennel very small and then mix with all the remaining ingredients. If the fennel is not in tiny bits it won't cook properly in the time it takes to cook the fish. Put out 4 packages of foil and dab half the mixture over the bases, put fish on top and spoon the rest of the mixture over the fish. Wrap up carefully to make a package and leave for an hour to marinate. Bake in a preheated oven (180°C/350°F) until cooked, 10–15 minutes depending on their size, and serve with some baby potatoes.

Serves 4

4 fillets medium-fleshed fish, such as baby snapper, dory, ocean trout or similar

Marinade
3 thick slices fennel (about ⅓ of a bulb)
2 cloves garlic, finely chopped
1 teaspoon grated ginger
1 small shallot, finely chopped
grated rind of ½ lemon
2 tablespoons lemon juice
1 teaspoon salt
4 tablespoons olive oil
generous pinch of cayenne pepper
1 tablespoon fennel tops

hint

Socrates said that a stalk of fennel eaten with a glass of water was the only cure for an evening of culinary excess.

fennel goes with

butter
oil
fish
seafood
chicken
ham
lemon
garlic
tomato
chilli
lettuce
onions
pine nuts
cheese
anchovies
cream

fennel in the style of parma

Typical of dishes from the Italian region of Parma, with its mix of Parmesan cheese, fennel and some meat, this recipe does not have many ingredients but the combination of light, soft fennel and hearty pork is quite rich and interesting. It is perfect for a casual lunch as you can assemble it all in advance. You can use any kind of tasty, spicy sausage in the dish but it should preferably be made from pork. I like to serve some of crusty potato wedges or something crisp to accompany it.

Trim away the tough, slightly stringy outside layer and cut the inside of the fennel into 8 segments, depending on its size. Bring a large pot of salted water to a boil and cook the fennel until quite tender when pierced with a fine skewer. Drain well. Cook the sausage slowly in a frying pan – you want to have a crisp skin and good shape without it bursting. If there is not enough fat for sausages to sizzle, add a little bit of butter or oil. When sausage is cool enough to handle cut into thick slices. Put half the fennel wedges into an ovenproof dish, put half the cheese on top and then arrange the sausage slices over this and the rest of the fennel on top. Melt the butter, trickle over fennel and then top with the rest of the cheese. You can do this in advance but don't leave made up for more than 6 hours.

Preheat oven to 180°C/350°F and bake for about 30 minutes or until the top is golden and the fennel is sizzling hot. Scatter a bit of the feathery green tops over. Serve a few pieces of fennel and some sausage for each person with some of the buttery juices that form on the base of the dish.

Serves 4

4 medium-sized fennel
salt and pepper
4 fat pork sausages
60 g (2 oz) butter
½ cup/2 oz grated Parmesan cheese
a few strands of fennel tops, for garnish

garlic

Allium sativum

Garlic gets planted just about everywhere in my garden, not just for eating but rather because it is one of the best of all companion plants to get rid of aphids and to keep the garden healthy. It will even survive tucked away in cool spots, which is not its ideal home. In shady areas the garlic will not produce big bulbs but the green tops can be picked to make a scented addition to an omelette or be stirred into scrambled eggs, scattered over salads, meats, chicken, into mashed potatoes and much more. An old reference book of mine states that garlic '... is so strong that it can only be used in small amounts ...'. Few people would agree with that now, for it is more the way you use it that determines the final taste than the amount. Garlic can be strident and strong, even harsh, and then gentle and nutty with a sweet mellow finish: Garlic is simply delicious and adds so much depth of flavour to most dishes.

Growing up we never had garlic in the house. It was listed among the things that nice girls didn't eat but, on reflection, how much more interesting life would have been if we had! No doubt bad breath was the main force behind us being deprived of garlic and I agree that masses of chopped raw garlic does leave you smelling like the bulb, yet gentle cooking leaves only a gentle aroma. Now it is rare to find anyone who still has a prejudice against garlic. Indeed, it is included in so many dishes that if you are dining out with a group it is likely that you will all have it included somewhere in your chosen menu, so will all be equally scented.

There is a legend that when the Devil left the Garden of Eden after the fall of Adam and Eve, garlic sprang from the left hoof-print, onions from the right. Other legends say that if you stuff the mouths of vampires with garlic cloves they cannot escape from their graves, while vampires will keep away from the dead if garlic cloves are scattered around the tomb.

The sheer strength of the bulb's taste created so many fables. It also originally made it respected as a medicine and good-luck charm rather than in the kitchen for its flavour. The volatile oil which makes everyone love or hate garlic has antiseptic properties and in countries where cholera is endemic, most of the population eats a small amount of garlic each day as a preventative measure. We are now learning that it is very good for you with many researches stating the benefits of garlic.

Garlic is a member of the lily family, along with onions, chives, shallots and leeks, and grows like a thick-leafed leek with long upright leaves and a round head of flowers.

planting

Garlic prefers well-drained but moist, fertile soil and is best in a sunny spot but will tolerate semi-shade. However, the bulbs will be tiny if grown in the shade. Dig the ground over well and don't fertilize too much as this results in garlic with less flavour. Plant cloves about 20 cm/8 in apart – although I like to plant clumps for the effect it gives so I put them in a small circle. Either buy garlic bulbs or keep some from last season's crop. They like to be planted when the ground is cold so late autumn is a good time. I have found that chilling a bulb from last year for 3–4 weeks has the same effect as waiting for cold ground and results in bigger bulbs. Use your plump cloves for the kitchen, smaller ones for planting.

Temperature Zone	Plant
Tropical	Autumn but chill bulbs first
Subtropical	Autumn but chill bulbs first
Temperate	Early winter
Cool	Late autumn–early winter
First picking	*Approx. 6 months*

varieties

The most pungent is *Allium sativum* with blue flowers. *Allium ampeloprasum,* elephant garlic, with pink flowers, is also available.

diseases and pests

Mainly onion thrips and you can hose them away. They seem to attack when the garlic is close to picking or if the weather is humid.

harvesting

Garlic bulbs can be harvested 6–9 months after planting. The tops will yellow but don't let them die right back or the bulbs can rot. You can pull the green tops any time or can dig up some bulbs while the tops are still green and use the white, peeled, baby stalks and bulbs as if they were miniature leeks. Let mature bulbs dry and then either plait them together using their leaves and hang up the resulting string, or just put them into an airy place. They will become damp and mouldy if stored refrigerated.

buying and storage

Garlic is grown throughout the world and we import large amounts from Asia, America and Argentina. Usually these bulbs are white and are often sold in mesh bags, while Australian garlic is large and either white or pink tinged. Garlic should have papery crisp skin, no damp spots and nor should any green shoots be appearing from the tips.

Occasionally you will find elephant garlic being sold. It is a monster variety but is quite mild and you need to use a large amount of it to produce the same flavour as a small clove of normal garlic.

When you harvest your own you will find it is quite mild and very juicy, as garlic's full strength develops only after it has been dried. Once dried garlic should keep for months in an airy place.

nutrition

The very thing that makes many people dislike garlic, the compound that causes the odour, is the most beneficial for our health. An enzyme is released when garlic is crushed or finely chopped, causing the odourless sulphur compound known as alliin to convert to allicin – the unmistakable smell of garlic. This compound and antioxidants that garlic also contains are its most valuable assets, as it has few minerals or vitamins.

cooking

Separate as many cloves as you want. Remove green, sprouting shoots in the centre of cloves if you intend eating the clove raw or marinating with it. Any discoloured or soft garlic will taste rancid so discard these bulbs.

To remove the skin easily put the clove onto a board and either thump with the flat side of a knife to crush it slightly or press down firmly with the end of a wooden spoon. Pull away the papery skin. Leave the skin on cloves if roasting with potatoes or vegetables in the oven, as it will prevent the garlic becoming too brown; the soft inside can easily be squeezed out.

I usually sprinkle a little salt on top of the garlic before I chop as it holds it steady and the garlic also gives out a little juice, which softens it quickly. Also use salt if you are crushing a clove, and smear the garlic with the flat side of a knife until you have a fine paste.

Add a whole clove to oil and warm gently, then leave until cool and use this infused oil to cook vegetables, especially potatoes, or brush on meat. For the mildest taste, put a couple of whole peeled cloves into a sauce, stock, soup or when cooking vegetables and remove before serving.

You can roast a whole bulb by cutting off the top part so the cloves are revealed, brushing the whole lot generously with oil and wrapping in a double thickness of foil. Bake in a moderate oven (180°C/350°F) for about 45–60 minutes, depending on the size of the bulb, until soft, then squeeze out soft garlic. Roasted garlic is delicious spread on crusty bread, mashed into potatoes or added to sauces and soups. It can be stored refrigerated for a few days, covered with a little olive oil to seal the top.

Overcooked garlic becomes very bitter so if you fry any to the point where it blackens you just have to tip it straight out. It will taste terrible and ruin your dish. Begin again, there is nothing you can do to rescue it.

garlic butter

hint

When chopping garlic finely, add a little salt to the board: it prevents the garlic slipping around, and also ensures the garlic gives out its juices and thus softens quickly.

This kind of garlic butter can be kept refrigerated or frozen and has many uses. Spread some on bread rolls and bake, or dab it over opened mussels, which are then grilled, or smooth it over a piece of fillet steak, or put over tomatoes for baking ... The breadcrumbs prevent the butter just melting away in a puddle. You can also mix some grated cheese into the butter and this gives it even more flavour if using as a topping. I have sometimes put this butter over tiny cooked clams in their shells – very time consuming – and baked them for a couple of minutes, serving a mound over the top of pasta which had been first tossed with fresh tomato sauce.

In a small pan cook the shallots in the white wine until softened – this only takes a few minutes. Cream or process the butter with garlic and parsley, add the shallots and crumbs and mix well. Pack into a crock or leave to firm and form into a sausage shape. You can wrap in paper and then foil and store in the freezer for months so you always have some on hand. Cut slices and leave at room temperature for about 15 minutes before using so it is soft.

2 tablespoons finely chopped shallots

¼ cup/2 fl oz dry white wine

200 g/6½ oz butter, preferably soft

6 cloves garlic, crushed

3 tablespoons finely chopped parsley

3 tablespoons breadcrumbs, made from stale white bread

salted lamb with a purée of beans and root vegetables

The lamb does not end up highly salted, but rather tastes a little cured and well-flavoured with the various spices. Any sort of purée can be used underneath or alongside the lamb, instead of this garlic and potato one, if you prefer.

Cut the lamb into double chops. Mix the salt with pepper, cumin, garlic and thyme in a bowl, rub this on the chops and put them into a shallow dish. Top with a plate, weigh this down and leave for 1 hour. Discard the liquid and wipe the salty mix from the chops.

While chops are marinating, cook the potatoes with sweet potatoes and garlic until soft. Drain well and purée. Drain the beans, rinse and then purée too and mix into potato. Season with lemon, salt and pepper, butter and lighten with olive oil.

Preheat oven to 180°C/350°F. Brown chops on both sides in a little oil. Transfer to the oven, bake for about 10 minutes then remove, wrap and let rest for at least 10 minutes. Serve on a bed of purée.

Serves 6

3 racks of lamb
(each about 8 chops)

1/3 cup/2 oz sea or Maldon salt

2 teaspoons crushed black pepper

1/2 teaspoon ground cumin

2 cloves garlic, crushed

1 tablespoon chopped fresh thyme or 2 tablespoons fresh rosemary pieces

olive oil

500 g/1 lb potatoes, peeled

500 g/1 lb sweet potatoes, peeled

10 cloves garlic, peeled

1 x 400 g can cannellini beans

2 teaspoons lemon juice

salt and pepper

45 g/1 1/2 oz butter and a little olive oil

crispy marinated garlic chicken

Succulent and with a golden skin, this chicken can be served with some sweet chilli sauce, cucumber salad and plain rice. In countries like Thailand where marinated chicken is cooked over an outdoor grill the skin becomes very crisp; to achieve a similar effect at home bake in the oven and then grill the top until very brown.

Cut slashes into the chicken so the marinade will penetrate the meat. Put all the remaining ingredients except oil and coconut milk into a food processor and grind coarsely. Add oil and coconut milk and mix again. Spread over the chicken. Put into a glass or china dish and marinate for a minimum of 6 hours (up to 12).

Preheat oven to 180°C/350°F. Transfer chicken to a metal baking tray lined with a sheet of non-stick baking paper/parchment. Bake for about 45 minutes, depending on the size of the chicken or until cooked through and well browned on top. Transfer to a pre-heated griller/broiler and grill, but watch so it doesn't burn.

Serves 4

4 large chicken marylands/legs
(thigh plus drumstick)

Marinade

1 teaspoon pepper

1 teaspoon salt

1 teaspoon ground turmeric

1 teaspoon brown sugar

8 cloves garlic, finely chopped

2 tablespoons chopped coriander/cilantro roots

2 tablespoons oil

1/4 cup/2 fl oz coconut milk

garlic goes with

capsicum/bell pepper

carrot

chilli

eggplant/aubergine

onion

potatoes

spinach

tomatoes

lemon

parsley

coriander/cilantro

rosemary

thyme

fish

shellfish

poultry

beef

lamb

pork

bread

olive oil

butter

Parmesan cheese

any firm cheese

goat's cheese

packages of garlic

easy ideas

*Garlic Sauce
for Steak*

For 4 people
cook 4 flattened
pieces of
trimmed fillet
steak in a frying
pan in a tiny bit
of oil, sautéing
over high heat
until they have
changed colour
on the outside.
Transfer to a
plate and put a
second plate
on top to keep
them warm.
Add to the pan
in which they
were cooked
2 cloves finely
chopped garlic,
I tablespoon
Worcestershire
sauce, 1/3 cup/
3 fl oz chicken
stock and
I tablespoon
chopped parsley.
Boil madly until
the sauce has
reduced by half;
add a knob
of butter and
serve the steaks
with the sauce
spooned on top.

This is a well-known way of baking garlic, which I am including for anyone who is not sure of how to do it so the garlic becomes soft and buttery and quite sweet. I serve it as a first course: guests spread the garlic on hot toast or some thin baked slices of French breadstick. It can be also served alongside lamb dishes, the garlic pulp could be squeezed into soup or mashed potatoes, or into the sauce for steaks. The garlic shrinks a little so you don't get as much as you think from each whole garlic head but if the amount startles you, just cut it by half.

Preheat oven to 180°C/350°F. Take off the papery skin but leave the garlic cloves joined. Slice across the top with a very sharp knife to give a flat top and just barely reveal some garlic. Put heads into a saucepan so they fit snugly, add milk to just come to the top and bring very slowly to a boil. Drain. Have a square of foil for each piece of garlic and brush generously with oil. Put one head of garlic onto each piece of foil and season. Put about a teaspoon of water over the top, wrap up so no steam can escape and put into a shallow container. Bake in oven for about 45–60 minutes or until they are soft. You need to check them, as you don't want to risk the garlic drying out. I rather like them a bit brown so often open the foil for the last 5–10 minutes and let the tops colour a bit. If not ready to serve immediately leave loosely wrapped in the foil with a small towel on top and they will keep warm for 30 minutes. To serve, open packages and put one head of garlic on each plate. Provide plenty of napkins – this tastes wonderful but is a bit messy to eat.

Serves 6

6 whole garlic heads

milk

2 tablespoons olive oil

1/2 teaspoon salt and pepper

6 teaspoons water

baked marinated garlic prawns

Succulent and flavoursome, this is an easy dish to cook for friends, as you don't need to hover around it – just time the prawns in the oven and serve.

Mix all the marinade ingredients. Add the prawns. Refrigerate and leave for about an hour but give them a stir once or twice.

When ready to cook the prawns, heat the oven to 200°C/400°F. Put the prawns into a container, preferably metal, along with the marinade. Roast for about 5–6 minutes – even 8 minutes – depending on their size. There is no need to turn them over. Put a tiny amount of mixed lettuce on the base of a plate, top with the prawns and their garlic-flavoured liquid (the lettuce will wilt slightly). Serve immediately as a warm salad.

Serves 6 as a first course, 4 as a main course

24 shelled prawns, tail left on

Marinade

1/3 cup/3 fl oz lemon juice

3 cloves garlic, finely chopped

I small chilli, deseeded
and finely chopped

1/2 teaspoon salt

1/2 teaspoon pepper

3 tablespoons olive oil

garlic and potatoes with garlic-scented oil

easy ideas

Garlic Chicken

Cut 1 small chicken (about 1 kg/2 lb) into halves through the backbone and brown them in a large frying pan on both sides in plenty of olive oil, seasoning as you turn chicken over. Tip in 1 cup/8 fl oz white wine – watch as it will splatter – add 20 cloves garlic in their skins and a couple of sprigs of thyme and cover. Cook very gently until tender. You will have lots of garlicky sauce around the chicken. Cut chicken into quarters. Boil sauce briskly to reduce it and spoon over each serving along with the garlic cloves, which will be buttery and soft. The garlic can just be squeezed gently out of the skin and over the chicken by each person at the table.

Potato has a great affinity with garlic, absorbing its aroma and holding it. This is quite a simple way of mixing it into potatoes, just by cooking the garlic in oil and then adding the garlic oil to the potato. Mix in hot milk to give a fluffy, light consistency – quantity may vary according to how much the potato will absorb. This dish is quite rich and best with meats like lamb, veal or sausages.

Cook the potatoes in salted water until tender. While they are cooking put the garlic into a small saucepan with olive oil, warm gently, cover and cook over a low heat until the garlic is tender and pale gold; don't let it brown or it will be bitter. Drain the potatoes and mash them or put them into through a moulin. Peel the garlic or squeeze out the pulp and mash into the oil. Gradually add this to the potato, seasoning well. Then add some hot milk, whisking it in so the mixture holds a shape but is quite fluffy. Lastly add the parsley and as the potato will now be cool, reheat by standing the bowl over a saucepan of hot water – or you can microwave it – before serving.

Serves 4

1 kg/2 lb floury potatoes
10 cloves garlic, unpeeled
½ cup/4 fl oz olive oil
salt and pepper
a little hot milk
3 tablespoons finely chopped parsley

baked garlic potatoes

Nothing smells more aromatic than potatoes and garlic baking together in the oven. They are a good accompaniment for just about any kind of dish and you always need to do a bit extra, as people seem to like second helpings.

Preheat oven to 180°C/350°F. Heat a metal baking dish in oven. In a bowl mix melted butter and oil. If the potatoes are large cut them into halves. Coat the potatoes with the butter and oil, turning them over in the mixture. Put some baking paper/parchment in the base of the heated metal tin. Arrange rosemary on top, then tip on potatoes. Scatter with garlic. Return to the oven and bake until crisp on the outside and soft inside – about 45–60 minutes, depending on size. Just before serving, season well with salt and pepper and toss to coat.

Serves 4–6

3 tablespoons olive oil
45 g/1½ oz butter, melted
1 kg/2 lb small baking potatoes
some rosemary sprigs
12 whole cloves garlic, unpeeled
salt and pepper

garlic nut rice

In the same way that Chinese fried rice is best when made with cooked rice that has been allowed to cool and dry for hours, this dish uses cooled dry rice. Instead of soy and vegetables for flavouring, it includes nuts and citrus. It goes well with chicken or meats but is good on its own for a healthy lunch.

The rice must be left to dry, uncovered, in the refrigerator for at least 12 hours before continuing with this recipe.

Cook the mustard seeds in a pan until they begin to jump. Add oil, garlic and ginger and fry a few seconds, add nuts, lemon and orange juices. Add to the rice and toss to flavour the rice, warm it through and separate the grains. It can then be left to cool, as it is very nice as a cold but not chilled dish, or serve warm as soon as you have prepared it.

Serves 4

3 cups cooked long-grain white rice

1 tablespoon mustard seeds

1 tablespoon oil

2 cloves garlic, crushed with a little salt

2 teaspoons shredded ginger

½ cup/2 oz roasted cashew nuts

½ cup/2 oz roasted peanuts

4 tablespoons lemon juice

4 tablespoons orange juice

garlic chicken salad

Soft garlic is pushed under the skin of the chicken, which is then baked, cut into portions, coated with a herb sauce and left to cool. The taste is intensely aromatic and so much more interesting than most bland chicken salads. Serve with other cold dishes, including a few spicy greens, a little potato salad or an interesting rice dish, but be sure to eat on the day you have made it, for if chilled for long the chicken loses some of its fresh flavours.

Cook the garlic in plenty of water for about 15 minutes or until tender. While the garlic is cooking, carefully loosen the skin from the flesh of the chicken and preheat oven to 180°C/350°F.

Drain garlic and let cool, then squeeze out the garlic flesh and push bits under the chicken skin. Season the skin generously. Dab on some oil and bake in oven for about 1–1¼ hours or until cooked through, basting occasionally. Remove and wrap in foil. Pour a cup/8 fl oz water into the baking tin and heat, mixing to dissolve meat juices, strain and then refrigerate juices so you can skim the fat from the top.

Mix everything together for the marinade. Cut the chicken into small portions and put into a bowl. Mix the meat juices into the marinade and pour over the chicken. You can serve immediately, but best left for an hour for flavours to mellow. You can cover and refrigerate for up to 12 hours, if necessary, but no longer. Remove from fridge 20 minutes before you intend to eat so the liquid will not be too cold and serve the chicken on some lettuce, spooning plenty of the marinade juices over the top.

Serves 4

10 cloves garlic, unpeeled

1 chicken, about 1.5 kg/3 lb

salt and pepper

some olive oil

Marinade

⅓ cup/3 fl oz olive oil

1 tablespoon white wine vinegar

1 tablespoon lemon juice

1 tablespoon tomato sauce

2 teaspoons Worcestershire sauce

1 tablespoon finely chopped chives

2 tablespoons finely chopped parsley

2 tablespoons finely chopped shallots

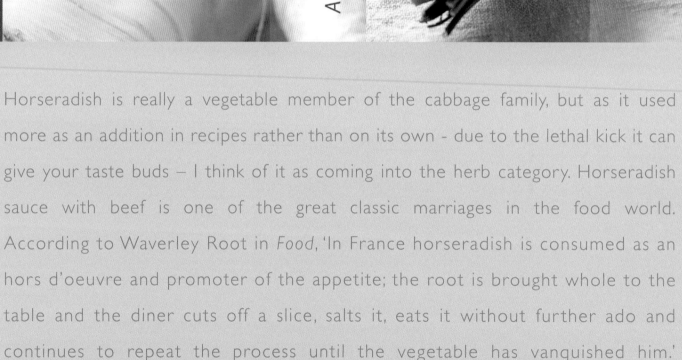

horseradish

Armoracia rusticana

Horseradish is really a vegetable member of the cabbage family, but as it used more as an addition in recipes rather than on its own - due to the lethal kick it can give your taste buds – I think of it as coming into the herb category. Horseradish sauce with beef is one of the great classic marriages in the food world. According to Waverley Root in *Food*, 'In France horseradish is consumed as an hors d'oeuvre and promoter of the appetite; the root is brought whole to the table and the diner cuts off a slice, salts it, eats it without further ado and continues to repeat the process until the vegetable has vanquished him.'

planting

Plant roots or crowns in spring. Like carrots, horseradish needs the ground cleared of any little stones or you will get split roots, which are difficult to grate. Horseradish prefers full sun but can be grown in partial shade. It likes rich, well-drained soil. It can spread as it is quite vigorous so I have confined mine to pots but these don't grow quite as big as roots in garden beds. Dig a trench and put them narrow end down, about 60 cm/2 ft apart. The thick end should just be covered so the depth you plant them will depend on this. One row about 3 m/10 ft long should give you eight plants.

harvesting

Leave until the second year after planting before harvesting. Wait until the leaves are large and beginning to die in late autumn to get the best flavour. When you dig horseradish up be sure to leave a few little bits in the ground so you have a crop for the next year or if you need the space in your garden, take them out and store in damp sand over winter, then plant again.

buying

Mostly we just buy horseradish in jars already mixed, but occasionally you can buy the root at markets or in some shops, usually in late autumn. It looks a slightly hairy, unattractive piece of produce but there is nothing that can give the palate the 'wow' factor with quite the same type of heat as a bowl of horseradish sauce made from freshly grated root.

nutrition

Apart from being a high source of Vitamin C – if you eat enough of it, of course, which is highly unlikely – horseradish has strong antibiotic qualities, which protect the intestine from harmful bacteria.

horseradish sauce

Grating horseradish does create a lot of fumes, so either do it sitting outdoors or, if that is not realistic, then grate in a food processor. Just scrape away the hairy bits on the outside of the root first along with the darker skin.

Mix the horseradish with sugar and vinegar and then just before serving mix in the cream and season. For an even hotter mix add less cream.

1/4 cup grated fresh horseradish

1 tablespoon sugar

1 tablespoon vinegar

1/4 cup/2 fl oz sour
or lightly whipped cream

salt and pepper

horseradish goes with

beef

potatoes

smoked trout

smoked salmon

uses

The baby leaves can be used in salads to stimulate the appetite.

lavender

Lavandula vera

I adore the blue-green spiky leaves of lavender, love the perfume it gives out so freely and generously, but have reservations about the degree it is often used in cooking. However, it is well worth including as a plant in the garden, whether it be as herb or for flowers. When you put in clumps of lavender their scent will attract the bees for fertilizing your garden, while branches lend a fragrance to cupboards and rooms and lavender stems look wonderful and spiky in vases either on their own or with a mix of perennials. Put some lavender along a path so you will enjoy its perfumed fragrance as you walk around the garden. From early days the Romans added it to their bathwater and its scent made it suitable for a strewing herb.

lavender biscuits (recipe page 179) ▶

There are lavender farms dotted around in many areas and they not only sell many varieties of lavender plants but also lavender goods that have become so popular. Soaps, pot pourri mixes, little fragrant pillows, biscuits, cakes, oils, cheese ... lavender is included in all manner of products.

I have eaten lavender in chicken, with lamb, and stirred into cheese, but prefer it mainly in dishes like cakes or puddings that can cope with a perfume, or biscuits which end up with a lovely crunchy taste. Be careful to avoid blooms that have been sprayed with insecticides and choose flowers free of insects and blemishes. I have never bought lavender for cooking and suggest you should use your own so that you can be sure it is not treated in any way. One bush will give enough stalks to cook a few batches of biscuits.

planting

Buy plants or get hardwood cuttings from friends as it grows quite easily.

Cutting can be taken in spring and summer. Or you can layer a bush: stake a low-growing branch down to the soil, push more soil over the woody part and in a couple of months you will have a whole new root system to replant. If you are buying visit a good nursery or a lavender farm and choose ones that appeal to you personally, as there are about 20 varieties whose flowers range from white to pink and the traditional purple and mauve. Bushes vary in shape from very tall and wide, to tall and narrow, to tiny, neat ones that don't take up much room – these tiny ones are best in vegetable gardens. Lavender can be planted from pots any time of year.

Lavender love the sun and are forgiving if not watered too much. They are quite hardy plants, but like a bit of lime. If you live in a very hot climate lavender won't flower as well as a more temperate area, as it loves some cold periods. Hot-climate gardens are best to feature French lavenders or

Canary Island lavender. Once lavender has flowered it is important to prune to encourage bushy growth, otherwise it gets woody very quickly.

harvesting

Pick flowers as they fade, to encourage further blooming, but for use in the kitchen I find it best to pick early in the morning, selecting flowers that are beginning to dry on the bush.

cooking

For cooking the best variety to use is the 'true lavender', usually known as English. If you have to wash it do so gently and then pat dry on kitchen paper. Pull the flower tops away from the stems. They should be dry for cooking rather than soft and fresh.

hint

If lavender is fresh and soft you can dry it for cooking in the oven at 50°C/125°F for about an hour. Or put on kitchen paper towel in a microwave on HIGH for a minute.

I prefer to let lavender dry naturally on some paper in the kitchen, or tied in a bunch and hanging. When dry rub gently and then sieve lightly. Store in a cool cupboard in a container.

lavender biscuits

Lavender gives these biscuits an almost musky flavour. They have little crunchy bits in them, which give a lovely texture. The biscuits will keep in an airtight tin for a week.

Preheat oven to 180°C/350°F. Cream the butter with castor/superfine sugar until light and fluffy and add the egg and vanilla and mix again. Stir in the lavender flowers and sift the flour over the top. Mix well, it should be a soft biscuit mixture. Put some non-stick baking paper/parchment onto a tray and spoon out rounded teaspoons of the biscuit mix. Using a fork flatten each one gently as they are nicest if quite crisp. Bake in oven for about 15–20 minutes – they should be a deep golden color. Transfer to a rack and while they are warm sift a bit of icing sugar over the top, not so much they are totally covered but enough so they have a speckled and frosted appearance. Let them cool completely before storing with some wax or greaseproof paper between the layers to protect the sugar topping.

Note
To make 1 cup/4 oz self raising flour, add 1½ teaspoons baking powder and ½ teaspoon salt to 1 cup/4 oz plain/all-purpose flour.

Makes about 40 biscuits

125 g/4 oz butter
100 g/3 oz castor/ superfine sugar
1 large egg
½ teaspoon vanilla essence
1 level tablespoon dry English lavender flowers
185 g/6 oz self-raising flour (see Note)
some icing/confectioners' sugar

lavender goes with

cakes
pudding biscuits
some cheese
honey
in marzipan

lavender lemon rice

Eat this warm or tepid for the best taste as it then displays all the fragrance of lavender and freshness of lemon and is a far cry from stodgy old rice puddings. You don't need any fruit alongside, just a bowl of fluffy whipped cream.

Put the lavender and lemon rind into a saucepan with half the milk and warm very slowly. Turn off the heat and let it stand for about 4 hours, so the flavours of lavender and lemon are infused into the milk.

Preheat oven to 160°C/325°F. Pour infused milk through a sieve and discard the lavender and rind. Mix with the remaining ingredients and pour into a shallow dish. Bake in oven so the pudding cooks very gently and the rice will thicken it to a lovely creamy texture. It usually ends up with a crust on top, which is delicious and seals in the rice and liquid. When you take it out of the oven let it rest for about 20 minutes before serving.

Serves 4

1 tablespoon dry English lavender flowers
grated rind of 1 lemon
4 cups/2 pints milk
4 tablespoons short-grain rice
3 tablespoons sugar

leeks

Allium porrum

Leek is a corruption of 'loch', the word which Romans used to describe any medicine they could lick to cure a sore throat. It is said Nero kept a leek in his mouth to add timbre to his voice. The leek is also the symbol of the Welsh, who wore leeks on their hats to distinguish themselves from their enemies in the twelfth century. Leeks grow wild in Wales and Scotland and are in many dishes from those countries, such as Cock-a-leekie, a soup made from chicken and leeks with prunes, which add an unusual sweet touch. These traditional recipes would have been made with wild leeks, which are bright green, strong in flavour and slightly bitter, and for that reason sweet ingredients were often added. The wild forms have been much improved now, being bred into the sweet, gentle varieties we can buy and grow.

Leeks were once a very popular vegetable, then went out of favour in the sixteenth and seventeenth centuries. Much of this was probably due to poor cooking. Leeks that are left far too long in a saucepan develop a slimy texture and, if not washed really well, the soil heaped up against the stems to keep them white get into all the layers of leaves and leave a gritty taste. It is understandable that in times when so many vegetables were overcooked, leeks would have joined this school and ended up a sloppy, unattractive dish. There was also the strong belief they gave you bad breath and, like onions and garlic, leeks were not socially acceptable at dinner parties.

It has always surprised me that vichyssoise is regarded as a summer soup, for the base is reliant on good leeks and potatoes and leeks are not at their best in the middle of summer. Leeks are a cooler weather vegetable, the very finest ones are the early season in October, then later after the heat of summer has passed. Perhaps the soup may have originally been a hot one.

Leeks are a more delicate base than onions for stews or soup, have a marvellous flavour in pies or tarts and go well with oil and vinegar in salads.

planting

Leeks look lovely in the garden, all the folds of green gradually wrapping around each other as they stretch up to the sky, tall and straight. They will just about grow anywhere, except when it is hot; then they shoot to seed before you can gather them up. Leeks are thus are only suitable to grow in gardens in temperate zones.

Plant seedlings in spring if you want a quicker result and so avoid the summer sun. Then put in a second crop in autumn so you have leeks for late winter. They need good drainage or the soil packs solid around them. Choose a bed in the sun and dig in a bit of fertilizer. Plant seeds in double rows – the rows about 30 cm/1 ft apart – and thin them out later. Put seedlings about 15 cm/6 in apart, making a 10 cm/4 in deep hole and dropping each seedling into this so only a bit of the green will be above the surface and don't fuss about filling them in. Just water gently and the water will push the soil around them. Some may fall but over the next day or so just straighten them up. Give them plenty of water and a bit of liquid fertilizer every month as they are growing.

Temperature Zone	Sow or Plant
Tropical	Not suitable
Subtropical	Autumn
Temperate	Spring and autumn
Cool	Spring and autumn
First picking	4 months

varieties

- London Flag
- Malabar
- Lyon
- Musselburg
- Welsh Wonder – the most widely grown variety commercially
- Elephant Leek – an heirloom seed with the bluest leaves and ornamental flowering stems.

special handling

To get white stalks on garden-grown leeks you need to blanch them. As they grow keep piling little bits of soil up and around the stalks to keep them from turning green. If this seems too much bother just let them go, for they still taste wonderful, just greener in colour and stronger in flavour.

diseases and pests

Snails fancy them, as do slugs and in dry weather you may get onion thrip. Get rid of the thrip just by hosing the insects away. If leeks are growing strongly they will cope well without any spraying.

harvesting

Whenever you like but definitely before they go to seed. Usually you can begin 3 months after planting and I love including the baby ones in salads. If you take the top half of the leaves off it encourages greater growth of the stalks – but as I also grow them for decoration I don't do this. With young home-grown leeks much of the green can be used, as it is quite tender and sweet.

buying and storage

The white thick stem and the pale green top are the edible parts. Leeks come in a variety of sizes, from large to small. Just be sensible and, if you are buying several, choose ones the same size, so when you cook them they will take the same amount of time. For some strange reason leeks are often sold in bunches of three, where one large leek has been bundled up with two smaller ones. This makes timing difficult for the cook. For salads or cooking whole choose young thin leeks; for using sliced in soups, stews or casseroles you can buy larger ones. Never select a bunch of leeks with yellow leaves or discoloured dry parts on the top.

As the end of winter comes sometimes leeks develop a woody stem inside, right through the centre. This can often be detected from the top and such leeks should not be bought, but if you cut one and find this hard centre discard it: the woody part will never become tender, no matter how long it is cooked.

Leeks keep in the refrigerator for up to a week in a vegetable bag.

nutrition

Leeks are a good source of Vitamin C, and also include some Vitamin A, iron and folate.

cooking

Clean leeks well for dirt lurks in all the leaves. If slicing just drop into a bowl of water and swish them around, then take them out with your hands and transfer to some kitchen paper towel to drain. If using whole cut off as much green as you want, then take off the outside layer and cut a few slashes down the sides of the leek from the top. Stand the leek with the green part down in a jug of warm water. This loosens the dirt quickly so you can easily rinse it out. Drain well, especially if stewing or cooking in oil or butter, or they will leak out water into the pan.

stir-fried leeks and lamb

leeks go with

garlic

potatoes

onion

tomatoes

butter

oil

cheese, especially melting and Parmesan

milk and cream

lemon

nutmeg

bay leaves

chives

parsley

anchovy

prawns

bacon

ham

prosciutto

eggs

pastries

This well-flavoured dish is an unusual stir fry as they are generally made from pork, seafood, poultry or beef rather than lamb. The lamb must be barely cooked, and the leeks crunchy. If you have a preference for another meat it can easily be substituted for the lamb.

Cut the meat into fine, thin rectangles, about 5 x 2.5 cm (2 x 1 in). Mix all the marinade ingredients together. Add meat and stir. Leave to stand, covered, for about 30 minutes.

Remove the meat to a plate. Wash and cut the leeks into thick slices. Only use the pale stalk and not the coarse, green ends which you can put aside for some soup or stock. Heat half the oil in a wok. Add leeks and stir fry until tender, remove to a plate, reserving marinade in bowl. Add the remaining oil to wok. Add garlic and fry, tip in sherry (it will splatter so be careful). The alcohol will boil away immediately, giving a lighter flavour. Add meat and separate it as the pieces cook – chopsticks are good for this job if you are adept at handling them. When the meat has changed colour on the outside, return the leeks to wok. Mix the stock into the bowl in which you marinated the meat so as to pick up all the flavours. Tip this around the edge of the wok and stir well to get any sticky bits from the side of the wok. Stir and serve with plain rice.

Variation
This dish should have some lightly thickened juices but if you want a thicker sauce add a teaspoon of cornflour/cornstarch, mixed with cold water, when you add stock.

Serves 4

500 g/1 lb lean lamb (e.g. leg or fillet), trimmed of fat

4 leeks

1/4 cup/2 fl oz oil

2 cloves garlic, finely chopped

2 teaspoons sherry

1/3 cup/3 fl oz chicken stock

Marinade

2 teaspoons dark sesame oil

2 teaspoons peanut oil

1 1/2 tablespoons dark soy sauce

1 teaspoon rice wine or sherry

1 teaspoon white vinegar

3 teaspoons sugar

1 teaspoon ground black pepper

2 teaspoons cornflour/cornstarch

oyster and leek pasta

This dish is rather extravagant and is perfect for a Sunday lunch or for a romantic, intimate supper. I first came across it in Alice Waters' book, Chez Panisse Pasta, Pizza & Calzone. Alice Waters uses the tiny Olympia American oysters, baby ones about the size of big thumbnail that are very sweet and delicate in flavour.

There is no exact substitute here, but small Sydney or Tasmanian oysters are fine, and I have had great success with the dish using baby mussels. Depending on your budget, you can be generous or frugal with the quantity of oysters. Buy the finest linguine you can, as you need a pasta which is exquisitely light to balance the sauce – and a glass or two of champagne is somehow perfect for the dish and no doubt for the cook.

Try to keep the oyster juices and tip this into a bowl. (However, in Australia you will usually buy oysters already opened and rinsed, so there won't be much juice unfortunately.) Cut leeks across into pieces about 3 cm/1 in, then lengthwise and then into fine strips. Cut the pancetta into little dice, chop parsley and remove thyme leaves from stalks.

Melt the butter, add the leeks and sauté gently for a few minutes. Tip in the stock, add thyme and cook until the leeks are tender. By this time, the sauce should have reduced. Add the cream and bring to a boil. Sauté the pancetta, until crisp, in a small pan. Mix parsley, oysters and their juices into the leek cream and keep warm. Cook the pasta in plenty of boiling, salted water and drain well.

Mix the sauce into the linguine. It will be on the thin side but should coat the strands. Season with plenty of black pepper and scatter with pancetta to serve.

Serves 2 as a main course, 4 as a first course

1–2 dozen oysters
3 leeks
4 thin slices spicy pancetta
some sprigs of fresh parsley
some sprigs of fresh thyme
45 g/1 ½ oz unsalted butter
¾ cup/6 fl oz chicken stock
½ cup/4 fl oz cream
200 g/6 oz linguine
black pepper

hints

If using leeks in a salad, after boiling drain them on several layers of kitchen paper towel on a plate. Put plastic wrap on top, then a second plate and a weight and leave for an hour. The water inside all the circles of the stalk will gradually leak out.

Leeks go well with most kinds of fish and meat, and their mild and delicate flavour enables them to team so well with casseroles.

leeks braised with cider

easy ideas

Leek Salad

Cook 2 leeks per person in salted water until tender and drain well. Make up oil and vinegar dressing, using 4 parts oil to 1 part red wine vinegar and, for every 6 leeks, add a teaspoon French mustard, a skinned diced tomato and a teaspoon brown sugar. Pour over the leeks and garnish with finely chopped parsley and some strips of anchovy.

Leeks are cooked in cider with hot mustard mixed through the sauce. This is especially good as a side dish with pork or game, things that can cope with something both spicy and slightly sweet. The sharpness of the mustard is lessened by the slightly fruity flavour of the cider.

Preheat oven to 180ºC/350ºF. Leave just a little of the green top on each leek. Heat the butter in a flameproof casserole and add the mustard. Stir until it is well blended and then pour in the cider and bring to a boil. Add the leeks and season well. Cover and cook in oven until the leeks are quite tender, approximately 30–40 minutes; test them with a fine skewer, as they should be soft rather than firm. Just before serving, scatter parsley over the top.

Serves 4

8 small leeks

30 g/1 oz butter

1 teaspoon dry English mustard

1 cup/8 fl oz cider

salt and pepper

2 tablespoons finely chopped parsley on each leek

leeks in a parcel

hint

Overcooked leeks can become soft and slippery and are not always pleasant to eat, so be careful to check them occasionally for tenderness, rather than just relying on timing.

The 'parcel' is a fine crust of filo pastry. You should assemble your parcel on the day you are eating as otherwise the leeks will soak into the crust, which spoils the contrast of a crisp case with a creamy soft filling. If it helps your planning, the filling can be completed the day beforehand. As this is quite a substantial dish you could serve it either as a meal or first course. These go well with cherry tomatoes that have been tossed in a little olive oil until the skins split, and then seasoned well with salt, pepper and a teaspoon of sugar. There should be some juice around the tomatoes so you get a little tomato-flavoured sauce.

Put the leeks and butter into a heavy-based saucepan and cook, giving them an occasional stir, until soft and slightly gold. Pour in the wine, bring to boil and cover. Let cook until quite soft, then remove the lid and boil until there is just a little juice around leeks. Remove and put in a bowl to cool. Mix in the crumbs and currants.

Heat the oil and cook the pine nuts, stirring them until they are golden. Drain on kitchen paper towel. Add to the crumb mixture with egg, mix and refrigerate. The mixture will become firmer as the crumbs absorb any liquid and swell, so you really need to do this at least 4 hours in advance.

Preheat oven to 180ºC/350ºF. Divide the mixture into quarters. Put sheets of filo pastry on a board and brush very lightly with melted butter. Cut in halves, making four pieces. Put some leek filling along each piece and roll over like a sausage roll, tucking in the sides, producing a cigar shape. Brush the top of roll with more butter. Continue until you have used up leeks and pastry, and then bake in oven for about 15–20 minutes or until crisp and golden. Serve immediately.

Serves 6 as a first course, 4 as a main course

6 leeks, very finely sliced

45 g/1½ oz butter

¼ cup/2 fl oz dry white wine, vegetable stock or water

½ cup/2 oz breadcrumbs, made from stale bread

1 tablespoon currants

2 teaspoons oil

⅓ cup/1 oz pine nuts

1 egg

2 sheets (or 4 for a thicker layer) filo pastry

extra butter

leek frittata with prosciutto

hint

Never serve really under-cooked leeks, for they are difficult to eat, do not taste good and can almost choke you, for the long bits get stuck in your throat – which can be a bit dramatic at a dinner party.

The cheese gives a nutty flavour to the frittata, while the prosciutto, crumbled on top, provides a salty, spicy taste and crunchy texture. I like to serve this style of dish directly from the frying pan in which it was cooked, taking the pan to the table balanced on a big board – so I don't burn a hole in the table – and cutting the frittata into thick wedges with a knife (or with a wooden spatula if a non-stick pan has been used).

A frittata does not need to be served piping hot. Like many egg or custard dishes it is often more flavoursome if the mixture is just tepid.

Cut the leeks into thin slices, using some of the green tops. Melt the butter in a saucepan and add the leeks. Cook for about 5 minutes or until the leeks have wilted, then cover and cook gently for around 20 minutes or until they are very soft. Season well and cool slightly.

Beat the eggs in a bowl, add sour cream and leeks and stir in the Jarlsburg. You can leave the mixture for several hours before cooking at this point.

Put the olive oil in a 23 cm/9 in diameter frying pan and heat. When the oil begins to give off the first signs of haze, add the mixture. It should set immediately on the base. Turn the heat down very low as you don't want it to burn and cook for about 8–10 minutes or until the base is well set. Carefully slide out on to a plate, then flip back quickly into the pan with the uncooked side down. It is not difficult to do but if you prefer, you can put the pan under a preheated griller/broiler to cook the top.

While the frittata is cooking, spread the prosciutto on to a foil-lined tray and cook under a preheated griller/broiler until crisp. Drain and crumble into small pieces. Scatter over the top of the frittata before serving.

Serves 6

6 medium-sized leeks

60 g/2 oz butter

salt and pepper

6 large eggs

$^{1}/_{3}$ cup/3 fl oz sour cream

$^{1}/_{2}$ cup/2 oz finely diced Jarlsburg cheese

2 tablespoons virgin olive oil

4 slices prosciutto

easy ideas *Leeks Baked in Olive Oil*

Cut into pieces about 7.5 cm/3 in long and put into a small casserole, seasoning well. Pour over some virgin olive oil and a tablespoon of lemon juice, add a few unpeeled cloves of garlic to the oil and cover. Bake in a moderate oven (180°C/350°F) until tender, about 45 minutes. Discard the garlic and serve lightly drained just with lots of pepper on top.

welsh leek pie

In days of yore, this inexpensive dish would have been served during Lent or in lean times, using wild leeks gathered from the countryside. Nowadays, it is more of a luxury because of the cost of leeks, but it is perfect for a light meal. The pastry is made in the old-fashioned way, as with Cornish pasties, using both lard and butter to give a light pastry with a soft texture. If the thought of lard fills you with horror you can make the pie using a plain butter pastry or, as a short cut, a commercial one.

To make pastry, sift flour and salt into a bowl or put them into a food processor. Add the butter and lard, cut into small pieces. Rub into the flour or process until crumbly. Stir in the cheese and mix thoroughly. Make a well in the centre, add about ¼ cup/2 fl oz cold water to begin with, and mix well with a fork. Then add more cold water until it holds together. Pastry should be moist, not dry. Knead once or twice, then divide into two for the pie.

Rinse the leeks well and cut into pieces about 2.5 cm/1 in long. Melt the butter, add the leeks and shake until coated with butter. Add the stock, seasoning and herbs. Cover and cook for about 15 minutes or until the leeks are tender. Drain carefully, keeping the liquid (if you let the leeks drain in a colander for 30 minutes they will be even better). Return the reserved leek juices to the pot and boil until reduced to about ¼ cup/2 fl oz.

Beat the egg and cream together with cheese. Add the reduced leek juices. Roll out one portion of pastry. Butter a 20-centimetre/8 in diameter pie dish, line with the pastry and press it firmly up to the edge. Put the leeks into this. They can be heaped in a dome in the centre. Spoon the egg mixture slowly on top; shaking dish gently so egg trickles slightly through the leeks. Roll out the second portion of pastry and place on top, pinching it together on the edges. If you want a deep-coloured crust, brush the top with some milk or beaten egg.

Preheat oven to 180°C/350°F. Prick pie several times in the centre and bake for about 35–40 minutes or until the pastry is firm and golden brown. Before serving, rest the pie for 10 minutes to allow the juices to settle.

Serves 6

9 small leeks
(6 if they are very large)

30 g/1 oz butter

½ cup/4 fl oz chicken
or vegetable stock

salt and pepper

1 bay leaf

a sprig of thyme and
a sprig of marjoram

1 large egg

⅓ cup/3 fl oz cream

⅓ cup/2½ oz grated
Jarlsburg or Swiss
Gruyère-style cheese

Cheese pastry

2 cups/8 oz plain/
all-purpose flour

1 teaspoon salt

125 g/4 oz butter

60 g/2 oz lard

⅓ cup/1½ oz grated
Parmesan cheese

some cold water

hint

If you grow leeks from seed don't throw out the little fine leeks that you remove so the bed is not too crowded. Chop them into scrambled eggs, scatter over a salad or add to sandwiches for a sweet, chive-like flavour.

Melissa officinalis

lemon balm

Apart from its flavour – which is lemony and quite sweet – lemon balm is a very pretty herb which I grow as a decorative plant. The leaves are light, heart-shaped and deeply veined and throughout summer, if you allow it, there will be masses of white and creamy yellow flowers that bloom for months. To use lemon balm for cooking you should keep cutting the flowers off, so I leave some bushes to flower and cut others for kitchen use. Bees love lemon balm and the name of this genus, *Melissa*, came from the Greek word for bees. It has a similar flavour to lemon verbena but is more delicate, so you can use it generously. In the Middle East lemon balm is made into a refreshing and fragrant hot drink, in much the same manner as we make mint tea.

planting

Really easy to grow, just put in a cutting if you have a gardening friend or buy a little plant in a nursery or a packet of seeds. Sow or plant in early spring, for although lemon balm is a perennial it dislikes frosts. Give the baby plants plenty of room: weed them by hand until the lower leaves are well established. When you pick leaves you will en-courage new growth. I find it self-seeds quite well, neither being too intrusive nor difficult, and it mingles quite happily with other garden plants as a low border. Lemon balm usually has plain green leaves but you can also buy a variegated type that has yellow and green leaves. The variegated one doesn't grow quite as strongly but looks very pretty in borders or in the herb garden.

harvesting

Summer leaves are stronger and tougher than spring ones. In general, just pick as required.

buying

I have never found this in shops but, like most herbs, if you find some and buy, make sure it is fresh looking, sprightly and fresh smelling.

easy citrus and lemon balm mousse

Lovely, fresh and light, this mousse has a mix of citrus tastes. Be sure to use young leaves as they are added raw to the mousse so they must be quite tender.

Beat the yolks with sugar until frothy and add the citrus rinds. Mix gelatine with the orange and lemon juices in a cup or jug and stand this in a saucepan containing enough water to come halfway up its side; heat until the water simmers and the gelatine has completely dissolved. Stir juices into the egg yolk base. Beat the cream until it holds soft peaks. Beat the egg whites until stiff, mix with cream and then fold this into the citrus and yolk base a little at a time, adding the lemon balm as you do so. Spoon into individual dishes or a large serving dish and chill for several hours. You can leave for 24 hours, chilled, if the mousse is tightly covered.

Serves 4

lemon balm goes with

fish

chicken

fruit salad

drinks

salads
(use baby leaves)

easy ideas

Baked Fruit with Lemon Balm

Mix together ground almonds, sugar and chopped lemon balm. Core apples or pears and stuff them with mixture. Bake in oven until soft.

2 eggs, separated

3 tablespoons castor/ superfine sugar

2 teaspoons grated orange rind

1 teaspoon grated lemon rind

2 teaspoons gelatine

1/4 cup/2 fl oz orange juice

2 tablespoons lemon juice

3/4 cup/6 fl oz cream

1 heaped tablespoon finely chopped lemon balm leaves

uses

Lemon balm helps promote relaxation and good sleep. It is also used as a remedy for fever and against vomiting and nausea. You will find it in some perfumes, in liqueurs and furniture polishes.

This herb was a favourite of ancient beekeepers, who rubbed leave over their beehives to encourage the bees to return, and bring other bees to the hive. The generic name, *Melissa*, comes from the Greek word for bee.

Cymbopogon citratus

lemon grass

It was only when I turned to some of my reference books that I realised lemon grass was not considered worth a mention in books published more than ten years ago. Yet it is an old perennial, a staple, in Asian cooking – although a more recent addition to the gardens and markets here. When I first began cooking Thai or Vietnamese food I used to find lemon grass was mainly obtainable only as a dried stalk, with nowhere near the pungency that the fresh herb gives, and it left a disappointing, flat taste. You can buy it fresh in the markets or in most Asian shops now but it is also very easy to grow. The plant's scent is sweet and very fragrantly lemon, while the stalks are tall. Lemon grass is actually a grass, and forms clumps. These will make a big tufted display in the herb garden or you can allow the clump to produce a green mass at the back of any flower garden. The leaves have sharp edges so it is a good idea to keep it away from paths, as it can be unpleasant if anyone brushes against it.

Use lemon grass whenever you want a delicate and fresh lemon taste, whether it be in a savoury dish or sweet dessert.

planting

Lemon grass loves full sunlight and needs well-drained soil. It doesn't mind if it is exposed to winds but very heavy frost may appear to kill it although usually it will recover once the ground heats up again. It is a perennial but in winter it looks very untidy and gets spotted and messy so I usually cut it back. As soon as the weather warms up it will produce masses of new shoots, which come up through the old grass.

Every so often my clump becomes so large I have to divide it, for if it forms too big a mass the centre can get wet and develop a bit of mould.

Plant clumps in spring to late summer so they are established before cool weather arrives. You can buy plants at a nursery or else get a root system going yourself. Buy some stalks of lemon grass that have the root end left on and put them into water, keeping the water clean by changing it every few days. Within 7–10 days tiny roots will form on the end. Put the lemon grass into a pot with some potting mix and keep it well watered until it looks healthy and established, then carefully transfer to the garden. It can be grown in a pot if you prefer but you will need quite a large one to allow the clump to expand.

harvesting

When you need some, pull away one piece of the grass. It can be a bit tough as it gets older and sometimes you need to cut it away with a small sharp knife. You only use the inner part of the stalk near the root end chopped in dishes, although the end of the stalks can be put into soups or stocks for flavouring.

buying and storage

Lemon grass is generally sold in a bunch of a few stalks, in Asian shops or good greengrocers. As the tops are generally cut it can be hard to tell how fresh it is but this herb is quite hardy and will keep its flavour well.

If you want to dry your own lemon grass put it in a dark, well-ventilated spot and spread out well on some brown paper. Keep stalks apart or they can go mouldy.

hot poached fruits in lemon grass syrup

hint

As lemon grass is very tough to cut, if you just need to bruise it instead bang down on the stalk with a meat mallet. It will split the piece open quite easily.

The spices can be left among the fruits or removed before refrigeration. Although the cardamom pods soften during cooking, they are a bit chewy and I prefer to pick these out and discard them. This quantity makes enough for 4 people and can be easily doubled. The lemon grass gives the dish a very refreshing and lingering aftertaste. I often serve it warm, reheating just before serving, but it can be eaten as a chilled dessert if you prefer.

Peel, core and cut the apples and pears into quarters. Place in a saucepan with the apricot halves, sultanas, prunes, orange rind, cinnamon stick, cardamom pods, ginger, lemon grass, water and sugar. Bring slowly to a boil. Simmer partly covered for about 45 minutes or until the fruit is very tender. Remove from heat and cool. Take out the lemon grass and cardamom. Add the almonds. Store, covered, in the refrigerator. This will improve if you allow it to mature for a day before warming again and serving.

Note
Although popular as a cooking apple, Granny Smith apples 'fluff' easily when poached, so for a firm, neat shape use eating apples instead.

Serves 4

2 eating apples (see Note)

2 pears

½ cup/3 oz dried apricot halves

¼ cup/1 oz sultanas

8 prunes

6 thin strips of orange rind

1 cinnamon stick

6 cardamom pods, lightly cracked open

1 slice peeled, fresh ginger, finely shredded

2 stalks lemon grass, crushed lightly but left in big pieces

2 cups/1 pint water

¾ cup/6 oz sugar

12 blanched almonds

spicy vietnamese chicken

Chicken legs stuffed under the skin with a very spicy, aromatic, Vietnamese-style mixture are a different way to enjoy poultry. Serve them with a typical Vietnamese dipping sauce and soft lettuce which can be used as a wrapping so the spicy chicken is eaten with a soothing green leaf.

Put garlic and salt into a pestle and mortar and crush. Trim the ends from the lemon grass, remove outer leaves and chop inside finely, then add to mortar with shallots, chilli and sugar and crush. Mix in fish sauce. Loosen the skin from the drumsticks with your fingers and push some of the mixture between flesh and skin. Then pull skin back over. Cover chicken well (it will smell very fragrant but strong) and refrigerate for at least 12 hours, turning over once, as some liquid will form under the chicken.

When ready to cook brush the drumsticks lightly with oil and either bake in a moderate oven (180°C/350°F) for about 30 minutes, depending on their size, or barbecue until cooked.

To make dipping sauce, mix everything together and stir well. Refrigerate, covered, if not using immediately. Serve chicken with lettuce leaves and the dipping sauce on the side.

Serves 6

5 cloves garlic, finely chopped

1 teaspoon salt

2 stalks lemon grass

2 tablespoons finely chopped shallots

1 chilli, deseeded and chopped

1 tablespoon sugar

1 tablespoon fish sauce

12 chicken drumsticks

Dipping Sauce

2 cloves garlic, crushed

1 small chilli, deseeded and chopped

2 tablespoons sugar

2 tablespoons lemon juice

2 tablespoon rice wine vinegar

2 tablespoons fish sauce

2 tablespoons water

1/3 cup/1 1/2 oz grated carrot

hint

When chopping use only the root end. It is very hard so watch it does not slip as you chop, or you may cut yourself. Cut into halves lengthwise, strip away the toughest outside part of the stalk and then chop the rest into very tiny pieces. It will still be quite firm even when cooked so cut it up small. For flavouring a dish, leave in big pieces and remove before serving.

malaysian fragrant rice with fresh herbs

In Malaysia the herbs for this rice dish are usually sold in bundles, called ulam *herbs, already sorted in the markets, and in each bunch there is a good variety of different kinds. Obviously Malaysian herbs vary from ones we grow or can buy, and you should choose different herbs for this recipe according to what is in season, but I have suggested a few. Most of the herbs used in Malaysia are found only in that country and have no equivalent English name, but they are generally classified as 'fragrant herbs'.*

Rinse the rice. Put the remaining ingredients into a saucepan and add the rice, bring to a boil and cover. Cook for 15 minutes. Remove from the heat and leave to rest for 10 minutes. Mix together all the herbs.

You will find the aromatic ingredients cooked with the rice have floated in the water and will be sitting on top. If you don't want these pieces in the rice remove them first at this stage. Fork the rice up, adding the herb mixture as you do.

Serves 6

1 cup long-grain rice

2 stalks lemon grass, roughly bruised

2.5 cm/1 in piece of fresh ginger, bruised

4 lime leaves

3 tablespoons coconut milk

1 3/4 cups/14 fl oz water

1 teaspoon salt and some pepper

Herb Mixture

6 leaves basil, cut into strips

1/4 cup/1/2 oz chopped coriander/cilantro or whole tiny leaves

1/4 cup/1/2 oz tiny yellow celery leaves, chopped

2 tablespoons finely chopped parsley

2 baby lemon leaves, finely chopped

1 large spring onion/scallion, finely chopped

1 shallot, very finely chopped

lemon grass goes with

all Asian foods
garlic
fish
seafood
chicken
beef
pork
basil
coriander/cilantro
soy sauce
chilli
fish sauce
palm sugar
coconut milk

baby pork and lemon grass pies

These little pies combine the comforting taste of warming minced meat with the modern flavours of lemon grass, ginger and chilli. They can be made in small metal tins, either the ones for mince pies or cup cake containers. For a slightly larger pie, muffin tins are good. Many butchers sell minced pork and it is much easier to use this than trying to mince pork at home. Don't feel guilty if you can't make pastry yourself and have to buy it, for there are some good puff pastry sheets in the shops – I prefer the butter type. Bought shortcrust, for my taste, is not as good as commercial puff pastry, as the makers don't really put enough butter into the mix so it ends up a bit hard instead of melting.

Heat the oil in a saucepan and fry the onion, garlic, lemon grass, ginger and chilli gently for about 5 minutes. Turn up the heat, add the pork and continue cooking until it has changed colour. Stir constantly to break it into small pieces or it will be very lumpy. Pour in the water, soy and sugar, then season well. Cover and cook for about 20 minutes or until the pork is very tender. Thicken the juices by mixing the cornflour with a little cold water to make a thin paste and adding it to the pork mixture. Stir until it has come to a boil and liquid has thickened. Remove pork from heat and allow to cool. The cooked mixture can be refrigerated for up to 2 days before use.

Lightly butter a small pie tray. Roll out shortcrust pastry, if using, until quite thin (even if using commercial shortcrust sheets, as I find them too thick for my taste). Cut circles of pastry, larger than the top of the cases by at least half the diameter. Press into the base and up the sides of each mould and fill almost to the top with the cool pork mixture. Cut out circles to fit the top and pinch the edges together. Beat the egg with a couple of teaspoons of water and brush this eggwash over the top and edges of the pies. Make a small hole in the pastry tops with the point of a sharp knife.

Preheat oven to 200°C/400°F and bake the pies until well coloured and the pastry is crisp – about 15–20 minutes for small ones and 20–25 minutes for larger pies. Leave them to rest in the trays for a minute or two then carefully remove to a rack or serving platter. Reheat when needed in a moderate oven for about 8–12 minutes, depending on size.

Variation
You can make one great big pie instead of lots of small ones, or put the mince into a pie dish and just top with pastry if you don't like too much pastry in a dish.

Makes about 24 baby pies

2 tablespoons oil

1 large onion, finely diced

2 large cloves garlic, finely diced

2 stalks lemon grass, finely chopped

1 piece fresh ginger, 2 cm/¾ in long, finely diced

1 small chilli, finely chopped

500 g/1 lb pork, finely minced

1 cup/8 fl oz water

2 tablespoons soy sauce

1 tablespoon sugar

salt and pepper to taste

2 tablespoons cornflour/cornstarch

4 sheets packet puff pastry or equivalent amount of home-made shortcrust pastry

1 egg

uses

Lemon grass tea is relaxing and is used by herbalists to aid respiratory and digestive problems. The tea is supposed to heighten 'psychic powers' and it is good to drink before bedtime, you will find it very refreshing and soothing. Just pour 2 cups boiling water over ¾ cup of finely chopped lemon grass leaves and leave for about 10 minutes or until very fragrant. Strain and reheat it, sweetening with a spoonful of honey if you like.

lemon verbena

Lippia citriodora

Recently I read in a gardening diary that lemon verbena was an unattractive plant in the garden, which surprised me. It can look leggy if you don't cut it back but when trimmed it keeps shooting fresh leaves and becomes quite full in appearance. And what a stunning lemon flavour this plant has. I adore the way it scents the air and flavours a dish with the gentlest, yet rounded citrus-lemon taste. One of the interesting qualities of lemon verbena is that it gives a lemon flavour without the acidity of lemon. Lemon verbena perfumes your hand if you pull a leaf and a couple of stalks can be mixed into a bowl of flowers to add a scent to a room. It is a wonderful herb to plant and yet I don't see it in as many gardens as it deserves. Mine is placed very close to a pathway so everyone who passes can be seduced by its scent.

lemon verbena cake (recipe page 199) ▶

Yet strangely it is the leaf that is the aromatic part of the plant, for the lilac flowers, which grow on slender spikes in summer, are quite without scent. Lemon verbena is deciduous – in fact I often think the grey branches look quite dead in winter – but in spring will burst forth with soft-coloured green leaves which are dull underneath, shiny on top and grow in threes.

Lemon verbena was introduced to Britain from Chile in the eighteenth century. Lemon verbena tea is a popular drink in France and Spain.

planting

Get a cutting or buy a small plant. It can be planted from a pot any time. Lemon verbena doesn't need too much nourishment – or too much of anything in particular, even fertilizer – except is grateful to be placed somewhere slightly sheltered, for it dislikes cold, wet weather and frost. If I don't need to pick the leaves, as soon as the branches are becoming long, I prune a few back all over the plant, which keeps it full of new young leaves for cooking.

harvesting

Just pick leaves whenever you want.

buying and storage

If you can't get lemon verbena fresh, it can sometimes be found dried. It retains its fragrance quite well as long as you buy some that has not been in the shops for a long time. Fresh, it lasts only a few days in water but the fragrance lasts far longer, even when it appears wilted.

lemon verbena syrup

uses

Verbena is a sedative, will settle nerves and sooth asthmatic coughs. If used as a lotion, it helps inflamed eyes and sores in the mouth or throat. The scent of lemon verbena is used in soaps and cosmetics.

Use this over ice cream, on a plain pudding, mixed with berries in season or serve it with the lemon verbena cake.

Cover the peel with water in a saucepan, add a good pinch of sugar then cook until the peel is tender. Drain the peel, chop finely and put into a basin.

Combine the rest of the sugar with the juices and verbena leaves in a saucepan and bring slowly to the boil. Thicken with cornflour/cornstarch diluted with enough cold water to make a thin paste. Pour the syrup through a sieve onto the cooked peel. Cover with plastic wrap and refrigerate. This keeps for about 4 days.

Makes about 1 cup

peel of 2 limes or 2 lemons

$2/3$ cup/5 oz castor/superfine sugar

$1/2$ cup/4 fl oz orange juice

$1/3$ cup/3 fl oz lime or lemon juice

1 tablespoon finely chopped lemon verbena leaves

2 teaspoons cornflour/cornstarch

lemon verbena cake

This is a cake made without butter but with olive oil instead. It has a firm crust and is speckled with little leaves of lemon verbena. You need 2 table-spoons of chopped leaves in this recipe and it takes quite a long branch picked of its leaves to produce that quantity.

Preheat oven to 190°C/375°F and butter, then dust with flour a 25 cm/10 in springform cake tin. Sift flour, salt and baking powder into a bowl. In a separate bowl, combine the sugar and oil well together and mix in eggs and peel. Add half the milk, then half the flour to the egg mixture. Mix together until well combined. Finally stir in the remaining milk and flour, and then add the lemon verbena. The mixture will have a wet consistency. Pour the batter into the cake tin and bake in oven for 30 minutes then reduce heat to 160°C/325°F and bake a further 20 minutes or until a fine skewer put into the centre comes out clean. Sometimes this cake takes longer, so be sure it is cooked as the crust on the cake can be deceptive. Remove from oven and allow to cool for 20 minutes, then remove from tin and place on a rack to cool completely. Sift icing/confectioners' sugar over it when cold – or you could ice with some lemon icing.

$2\frac{1}{2}$ cups/10 oz plain/all-purpose flour

$\frac{1}{2}$ teaspoon salt

2 teaspoons baking powder

2 cups/1 lb sugar

$\frac{3}{4}$ cup/6 fl oz light olive oil

3 eggs

rind of 1 lemon (ensure there is no pith), finely chopped

1 cup/8 fl oz milk

2 tablespoons finely chopped fresh lemon verbena

some icing/confectioners' sugar for dusting

hint

Cakes made with olive oil usually go brown on top and can appear cooked before they are, so check carefully with a skewer before removing from oven.

easy ideas

Lemon Verbena Quench

Steep leaves in boiling water for about 5 minutes, then strain and sweeten with sugar to taste. Drink warm or let cool then mix with mint and lots of crushed ice.

Lemon Verbena Fish

Lightly oil some chunky pieces of fish or portions of well-seasoned poultry cook on a bed of lemon verbena in the oven or wrapped tightly in a foil package.

Lactuca sativa

lettuce

Apart from their crisp or soft texture and bright green freshness, I treasure lettuce plants for their use in the borders of my garden. Just picking baby lettuce among the flowers makes you really appreciate what a wonderful green it is. Lettuce provides an edging and structure to my garden in the same way that trimmed box trees do in formal gardens. Using lettuce as border plantings means you end up with far too many, of course, but sharing the bounty from a garden is rewarding. They make very welcoming presents for friends, family and neighbours, and you can eat your own tiny, sweet fresh lettuce every day in salads. It is best to put in one type should you decide to plant them as a border, then they will grow quite evenly and, as you pick, take every second one, allowing remaining ones to fill out the spaces.

Of all the salad plants lettuce is the most widely eaten. It is not a new vegetable, for it was listed among the plants growing in the gardens of King Merodach-Baladan in Babylon. In Egyptian tombs lettuce seeds have been found, but this type of lettuce had leaves from one central stalk and looked rather like our lettuce do when they go to seed in the garden.

Lettuce is one of the easiest of all greens to grow and a lettuce is the starting point for all kinds of salads. A salad is the best kind of fast food, when you think of it, besides being among the healthiest of dishes. Once you become used to plucking baby leaves of your plants you will be able to mix up a bowl adding new interest to the lettuce with tiny beetroot leaves, salad burnet, baby turnip leaves or radish sprouts.

There is a big difference in growing your own lettuce rather than relying on bought. Instead of needing to buy three or four lettuces to provide variety in a bowl of greens you can wander around and pluck just a few leaves from many types, to give you a range of colours and textures. Grow a nasturtium plant near the lettuce so you can pick a few of its leaves also, while its flowers make a colourful garnish for a salad, as do violas, pansies or marigolds, but for these plants only use the petals and scatter them on top at the finish. Alternatively pick lettuce when they are very tiny and serve one per person, or use in cooked dishes like any green.

Some packets of mixed lettuce seeds include chervil, which has fern-like leaves and adds a piquancy to salads, and it will grow happily through the lettuce to give a fragile dark-green spray over them. I grow some bitter salad greens such as endive and radicchio, an increasingly popular form of chicory, but I find most Australians like only a minimum of bitter-tasting varieties in their salads.

Lettuce are one of the best vegetables to grow in pots, and are excellent as an edging in a large shallow pot or a basket with some flowers in the centre. Complete the pot planting with flowers or herbs which could be an accompaniment in a salad, so when you pick the lettuce you can pluck off a few flowers at the same time.

planting

Lettuce are rewarding because they are fast growing and quite hardy. They love a free-draining soil but also need water and respond to generous amounts of compost or manure. In summer you may have a problem with them going to seed quickly, so plant summer lettuce in a more shaded area at that time and try mesclun or varieties like mignonette. I put mulch of lucerne around where I grow lettuce to keep the soil moist but leave a little free around the stalk.

If you plant seeds you will end up with the seedlings too close together so thinning them is important or the lettuce will not grow well or form hearts. Transplant the thinnings elsewhere. Lettuce are obliging and will not all be ready at the same time, so give you a range of lettuce sizes over the months.

Keep fertilizing. I use a liquid feed which keeps them growing. When watering try not to splash the plants too much as lettuce can get lots of grit in their centres. Having straw or mulch around helps avoid this.

The planting time for each climate zone depends on variety, as some are more suitable for winter, while others will thrive only in spring and summer, and yet others in hot or tropical climates will bolt to seed and never form hearts. Check packets carefully.

varieties

Lettuce are divided into two main types: ones with a firm head and those that are loose leafed.

Loose-leafed lettuce include

- Lollo Rosso – frothy ruffled leaves
- Lollo Bionda – a pretty pink shade
- Rouge d'Hiver – ('Red Winter') a brown cos with a central green head
- plain cos – with its tall upright stems is marvellous used as a baby lettuce.

You can also plant bronzed lettuce – for instance, Red Velvet, Red Oakleaf, Red Coral – and green or brown mignonette. Varieties of Asian lettuce are now available at nurseries.

Head lettuce is the type you mostly buy in supermarkets. There is nothing wrong with it but it has a less pronounced flavour than loose-leafed, although it has good storage qualities, and I find it more difficult to grow a good hearted lettuce in my soil.

Then, of course you can scatter a mesclun mix into the garden bed, to give a tapestry of colour and range of leaves. Seeds are cheaper than punnets and provide a large bed of greens from one packet.

diseases and pests

Slugs like salads, especially the baby leaves, as do snails and cutworms. Trap snails and slugs by treating them to a saucer of beer and hose or pinch out any aphids if you get them.

harvesting

From about 5 weeks on for seeds, 4 weeks for seedlings, depending on their size. If wanting loose-leafed lettuce pick when big enough for your use. Headed lettuce needs to be left until it has formed a compact centre. Pick lettuce only on the day you want to use them for the freshest taste – but of course they can be stored much longer. If you just pick the leaves you will get new shoots coming through from the base, although I don't find them as vigorous.

buying and storage

All lettuce should look fresh, never appear wilted, have brown or broken edges or slimy patches. It should smell of the garden and the fresher it has been picked, the sweeter the flavour. If buying lettuce with a head, it should feel full and firm. Try to buy lettuce at the most the day before you want to serve it.

Everyone has a different opinion as to how to keep lettuce best: some find washing the lettuce first and then wrapping it in a linen towel and storing inside a plastic bag good, while others leave the whole lettuce just in a plastic bag. I don't have great success if it is washed before storing, and I find delicate home-grown lettuce can become soggy and discolour rapidly.

nutrition

The nutrients in a lettuce depend on its colour. The darker the leaf, the higher will be the content of the various carotenoids. Thus the pale leaves of iceberg lettuce have far less carotenoids than a deep green mignonette. All lettuce contains Vitamin C and of course some fibre.

cooking

Regardless of whether you intend to serve it in salads or cook it, lettuce needs a good wash. Put into a sink or large basin with lots of cold water and be sure all the little crinkly bits are washed, as dirt or tiny bugs can hide in them. Lift out of the water so you leave the bits of soil behind and never store wet. Use a salad spinner to get rid of the moisture and don't fill it too full. After spinning roll lettuce up in paper towelling and a tea towel and store for a couple of hours in the refrigerator before using so the leaves will be cold and crisp.

Oil will not hold on lettuce leaves if they are too damp so it is important they are always dry before dressing a salad or it will be tasteless. For cooking of course it matters little if the leaves are damp.

lettuce and lemon grass soup

Palest green, a little murky at times, I admit, as some lettuce change colour quickly and lose their green, but the delicate flavour of lettuce makes an excellent soup, even better when lemon grass is added to lend a fresh citrus finish.

Cook the onion and garlic in butter in a large pan until slightly softened, add the lettuce and fry for a few minutes, then add parsley, potato, stock and lemon grass and bring to a boil. Simmer for 25 minutes or until all the vegetables are quite soft. Remove the lemon grass or strips of lemon rind and process the soup. Reheat, adding the milk or cream only when heating.

Serves 4

30 g/1 oz butter

1 small onion, finely chopped

1 clove garlic, finely chopped

1 head lettuce or 2 small green mignonette, shredded

2 tablespoons finely chopped parsley

1 large potato, peeled and cubed

4 cups/2 pints stock, either chicken or vegetable

1 stalk lemon grass or several strips of lemon rind

1/2 cup/4 fl oz milk or a little cream

asian lettuce pork parcels

Wrapped food is always interesting – it is the excitement of eating a surprise inside a parcel – and kids love it too. You could use this idea with other minced meats such as chicken if you like. Use a soft-leafed lettuce for this dish and remove the largest outside leaves. Drop into boiling water and heat for a few minutes or until soft enough to roll over. Drain very well as lettuce leaves hold water, and cool before attempting to use them.

Mix all filling ingredients together, using your hands so the mixture is very well blended. Divide into about 8 oblong patties. Flatten them slightly. Put a lettuce leaf on the bench. Cut out the white stalk and roll leaf over to enclose the patty (use two overlapping leaves if one is not large enough to enclose the meat). Repeat until you have 8 parcels.

Preheat oven to 180°C/350°F. Scatter the ginger on the base of a shallow ovenproof dish. Put the lettuce parcels on top, join side down. Mix the stock with sugar and garlic and pour over the top. Cover and bake in oven for 20 minutes, remove the lid and cook a further 15 minutes or until the lettuce is very soft. Drain carefully and serve with a spoonful of juice and some rice alongside.

Serves 4

8–12 large lettuce leaves, blanched and drained

2 tablespoons shredded fresh ginger

1/2 cup/4 fl oz chicken or vegetable stock

2 teaspoons brown sugar

2 cloves garlic, finely chopped

Filling

500 g/1 lb finely minced pork

1 small onion, finely chopped

2 cloves garlic, finely chopped

1 tablespoon sweet Thai chilli sauce

2 eggs

1 teaspoon salt and some pepper

3 tablespoons finely chopped coriander/cilantro stalks

1/2 cup/2 oz finely grated carrot

1/2 cup/1 1/2 oz breadcrumbs, made from stale bread

lettuce soup

Lettuce can be combined with other vegetables to make interesting soup. It keeps well for 24 hours, refrigerated, but no longer.

Wash the lettuce well and shred fairly finely. Heat the oil in a saucepan, add the onion, celery, carrot and garlic and fry gently until the vegetables are slightly limp. Turn up the heat, add the lettuce with the water still on its leaves and cook, stirring until it is slightly softened. Dice the potato and pour in wine, stock or water. Bring to a boil, cover the pan and cook until the vegetables are quite tender – about 20 minutes. Purée the soup in a blender or a food processor and check for seasonings. If it is too thick you can add a little additional stock or water or else thin down with some milk or cream.

Serves 4 generously

1 head lettuce

1 tablespoon oil

1 medium-sized onion, roughly diced

1 stalk celery, sliced

1 medium-sized carrot, finely chopped

1 clove garlic, chopped

1 medium-sized potato

1/2 cup/4 fl oz dry white wine

3 cups/1 1/2 pints veal or chicken stock or water

salt and pepper

lettuce goes with

carrots

onion

peas

potatoes

dried beans

bacon and ham

chicken

vegetable or veal stock

dressings

balsamic

garlic

herbs

oil and vinegar

Asian flavourings

fish sauce

lime or lemon juice

palm sugar

coriander/cilantro

chilli

ginger

mint

parsley

toppings

eggs

bacon, ham or prosciutto

capsicum/ bell pepper

sun-dried tomatoes

olives

nuts of any kind

different peppers and salts

lamb and lettuce bundles

easy ideas

Lettuce and Curried Egg Rolls

Finely shred sufficient lettuce to make about 2 cups and mix with 3 mashed hard-boiled eggs, plenty of salt and pepper, and enough mayonnaise to bind mixture. Add 2 teaspoons curry powder. Put big spoonfuls along a thin piece of puff pastry and roll over, like making sausage rolls. Prick the top, brush it with egg beaten with 1 tablespoon of water and bake in a hot oven (200°C/400°F) until the pastry is golden brown and cooked – about 20–25 minutes. Cut into bite-sized pieces and serve as a snack, with drinks or as an accompaniment to vegetable soups.

This recipe is similar to the Chinese dish of squab, which is served at the table so diners can wrap the savoury meat in crisp lettuce, but my version is made with finely chopped lamb.

Soak the mushrooms in hot water for 30 minutes. Drain, discard the tough stems and cut the caps into fine pieces. Cut the lamb fillets into halves lengthwise and then into fine shreds. Mix with oil and rub with your hands to lightly coat the meat. Add cornflour, soy, and ginger. Heat the oil, add garlic and chilli fry for a few seconds, add lamb and stir fry for 2 minutes, mix in onions, water chestnut, sugar and soy and fry until the meat is just cooked. Add lightly beaten egg and stir until creamy. Mix coriander leaves through. Put into a bowl with a plate of lettuce leaves on the table. Wrap the lettuce around the lamb.

Serves 4

3 dried mushrooms

500 g/1 lb lamb fillets, trimmed of sinew

1 tablespoon oil

1 teaspoon salt

2 teaspoons cornflour/cornstarch

2 tablespoons light soy sauce

2 tablespoons ginger juice

4 tablespoons oil

3 cloves garlic, finely chopped

1 chilli, finely chopped

bunch of spring onions/scallions, chopped into small pieces

¼ cup chopped water chestnut

2 teaspoons brown sugar mixed with 1 tablespoon soy sauce

1 egg, lightly beaten

⅓ cup/¾ oz chopped coriander/cilantro leaves

lots of soft lettuce leaves, preferably butter or mignonette

lettuce baked savoury casseroles

In the same way you can make an egg dish with spinach or silverbeet, shredded lettuce can be mixed with eggs and cheese to make a textured, baked casserole. The lettuce can be any kind of soft leaf, such as butter lettuce or green mignonette, or you could use a mix of different leaves. Serve one of these casseroles with spring lamb racks or on their own for an interesting first course or light lunch.

Preheat oven to 180°C/350°F. Cook the lettuce in butter, stirring so lettuce is coated and wilts, add the parsley, salt and cayenne and cover, cook 10 minutes until tender, remove the lid and cook until the moisture has evaporated and the pan is almost dry. Purée. Mix in all the remaining ingredients except Parmesan. Pour into individual casseroles each of about 1 cup/8 fl oz in volume which have been generously smeared with butter. Top with cheese and bake in oven standing in a pan with a little boiling water around for about 45 minutes or until they are quite firm on the edges and set but a bit creamy in the middle. Let them stand for at least 5 minutes so they settle before serving.

Serves 6

500 g/1 lb mixed lettuce leaves, shredded

30 g/1 oz butter

2 tablespoons parsley sprigs

1 teaspoon salt and pinch of cayenne pepper

pinch of nutmeg

¼ cup/1 oz breadcrumbs, made from stale white bread

½ cup/2 oz grated Jarlsburg cheese

4 eggs, lightly beaten

¼ cup/4 fl oz milk

¼ cup/4 fl oz cream

3 tablespoons grated Parmesan cheese

lettuce and vegetable gratin

hint

Use a bed of
outside lettuce
leaves on the
base of a baking
dish when
roasting chicken
to keep the bird
moist. It won't
stick to the pan.

*As a main dish, this does four generously, you can eat it with toast fingers,
a little rice or some baby boiled potatoes. As a side dish, it is also very
good with thinly sliced ham. You can use a butter lettuce that has soft leaves
and, if it is tiny, you may need more than one. Green mignonette is also
very good and the more common lettuce, iceberg, is fine but will take a
little longer to cook.*

Hard boil the eggs and cut into quarters or chunky pieces. Melt the butter
and add the onion and carrot. Sauté until the onion is slightly limp. Wash
the lettuce well, cut into shreds and add to the pan with the water that is
still on the leaves. Sauté and give it an occasional stir until the lettuce is
limp. Put a lid or a plate over the pan and leave over a low heat for about
5 minutes or until the vegetables are tender. Set aside.

For sauce, melt the butter and add the flour. Cook, stirring, until the flour
has fried and add the milk. Bring to a boil, stirring constantly. Season with
salt and pepper, then turn the heat to low. The sauce will have a thin
consistency. Let it simmer very gently for about 10 minutes – it will thicken
a little. Add the mustard and mix the lettuce and vegetables plus the hard-
boiled eggs into the sauce. Put into a shallow gratin dish: one that holds
about 4 cups/2 pints. Scatter the crumbs and then the cheese on top.

Preheat oven to 180°C/350°F. If you are cooking the dish as soon as you
have prepared it, bake it for about 15 minutes or until the edges are
bubbling and the cheese has melted into a golden layer. It will take longer
if the dish was prepared beforehand, about 25 minutes at least.

Serves 4

4 eggs

45 g/1½ oz butter

1 white onion, finely sliced

1 medium-sized carrot,
cut into thin matchstick
strips or diced

1 large lettuce

Sauce

45 g/1½ oz butter

1½ tablespoons flour

2 cups/1 pint milk

salt and pepper

1 teaspoon French mustard

Topping

⅓ cup/1½ oz breadcrumbs,
made from wholemeal bread

⅓ cup/1½ oz grated melting
cheese, such as Jarlsburg,
Emmental or Gruyère

easy ideas *Lamb and Lettuce Casserole*

Gently fry 2 large chopped onions in a generous amount
of olive oil in a large frying pan. Remove to an ovenproof
casserole. Brown 8 small lamb chops, trimmed of fat, in the
same pan. Season chops well as they are cooking and then
transfer to casserole (you can put them in 2 layers on the
onion). Strew a dozen whole cloves of garlic around the
edge, pour of 1 cup/8 fl oz chicken stock or seasoned
water and cover. Bake in oven at 180°C/350°F for about

30 minutes or until chops are almost tender (or if you
prefer this dish can be cooked in a wide saucepan directly
over heat). Chop a washed cos lettuce roughly, discarding
any tough outside leaves, and pile over chops; season. Cook
another 20 minutes or until all is tender. Serve with the
juices, which should be relatively fat-free if you trimmed
the chops well.

sautéed lightly curried creamy lettuce

This is nice as a vegetable with a chicken dish or with some scrambled egg and toast. The best type for this is a soft-leafed lettuce, such as green mignonette or butter. Crisp head lettuce does not have enough taste.

Melt the butter in a frying pan. Add the onion and cook gently until limp. Mix in garlic and cook for 30 seconds and then add the lettuce with the water left on the leaves. Cook, giving an occasional stir until lettuce has softened. Add the curry powder and fry until it is aromatic and then season with salt and pepper. Lastly, add the cream and stir so the strands of lettuce are just coated with sauce. Don't leave on the heat too long once the cream has been mixed through or it will cook away.

Serves 4 as a side dish

30 g/1 oz butter

1 small onion, finely diced

1 clove garlic, crushed

1 lettuce, washed and shredded

2 teaspoons mild curry powder

salt and pepper

¼ cup/2 fl oz cream

lettuce and prosciutto tart

It is rare that people think of lettuce in a tart or quiche, but lettuce has a gentle flavour with a soft colour that lends itself well to additions such as prosciutto, bacon, cheese or some baby cooked peas. No need to use only the tiny inside leaves, for as long as they are not too tough the outside leaves of a soft lettuce such as mignonette, cos, iceberg or butter are fine.

Cook prosciutto until crisp in a frying pan. Remove to a large bowl and add lettuce, onion, oil and butter to the pan, and cook, stirring occasionally, until lettuce and onion are soft and any liquid around them has almost cooked away. Mix, along with any juices, into prosciutto and cool, then add remaining ingredients and stir well. Pour into baked pastry case and cook for about 35 minutes or until filling has set. Let tart sit for 5–10 minutes before cutting into slices.

Serves 4 as a main meal, 8 as a first course

1 pastry case, baked blind, about 20 cm/8 in diameter

3 slices prosciutto, in small pieces

1 medium-sized lettuce, finely shredded

1 onion, finely chopped

2 tablespoons olive oil

45 g/1½ oz butter

3 eggs

¾ cup/12 fl oz thick/double cream

salt and pepper

¼ cup/1 oz grated Gruyère cheese

¼ cup/1 oz grated Parmesan cheese

easy ideas

Chicken and Lettuce Stir Fry

Pour a jug of boiling water over 100 g/3 oz fine egg noodles; leave for a couple of minutes then drain. Thinly slice 2 skinned and boned chicken breasts. Fry chicken in very hot oil in a wok for a couple of minutes until golden. Remove, turn down heat and toss 2 finely chopped shallots and 2 chopped garlic cloves into the oil, followed by 1 washed, shredded lettuce (e.g. cos or butter). Everything will steam in the water from the lettuce leaves in a couple of minutes. Stir in either 2 tablespoons of sweet chilli sauce or satay sauce or some Chinese mushroom sauce to taste. Return chicken and noodles to wok and mix to warm them through. Some basil or coriander leaves can be added at the finish.

walnut dressing

This particular salad dressing is quite rich so any salad it accompanies is best served as a course on its own rather than with meats.

Whisk oils with lemon juice and mustard. Place the walnut pieces in a frying pan with the additional walnut oil and sauté them, moving and stirring so they colour evenly (if you leave them they can burn easily). Remove to some kitchen paper towel to drain. At the last moment toss lettuce with the dressing. Scatter the walnuts and cheese on top.

The first person to serve the salad should move the lettuce so the cheese and walnuts are fairly naturally distributed. If you feel this isn't going to work, toss the cheese through first and place the walnuts on top for presentation.

3 tablespoons vegetable oil

1 tablespoon walnut oil

3 teaspoons lemon juice

1 teaspoon Dijon or French mustard

1/3 cup/1 1/2 oz walnut pieces

extra 2 teaspoons walnut oil

1/4 cup/1 oz finely grated Parmesan cheese

red capsicum dressing

This dressing is a lovely deep salmon colour and has a slightly smoky flavour from grilling the pepper.

Chop the capsicum/bell pepper into pieces, purée in a food processor, adding the oil gradually. Remove to a bowl and mix in the vinegar, green peppercorns, mustard and stir. You will find it will probably be too thick, so thin down a little with some hot water, adding it just a small spoonful at a time until the dressing has a light, coating consistency. It can be made several hours before you intend to use it.

1 large red capsicum/bell pepper, grilled and peeled

1/2 cup/4 fl oz vegetable or very light virgin olive oil

1 tablespoon white wine vinegar

1 teaspoon green peppercorns, lightly crushed

1 teaspoon French or Dijon mustard

a little hot water

yoghurt salad dressing

A salad dressing for those who are on a fat-free diet and do not want to use any oil dressings. The apple juice concentrate cuts the sharpness of the yoghurt. It is best used with a green salad which has had some diced cucumber tossed through, rather than just on plain greens.

Whisk the yoghurt and apple juice concentrate together and add pepper and ginger. Keep chilled if not using immediately. It is best used within a couple of hours.

1/2 cup/4 fl oz non-fat yoghurt

1 tablespoon apple juice concentrate

a little black pepper

1/4 teaspoon grated fresh ginger

easy ideas

Curried Pork and Lettuce Cups

Using a crisp iceberg lettuce, or softer mignonette or butter lettuce, gently remove leaves, trim edges around with scissors to make 12 round cup-shaped pieces about the size of a saucer. Heat a little oil in a frying pan and cook 500 g/1 lb minced pork with 2 cloves chopped garlic and 1 tablespoon curry powder. Keep stirring so the pork breaks into small pieces as it cooks; season well. Pour 1 cup/ 8 fl oz coconut milk over the top and cook until pork is tender and sauce thick. Mix in a little chopped mint or basil and spoon into the lettuce cups.

mustard egg dressing

Adding a hard-boiled egg to a dressing gives a thicker quality, as does mustard, so this is a good dressing for a salad to go with meats.

Mash the egg and mix with mustard. Shake everything else except chives together in a screw-top jar, pour over the egg mixture gradually, stirring with a fork. Mix in chives just before using the dressing.

1 hard-boiled egg

2 teaspoons French mustard

6 tablespoons olive oil

1 tablespoon wine vinegar

1 tablespoon lemon juice

1 teaspoon brown sugar

salt and pepper

1 tablespoon finely chopped chives

tomato capsicum dressing

The colours are vibrant and so is the flavour.

Purée the tomato and capsicum together until a thick pulp. Add oil, vinegar, sugar and purée again. If too thick add a little bit of hot water.

2 red, ripe tomatoes peeled and some seeds discarded

1 capsicum/bell pepper, grilled until the skin has blackened and peeled, then chopped

6 tablespoons olive oil

2 tablespoons wine vinegar

1 teaspoon sugar

few spoonfuls of hot water (optional)

spicy asian dressing

This dressing is interesting if you toss it through lettuce with shreds of chicken. However, if you are intending to just use it for a plain salad be sure to include some mixed leaves of basil, mint, coriander along with the lettuce so the spicy, sweet, fresh and sharp flavours of the dressing will be shown at their best. It is very good as a dressing with cooked prawns too.

Mix everything together in a jar and shake well. If making any time in advance add the coriander just before serving.

1 tablespoon soy sauce

1 tablespoon sweet Thai chilli sauce

1 tablespoon ginger juice (made by squeezing grated fresh ginger)

4 tablespoons oil

1 tablespoon Chinese rice wine

1 tablespoon lemon juice

2 teaspoons brown or palm sugar

2 tablespoons roughly chopped coriander/cilantro leaves

easy ideas

simple salad dressings

The simplest dressing for salad is a mix of 4 tablespoons olive oil and 1 tablespoon wine vinegar or lemon juice, seasoned well with salt, pepper and perhaps herbs. Don't store jars of ready-made vinaigrette – or any kind of dressing – as they develop 'off' flavours. Do it fresh every time, for it takes so little time to make up a dressing and your salad deserves the best. For the same reason dress the salad with the best oil and vinegar you can afford. Choose an oil that suits your own tastes, as some people like a lighter flavour than others.

marjoram

Origanum majorana – sweet marjoram
O. onites – pot marjoram
O. vulgare – wild marjoram or oregano

There are three varieties of marjoram, but the main one for the cook is the sweet marjoram. Its rounded small green leaves are fragrant and soft, it has a white flower and the best flavour. It goes well with meats or in marinades. Pot marjoram is a strong vigorous plant but is a bit strident in its flavour and has white flowers or is pink flowering. It is the plant loved by Greek people, who call it 'rigani'. Wild marjoram is the strongest and spiciest and can be invasive; it forms quite a strong dense mat, the leaves are dark green and heart shaped and it has a purple-pink flower. The other name for this wild variety is oregano. These different names can be very confusing. (I also grow a golden variety as it has such pretty yellow leaves, but it does not quite have the flavour of the green plant.)

greek baker's lamb (recipe page 213) ▶

All can be used in a similar way but I find the difference in taste between them does not depend so much on the variety but on where it grows. Grown in the sun it is stronger than the same plant in dappled shade, in a stony part of the garden it again has a different flavour. Just be sensible and mix into dishes so it tastes right to you, remembering that it is quite a highly flavoured leaf. If you find the variety you have planted is not highly flavoured enough, be content with picking bunches of it for vases on its own or enjoy it when it is in flower.

planting

Marjoram is a perennial but may protest if the winter is cold and wet and die back. When it becomes warm again in spring it should come back up. You can plant from seeds but unless you want lots of plants it is more sensible to buy a plant from a nursery or get a cutting from a friend. It grows very easily from cuttings taken early in summer or by root division. Seeds or plants can be put into the garden from spring to autumn.

I have a number of plants, and while some patches are in full sun one is under an old fig tree and it thrives, forming a soft green mat of growth, which keeps almost all the weeds away. The hotter the climate the stronger the aroma of marjoram. The flowers attract all the neighbouring bees in spring.

harvesting

Just pick whenever you want to use fresh. For drying, collect the marjoram leaves and flowers during their flowering season but before they have opened.

buying and storage

This is one herb that many people prefer to buy in its dried form rather than fresh. The best places to buy it dried are Greek delicatessens – or of course you can dry your own. Pick a bunch, making sure there are unopened flowers on the stalks, and tie loosely, don't have too many in each bunch. Hang them in a cool place or the kitchen until well dried, depending on the weather this can take from a few days to a week. Then it is best to strip off the dried leaves and flowers and put them into a jar so they don't get dusty. Store in a dark place and use them as long as they have a rich aroma.

marjoram chicken

marjoram goes with

eggplant/aubergine
tomatoes
meat
casseroles
marinades
dried bean dishes
soups
stuffing for poultry

A simple way to roast chicken. It will finish with a crisp golden skin, moist flesh and fragrant flavour with lots of delicious marjoram-flavoured juice to spoon over the portions. This is especially good with some crispy roast potatoes and a dish of baked tomatoes, which will have an affinity with the marjoram taste.

Preheat oven to 200°C/400°F. Rinse the chicken and pat dry. Put the lemon inside with the garlic and some marjoram. Put more marjoram on the base of an ovenproof dish, which has deep sides and scatter with the diced onion. Season the chicken with salt and pepper, trickle over a little oil and smear or dab some butter over the breast. Sit it on top of the bed of marjoram and onion and roast for about 20 minutes, then pour over half the stock, turn the oven down to moderate (180°C/350°F) and continue cooking for another 30 minutes. Pour on the rest of the stock and cook until the chicken is ready, test by putting the point of a knife into the thickest part of the leg and checking the juices run out clear. It should be ready in another 20 minutes or so. Take out the chicken while you pour the juices from the container through a sieve into a small saucepan. If there isn't enough add a dash more stock to the pan and scrape it around to get up any of the brown bits on the bottom.

Serves 4

1 chicken, about 1.5 kg/3 lb
1 lemon, quartered
8 cloves garlic, unpeeled
handful of marjoram
1 onion, diced
salt and pepper
olive oil
30 g/1 oz soft butter
1 cup/8 fl oz chicken stock

greek baker's lamb

In tiny Greek villages you can see the women walking quickly to the village baker carrying a big covered tray, then at lunchtime they return and pay the baker a few drachmas to collect the tender stews that he put into his oven to simmer away for hours. These pungent and warming stews would include 'rigani', the dried oregano, but they can be flavoured with fresh oregano and this is an especially good dish if you use young spring lamb and young oregano or marjoram. It is very good served with some small potato pieces, which you can cook in the oven at the same time in a mixture of oil and butter so they are soft inside and crispy on the outside.

Put the lamb racks, fat side uppermost, into a casserole with deep sides in a moderate oven (180°C/350°F) for about 15 minutes so you get rid of some of the fat. Meanwhile fry the onions very gently in oil until softened and pale gold so they have a sweet flavour, add the tomatoes and cook a minute with salt, pepper and honey. When there is plenty of juice mix in the stock or water, cumin and oregano. Wipe out any fat in the pan with the lamb; pour in the tomato mixture. Cover with a tight-fitting lid, return to the oven, turn it to barely moderate (160°C/325°F) and let the lamb cook for about 45 minutes, spooning the sauce over the top occasionally. If it becomes dry add a bit more stock.

Cook the beans in salted water until tender. Chop into small pieces. When the lamb is ready, add the beans and lemon juice to the sauce and warm again for a few minutes. To finish, mix the parsley with lemon rind and garlic. Slice the lamb into chops. Spoon a bit of sauce onto plates, keeping some aside, put the lamb on top, mix the garnish into the rest of the sauce and spoon a little more on top.

Serves 6

2 racks of lamb,
about 12 chops in each

2 onions, thinly sliced

3 tablespoons olive oil

750 g/1½ lb tomatoes,
peeled and roughly chopped

sea salt and pepper

1 teaspoon honey

1 cup/8 fl oz chicken
or veal stock or water

3 teaspoons ground cumin

2 tablespoons oregano leaves

several handfuls
of young green beans

juice of a small lemon

⅓ cup/½ oz finely
chopped parsley

2 teaspoons finely chopped
lemon rind cooked for
5 minutes in water

2 cloves garlic, finely chopped

uses

Marjoram has antiseptic qualities and can aid the common cold and sore throat if made into a tisane. It can be used to clear nasal congestion if used dried and powdered. It also improves circulation.

hint

There are times when it is not possible to find fresh herbs and you must use dried. As these are stronger than fresh, use only a third of the amount specified in the recipe for fresh herbs. Add early in the cooking, so the heat releases their essential oils and aromas.

mint

Mentha viridis or spicata – spearmint
M. piperita – peppermint
M. rotundifolia – apple mint
M. cordifolia – wintermint

Mint is one of the best-known herbs in the world. There is a big variety of mints and hybrids available. The best known is the mint known often referred to as 'common' mint: it is a spearmint with long narrow leaves and it dies down in winter, so you need to buy mint then if it is the only one you grow. Peppermint contains the greatest amount of menthol, which gives the typical fresh, cooling flavour we expect from mint, and it grows wild on the hillsides of Provence. Apple mint has a round leaf with an excellent, fresh, clean, mint-sweet taste but is the worst for spreading throughout the garden. The big advantage of wintermint is that you will have it during winter as, unlike spearmint, it does not die down yet it has a similar flavour.

racks of lamb with mint gremolata and potato salad (recipe page 218) ▶

Mint was once a very important strewing herb, used to perfume rooms, and was frequently mentioned by Hippocrates and Pliny for its medicinal value. The Romans used it to stimulate the appetite and to flavour dishes and first introduced it to England where it became famous for its association with lamb. The Greeks are very clever with their use of mint – it originated in Greece, where it is still the most popular herb.

Famous sauces don't always come from the famous chefs of the world. You just have to consider the bread sauce of England served with chicken, the cranberry of America with turkey on Thanksgiving Day and applesauce with pork from Germany. Once every Australian home had a patch of mint – no doubt from the number of English people who came here – and with every leg of lamb came a jug of mint sauce. It was a part of our history, with father carving the leg for the family, mother making up the mint sauce. The two flavours combined so the sweet but tart mint sparked up the gravy, counteracting what was often a strong lamb taste, and I believe was also used to help add moisture to a meat that was usually seriously overcooked.

In modern menus mint is more likely to be added to a pesto with some basil and parsley, be stirred through chicken salad or added to coconut sauce. You can buy a bunch in every greengrocery shop or supermarket but it is the easiest of all herbs to grow and gives a fragrance which goes beyond the kitchen. Tuck a few sprigs in with a vase of flowers, slip a sprig into summer drink, rub on your hands after chopping something strong and aromatic or just enjoy the fragrance it sends out as you pass a clump in the garden.

As well as making mint sauce, you can add equal quantities of mint and parsley to potato salad, chop into an orange sauce for lamb fillets, add to tabbouleh, yoghurt and cucumber salads or put sprigs into a steamer or the water around boiled potatoes, carrots and peas. Push some into the syrup for fruit salad – it is especially good with pineapple.

planting

Mint is easy to grow, in fact too easy, as it can be a nuisance if not carefully restricted and is no respecter of another plant's space. You can grow mint in a pot or else push pieces of slate into the ground around your clump. As it needs lots of moisture add some water-saving granules to your pots. Buy a plant, or ask for a piece of mint with a small root section from a friend – most people are happy to share, as it is so prolific and division may be done any time from the runners, but is most successful in autumn or spring. However, you can plant mint any time except the middle of winter.

If mint gets rust on the foliage you will have to immediately cut these leaves off or dig out and destroy the plant and try again by putting a new runner in another bed. Rust mainly happens when the plant is subject to very sudden changes of temperature or the weather is humid and the mint is crowded out by other plants.

harvesting

Pick as required. You can dry mint by hanging bunches of stalks in the kitchen until the leaves have dried, then pulling off the leaves and storing in a glass jar with a good seal. The flavour is not the same, however, for mint changes when dried and is not as 'minty' somehow.

buying and storage

Leaves should be bright and green. Mint blackens quickly if kept in water so avoid any dark stalks in the shops. Don't wash mint but store in kitchen paper inside a plastic bag in the refrigerator.

traditional mint sauce

There is a knack to serving mint sauce: it should be served with a spoon as you need to scoop up the chopped bits of mint from the bottom. Pouring it from the jug over the roast gives only flavoured liquid, none of the fresh mint pieces.

Put the mint leaves into a bowl and pour on the boiling water. Move and muddle mint around in the liquid with a spoon so the water releases the herb's flavour. Before it cools too much add sugar and stir to dissolve. Add about 3 tablespoons vinegar and then leave for a minute, taste and add more vinegar so you have a sharp but sweet taste. Season with a little salt. Let the whole thing marinate for several hours so it becomes really minty.

½ cup/1 oz very finely chopped mint leaves

3 tablespoons boiling water

3 tablespoons sugar

enough vinegar to give a sharp flavour

salt

chicken and mint salad

A fresh-tasting summer salad, which has the interesting combinations found in Vietnamese and Thai cooking of sweet and sour, spicy and cool. You could serve it on a bed of cooked cold noodles, which would make it a far more substantial dish, and it would then be easily enough for 4 people. This amount makes 2 generous servings.

Process all the dressing ingredients roughly; pieces of herb should still be visible. Check flavour: it should be a little spicy, sweet, sharp and aromatic. Adjust if necessary.

Mix chicken, cucumber, carrot and cabbage in a bowl and add enough of the dressing to moisten, let it stand for 30 minutes refrigerated, toss again. Serve with some more dressing on top and lots of peanuts.

Serves 2–4

2 cooked chicken breasts, skinned and shredded into tiny strips

½ cucumber, peeled, cut lengthwise, deseeded and sliced finely

1 small carrot, grated

2 cups/7 oz finely shredded Chinese cabbage – don't use the stalk

chopped dry roasted peanuts

Dressing

⅓ cup/½ oz mint leaves

¼ cup/½ oz coriander/ cilantro leaves

1 chilli, deseeded and finely chopped

2 cloves garlic, chopped

2 tablespoons brown sugar

1 tablespoon rice vinegar

3 tablespoons lemon juice

2 tablespoons fish sauce

4 tablespoons vegetable or light olive oil

¼ cup/2 fl oz orange juice

mint goes with

carrots

potatoes

tomatoes

baby peas

basil

parsley

all kinds of drinks in summer

chicken

lamb

cucumber

yoghurt

Asian food

chilli

garlic

ginger

lemon

lime

fresh fruit syrups

poached fruit

uses

You can make your own mint tea by putting a table-spoon of green tea leaves into a big pot along with a handful of fresh mint leaves and a strip of lemon peel. Pour on 1 litre/2 pints boiling water and let it infuse for about 5 minutes. Pour through a strainer into cups and sweeten with a little honey or leave it plain.

racks of lamb with mint gremolata and potato salad

uses

Mint, especially
eau de cologne
mint, adds frag-
rance to pot
pourris. Mint oil
is an important
flavouring in med-
icine, cordials and
sweets. Pepper-
mint tea has a
great reputation
as a digestive
if taken after a
meal, is good for
pain or flatulence,
stomach cramps
and some head-
aches. It is said
that rubbing
fresh leaves on
rheumatic joints
brings relief.

Gremolata is the traditional topping for Italian osso bucco, usually made with garlic, lots of chopped parsley and lemon. This version substitutes mint for the parsley. When it is added to the top of the meat and wrapped up with it, the joint's warmth brings out a gentle minty taste in all the juices which form around it.

For potato salad, boil potatoes in salted water until tender. Cool slightly, peel and chop roughly into bite-sized pieces. Mix the olive oil, vinegars and mayonnaise together to make a dressing. Put a layer of potatoes into a bowl, then some dressing, lemon rind, parsley, mint and onion, and season well. Continue layering until potato is finished and leave to stand for about 3 hours.

Make gremolata: cook the lemon rind in a little water for 10 minutes then drain and chop very finely. Mix the lemon with remaining ingredients and set aside.

Preheat oven to 200°C/400°F. Trim the fat from the lamb and season the outside with pepper. Rub on oil, then a little balsamic vinegar. Roast for 15–20 minutes, depending on preferences. Remove and season with salt and scatter with the gremolata. Wrap meat in foil and leave to cool. Cut into chops just before serving.

To serve, toss the potato salad. Arrange on a platter with the cut lamb racks on top or around the edge.

Serves 4

2 racks of lamb,
about 8 chops each

pepper

2 tablespoons olive oil

1 tablespoon
balsamic vinegar

salt

Potato Salad

1 1/2 kg/3 lb small waxy potatoes,
such as Southern Gold

1/2 cup/4 fl oz olive oil

2 tablespoons red
or white wine vinegar

1 tablespoon balsamic vinegar

2 tablespoons mayonnaise

grated rind of 1 lemon

1/4 cup/1/2 oz finely
chopped parsley

1/4 cup/1/2 oz finely
chopped mint

1 red onion, very finely chopped

salt and pepper

Mint Gremolata

rind of 1 lemon, carefully
removed with a peeler

4 cloves garlic, crushed

1 teaspoon salt

3 tablespoons finely chopped mint

1 tablespoon finely
chopped parsley

Allium cepa

'The onion,' wrote French gourmet writer Robert J. Courtine, 'is the truffle of the poor'. My disagreement is not with likening it to a truffle but that the onion should be only for the poor. It is one of the great flavourings in just about every cuisine, and for just about everyone who loves cooking. Pungent when raw, cooked onions add sweetness and seem to bring out other flavours, when gently simmered in a casserole almost melts into the sauce, can be crispy and strong, soft and tender, are happy to take a role as a backbencher but are equally good at front of stage. They are part of the big family of lilies, along with the tulip, the yucca, red-hot poker and asparagus, and they are related to garlic. Native to central and western Asia the onion has been cultivated for thousands of years. In an inscription in the oldest written language, Sumerian, it says that 'The oxen of the gods ploughed the city governor's onion patches'.

Once the poor mainly ate onions with bread. Perhaps onions' strength of flavour and smell were not sophisticated enough for rich people, yet Egyptian mummies, who we presume were from the richest classes, were given a supply of onions meticulously wrapped in bandages for their dinners in the afterlife.

Like most strong-tasting foods onion has been credited with healing powers, from warding off evil spirits to fixing baldness. We mainly eat it for the flavour it gives dishes, but science now is verifying its health benefits.

These are hardy vegetables, grown as annuals. Onions have hollow leaves and bulbs that vary in colour from red to cream. The taste of home-grown onions, like tomatoes from the garden, shows how much flavour they can develop as against a commercial product.

A problem for many people seems to be how to stop weeping and resembling a red-eyed, red-nosed mess when cutting up masses of onions. I have read handy hints ranging from sipping a glass of water as you chop, talking to yourself while holding a toothpick in your teeth, wearing goggles ... nothing really works well. Onions are far less potent if chilled. I keep a couple in the refrigerator, especially in summer when the fumes are worst. Otherwise make sure you stand to chop where there is some circulating air and leave the root end on until the last minute.

I love raw onion but not everyone does. I have found the best way to get the crunch and flavour of onion with the raw heat is to slice thinly and put into a jug of iced water in the refrigerator so the onion becomes quite chilled. After a few hours you will have onion taste and crispness but without that heat. Most people can tolerate – and even like – this iced, very crisp onion scattered on top of salads or diced into a mixed salad.

planting

Plant in cold weather or at the end of summer. Make sure your soil is weed free or the weeds will take all available food and water while the onions act cowardly and give up the fight. Weeding must be done by hand as the onions' tiny roots mustn't be disturbed. You don't have to fertilize the ground before planting but do need to work it over so there are no lumps. Then sprinkle on a little liquid fertilizer every month. Too much, however, makes them grow lots of tops, not so much on the bottom end.

You can buy seeds but these take ages to grow, so if impatient it is best to plant seedlings, although there is not as much variety in the types available. They are slow to plant in that you have to divide the punnets of seedlings and make little long holes to drop the onions into. Use a stick to make the holes more quickly, then drop a seedling into each hole.

Onions can be grown between other vegetables like cabbages or cauliflower, and you can tuck them between low-growing flowers such as pansies as they don't need much space. If you grow onions really close the resulting bulbs will be tiny, wide apart you get bigger ones. Mulch around them well, which also keeps the weeds at bay.

Temperature Zone	Sow or Plant
Tropical	Not suitable
Subtropical	Late summer–late autumn
Temperate	Early autumn–mid winter
Cool	Mid autumn–early spring
First picking	*Timing varies with variety and climate, but many months*

varieties

There are many types. Unfortunately, they are often not labelled accurately, either on the seed packet or seedling punnet; you are mostly only given the information 'brown', 'white' or 'red', which is not very helpful! Remember that soil and growing conditions will affect the taste of the onion as much as the variety you plant.

- Purplette – a red-skinned mini onion
- Red Bunching – another red
- White Welsh – a bunching onion
- Barlotta – an heirloom variety and a flat white, which can be picked small for pickling or eaten as a large onion

Early season varieties

- Early Flat
- Early Grand
- Early Barletta

Mid season varieties

- Mild Red
- Odourless

Late season varieties

- Brown Spanish
- White Imperial Spanish

These are only a few of the many onion strains available to the gardener. In fact the large variety may surprise you when you look around, as only a few are grown commercially and the more unusual ones don't get planted for the markets. Just shop around and read the directions on seed packets as to which onion seeds it contains and when to plant them.

diseases and pests

Snails fancy them and onion thrips and maggots are pests. If you get maggots in the garden you need to spray.

harvesting

Pull green onions from the ground when they are young and the bulbs only partly formed, using the leaves and the baby bulbs fresh in dishes. This is the spring onion, shallot, scallion – these names all refer to much the same thing, just an immature onion. All you need to learn is what it looks like.

If onions are left in the ground and then harvested when the leaves have dried you have longer-keeping dry onions. Lift bulbs completely out of the soil so they don't begin growing again, be sure to dry them properly until the skins are papery and dry and store in a cool place with plenty of air circulating them.

buying and storage

Avoid any wet or moist-skinned onions as they will deteriorate very quickly and for this reason be cautious about buying them in plastic bags. They should smell sweet and have no sprouting ends. Keep them with some air around when storing, I find they keep well in a big loose wicker basket and look decorative in the kitchen. Usually the sweeter the onion, the softer it will be and sooner you need to use it. So mild onions for salads need to be refrigerated, while really dry onions with their skin on are stored out of the refrigerator – except if you have peeled too many for any reason. Rather than waste them you can wrap peeled onions tightly in plastic and keep in the refrigerator, but use within a day.

Commercial onions and their uses

- Brown onions. For most kind of cooked dishes, especially stews and casseroles, frying or baking.

- White onions. For all of the above. These can have a little more sweetness for frying than brown onions.

- Red onions. These can vary a bit in appearance, and are mostly sold with tops on and tied in bunches. They are often called Spanish onions and are sweeter than the brown and white. They are used raw more often as they are not supposed to leave as strong a taste in your mouth. I question that however at times.

- Yellow Spanish. These have softer skin than other onions and are mildly flavoured, but not odourless, although they are often so called. They soften very quickly so need to be used soon after buying.

- Green onions. They can be strong but need to be eaten very fresh and are often used both raw and cooked.

- Shallots. These little brown bulbs joined at the base are occasionally called eschalots and are popular in France as well as being an asset in Asian dishes. They have a very good flavour and cook to a sweet and tender consistency very quickly. They grow quite easily with similar conditions to large onions. Just stick some singly into the ground and you end up with a big clump around each.

nutrition

Young green onions have the highest levels of nutrients of the onions and are a good source of Vitamin C. The green tops provide beta-carotene and folate, which is converted to Vitamin A. Dry onions provide some Vitamin C too and small amounts of minerals and vitamins, but it is other compounds which are considered nutritionally important. It is believed their sulphur compounds may have anti-cancer effects while the anti-oxidants they contain protect the body against coronary heart disease. Along with tea and apples, onions are one of the highest sources of anti-oxidants in our diet.

cooking

Onion requires very little preparation, Don't chop onions in a food processor, it changes their flavour and they bruise, so you rarely get the same sort of golden colour and often they taste bitter instead of sweet when cooked.

Leave the root end on when slicing, for it holds the onion together. Cut onion into halves, then with the cut side down – so you have a steady surface – slice from the other end right up to the root. Leave on the root end too if you are chopping them. Cut two slices into the onion lengthwise so they are close to the root end, and then cut crosswise, being careful to keep the knife at a downwards angle so even if it slips your fingers aren't cut.

To make little onions and shallots easier to peel dip into boiling water for a few minutes.

Green or spring onions should have any dry or damaged outer leaves peeled away. Cut off the root before chopping or slicing. Most recipes use some of the green top, which also has lots of strong flavour; the recipe will usually stipulate this. Onion recipes are often quite explicit as to how you cook them, for the method will give the final result of sweet, or firm, or crisp. Cooking onion is not only about texture but also about changing the strength of the taste.

bread rolled crispies

spring/green
onions/scallions
go with

fish

chicken

pork

patties

salads

noodles

bean shoots

coriander/
cilantro

soy sauce

fish sauce

chilli

garlic

ginger

Crusty little rolls baked in the oven have a filling of spring onion, ham and cheese, just the kind of nibble that everyone usually loves and easy to make in advance ready for baking later. I find most people can easily consume four of these without any effort.

Preheat oven to 200°C/400°F. Roll out the bread with a rolling pin so it is quite flat. Cook the spring onion/scallion for a minute in oil and butter until softened and transfer to a bowl. Chop the ham very finely, it will have a much nicer texture than if you mince it and mix with onion. Add cheese, egg yolk, Tabasco or pepper and mix well. Spread a layer onto each piece of bread. Roll bread up; if you think they may unroll, toothpick the edges temporarily. Have a baking tin pan ready lined with non-stick baking paper/parchment.

Melt butter. Dip the outside of the rolls lightly into the butter on all sides and also on the base and put each one onto the tray, join side down. Alternatively you can brush rolls with butter but this needs to be generous or you won't find they taste buttery and crisp, instead just dry. When ready bake in a oven for about 15–20 minutes or until crisp. Serve whole or cut into pieces for cocktail savouries.

Makes 16

8 slices fresh white or brown bread, crusts removed

½ cup/2 oz chopped spring onion/scallion, including green tops

1 tablespoon oil

30 g/1 oz butter

125 g/4 oz finely sliced ham

½ cup/2 oz grated tasty/cheddar cheese

1 egg yolk

dash of Tabasco or plenty of pepper

125–150 g/4–5 oz butter

grape harvester's soup

This is vastly different soup to the traditional onion soup of France, which is made with long-cooked onions and rich chicken stock. This one relies not only on onions but tomatoes for flavouring. A non-acid light wine should be used in the soup or the combination with tomato could be too sharp.

As it is a soup eaten in vineyards in Europe, the wine originally used would have been the new season's vintage, so it is best made with a fresh young wine. Then, naturally, you sip the rest of the bottle with the soup.

Heat the oil in a heavy-based saucepan, add the onions and cook gently until they are soft and golden. Add the sugar and cook, stirring occasionally until the onions are well coloured and tinged with brown specks. This slight caramelization of the onions gives the soup its rich flavour. Mix in the garlic and flour and let it fry, add the tomatoes and wine and stir until it comes to a boil. Simmer gently for 5 minutes, then add stock or water. Cover and cook over a very gentle heat for 45 minutes.

Lightly toast the bread. Cut garlic in half to expose its juices then rub the warm toast with the garlic surface, and place a slice of toast in each soup bowl. Pour the boiling soup over the top of the toast so it absorbs some of the liquid and serve immediately.

Serves 4

3 tablespoons olive oil

750 g/1½ lb onions, thinly sliced

1 teaspoon sugar

3 cloves garlic, finely chopped

2 teaspoons flour

750 g/1½ lb tomatoes, peeled and roughly chopped

1 cup/8 fl oz young red wine

5 cups/2½ pints vegetable or chicken stock or water

4 medium-thick slices day-old country-style bread

extra 1 large clove garlic

florentine onion soup

Ground almonds are more reminiscent of Spanish cooking but this Italian soup includes them, along with plenty of onions and cinnamon. It is quite unlike French onion soup but is also very flavoursome and the ground almonds give it a fine nutty texture. The chunk of bread in the bottom of each soup bowl absorbing the liquid makes it quite a filling dish.

Heat the oil and gently fry onion and carrot until limp, giving them a stir every so often. Cover and cook until soft, remove the lid and scatter on sugar. Fry for about 5 minutes, stirring until there are some deep brown specks on the onion. Pour over the wine and cook until it has almost gone. Add half the stock, cinnamon stick, cover and simmer the mixture very gently for about 25 minutes to bring all the flavour of the onions out into the stock. Mix the almonds with vinegar and slowly add the reserved stock. Pour this into the pan and stir until it has come back to the boil, cover and cook again for 15 minutes. The soup can be completed to this stage several days beforehand and warmed again.

When ready to serve cut bread into halves and brush each one thickly with oil. Either sauté in a pan until crisp or bake in the oven until golden. It doesn't matter if you do this a little while in advance, as bread doesn't need to be hot. Put the bread into deep soup bowls and taking a cup of boiling soup together with a good mix of onion pour it slowly over the top of the bread. Scatter on plenty of shavings of Parmesan cheese.

Serves 6 as a first course, 4 as a meal

4 tablespoons olive oil

5 large brown or white onions, halved and sliced

1 large carrot, finely chopped

1 tablespoon sugar

½ cup/4 fl oz dry white wine

6 cups/3 pints chicken stock

1 cinnamon stick

⅓ cup/1½ oz ground almonds

2 tablespoons white vinegar

4–6 slices sourdough or a crusty country-style bread

a little more virgin olive oil

shavings of Parmesan cheese

eggs in creamed onion sauce

An easy dish to eat and a gentle, comforting combination. Hard-boiled halves of egg are coated with a very soft onion sauce that has quite a sweet, creamy flavour. This sauce has many other uses, for instance try it with lamb, serve with veal chops or roasted veal, or use over a dish of spinach instead of a cream or cheese sauce. It reheats well.

Heat the butter with oil in a saucepan and cook the onions gently until soft and golden, stir every so often so they colour evenly. Scatter on the flour and turn onions over, then add the milk and cream, season well and stir constantly until sauce comes to a boil. Simmer a couple of minutes, add mustard, cool a little bit and process so you have a creamy purée. Pour a little into a shallow ovenproof dish, about 20 cm/8 in diameter. Cut the eggs into halves lengthwise and then into quarters and arrange on top. Spoon rest of sauce over so every egg piece is completely covered. Mix cheese and crumbs and scatter on top. You can prepare in advance to this stage and refrigerate for up to 12 hours.

To serve, preheat oven to 180°C/350°F and bake for about 20 minutes.

Serves 4

60 g/2 oz butter

1 tablespoon oil

3 large white or brown onions, halved and finely sliced

2 tablespoons flour

2 cups/1 pint milk

2 tablespoons cream

salt and pepper

1 teaspoon French mustard

6 hard-boiled eggs

⅓ cup/1½ oz freshly grated Parmesan cheese

⅓ cup/1 oz breadcrumbs, made from stale white bread

dry onions go with

just about everything but especially:

chilli

garlic

ginger

chicken

beef

lamb

olive oil

butter

pastry

yeast dough

tomatoes

all fresh herbs

cheese

eggs

creamy sauces

olives

sun-dried tomato and capsicum/ bell pepper

fresh tomato and capsicum/ bell pepper

cheese onion slice with semi-dried tomato

shallots
go with

steak

wine

eggs

cream

cheese

potatoes
and roasted
vegetables

lamb

tomatoes

All manner of interesting toppings can be put onto bases of pastry. This version relies on sweetly cooked onions topped with a creamy cheese sauce mixed with a little sun-dried tomato – or you could substitute capsicum pepper – to add bite. If you don't want to make this crust, any crisp shortcrust or a layer of puff pastry will do.

Preheat oven to 190°C/375°F. Process flour, salt and butter together and then when crumbly add cream and lemon juice and mix to a paste. Wrap dough in plastic for 30 minutes to rest, refrigerated. Roll out between waxed paper, put in a greased Swiss roll tin, cover with buttered foil, and bake for 5 minutes, then turn heat down to 180°C/350°F for about 12 minutes. Remove the foil and bake for another 7 minutes or until golden and firm.

For filling, heat oil and butter together and cook the onion very slowly until soft, stirring every so often. Heat the extra butter in a separate pan, add flour and fry until it is grainy; add milk, bring to a boil, stirring, and cook until quite thick. Remove and cool slightly, add egg and cheese, tomatoes and season. Spread onion over the base of the pastry, then top with sauce and bake again in the oven for 15 minutes or until firm. Cool for 5 minutes before slicing. If you want to keep this slice for reheating, store in the refrigerator and reheat in a moderate oven for about 12 minutes or until warmed through.

Pastry

1¾ cups/7 oz flour

½ teaspoon salt

125 g/4 oz butter,
cut into small pieces

4 tablespoons cream

1 tablespoon lemon juice

Filling

2 tablespoons oil

30 g/1 oz butter

2 onions, finely chopped

extra 45 g/1½ oz butter

3 tablespoons flour

2 cups/1 pint milk

1 egg

1 cup/4 oz grated
Jarlsburg cheese

¼ cup/1 oz grated
Parmesan cheese

¼ cup/1 oz finely chopped
semi-dried tomato or
capsicum/bell pepper

dash of salt, cayenne pepper
and black pepper

extra Parmesan cheese,
to top the slice

easy ideas *Mushrooms Stuffed with Sweet Onions*

Roughly chop 4 onions and gently cook in about ⅓ cup/ 3 fl oz oil and 60 g/2 oz butter in a saucepan until golden and soft, stirring every so often. Add ½ cup/4 fl oz red or white wine and 1 tablespoon sugar; boil quickly until the wine has cooked to a sticky sauce. Oil the outside of some mushrooms well (how many depends on their size) and remove stalks. Fill with onion mixture and scatter over a little fresh thyme. Bake for about 15–20 minutes at 180°C/350°F, or until mushrooms are soft.

cornmeal pizza with sweet onion topping

hint

Red onions cook quickly to a soft texture in dishes and have an interesting colour.

This is so much nicer than any pizza you could ever buy, just because of its total simplicity. Including cornmeal in the pizza base gives crispness and an interesting crunchy texture. This recipe makes two bases, 20–23 cm/8–9 in across. Even if you haven't handled yeast before, a pizza is one of the easiest ways to begin as it doesn't matter if the base is a bit uneven, while the mix is quite forgiving if left too long or used before it has completely doubled.

Sweet, caramelized onions are one of the most scented toppings you can use. You may feel there is a bit too much oil in the onions but for a pizza topping you need a certain amount to moisten the bread and prevent the onions from going black when the pizza is baked. You can make the pizza with only cooked onion or put another topping over them and I have listed a few suggestions . Don't add too many different things, though, for somehow instead of adding to the finished flavour, this just dilutes it.

The onion topping can be made in advance. Put onions into a wide saucepan with the butter, oil and bay leaf and heat for about 10 minutes until the onions are beginning to wilt, stirring regularly so the onions at the base come to the top. Cover and cook over a medium heat until the onion is very soft. Remove lid, scatter on the sugar and cook, stirring, until you have a richly browned pan of onions. It is good to get a few very dark sections, this will add to the flavour, but don't let any actually burn. When onions are cooked transfer to a bowl and keep refrigerated until you want to use them.

For pizza base, put the yeast, sugar and water into a small basin and stir. Let it stand until the bubbles form on top. Put the flour, polenta/cornmeal and salt into a basin and stir to mix. When the yeast is bubbling, pour the oil and milk into it and tip the liquid into the centre of the dry ingredients. Mix with a fork, adding a little more warm water if too dry. Put into an electric mixer if you have dough hook and beat for about 5 minutes. If not, put out on to a bench and knead for 5–6 minutes by hand. If sticky, just add a few more spoonfuls of flour. Put dough into a lightly oiled bowl. Cover with a piece of lightly oiled plastic wrap and leave in a warm place for about an hour or until it has doubled in volume. Remove from the bowl and flatten into a rectangle. Fold this over into three layers, press down again and return to the bowl, cover with the plastic wrap and let it rise until doubled once more (about an hour).

Pizza Base

2 teaspoons dry yeast

1 teaspoon sugar

¼ cup/2 fl oz warm water

1 cup/4 oz plain/all-purpose flour

1/3 cup/2 oz polenta/cornmeal

1 teaspoon salt

1 tablespoon olive oil

⅓ cup/3 fl oz milk

handful of Parmesan cheese (optional)

Sweet Onion Topping

1 kg brown onions, halved and thinly sliced

45 g/1¼ oz butter

½ cup/4 fl oz olive oil

1 bay leaf

1 tablespoon sugar

Take dough out and divide into two pieces, tuck the ends of each piece under to form a ball and roll out on a lightly floured bench very, very thinly to make a round flat pizza base. Put onto oiled pizza trays. It requires lots of experience to move a base once covered with topping without it stretching and losing shape, so always best to put it onto the trays first.

Preheat oven to 210°C/425°F. Brush bases with some of the oil from the onion (if the oil has set firmly around the onions, just warm them a bit – or leave out at room temperature for an hour so you can separate oil from onion). Cover with the caramelized onion and bake in hot oven until the base is quite crisp and the topping ready, about 15–20 minutes. Onion can be topped with some Parmesan cheese before baking if you wish.

Other Toppings

- Brush with fresh tomato sauce (see p.350) mixed with some of the onion oil and then top with onions. Scatter on a few pieces of rosemary.

- Put strips of anchovy here and there over the top of the onion.

- Arrange some cooked bacon, some shredded proscuitto or strips of very smoky ham under the onion.

- A few oily, grilled capsicum/bell pepper strips can be mixed through the onion to lend a smoky flavour. Scatter a bit of Parmesan over before baking.

- Mix the onion oil with several tablespoons of fresh chopped herbs and dab over the top of the crust before putting onions over this.

marinated onion salad

The secret of this salad is to make it well in advance and leave for at least a day before you serve it. Refrigerated, it keeps for five or six days. It is difficult to say how many this will serve. It should be enough for four to six but the longer it is kept, the more the onions soften and the fewer it will feed, so remember that when you slice them. If you are not using large onions, it doesn't hurt to add an extra one. Put out with cold meats or salads, use as part of an antipasto platter. It is also very good on crusty bread as a snack.

Cut onions in half and then into very thin slices. Mix all the remaining ingredients in a bowl large enough to hold all the onion. Add the onion slices and stir so they are thoroughly coated with the mixture. Leave this at room temperature and give it a stir several times over the next few hours. Transfer to the refrigerator and cover. Leave for at least a day before using, stirring once each day. As the onion softens, there will be quite a lot of liquid around it, so before serving drain the onion slightly, leaving it moist. The liquid should be discarded once you have used the salad. Begin again with a fresh marinade.

Serves 4–6

3 large onions, either white or red

1 cup extra-light olive oil

5 tablespoons lemon juice

2 tablespoons sugar

1 tablespoon ground cumin

1 teaspoon ground turmeric

2 teaspoons salt

1 teaspoon white pepper

roasted onion wedges

One of the easiest – and one of my favourite – ways of eating onions with some roasted meat. They can just go into the oven at the same time as the meat and finish with glazed caramelized edges. I find most people can manage more than one so you may like to do several onions each.

6 medium-sized onions
45 g/1 ½ oz butter
1 tablespoon olive oil
salt and pepper
sugar

Preheat oven to 200°C/400°F. Peel the onions but leave on the root end. Cut through the centre so you form wedges – depending on their size you should have approximately 6 wedges to each onion. Pack them into a smallish pan, preferably china, or an earthenware dish so they are quite close together and sit upright. Then push a little piece of butter into the centre of each onion, trickle some oil on top and scatter with plenty of salt, pepper and sugar. Place them in oven for about 15 minutes. Turn them over, return to the oven and cook for a further 25 minutes or until soft and very golden brown (f you use large onions they will take longer to cook). Just watch they don't begin to burn and go black instead of just turning a lovely brown from the sugar, if they look like becoming too dark cover with foil. Serve an onion to each person with a bit of juice; the idea is to leave the onion in the skin so the soft, sweet section in the centre can be scooped out.

Serves 6

easy ideas *Onion and Fish Parcels*

Season 4 fillets of white fish (e.g. snapper, dory, flathead) and squeeze on a little lemon juice. Finely chop 2 large onions and cook them in a little oil and butter, stirring until soft and golden. Season and mix in ¼ cup/½ oz chopped parsley and if not moist add a couple of tablespoons olive oil. Prepare 4 pieces of foil that are double the size of a fish fillet. Put a little onion on the foil, then place fish over it, top with rest of onion, spreading it out thinly. Fold foil packages over to enclose fish, sealing edges well. Bake in preheated moderate oven (180°C/350°F) for about 12–15 minutes – or even longer if thick fish fillets have been used. Serve in the parcels so each person can enjoy the aroma when they open the foil. The same method can be used for shelled raw prawns/jumbo shrimp.

Glazed Baby Onions

Peel 24 baby onions and boil for 10 minutes in salted water. Drain. Transfer to a frying pan and cook in a little oil for a further 5 minutes, shaking pan every so often. Add 1 tablespoon sugar and cook, stirring and being careful it does not burn, until slightly coloured. Pour in 1 cup/8 fl oz seasoned chicken stock, cover and cook until onions are tender. Then remove lid and boil, shaking pan occasionally, until there is just a bit of syrupy liquid left around the onions.

onion and shallot risotto

There is nothing difficult about making risotto, it is just the problem of being bound to the stove for the time it takes the rice to absorb the liquid and change from a starchy hard grain to one which is tender and plump with flavour. The process takes about 20 minutes as a rule, so risotto best for serving to friends you don't mind hanging around you in the kitchen while you chat and share a few drinks. Risotto is well worth the wait. I am immediately suspicious in a restaurant when I am served a dish of risotto soon after ordering, knowing it will have been made in advance and just reheated – for reheated risotto never has the creaminess of the freshly made version. Arrigo Cipriani, from the famous Harry's Bar in Venice, says that he feels strongly that 'certain dishes should not be preceded by an appetizer. Risotto is a case in point. Nothing but nothing should come before the first mouthful of a good risotto ... it is an event and waiting for it only heightens the experience.'

Heat half the butter with oil in a heavy-based deep frying pan and add the onions and shallots. Cook very gently for about 45 minutes until they are soft, tinged with gold and brown in sections. The shallots should be tender. Remove these and reserve for later. Add the garlic and sugar, fry a minute, then remove onion mix from pan. This part can be done well in advance.

Add the rest of the butter and the rice to the pan and stir until the rice is evenly coated with butter. Warming the wine and stock together, add a cup to the rice, return the onion and garlic and keep stirring. Add hot stock, about a cup at a time, as it is absorbed. The stock should come level with the top of the rice each time, but don't add so much it covers it with liquid. When the rice is tender – and tasting it is the only sure test – quickly peel cooked shallots and return to the pan. Add the extra butter, another cup of very hot stock and cheese. Cover with a lid or plate, let stand for 2 minutes and then stir quite briskly. (Depending on all manner of things you may have some stock over or may not have enough, it seems to vary according to the pan and the heat you use so don't fuss about the amount; it's more important that the rice should be tender yet still a little firm in the centre.) Mix parsley through risotto and serve absolutely instantly.

Serves 6 as a first course, 4 as a main meal

90 g/3 oz butter

2 tablespoons oil

4 white or brown onions, thinly sliced

12 shallots, unpeeled

2 cloves garlic, finely chopped

1 teaspoon sugar

1 cup/7 oz arborio rice

1 cup/4 fl oz dry white wine

about 4 cups/2 pints chicken stock

extra 30 g/1 oz butter

1/3 cup/1 1/2 oz grated Parmesan cheese

3 tablespoons finely chopped parsley

onions in cider with pine nuts

A simple roasted onion dish, the sweetness in the cider will cook to a golden glaze, then top with pine nuts and you get a contrast in textures. These go with just about anything.

Preheat oven to 180°C/350°F. Put onions into a small ovenproof casserole which they will fit quite snugly and trickle on oil. Cover and cook in oven for about 30 minutes or until tender. Pour over the cider, return to oven and cook uncovered for a further 20 minutes or until the cider has reduced to just a little sauce. While onions are cooking fry the pine nuts in a small pan in a little oil, stirring constantly until golden. Drain. To serve, scatter nuts over the onions.

Serves 4

12 small onions, peeled

2 tablespoons olive oil

1 cup/8 fl oz cider

1/3 cup/2 oz pine nuts

some additional oil

green onion sauce

A delicate pastel green sauce that can be spooned over steamed vegetables or used with light meat such as spring lamb, fish or poultry. Trickled on some tiny new potatoes it makes a lovely side dish, which will go with most main courses.

Put the onions and butter into a saucepan, stir, and cook with a lid on for 5 minutes, and then add stock and cream. Cook covered until soft and process. The sauce is meant to be thinnish but you can boil quickly for a few minutes to reduce and thicken slightly if you wish.

Makes enough for 4

1 large bunch spring onions/scallions, chopped

30 g/1 oz butter

1/4 cup/2 fl oz chicken stock

1/2 cup/4 fl oz cream

onion and pear sauce

A interesting and usual sauce to serve with chicken or any kind of poultry, particularly good if you have a few spices on the outside of the poultry. Be sure to use a firm pear, for a sweet one will not give the right, tart flavour. The sauce can be made in advance and refrigerated for a day, then reheated as you need it.

Cook the onions gently in a saucepan in butter until soft and translucent. Turn up the heat and fry for a few minutes, stirring until golden, add the turmeric and fry 30 seconds, then add wine and simmer for 5 minutes. Add the pear, sugar and lemon along with currants and stock. Simmer gently until the pears are tender; if the sauce is cooking away too much, cover with a lid. Finally mix cream and flour and stir into the sauce until lightly thickened.

Serves 4

2 onions, halved and thinly sliced

45 g/1 1/2 oz butter

1 teaspoon ground turmeric

1 cup dry but not acid white wine

1 large firm pear, peeled, cored and finely chopped

2 teaspoons brown sugar

1 tablespoon lemon juice

1 tablespoon currants

1 cup/8 fl oz chicken stock

2 tablespoons cream mixed with 1 teaspoon flour

caramelised onions

This style of sweet, well-coloured onions is one of the most popular ways of cooking them. The slow, long cooking enables the natural compounds present in onions to change to sugar. The red wine adds more flavour and the addition of sugar balances out the wine. You can keep these caramelized onions for a few days and reheat them. They have many uses – try adding a few to a sauce for pasta, as a topping on pizza, tuck some inside baked potatoes or serve with sausages as a relish.

Put the onions into a heavy-based saucepan with oil and butter. Cook very gently until they are coated with butter, then cover and continue to cook until they are soft, stirring every so often. They take about 30 minutes. Remove the lid, add the sugar and wine, season and let onions continue cooking over a higher heat, stirring, until they become quite coloured. The wine will cook right away and you need to watch onions; they should end up quite dark in colour but be careful you don't let them burn. Near the finish mix in the balsamic vinegar, cook for a further minute and remove from the heat. Cool a bit before storing, tightly covered, in the refrigerator.

Makes enough for 4

4 large brown or white onions, thinly sliced

2 tablespoons olive oil

30 g/1 oz butter

1 tablespoon brown sugar

1/2 cup/4 fl oz red wine

salt and pepper

2 teaspoons balsamic vinegar

easy ideas

Onions in Wine and Cream

Slice about 3 large onions and cook in a frying pan in a mix of oil and butter until soft and golden, stirring every so often. Tip in 1/2 cup/4 fl oz white wine and boil until liquid has cooked away, then season, add 1/2 cup/4 fl oz thick/double cream and heat until bubbling. Spoon over toast for a snack, or over steak.

parsley

Petroselinum crispum – curly parsley
P. hortense filicinum – flat leaf parsley
P. crispum var. tuberosum – Hamburg parsley

Parsley is a native of Sardinia. It is one of the most popular of all herbs and it is one herb which has few boundaries, going with almost all food. Some few years ago it developed a reputation as old-fashioned, and so restaurants and home cooks alike began to tuck bits of dill, coriander or basil over food instead, forgetting that parsley is still one of the most versatile of all flavourings. It is back in fashion and appreciated for the bright green touches it gives food, the tangy garden freshness of its flavour and its health benefits. It is a rich source of proteins, vitamins, iodine, magnesium, iron and other minerals – you can chew some sprigs of fresh parsley every day instead of taking iron tablets. One of its great benefits for the cook is that parsley seems to gently draw out the best of flavourings from the other herbs, which may accompany it. But it must be fresh; the secret of a wonderful parsley flavour is to chop by hand as close to using it as you can.

It is strange that it became surrounded by stories of black magic in medieval England, where the seed was believed to have to go back to the Devil seven times before the plant would grow and that to transplant it would bring bad luck to the gardener who touched it. It is surprising that anyone bothered to grow parsley!

It is equally hard to imagine the modern kitchen without it. Potatoes without a touch of green parsley, especially in potato salad, would be boring. Creamy sauces can suddenly come alive with some added parsley or a garnish of it on top, and scrambled eggs with a dusting of parsley is an easy and marvellous breakfast combination.

I have never grown or tasted Hamburg parsley but I am told that the long taproot is like a parsnip in size, it is peeled and cooked and you eat it like a vegetable. It has a delicious parsley–celery flavour.

planting

Parsley likes rich soil, plenty of moisture and will grow just about anywhere, although it loves nitrogen so grows well around lemon trees. Semi-shade is best in very hot climates, and if you grow it in full sun be sure to keep it well watered. The common parsley is not quite as hardy as the flat-leaf variety. Grow both the curly parsley for garnishing and adding to almost any dish or sauce, and the flat one for a rich, slightly sweeter taste.

It is rare there is not a parsley plant thriving in my garden, regardless of the time of year, but if you are sowing seed the first time wait until spring or when the ground is becoming warm. Parsley plants should last for a year, then can be cut back quite hard once seed heads form and will crop again, but eventually far fewer green leaves will be produced on the stalks, so you must begin afresh.

When you pick, however, always leave a couple of plants to go to seed so you will have lots of little parsley plants self-seeding in the garden. Parsley takes a while to come through the ground and to hurry the seeds up you can soak seed the night before. If you have bought a packet look at the use-by date and make sure you are using very fresh seeds.

harvesting

Pick often, it encourages the plant to produce more leaves and baby parsley is so much nicer than large tough sprigs.

buying and storage

Because parsley is such a popular herb there is usually no problem with buying really fresh bunches. It should smell sweet and not have leaves which are too large or coarse. The leaves should feel moist, not dry, and be sprightly. The stalks should smell fresh. You can keep parsley in water. Be sure to change the water every day or it becomes stale and will smell disgusting.

I don't bother to dry parsley, as I find there is not a great deal of flavour in dried parsley. However, if you know you can't keep a crop growing all year, home dried is better than commercial dried parsley in the spice jars. Put big branches of parsley on a piece of non-stick baking paper/parchment into a slow oven (150°C/300°F) until it is crisp and then crumble roughly and put into a jar.

small cheese and parsley timbales

parsley goes with

just about anything

potato

all kinds of root vegetables

oil

butter

cheese

beans

meats

garlic

ginger

The timbales will puff up – although not as lightly as a soufflé – and they also have a rich and melting texture which makes this a very good lunch dish or first course. If you serve it in cold weather, some sautéed or oven-baked tomatoes are a good accompaniment; on warmer days, a mixed salad is ideal.

Butter 6 individual moulds or ramekins, each holding about 1 cup/8 fl oz of mixture.

Melt the butter and add flour and fry, stirring for a few minutes until the flour has lightly fried but don't let it colour. Add milk and bring to a boil, stirring constantly. Beat the eggs and yolks together in a bowl. Remove white sauce from the heat and add the eggs, stirring well. Mix in the blue cheese, salt and pepper and Gruyère or melting cheese.

You can prepare the dish in advance to this stage several hours beforehand but don't refrigerate or it will become too firm.

Preheat oven to 180–190°C/350–375°F. Beat the egg whites until stiff and fold them, one third at a time into the mixture along with the parsley. Spoon into the buttered dishes. Bake in oven for about 20 minutes or until you have lightly puffed, golden timbales. Hurry them to the table as they do collapse quickly, like a soufflé.

Serves 6

45 g/1 ½ oz butter

2 tablespoons plain/all-purpose flour

1 cup/8 fl oz milk

2 eggs

2 egg yolks

2 tablespoons blue cheese

salt and pepper

½ cup/2 oz grated Gruyère or a Swiss-style melting cheese

2 egg whites

3 tablespoons chopped parsley

leek and parsley frittata

hint

Baked mushrooms can be dry on the bottom. A good trick is to brush the base of them first with plenty of olive oil. It will soak in but enable them to cook better.

The strong flavour of parsley is balanced by the sweetness of mild leek, and it is given sparkle with some scattered red capsicum on top. Chop the parsley by hand as it will bruise in a food processor. Being an important part of the dish, it should be fine and light, without any moisture.

Heat half the oil in a saucepan then add the leeks and cook very gently, stirring occasionally, until softened. Remove to a bowl and mix with the parsley. Put the diced capsicum/pepper in the same saucepan. There should be sufficient moisture; if not, add a dash more oil. Cook over a medium heat until the capsicum/pepper is wilted, remove to a plate and set aside.

Beat the eggs with salt, pepper and cream and tip into the leek and parsley mixture. Stir well. Heat remaining oil in a heavy-based frying pan. When very hot, add the frittata mixture and turn the heat down immediately. It will sizzle and set on contact with the oil. Cook gently so the frittata is half cooked through before the bottom becomes too brown. Scatter the diced capsicum/pepper on top. When the egg is partly set, transfer pan to the griller/broiler and cook until almost totally firm. Scatter with cheese for the last minute and return to the griller/broiler so that the cheese forms a golden topping.

Serves 6

5 tablespoons virgin olive oil

white section of 2 leeks, finely sliced

½ cup/1 oz finely chopped parsley

1 small red capsicum/bell pepper, cut into tiny dice

4 large eggs

salt and pepper

⅓ cup/3 fl oz cream

¼ cup/1 oz grated Parmesan cheese

eggs baked with buttermilk topping

When I bake eggs in the oven, I always use a little cream on top to keep the yolk moist and runny; the same result can be achieved using buttermilk. This light topping gives an interesting tartness and it is not as rich as cream, while the parsley lends further freshness. A dish you can use for a light lunch or brunch.

Preheat oven to 180°C/350°F.

Dice the bacon and put into a pan. Cook until the fat is transparent and the bacon crisp. Transfer to some kitchen paper towel to drain. Remove the crusts from the bread and cut into tiny cubes. Heat the oil and add the bread, cook until it is golden and crisp. Drain on kitchen paper. Bacon and bread cubes can be prepared in advance. Divide the bacon and bread cubes between 4 small casseroles. Scatter with half the parsley. Break an egg into each casserole and season with some salt and pepper. Spoon a little buttermilk over the top of the egg.

Cook in oven for about 12–15 minutes. The eggs should still have creamy yolks, so watch them carefully. Don't leave them until the yolks become hard or the dish will lose much of its charm. Serve immediately with the rest of the parsley on top.

Variations
Add some finely chopped chives to the bacon and bread, season with a dash of Tabasco for a spicy dish, or fry a clove of garlic in the oil to flavour it lightly (discard garlic).

Serves 4

4 bacon rashers

2 slices bread

2 tablespoons light olive oil

2 tablespoons finely chopped parsley

4 eggs

salt and pepper to taste

4 tablespoons buttermilk

hint

Parsley needs washing, as it can be gritty. Rinse in a bowl of cold water and transfer to some kitchen paper towel, patting it quite dry. Leave out for 10 minutes so it dries more and then remove the sprigs and chop finely with a large, very sharp knife. Never use a food processor unless parsley is part of a mixed and minced herb pesto, as the blades just bruise the leaves. Parsley chopped in advance and left stored, even in the refrigerator, loses most of its fresh flavour; it will smell and taste quite stale very quickly.

fish baked in a coat of almond, herbs and yoghurt

This is an interesting, healthy way of cooking fish; the yoghurt coating and crisp topping give the fish a fresh, sharp flavour. It goes well with steamed baby potatoes and a green salad. The yoghurt won't separate when the fish is cooked as the addition of flour stabilizes it.

Preheat oven to 180°C/350°F. Squeeze a little lemon juice on top of the fish. Line a baking tray with non-stick baking paper/parchment and put fish on it. Mix yoghurt and flour, add spring onions/scallions and spread over the top of the fish. Mix the crumbs with almonds, parsley, basil and oil and pat the crumb topping over the yoghurt. Bake fish for about 12 minutes or until cooked – timing is difficult to give exactly as it depends on the thickness of the fillet.

Have the griller/broiler on and, before serving, grill for a minute or two so the topping becomes golden and crisp.

Serves 2

2 fillets of white fish (blue eye, trevally or snapper)

a little lemon juice

1/3 cup/3 fl oz low-fat natural yoghurt

2 teaspoons plain/all-purpose flour

2 tablespoons finely chopped spring onion/scallion

1/3 cup/1 oz breadcrumbs

2 tablespoons finely chopped toasted almonds

3 tablespoons finely chopped parsley

1 tablespoon shredded basil

1 tablespoon oil

stuffed mushrooms

Stuffed mushrooms bubbling away in the oven with a savoury filling are something you can put on while you sit around and chat, as they are quite forgiving and don't need watching. Use quite large ones, so they will be thick and meaty, and just take out the stalk so there is a central cavity to fill. Little button mushrooms are not much use for a dish such as this and they don't have enough flavour to cope with the stuffing anyway.

Remove the stems from the mushrooms and chop these very finely. Put into a pan with the garlic and olive oil and leave to cook gently until softened. Remove to a bowl; mix in the ham, parsley, pepper and season with chilli. You can prepare to this stage beforehand and leave refrigerated, covered, for about 6 hours.

Preheat oven to 180°C/350°F. Fill mushroom caps with the mixture and flatten gently so it holds a good shape on top. Put into a buttered shallow baking dish. Bake for 12–20 minutes or until the mushrooms are tender. They will shrink a little and give out some juices. Serve as soon as they are cooked with bits of toast or bread so everyone can mop up the juices.

Serves 6 as a first course, 4 as a mushroom lunch

12 large mushrooms

1 clove garlic, finely chopped or crushed

1 tablespoon olive oil

1/2 cup/4 oz finely diced or minced ham

3 tablespoons finely chopped parsley

some pepper

3 slices chilli, finely chopped, or 1 teaspoon chilli sauce

marinated steak with californian sauce

The steak, which is first marinated, is then put into this really simple sauce that you add to the pan after the steak is cooked. The meat ends up with a lingering herb flavour and buttery taste.

Pat the steak dry and put all the remaining ingredients into a shallow glass or china dish. Add the steak and leave 24 hours. Remove but don't pat dry. Heat a pan and cook the steak on one side until well browned. Don't turn it over all the time as you do this as it results in a 'confused' piece of meat. Press down once or twice to make sure it sits on the bottom of the pan. Then turn over and cook again on the second side. It will take a little less time to cook than the first side. Remove and salt, put on a warmed plate with another plate on top.

Discard any fat from the pan. Pour the vermouth and stock into it and stir to get up all the nice caramelized brown bits from the meat. Add the lemon and sugar and cook over a high heat until reduced a little. It should only take a minute or two. Add the butter and parsley and immediately remove from the heat. Stir until the butter has melted. Serve steaks coated with sauce.

Serves 4

4 porterhouse, T-bone or fillet steaks

4 tablespoons olive oil

2 tablespoons lemon juice

2 tablespoons finely chopped parsley

1 teaspoon chopped rosemary

1 teaspoon chopped thyme pepper

Sauce

1/4 cup/2 fl oz vermouth

1/4 cup/2 fl oz chicken stock

2 teaspoons lemon juice

scant teaspoon brown sugar

45 g/1 1/2 oz butter, cut into small pieces

2 tablespoons finely chopped parsley

easy ideas

Prawns with Lemon Parsley

Remove 4 strips of rind from a lemon using a vegetable peeler and simmer in plenty of water until tender (about 10 minutes). Drain and chop finely; mix with 1 clove crushed garlic and 1/3 cup/1/2 oz finely chopped parsley. Heat a little oil in a frying pan, toss 500 g/ 1 lb peeled raw prawns/jumbo shrimp until they have changed colour and are cooked through. Add a big knob of butter, a generous squeeze of lemon juice, scatter over salt, pepper and the lemon parsley mix and shake or stir mixture for 30 seconds before serving.

salad of parsley and fresh herbs

This salad is much easier to assemble if you have a herb garden and can just go out and pick baby bits of all the herbs with abandon. Once you have dressed the salad it must be served immediately but the herbs and lettuce can be kept in a plastic bag in the refrigerator to crisp for about six hours.

When buying parsley for this salad, choose a bunch that is not too large or it will be too coarse in texture and taste. If you don't have a mix of herbs on hand you can just make the recipe as a lettuce and parsley salad. This is a healthy salad and I find it more suitable for eating in small portions rather than larger ones, as the flavours are intense. It is good with a platter of cheese or as a side salad after the main course.

Rinse the herbs and lettuce and pat dry. If the lettuce is large break leaves into pieces. Put everything except flowers into a bowl, toss with the dressing and arrange on small plates. Remove the petals from the nasturtiums and scatter on top.

For dressing, mash the egg finely and mix with the mustard and sugar. Add the oils and lemon juice to taste. You may need more as the tartness of lemon varies considerably. Season with salt and pepper and mix the dressing well. If made in advance, stir again before using.

Serves 4–6

1 ½ cups/1 ½ oz baby sprigs of flat leaf parsley

½ cup/½ oz baby sprigs from curly parsley

18 baby basil leaves

8 small stalks salad burnet

18 chervil leaves

18 baby nasturtium leaves

some sprigs of the inner, pale yellow celery tops

8 baby mignonette lettuce leaves

8 nasturtium flowers, to garnish

Dressing

1 hard-boiled egg

1 teaspoon French mustard

¼ teaspoon sugar

3 tablespoons light olive oil

1 tablespoon walnut oil or extra 1 tablespoon light olive oil

3 teaspoons lemon juice

salt and pepper

parsley pesto

You can make this a day or more in advance, then store refrigerated with a bit of oil poured on top to keep the sparkling bright green colour.

Purée everything together except for the oil, adding it gradually after the first ingredients are a thick paste.

½ cup/½ oz firmly packed parsley sprigs

¼ cup/½ oz pine nuts

2 tablespoons grated Parmesan cheese

2 cloves garlic, chopped

1–2 tablespoons lemon juice

a little black pepper

salt to taste

½ cup/4 fl oz olive oil

parsley and walnut sauce

This recipe is rather like making a pesto, which is then stirred into yoghurt. It's a good sauce for some crispy raw vegetable sticks, for topping over potatoes, spooned on some fish or chicken or used on roasted warm vegetables such as chunks of pumpkin, eggplant or zucchini.

Process everything except yoghurt until a coarsely chopped paste. Stir into yoghurt and check for seasoning.

Makes about I cup/8 fl oz

1 cup/4 oz shelled walnuts or pecan nuts

1 cup/1½ oz flat leaf parsley

1 teaspoon ground cumin

½ teaspoon cinnamon

salt and pepper

2 cloves garlic, finely chopped

½ cup/4 fl oz natural yoghurt

mussels with a green sauce

Even people who are not crazy about mussels seem to love this way of serving them, chilled and fresh tasting from the vinaigrette, which coats each mussel with a bright green sauce. Serve them back in their shell so they can easily be scooped out with a teaspoon.

To cook the mussels heat the wine and water together with the aromatics in a large, wide saucepan and when boiling add the mussels, put a lid on top and leave a minute. Shake pan carefully then uncover and as mussels open remove them. Take half the mussel shell away, leaving the mussel attached to the other section.

To make the sauce, mash the egg with mustard, add all remaining ingredients. Spoon over the mussels. If doing this hours in advance it is easier to remove the mussels from the shells, put them into a bowl, cover with sauce, keep the shells in a plastic bag in the refrigerator and put back into shells when you want to serve.

Serves 6 as a first course

1½ kg/3 lb mussels, well scrubbed and beards removed

¼ cup/2 fl oz water

¼ cup/2 fl oz dry white wine

some slices of onion, parsley stalks and peppercorns

Sauce

1 hard-boiled egg

2 teaspoons French mustard

2 spring onions/scallions, halved and finely chopped

3 tablespoons finely chopped parsley

1 tablespoon finely chopped basil

1 tablespoon finely chopped chives

4 tablespoons olive oil

1 tablespoon lemon juice

1 tablespoon white vinegar

1 tablespoon mayonnaise

salt and dash of cayenne pepper

general herb hint

There are times when it is not possible to find fresh herbs and you must use dried. As these are stronger than fresh, use only a third of the amount specified in the recipe for fresh herbs. Add early in the cooking, so the heat releases their essential oils and aromas.

easy ideas *Parsley Egg Shreds on Smoked Salmon*

Put several slices of smoked salmon on chilled plates, season with pepper, a squeeze of lemon and tiny bits of finely chopped shallot. Whisk with a fork 3 eggs and season, then mix in 3 tablespoons finely chopped parsley and 1 tablespoon water. Heat a little oil in a small frying pan or crepe pan and when very hot pour in enough egg to coat the base thinly. It will set almost immediately. Flip over and cook for a few seconds on the other side. Remove with a spatula to a plate and continue making up all the egg, putting 'crepes' on top of each other. Fold stack over and cut into fine shreds. Scatter over the salmon and serve. This makes enough for 3 plates of salmon.

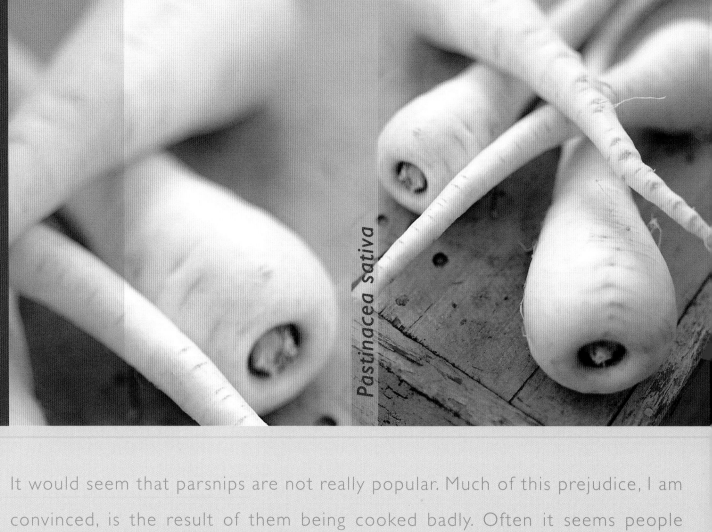

parsnip

Pastinacea sativa

It would seem that parsnips are not really popular. Much of this prejudice, I am convinced, is the result of them being cooked badly. Often it seems people have eaten parsnip prepared so badly they dismiss it from their minds forever. One of the nicest things about parsnips is they are one of the few vegetables which adore winter cold. Parsnips are the sort of comforting, nourishing food we love to eat during the chilly days that nature has dictated they marry with so well, for the sweetness, the best part of parsnips, comes when they have been left in the ground over cold weather. Crisp sausages, big succulent roasts, gently braised meats long simmered in wine and spices, spicy soups and other roasted buttery glazed vegetables baked in the oven.

cheese roulade with root vegetable stuffing (recipe page 244) ▶

planting

Usually grown as annuals, parsnips belong to the same family as carrots, celery and parsley, and have similar needs. Be sure to dig over the soil as any lumps or stones will give you funny-looking, deformed parsnips and the ground should be well drained so the long roots can develop. Soak the seeds before planting to improve germination. Parsnips need space so don't crowd them. Sow seeds about 1 cm/½ in deep in wide rows, 60 cm/2 feet apart and thin once through. Cut these little unwanted seedlings off at ground level rather than pulling them or you will disturb the remaining seedlings and weed carefully by hand until they are well established. They love the cold, needing some at the beginning and end of their growing time, and can even stand freezing temperatures. Give them plenty of water in the beginning, then cut this down when they are almost ready to stop the parsnip roots cracking.

Temperature Zone	Sow
Tropical	Not suitable
Subtropical	Autumn
Temperate	Spring–early autumn
Cool	Spring–late summer
First picking	After frost, about 4 months

diseases and pests

No diseases really but you may get some root maggots and these can be controlled by putting a piece of plastic around each plant, or chemically.

harvesting

Just leave them in until you are ready to eat them. Be sure to wait until you have had a few frosty nights, as low temperatures convert the root starch to sugar.

buying and storage

Choose parsnips that are not too tapered, as the spindly ends are of no use. They should be a beige colour, firm and sweet smelling. Avoid any huge specimens, for these will have woody cores, and bypass those with soft or brown spots. Never wrap in plastic, they sweat. You can keep parsnips in the vegetable container of the refrigerator for about a week.

nutrition

Best asset is their high percentage of fibre and they have some Vitamin E, Vitamin C and folate, with a scatter of other minerals and vitamins.

cooking

Cut off the spindly end and peel parsnips with a vegetable peeler, then trim away the root end. Check you don't have a hard core, if there is one through the centre, you need to cut it out. Slice and simmer in water, stock or cook gently in a little butter first, then cover with chicken stock until tender and drain. The stock can be used again in soups. If you roast them roll in some oil first and put onto non-stick baking paper/parchment as they often stick.

parsnip and carrot pie

If you truly hate parsnip you can just use carrot and some baked or steamed sweet potato for this pie.

Cook parsnip in salted water until tender and drain. Mash well. Mix in the egg, cream and season. While parsnip is cooking put the carrot into a separate saucepan with salted water and cook until tender. Drain well and mix with the mashed parsnip, together with herbs.

Preheat oven to 200°C/400°F. Put one piece of puff pastry onto a lightly floured bench. Put the mixture on top, leaving a rim. Then top with a second square of pastry, pinch the edges together and transfer to a buttered flat baking tray. Brush the top with egg and bake in oven for about 25 minutes or until the pastry is very brown. Leave for a minute before cutting into squares.

Serves 6

3 medium-sized parsnips, peeled and diced

1 egg

¼ cup/2 fl oz cream

salt and pepper

375 g/12 oz carrot, peeled and finely diced

3 tablespoons finely chopped parsley

2 teaspoons fresh thyme leaves

2 teaspoons fresh oregano leaves

2 sheets of puff pastry, about 30 cm/12 in square

1 egg, lightly beaten

parsnip and orange soup

Not a usual combination but very good. The orange gives a sharp, fresh flavour to the soup, which has a light thickness from the puréed parsnip. Even if you are not keen as a rule about parsnips, you will probably enjoy this soup, as the flavour mellows nicely with the combination. The same idea can be used with carrots too. The soup keeps well for several days.

Put the onion into a pan with butter and cook a couple of minutes or until slightly wilted. Add the parsnips and leave them to fry gently in the butter for about 5 minutes, being careful they don't stick. Scatter on the curry and stir until vegetables are coated and the curry smells aromatic. Mix in the orange rind, juice and stock and cook until the parsnips are very tender. Leave to cool a little and transfer to a food processor or blender and process to a purée. Return and heat again, seasoning at this stage if needed and taste. If you wish you can add a dash more orange juice to lift the orange flavour even more. This soup becomes quite thick when stored overnight in the refrigerator, but you can just add more stock to thin the soup down.

Serves 4

1 small onion, finely diced

30 g/1 oz butter

500 g/1 lb parsnips, peeled and sliced thickly

1 teaspoon curry powder

rind and juice of 1 large orange

3 cups/1 1/2 pints light chicken stock or vegetable stock

salt and pepper to taste

parsnip goes with

other root vegetables

onions

butter

oil

milk

cream

orange

lemon

stock

chicken

game

roasted meats

sausages

nutmeg

curry powder

mustard seeds

parsley

beverley's parsnip puff

I first created this as a young bride in the days when nobody I knew would eat parsnips, but with a stack of them in the cupboard and on a tight budget I needed to serve them alongside the meat. It was quite astonishing how the strong flavour changed to one with gentle, soft overtones. Everyone I know loves this dish, even quite dedicated parsnip haters, and it goes particularly well with pork, game, duck, chicken or any kind of roasted meat. Equally good is the way it reheats, so you can prepare hours in advance and cook at dinnertime.

Peel, slice and cook the parsnips in salted water until tender. Put through a moulin or purée. Add the butter while it is still warm and stir through. Mix in cream, nutmeg, egg and season well. Spoon into a buttered, ovenproof dish. Scatter the crumbs on top and dribble melted butter over this. It can be prepared to this stage in the morning.

Preheat oven to 180°C/350°F and bake for about 25 minutes or until very hot and the crumbs are crisp.

Serves 6

4 large or 6 medium-sized parsnips

60 g/2 oz butter

1/3 cup/3 fl oz cream

good pinch of nutmeg

1 large egg

salt and pepper

Topping

1 tablespoon breadcrumbs, made from stale bread

30 g/1 oz melted butter

cheese roulade with root vegetable stuffing

easy ideas

*Curried Apple
and Parsnip*

Cut 2 parsnips
and 1 peeled,
cored apple into
thin slices. Fry a
finely chopped
onion in a little
oil or butter,
add 2 teaspoons
curry powder
and fry a bit,
then toss the
parsnip and
apple slices in
this mixture.
Pour on 1/2 cup/
4 fl oz water,
season, cover
and simmer
gently until the
parsnips are soft
and surrounded
by golden, spicy
liquid. Serve
with chicken,
sausages or pork.

Fluffy and light, the cheese casing is rolled around a soft, buttery mix of root vegetables. There are three parts to this dish but the filling and the roulade coating can be done well in advance.

To make the filling chop up the peeled root vegetables and cook in salted water until tender. Drain and purée. Mix in butter and cream. Season well, add nutmeg if you like this flavouring too.

For coating, cook the onion in oil and butter until soft, remove from pan to a bowl and mix with parsley, crumbs and season. Cool. Scatter over the base of a swiss roll tin which has been lined with some buttered non-stick baking paper/parchment.

For roulade, preheat oven to 190°C/375°F. Melt butter, add flour and fry a minute, add milk and cook, stirring until it comes to a boil. Remove and let cool a little. Add cheeses and egg yolks, then season. Beat egg whites until stiff. Fold through a little at a time and spread evenly into the tin over the onion and crumb base – it will be a thin layer. Bake for about 20 minutes or until firm. Tip out carefully onto more non-stick baking paper/parchment and peel off the base paper. Spread the creamed filling on top. Roll up from the long edge, using the paper as a lever. Let cool.

You can reheat by wrapping whole roll in buttered foil – or slices of roulade brushed with butter – and put onto a sheet of baking paper in a moderate oven for about 8–10 minutes.

Serves 6

1 large carrot

3 small parsnips

1 small sweet potato

30 g/1 oz butter

1/4 cup/2 fl oz cream

salt and pepper

nutmeg (optional)

Roulade Coating

2 tablespoons oil

30 g/1 oz butter

1 onion, finely chopped

2 tablespoons finely
chopped parsley

1/2 cup/1 1/2 oz breadcrumbs,
made from stale bread

salt and pepper

Roulade

45 g/1 1/2 oz butter

1 1/2 tablespoons flour

1 1/2 cups/10 fl oz milk

1/2 cup/2 oz grated tasty/
cheddar cheese

1/3 cup/1 1/2 oz grated
Jarlsburg cheese

2 tablespoons grated
Parmesan cheese

3 eggs, separated

1/2 teaspoon salt and pepper

Pisum sativum

Peas, along with pulses, have a culinary history dating back thousands of years. Peas were a food that could be carried through from one season to the next when fresh produce was not readily available. Traces of early peas have been found in prehistoric lake dwellings at Herzogenbuchsee at Switzerland, well carbon-dated to almost 9750 years before the birth of Christ. These dried pulses were quite large, about the size of a big marble, and archeologists believe they were roasted and peeled before being eaten as the skins were quite hard. Dried peas are still regarded as staple food and eaten during winter months in countries that have learned to serve them with rich casseroles, under meat to give comfort and sustenance or to make soups.

The baby sweet, little green pea once grew wild, rambling through paddocks, and then was cultivated by the Italians in the late sixteenth century, gradually becoming the young peas we now know, and which you should plant. Unless you have a huge property there will rarely be enough to dry, so it is best to buy these in the shops and just enjoy the tiny fresh ones from the garden.

There is a charming story concerning the American President Thomas Jefferson, who had a wonderful garden in Virginia. In his notes he stated that peas were his favourite vegetable. There was some competition among his friends as to who could pick the first crop of peas each year. The winner would host a dinner to which the others were invited, with the baby peas the star of the evening. One year Jefferson's peas were the earliest, but he was a kind and gentle man and he kept this quiet so as not to spoil the pleasure his friends had from being first.

It is sad that many people have forgotten what a beautiful vegetable peas are – shelling appears to be such a deterrent that frozen peas have become the only way to buy them. Most people never consider buying fresh peas. Part of the problem has no doubt come from the many peas sold in the past that were too large, too hard and, when cooked, tough. In such cases all the bother of shelling was certainly wasted. Frozen peas have a taste that is close to fresh peas; they mimic it well, but lack the sweet aftertaste, the flavour and melting texture of the fresh vegetable.

Snow peas and sugar snap peas, which are modern varieties, have largely replaced peas as a fresh vegetable. There is no shelling involved with them, and they can be put into stir fries or eaten as a side vegetable.

I once read that the best way to enjoy young peas from the garden was just to cook them in their pods and serve with a bowl of melted butter for dunking. The peas are dipped into the butter and then sucked out of the shell with much mess and some noise ensuing. Having tried this, I suggest it is a dish best eaten privately – or with a close friend who is equally comfortable with such sticky, drippy, uninhibited eating. It is of course only worth doing if the peas are truly babies and much of the pleasure is in the juice, which is sucked out with the tiny peas. However this at least is one dish which the frozen pea companies can never copy!

planting

Peas don't mind some shade and need good drainage. Work in some fertilizer and remember to keep them well watered. You can never plant enough; it is one of the frustrating things about home-grown peas. They are just so delicious that you can eat about double the amount you would of bought peas. Plant so they can mature before the weather becomes hot, putting seeds about 5 cm/2 in deep and 5 cm/2 in apart in rows that are 45 cm/18 in apart. It is a good idea to have a baby trellis to support the vines as they fall all over the place and get tangled. Be careful when weeding around them, the roots are fragile and it is quite easy to yank one out accidentally. You will get a bigger crop from snow peas and snap peas as a rule than the common pea.

Temperature Zone	Sow
Tropical	Not suitable
Subtropical	Early autumn–mid winter
Temperate	Mid summer–late winter
Cool	Early winter–late spring
First picking	2–4 months, depending on varieties

varieties

Early ones

- Earlicrop
- Early Dwarf
- English Wonder
- Little Wonder
- Melbourne Market.

Mid season

- Giant Stride.

Tall varieties

- Petit pois
- Gulliver
- Yorkshire Hero.

Heirloom varieties

- Greenfeast – dwarf shelling pea
- Purple Podded Dutch – can be eaten fresh or used as a dried pea.

There are also climbing and dwarf snow peas and climbing and dwarf sugar snap peas.

diseases and pests

Birds like them, as do aphids, and anyone who loves peas tends to pick and eat them raw before they ever reach the kitchen. Hose aphids off and be tempted to do the same for anyone who eats the precious crop without asking. They are susceptible to blight, mildew, wilt and rot, but there are disease-resistant varieties available and the joy of your own baby peas are worth all the hassles. Just try not to handle the plants when they are wet to reduce the likelihood of disease. If any plants are affected remove immediately and don't put into your compost.

harvesting

From 44 days for some sugar snap peas to 65-80 days for podded peas, or even longer depending on the variety and warmth.

Pick as long as there is anything on the vine as the more you pick the more they produce. The pods should be filled but not bulging and snow peas should be picked as soon as the white flower drops from the end. Don't pick peas in the middle of the day, leave until later so you can pick near dinnertime and they will be incredibly sweet and tender.

Pea shoots are the growing tips of the plant and Cantonese cooks prize these. If you want to try them you need to pick the ends when the plants are young, plucking off the growing tips, but will lose many pods.

buying and storage

Taste one if you can, that way you will know by the sweetness how old the peas are and how tender they will be when cooked, as the sugar in peas turns to starch quickly after picking. Any dried-out wrinkly pods will contain peas that will echo the pod and be tough and wrinkled when cooked. Pods should be bright green and waxy to touch, full but not bulging, which would indicate peas left too long on the vine.

Snap peas should be crisp to feel, shiny and never have big developed peas inside; nor should snow peas.

Store in the refrigerator in a vegetable bag but use as quickly as you can. Snow and snap peas keep longer than peas in the pod, but for no more than 48 hours.

As you often need to know how many peas you need to buy, judge that in shelling you lose a little more than half the weight so 500 g/1 lb bought peas will barely be 250 g/8 oz when shelled.

nutrition

Peas provide lots of fibre in the diet, as well as iron, carbohydrate, Vitamin C, folate, thiamin and protein, and are among the top vegetables for nutrition. Snow peas have more Vitamin C and less fibre than podded peas, while snap peas have about half the nutritional value of green peas and snow peas.

cooking

Green peas

Shell them close to cooking and keep a few pods to flavour the water. Bring some lightly salted water to a boil, add a teaspoon of sugar and sprig of mint and when bubbling add the peas. Cook with the pan covered until tender, 5 minutes for home-grown peas, longer for most bought peas. Drain and add a knob of butter and pinch of pepper and shake so they are shiny and coated.

Snow peas or snap peas

Snap the stem end and pull the string downwards, then snap the other end and pull away the string, as this is unpleasant to eat, especially if they are large peas. Cook with a little oil quickly in a pan, tossing, then add a few spoonfuls of water to create steam and cook until crisp tender and bright green.

You can boil them for a few minutes if you prefer, then drain well and add a dash of oil or butter.

snow pea soup

The flavour of this is more delicate than pea soup. It is served with a fragrant ginger cream on top and makes a lovely first course before something rich, as the ginger acts as a digestive. As the soup uses a lot of snow peas I suggest you mainly prepare it when they are not too expensive.

String the snow peas and pinch away the ends. Heat the butter and cook the onion gently in a large saucepan until it is soft and pale gold. Add the peas and stock, bring to a boil, cover and cook gently about 15 minutes or until they are very soft. Process.

Grate the ginger and using a clean damp hand squeeze hard over a small bowl to get as much juice as possible from the pulp – you should get about 1½ tablespoons. Mix this into the cream.

Serve the soup in small bowls, trickle a bit of ginger cream on top and marble it using the handle of a fork.

Serves 4

750 g/1½ lb snow peas
45 g/1½ oz butter
1 large onion, finely chopped
4 cups/2 pints light chicken or vegetable stock
piece of fresh ginger about 5 cm/2 in long
½ cup/4 fl oz cream

peas go with

butter
oil
Parmesan cheese
onion
lettuce
chervil
mint
parsley
cream
rice
ham and bacon
lamb
prawns
eggs

pea soup with a fine dice of vegetables

The peas are puréed to make a soft green mixture that has finely diced vegetables throughout. The dish is sweet and flavoursome with a pretty, sap-green colour. As it is quite delicate it is important to chop the vegetables by hand into tiny pieces so they are like little bits of coloured confetti.

Shell the peas and put them and half a dozen pods into a saucepan. Add the stock and simmer gently until quite tender. Drain, take out the pods, keep the liquid aside and purée the peas in a food processor with about ½ cup/ 4 fl oz of the liquid (the rest is used to cook vegetables). Put the bacon into a pan, cover with cold water and bring to a boil. Drain, pat dry and cut into fine dice. Heat the oil in a pan. Sauté the vegetables and bacon until wilted, cover and cook until tender. Add the chicken stock in which the peas were cooked and the herbs tied together with string and simmer for about 10 minutes. Remove the herbs. Mix the cornflour with the milk and add to the liquid. Stir until it comes to a boil, then mix in the bowl of reserved pea purée and check seasoning.

Serves 6

1 kg/2 lb fresh peas in the pod
6 cups/3 pints chicken stock
3 rashers bacon
2 tablespoons light olive oil
1 medium-sized carrot, finely diced
1 small onion, finely diced
1 leek, thinly sliced
sprig of thyme
1 bay leaf
several stalks of parsley
1 tablespoon cornflour/cornstarch
½ cup/4 fl oz milk or cream
salt and pepper

miniature sandwiches of salmon and peas

easy ideas

Pasta and Peas

Cook a cup of
baby peas and
separately cook
about 100 g/
3 oz macaroni.
Drain the peas but
reserve about 1/4
cup/
2 fl oz of the water.
Fry several rashers
of bacon cut into
strips and add the
peas to the pan,
plus their water
along with 1/2 cup/
4 fl oz cream.
Boil madly for
a minute, toss
through pasta with
plenty of grated
Parmesan.

Peas produce a pretty, pale-green, pastel sandwich filling with small pieces of pink salmon studded throughout. This is best made at least an hour before serving and can be kept for 6 hours, refrigerated. Leave the sandwiches whole for storing, then cut into dainty strips and arrange on a bed of cress or some grape leaves for lunch.

Purée the peas. It is easiest when they are first cooked and still warm and wet. Drain the salmon, take out any bits of bone and keep the liquid – if the mixture is too dry you can add some of this to moisten later. Mash the salmon well with a fork, season with salt and pepper and lemon juice. Add spring onion/scallion, the pea purée, mayonnaise and taste. It should be fresh and light; add a little more lemon if you wish.

Remove the crusts from the bread and butter lightly. Spread half of them thickly with the filling and top with remaining bread. Wrap in plastic wrap and refrigerate. To serve, cut across the centre into halves and then cut into strips.

Makes 24 small sandwiches

3/4 cup/3 oz fresh peas,
cooked until tender

1 x 100 g/3 1/2 oz can red salmon

salt and pepper

2 teaspoons (or more)
lemon juice

1 tablespoon finely chopped
spring onion/scallion

1 tablespoon mayonnaise

6 slices brown bread

butter or margarine

potage paul

I have no idea where the name for this soup came from but when I was a young bride and first began giving the elaborate dinner parties fashionable in those days I used to serve Potage Paul as the first course. It is quite delicate and makes a beautiful starter before just about any kind of meat. Make it in advance and keep for a day if you wish, as the flavour stays very fresh for 24 hours. Serve it plain or with some sippets or croutons – tiny cubes of bread fried until they are golden and crisp in olive oil.

Melt the butter in a saucepan and sauté onion, garlic, lettuce and parsley until the onion has become a little limp. Add curry powder and fry briefly. Add stock and peas and bring to a boil, cover and simmer gently for about 25–30 minutes. Purée the mixture in a blender or put through a moulin, then return to pan.

Mix the cornflour with water and add to soup, heat and stir until it comes to the boil and thickens. Last, add the cream and taste. You may need to adjust the seasonings, this will depend on the stock.

Serves 4, generously

30 g/1 oz butter

1 white onion, finely chopped

1 clove garlic, finely chopped

3 large lettuce leaves, shredded

2 tablespoons finely
chopped parsley

1/2 teaspoon curry powder

4 cups/2 pints chicken stock

1 1/2 cups/7 oz shelled fresh peas

2 teaspoons cornflour/cornstarch

1 tablespoon water

1/2 cup/4 fl oz cream

salt and pepper to taste

indian rice with peas, cauliflower and cumin

As in most Indian dishes, the peas and cauliflower are well cooked when served. Crunchy vegetables do not seem to create the right balance if served with fragrant rice, so if you only have a few precious peas growing you could buy peas for a spicy dish like this.

Shell the peas and keep several of the small pea pods. Cut or break the cauliflower into flowerets and rinse. Drain on kitchen paper towel. Pour a 2-cm/³⁄₄ in layer of oil into a saucepan and fry the cauliflower in small batches over moderate heat until it is lightly coloured and becoming soft. Remove and drain on kitchen paper towel. Season with salt and pepper.

Discard most of the oil, leaving about 1¹⁄₂ tablespoons in the pan. Fry the cumin seeds until they are fragrant – about 8 seconds. Add the rice and stir until some of the grains become opaque. Pour in the vegetable stock or water and bring to a boil. Add the peas and some pods, plus the sugar, place a lid on the pan (it must be very tight fitting, otherwise put foil over the top first) and cook over low heat for 20 minutes.

Lift the lid and lay the cauliflower on top of the rice. Cover again and cook for a further 7 minutes. Turn the heat off, pull the pan aside and leave to rest for 5 minutes. When you serve this, carefully remove the cauliflower first and pile into a dish with the rice around it.

Serves 4

500 g/1 lb fresh peas in the pod

¹⁄₂ medium-sized cauliflower

some oil

salt and freshly ground pepper

1 teaspoon cumin seeds

2 cups/1 lb long grain, fragrant rice such as basmati

4 cups/2 pints vegetable stock or water

¹⁄₂ teaspoon sugar

easy ideas

Pea and Ham Sandwich

Cook 1 cup/8 oz peas in salted boiling water until tender and drain. Process to a purée and add salt, pepper and about 1 tablespoon of mayonnaise, or enough to make a spreadable mix. Put a thin slice of ham on buttered brown bread, top with pea purée and then put another slice of buttered bread on top. Press down gently, trim crusts away and cut into fingers.

peas with rice

This is really a simple, pilaf-style dish that contains young peas in almost equal proportion to rice – they lend it sweetness and colour. You can serve this on its own, or spoon a layer under some lamb fillets or pieces of chicken. I like to use fragrant rice such as basmati or jasmine, which has a delicate texture, in this recipe.

Cook onion in oil until it has softened. Add rice and stir until some rice grains become opaque and then tip stock in all at once. Bring to a boil, add peas, pea pods, sugar and mint and cover pan. Cook over low heat for 20 minutes and then remove from heat and rest for 5 minutes before removing lid, so the rice steams. Add butter and cheese and using 2 forks lift the rice so it all becomes mixed together without becoming sticky. You can discard pods if they are not really tender but they are rather nice to eat if they are baby ones.

Serves 4

1 small onion, finely chopped

3 tablespoons oil

1 cup/6¹⁄₂ oz long-grain rice

2¹⁄₂ cups/generous pint chicken or vegetable stock

500 g/1 lb peas, shelled, reserving 6 small pods

¹⁄₂ teaspoon sugar

1 sprig mint

30 g/1 oz butter

¹⁄₄ cup/1 oz grated Parmesan cheese

pea soufflé

Reserve this soufflé for a time when peas are young and sweet, spring has given you masses of exquisite peas and you know you have a few friends worthy of sharing in this silky, puffy, pastel-green soufflé. Buy, or pick, at least 500 g/1 lb peas, you will end up with about half this weight when shelled, which is enough for the soufflé.

It only makes enough for four people, and forget about serving anything else with it as it should be eaten on its own – with perhaps a little jug of melted butter.

Rinse the peas. Melt butter in a saucepan; add the onion and lettuce and cook stirring occasionally until the vegetables have softened. Add the peas, water, sugar and salt. Bring to the boil and cook until the peas are very tender. Drain peas. Put into a blender or a moulin and purée: you need 1–1¼ cups/8–10 fl oz of pea purée. Reserve any extra for later use.

Melt additional butter, add the flour and cook until it is foaming. Pour in the milk, add the pea purée and cook until very thick, stirring occasionally. Remove from heat and let cool for 5 minutes. Add the egg yolks one at a time and mix well. The soufflé can be prepared to this stage several hours in advance as long as you stir well before adding the whites to lighten the mixture. Don't refrigerate it at any stage.

Preheat oven to 180°C/350°F. Beat the egg whites until they hold stiff peaks and fold a third into the pea mixture, then fold in the remainder. Pour into a well-buttered, 5-cup/2½ pint soufflé dish. Bake for about 25–30 minutes or until it is puffed and set to touch on top.

Serves 4

500 g/1 lb fresh peas
in the pod, shelled

45 g/1½ oz butter

1 large white onion, finely diced

12 lettuce leaves, shredded finely

1 cup/8 fl oz water

2 teaspoons sugar

1 teaspoon salt

extra 30 g/1 oz butter

1 tablespoon flour

¼ cup/2 fl oz milk

3 egg yolks

4 egg whites

pasta with lamb and pea sauce

Save some of the pea pods to cook with the lamb, to give added sweetness to the rich brown gravy, although if they are not tender baby pods remove them just before serving. This pasta dish is not usually served with Parmesan cheese on top but you may like to serve a little dish of cheese on the table. It makes enough for 500 g/1 lb pasta. If you choose a pasta like a shell it will collect the sauce in its rounded cavities.

Heat the oil and fry the onion until it is soft and golden. Add the garlic and fry for 30 seconds. Add the lamb, turn up the heat and continue frying until the mince is well browned and quite fine. Add the water, lemon rind, salt, pepper, parsley and mint. Stir through tomato paste and cover the pan. Cook over low heat for about an hour or until tender and you have a good rich sauce. If the lid of the pot is not tight fitting you may need to add some extra water before adding the peas. Mix in the peas, cover and cook for about 15 minutes if fresh (less if frozen).

When the sauce is nearly ready, cook the shell pasta until just tender. Drain and carefully toss the sauce through, making sure it collects in the cavity of the shells. Serve immediately.

Serves 4–6

1/4 cup/2 fl oz virgin olive oil

2 onions, roughly chopped

2 cloves garlic, roughly chopped

750 g/1 1/2 lb very finely minced lean lamb

1 cup/8 fl oz water

2 strips of lemon rind

1 teaspoon salt

plenty of ground black pepper

1/4 cup/1/2 oz finely chopped parsley

1 tablespoon chopped fresh mint

1 tablespoon tomato paste

1 cup/5 oz shelled fresh peas

shell pasta

eggs and bacon tart jazzed up with peas

The best kind of tart imaginable for a brunch, it has the comforting taste of eggs and bacon with rich creamy cheese custard over the top. Although the amount of peas used is only small, it livens up the dish and stops it tasting too creamy.

Preheat oven to 210°C/400°F. Roll out the pastry a little on a floured board and use to line a big oval dish about 23 cm/9 in diameter or a square shallow casserole. Prick the pastry lightly. Put some paper on top, fill with beans and bake in oven until set, then remove the paper and cook a little longer until lightly coloured.

Cook the bacon in half the butter until crisp. Cook the peas in salted water until tender and drain. Cook the onions in the rest of the butter until softened, put a lid on top and continue to cook until very tender. Mix bacon with peas and onions. Put the mixture into the puff pastry shell. Break 8 eggs over the top of the mixture. Season the dish. Beat the 2 remaining eggs with half the cheese and all the cream, season this lightly and pour over the top. Top with remaining cheese and bake in a moderate oven until the filling has set. The time will vary according to the sort of dish you use but begin checking on it after about 25 minutes. Let it cool for 10 minutes so the custard settles and then cut into big fat wedges.

Serves 6

some butter puff pastry

200 g/7 oz bacon, cut into strips

60 g/2 oz butter

3/4 cup/3 oz peas

2 onions, halved and thinly sliced

10 eggs

salt and pepper

1/2 cup/2 oz grated tasty/cheddar cheese

1/4 cup/1 oz grated Parmesan cheese

1/4 cup/2 fl oz cream

sicilienne pea and prawn salad

Rather than being a starter for a dinner I like to serve this salad as a main dish. You can add a few more prawns if you think this amount is mean. Although called a 'salad', don't think you can prepare this hours in advance and serve later in the day, as the exquisite flavours are due to the freshness of prawns, the peas straight from the pan and the whole combined with warm juices stirred into a bright green parsley pesto. There is only a minor amount of pasta in the dish, just enough to provide a starchy, more substantial background to the peas.

Heat the water with salt, fennel, garlic and oil. Shell prawns. Cut into the back of each, remove the vein and cut it further so it is quite open, flatten slightly. Cook the prawns for about a minute in the water and remove when they have gracefully curled. Heat the olive oil in a pan and fry the onion and garlic until golden. Add the peas, 1 cup/8 fl oz water, season with sugar and cook until the peas are tender with a lid partly tilted over the top. Remove the peas and drain but keep the liquid.

Meanwhile cook the pasta and drain. Mix the peas with prawns, pasta and pesto while warm, adding a little pea liquid so it is not too thick, and stir. Season very well with pepper. If serving as a cold salad you may need to add a little more liquid later as it should be moist and the pasta tends to soak up the liquid as it stands.

Serves 4

2 cups/1 pint water

1 teaspoon salt

1 teaspoon fennel seeds

1 clove garlic, roughly chopped

1 tablespoon oil

16 green prawns

2 tablespoons olive oil

1 large onion, finely chopped

1 large clove garlic, finely chopped

1½ cups/7 oz fresh baby peas

1 teaspoon sugar

100 g/3 oz fine pasta such as spaghetti broken into pieces or baby macaroni

½ cup Parsley Pesto (see page 238)

easy ideas

Peas in Minted Cream

Cook about 500 g/1 lb shelled peas with 1 diced onion in salted water until tender and drain. Return to pot and add ⅓ cup/3 fl oz cream, and pinch of sugar and 1 tablespoon chopped mint. Boil for a minute. Serve with lamb or chicken.

potato

Solanum tuberosum

The little waiter in the restaurant in Dublin where I was dining informed me that the steak order would come with three vegetables. It did. Mashed potato, fried potato and potato salad and I didn't really mind very much at all. I sometimes think that I am just as infatuated by potatoes as the Irish are. Potatoes are indispensable in our lives now and much loved by almost everyone but it took hundreds of years before they became popular in Europe. This plant belongs to the deadly nightshade family – other members being the tomato, capsicum pepper and eggplant – and was regarded with suspicion. While the flower was admired, the tuber was never eaten. It was assumed there was something sinful about the potato and so pious people regarded them as sexy. In Boston in the nineteenth century, an American minister stated the potato was the reason for moral decay among the residents of the city. Because it required so little preparation to serve a potato dish, it led to wantonness among housewives as they had far too little to do with their spare time.

Potatoes grew in temperate regions along the Andes for thousands of years and the pre-Columbian culture there cultivated hundreds of varieties. Jimenez de Quesada brought them from Peru to Spain and then Sir Frances Drake carried them to England and gave Queen Elizabeth I a plant. She was not impressed with the potato because the cook let it grow, then discarded the potato tubers and stewed up the leaves.

Potato aromatic with garlic, fragrant with sprigs of rosemary or thyme, with crunchy brown skins or soft fragile papery ones, potatoes made into crispy, flat latkes or soft fluffy, buttery mash to mop up a sauce ... each has a different texture and taste. It is impossible to become bored with potatoes and the renewed interest in growing a wide range of varieties has given us many types to choose from.

You need to become conversant not just with the names but their uses and then decide what kind you will grow or buy. Baby potatoes, which are newly dug, will be waxy and their fragile papery skin, which should rub away easily, is the best indication of their youth. They are sugary and can be used for salads, or boiled and tossed with butter and herbs or sliced into casseroles. They are no good for mashing as they are low in starch. For baking and mashing, or making lovely crisp chips, you need potatoes

that are high in starch and low in sugar. These are termed floury potatoes. They cook to a lovely fluffy texture or bake with a good crust. Quite often tiny potatoes are sold in shops and although they look like new ones they are not and may not be suitable for salads; conversely, some big potatoes just dug from the ground in season have thin skins and could be.

Although it can be a little muddling to choose the right variety, there is much more emphasis on correct labelling now and more knowledgeable greengrocers take an interest in the subject, so just ask if you need potatoes for a specific reason. Potatoes such as Pontiac fulfil many uses, and depending on the season you can usually either bake them or cook for potato salad and I call these 'all-purpose' potatoes.

planting

Don't just put some potatoes into the ground unless they have been sold as seed potatoes, as potato from the market or greengrocer has often been chemically treated. You should buy certified disease-free potatoes. Most nurseries sell some types, usually not a big range but enough for most gardens. Once you have some in they generally just keep coming up constantly. Even when you dig them out a few little tiny potatoes will remain to shoot again. I see little reason to allow most of them to grow to a large size, as it is the sweet earthy taste of baby potatoes picked and cooked that day which is so exquisite.

Potatoes will just about grow anywhere in well-drained, fertile soil and like some lime. Put them in full sun, planting about 10 cm/4 in deep and 40 cm/15 in apart. Then keep them

well mulched and keep heaping up the soil so the potatoes near the surface of the ground don't turn green. New potatoes will form right along and up the stem. Keep fertilized as they are growing, usually once they are well through the ground.

Potatoes are ideal for no-dig gardens and I have seen them growing in old tyres, on and under mulch and straw; this is fun for children to watch and they love harvesting them.

Temperature Zone	Plant
Need a frost-free growing time of about 4–5 months	
Tropical	Late summer–early spring
Subtropical	Mid summer–early spring
Temperate	Winter–early spring
Cool	Early spring–early summer
First picking	*Depends on variety and area, about 4–5 months*

varieties

There are many and these are not always the ones sold in the shops.

Early crop

- Cliff's Kidney
- Arran Pilot
- Kipfler
- Epicure.

Later varieties

- Sutton's Supreme
- Sebago
- Sequoia
- Rua
- Katahdin
- Pontiac.

diseases and pests

Potatoes do have a few problems: aphids, slugs, snails, wireworms and tubermoth caterpillars. You really need to spray if you get any of these but in a very healthy garden the incidence is very low.

harvesting

From 6 weeks to 5 months from planting, depending on the time of year and variety. Watch for the potato to bloom and then you can dig them up, but if it doesn't flower some yellowing leaves indicate that the potatoes should be dug. During the growing season you can steal a few without the plant being aware. Gently put your hand into the mulch around the potato and take out a few, leaving the plant to keep growing. If using a spade for digging up the whole plant be careful you don't put it through the centre of the tubers; I find a fork is best for loosening the soil around potatoes. As the skin will be very fragile try not to damage it. I leave some dirt on the potatoes after I've dug them, just loosening it, but don't wash until you need to cook them, as potatoes keep much better with the natural soil around them.

buying and storage

Try to get unwashed potatoes, they keep better than washed, and avoid any that are sprouting or have any green bits, an indication the potato contains quantities of the toxin solanine which can cause illness. I never buy potatoes in plastic bags, as they sweat and deteriorate quickly. Store in a dark, well-ventilated cupboard. Little new waxy potatoes are best eaten within the week; older mature ones can be stored for a couple of weeks.

nutrition

Potatoes supply small amounts of potassium, thiamin and folate and large amount of Vitamin C and dietary fibre, with waxy potatoes having higher levels than floury ones.

cooking

Scrub them if they are new and tiny, peel if older, but a good part of their nutrients lies in the skin. Steam or boil baby potatoes; if boiling large ones you are often best to cut them into a pieces of similar size so they cook at the same time. Once tender, drain quickly and never leave them sitting in the water or they become quite waterlogged.

If you want to mash potato, do it by hand as a food processor gives a gluey result. You can put them through a moulin or mash well, and then beat in some butter so it melts into the warm potato and finally fluff by mixing in hot milk using a fork or wooden spoon. Cold milk makes the potato stiffen. I like them very soft and light, but some people prefer a stiffer mixture, it is just a matter of personal taste.

There are plenty of other ways to cook them: roasting, baking in foil packages, sautéing in a pan, adding to casseroles ... If you have any potato left over you can cut into pieces and sauté them in some olive oil until they are crusty and golden.

prosciutto, onion and cheese-filled potatoes

Scrub a large floury potato per person and rub with a little oil. Pierce each one with a fine skewer and bake in a moderate oven (180°C/350°F) for about an hour or until they are quite soft. Cut open the top and take out a spoonful of potato and then top with this rich mixture. You can return them to the oven for a few minutes before serving. It makes ample for 4 large or 6 medium-sized potatoes.

Fry the prosciutto in a dry pan until you have some moisture – it will smell very aromatic. Remove and cook the onion, covered, in the pan until soft. Mix with the prosciutto. Stir in the cheese, add cream and mix well. The onion should be warm rather than very hot or it will melt the cream. Prepare the filling hours in advance if it makes it easier.

Serves 4–6

6 thin slices prosciutto, finely shredded

1 large onion, finely diced

1/4 cup/1 oz grated Parmesan cheese

1/4 cup/2 fl oz light sour cream

grated potato bake

This potato dish goes well with roasted chicken, with steak or lamb chops, or in fact just about any kind of meat. The mixture sets nicely so you can cut thick wedges. Or think of it when you want something instead of a frittata for a light lunch on a weekend, served with a tossed green salad and cherry tomatoes.

Preheat oven to 180°C/350°F. Heat the oil with butter in a small saucepan and fry the onion until soft and golden. Add the bacon and garlic and fry for about 3 minutes. Transfer to a large basin and mix in the herbs. Grate the potato over the top, add the eggs, cream and cheddar cheese, season well with salt and pepper and mix everything with a fork. Grease the base of a shallow ovenproof casserole dish, about 22 cm/8½ in diameter and about 5 cm/2 in deep. Pour in the mixture and level the top. Bake in oven for about 45 minutes, or until golden and cooked through. Timing will depend on the starchiness of the potato. Test with a skewer. Mix the Parmesan cheese with the breadcrumbs and scatter on top, then scatter over the olives and return to the oven for a further 10 minutes. Remove and let it settle for 5 minutes before cutting into slices.

Serves 6

2 tablespoons olive oil

30 g/1 oz butter

1 large onion, finely chopped

2 rashers bacon, cut into strips

2 cloves garlic, finely chopped

2 tablespoons finely chopped parsley

1 teaspoon finely chopped fresh thyme

1 teaspoon finely chopped fresh marjoram

500 g/1 lb all-purpose potatoes, peeled

3 eggs

1/3 cup/3 fl oz cream

1/2 cup/2 oz grated tasty/cheddar cheese

1 teaspoon salt

1/2 teaspoon black or white pepper

2 tablespoons grated Parmesan cheese

2 tablespoons breadcrumbs, made from stale bread

1/4 cup/2 oz finely chopped black olives

potato goes with

So many foods it is hard to keep to any kind of a list

olive oil

butter

garlic

ginger

chilli

cheese

cream

milk

yoghurt

ricotta

mayonnaise

spinach and silverbeet

other root vegetables

pastry

fish

bacon and ham

sausages

just about all meats and poultry

stocks

curry

saffron

most herbs

eggs

potato and herb stuffing

Potatoes are often used in stuffing for poultry which is fatty or rich, so the stuffing absorbs the fat. No need to wait for that, this stuffing is very good in turkey or chicken, being served instead of a potato accompaniment. The amount below is enough for one turkey of 3–4 kg/6½–9 lb in size or two chickens. Make half the quality if you only have one chicken, or cook the rest in a buttered casserole in the oven with the bird, covering the top of the stuffing firmly with some buttered foil. If cooked in a casserole it only takes about 25 minutes and is served spooned alongside the carved meat.

Peel and cut the potatoes into 2-cm/¾ in cubes and cover with water. Season with salt and cook gently for 8–10 minutes or until just tender. Drain and place in a large bowl.

Melt the butter and cook onions and celery until softened. Place in the bowl with the potatoes, add crumbs, parsley, salt, pepper, orange rind, sage and eggs. Mix gently but thoroughly. Pack firmly into the poultry and roast as usual.

750 g/1½ lb all-purpose potatoes

60 g/2 oz butter

2 large onions, finely chopped

2 stalks celery, finely sliced

1 cup/3 oz breadcrumbs, made from stale bread

½ cup/1 oz finely chopped parsley

1 teaspoon salt and plenty of black pepper

rind of 2 oranges

1 tablespoon chopped sage leaves

1 large egg

1 egg white

a soufflé of root vegetables

This not a light airy soufflé, but is quite substantial with its base of potato, parsnip and carrot. I like it best served with some kind of a sauce, for example a mushroom sauce or one based on herbs. A creamy white sauce flavoured with some cheese, such as Parmesan, would also be suitable. Serve as a main course, accompanied by a salad.

Butter six individual 1 cup/8 fl oz soufflé dishes, or a large soufflé dish with a 6–7 cup/2½–3 pint capacity and preheat oven to 180°C/350°F. Peel and slice or dice the potatoes, parsnips and carrots. Cook them in salted water until tender and drain. Purée in a food processor and transfer to a basin. While they are still warm, mix in the garlic, salt and pepper. Add the cream and mix well. Add the yolks one at a time, beating well. Beat the whites until they hold stiff peaks. Reserve a tablespoon of cheese, which will be scattered on top, and then gently fold the egg whites and the rest of the cheese into the cream mixture.

Spoon into the moulds or large soufflé dish and scatter with the reserved cheese. Bake for 20 minutes in oven for small moulds, or 30 minutes for a large soufflé. It is important not to overcook this soufflé or it can be dry. The outside edge should be golden and firm to the touch, the inside slightly soft.

Serves 4–6

250 g/8 oz floury or all-purpose potatoes

250 g/8 oz parsnips

250 g/8 oz carrots

1 large clove garlic, finely chopped

½ teaspoon salt or to taste

½ teaspoon white pepper

⅓ cup/3 fl oz cream

4 egg yolks

6 egg whites

½ cup/2 oz grated Parmesan cheese

potato patties with peanut sauce

The potato patties are light and melting, the peanut sauce is spicy and hot, and they make a great combination as a light meal accompanied by a big bowl of salad.

Melt the butter and add the onion, cook gently until it is wilted and then turn up the heat and cook until there are some brown specks on the onion. Put in a basin. Put the potatoes through a moulin or mash well and season with salt and pepper. Stir in the onion and chill for an hour.

Take small handfuls and form into balls, then flatten them down into patties about 7.5 cm/3 in across. If the potato sticks to your hands, dampen the palms lightly. Chill again until ready to cook.

For the peanut sauce, heat the peanut oil in a frying pan and cook the raw peanuts until they are golden. Drain and grind finely in a blender or food processor. Heat the oil again and add the chilli. Cook until it is puffed, turning it over. When crisp, remove and cool. Crumble it finely. Add the garlic and onion to the same pan and cook until golden. Mix in the nuts, shrimp paste, brown sugar, lemon juice, salt, the crumbled chilli and water. If the pan is not large enough, you can transfer it to a saucepan. Cook until lightly thickened. Add coconut cream or coconut milk and simmer gently for about 5 minutes. If too thick, thin with a little water. The sauce keeps well for about 3 days, refrigerated. Warm it again before serving.

To finish the dish, heat a little oil in a frying pan. Add the potato patties and cook over medium heat until golden brown on one side. Turn over carefully and cook on the second side. Transfer to a plate and spoon a little warm peanut sauce on top of each. Or serve them on a large platter with a jug of peanut sauce on the table.

Makes 12 patties

45 g/1 ½ oz butter

1 onion, finely diced

3 large all-purpose potatoes, peeled and cooked

salt and pepper

some oil for frying

Peanut Sauce

2 tablespoons peanut oil

125 g/4 oz raw peanuts

1 small dried red chilli

2 cloves garlic, finely sliced

1 onion, finely chopped

1 teaspoon shrimp paste (blachan/belacan)

1 tablespoon brown sugar

2 tablespoons lemon juice

½ teaspoon salt, or to taste

1 cup/8 fl oz water

½ cup/4 fl oz coconut cream or coconut milk

hints

For an interesting coating on a baked potato rinse it first and rub some coarse kitchen salt all over the outside with your hands. It will stick to the damp skin, leave on only a fine coating and bake in a moderately hot oven (200°C/ 400°F). It will crisp nicely and have a crunchy, salty crust.

tuscan-style potatoes

I am not sure why these are called Tuscan potatoes as I have rarely eaten sour cream in Tuscany – perhaps it is the tomato paste mixture. These potatoes are tasty and look interesting and a bit of rosemary could be substituted for parsley if you served them with roast lamb.

Wash the potatoes and prick the skins. Rub a little butter or margarine on the skin. Bake at 200°C for about 1 hour. The skins will be crisp, the potato tender. While they are cooking mix the sour cream and tomato paste together. When the potatoes are ready, cut a cross on the top of each one and open out gently by squeezing at the base on both sides.

Fill opening and spoon sour cream mixture over the top and scatter with parsley. There will be generous amounts of topping, even for large potatoes.

Serves 4

4 medium waxy potatoes

½ cup/4 fl oz sour cream

2 tablespoons tomato paste

1 tablespoon finely chopped parsley

cornish pasties

easy ideas

Potato Goulash

Once eaten by poor people who could not afford the meat included in a traditional goulash, this goes with grilled meats or chicken. Cut 4 large potatoes into bite-sized pieces; cut an onion into half-rings and fry in plenty of oil mixed with a tiny piece of butter in a saucepan. When the onion is golden scatter on a table-spoon of sweet – not hot – paprika, stir then add the potatoes and enough chicken stock or water to just come to the top of them. Salt and simmer gently for about 20 minutes or until tender. The water will cook away a bit but the potatoes should have a little juice around them at the finish.

This is a vegetarian version of the lamb Cornish pasty. It is traditional to put some turnip and swede in these but if you loathe those vegetables then of course just omit and add another potato. Be sure to season quite heavily with salt and pepper as the vegetables absorb lots. The pasties reheat very well and beg to be served with a bowl of some spicy homemade relish.

Put all the vegetables into a bowl with plenty of salt, pepper and herbs. Stir until very well mixed. Don't leave too long at this stage or the diced vegetables will discolour. Butter a couple of oven trays well and preheat oven to 180°C/350°F.

If using ready rolled pastry, you can roll a little more on a floured bench to give a thinner case or roll out homemade thinly. Cut out rounds using a dinner plate as a guideline to size. Put vegetables on one side of each circle. Dot the vegetables with a few tiny pieces of butter. Dampen the edges and fold over to enclose, making a half-moon shape. Turn the edges of the pasty over to achieve the rope-like effect, which is the traditional seal.

This results in a flat pasty but, if preferred, the filling can be placed down the centre and the sides brought up to make a high pasty with a ridge across the middle. Transfer to a baking tin and brush the top well with some egg. Put two small cuts on top. When pasties are all prepared, bake in a oven for 25–30 minutes or until the pastry is well coloured and the vegetables are soft. There is nothing worse than a pasty which has vegetables a bit undercooked inside.

Makes 6 pasties

1 large onion, finely chopped

1 large carrot, peeled and finely diced

1 small turnip, peeled and finely chopped

125 g/4 oz swede, peeled and finely chopped

4 large waxy potatoes, about 750 g/1½ lb, peeled and finely chopped

plenty of salt and pepper

¼ cup/½ oz chopped parsley

2 teaspoons chopped fresh thyme or marjoram

6 sheets commercial shortcrust pastry (about 1 kg/2 lb) or equivalent of homemade shortcrust pastry

45 g/1½ oz butter

1 egg beaten with 1 teaspoon water

crushed potato salad with three mustards

Instead of dicing potatoes the new way of using them in potato salad involves 'crushing' them so you have uneven edges. The idea behind this is to create soft surfaces, which will absorb the dressing better.

Cook the potatoes until they are tender and peel. Squash and crack them lightly with a masher or fork so they are in rough pieces. Mix lightly with onion. Mix the oil, vinegar, English and French mustards and fold through. Warm the mustard seeds until they pop and leave aside. Roughly chop the egg. Cook the bacon until crisp.

To assemble put the potato over the base of a dish. Scatter with mustard seeds, then egg and bacon. Trickle the mayonnaise mixture here and there over this. You can garnish with chives or parsley if you wish. The salad should be tossed at the table, but lightly so the potato retains some shape.

Serves 6

750 g/1½ lb waxy potatoes

1 onion, preferably red, finely chopped

½ cup/4 fl oz olive oil

2 tablespoons white vinegar

2 teaspoons hot English mustard

1 tablespoon French mustard

2 tablespoons mustard seeds, either brown or yellow

3 hard-boiled eggs

3 slices bacon, cut into strips

⅓ cup/3 fl oz mayonnaise (see opposite) mixed with 2 tablespoons yoghurt, cream or creme fraiche

individual frittatas

A different way of serving a frittata, just spoon the mixture into well-buttered muffin tins and bake in the oven. This makes it a really easy dish for a brunch, as you don't have to watch the frittatas, just time the dish. Of course I should not really refer to this as a frittata, which is baked in a frying pan, but the mixture is exactly the same and just the method of cooking is changed. The tasty filling can be cooked in the traditional way in a big frying pan if you prefer.

Heat the oil in a frying pan and fry the onion and garlic for 5 minutes or until softened. Add the potatoes and toss in the oil for a few minutes or until they are sealed and turning golden. Cover and cook for 5 minutes, add the zucchini, cover and cook until the vegetables are quite soft. Transfer to a bowl and season. Cool, add both kinds of cheese, chives, cream and eggs.

Preheat oven to 180°C/350°F. Butter large muffin containers. Line the base of each one with non-stick baking paper/parchment to make it easier to turn out the muffins. Spoon mixture into the containers and put into oven for 10–12 minutes or until set on the edges and still a little creamy in the centre. Remove and leave for a few minutes before turning out.

Makes 12 muffin-sized frittata or a single pan-cooked 20 cm/8 in frittata

3 tablespoons olive oil

1 large onion, finely diced

1 clove garlic, finely chopped

375 g/12 oz waxy potatoes, peeled and cut into small cubes

1 medium-sized to large zucchini, cut into small cubes

salt and pepper

1/4 cup finely diced Jarlsburg cheese

2 tablespoons grated Parmesan cheese

2 tablespoons finely chopped chives or spring onion/scallion tops

2 tablespoons cream

5 eggs, lightly beaten

hints

Pancetta has a smoked flavour and lends itself well as an accompaniment to the creamiest potato, fry it until crisp and use as a topping on mashed or puréed potato or scatter over the top of tiny boiled buttery potatoes with parsley.

mayonnaise

This is an old-fashioned mayonnaise, which is quite sweet and mainly meant to be an addition to a dish rather than being used in large quantities. Tone the sweetness down by adding a bit of yoghurt, cream or suchlike to the portion you will use. It is good as a thin spread for sandwiches and keeps well for weeks in a jar, lightly covered with foil in the refrigerator. If you prefer you can use any mayonnaise of your choice in the Crushed Potato Salad above, such as an oil mayonnaise.

Put all ingredients into a saucepan and whisk. It will curdle. Heat, stirring or whisking, until it comes to a boil. It will now be smooth. Cool, stirring occasionally, and store refrigerated.

2 eggs

1 teaspoon mustard

1 teaspoon salt

1 tablespoon cornflour/cornstarch

1/2 cup/4 oz sugar

1 cup/8 fl oz milk

1 cup/8 fl oz white wine vinegar

stuffed potato cake

easy ideas

Hot Potatoes with Smoked Salmon

Cook about 18 baby potatoes in salted water until tender. While they are cooking mix together ⅓ cup/ 3 fl oz sour cream, 2 tablespoons finely chopped parsley, some black pepper, a little finely chopped red onion and ½ cup/4 oz finely chopped smoked salmon. Drain the potatoes well, put them into a bowl and spoon the mixture over the top. At the table they should be mixed so the cream melts a little and the smoked salmon is stirred through. Just eat this on its own.

Creamy potato is pressed into a mould and then filled with a savoury mixture before being topped with more potato, to make a very comforting and substantial meal. It is unlikely you would do this at the last moment so you can make the dish up hours beforehand and leave aside until you want to bake it. No reason all kinds of fillings can't be put into the centre, even some cooked meat if you like. I serve it with a spoonful of almond parsley pesto on top, allowing this to soften a little in the warmth of the potato.

Cook the potatoes until soft in salted water, drain well and put through a moulin. Don't process or you will end up with a heavy, gluey potato. Add the butter, milk, then beat lightly with a fork as you add the eggs and yolk. Mix in Parmesan cheese and season.

While the potato is cooking, cook the onions and capsicum/bell pepper in a little olive oil until quite soft. Chop the spinach and mix through. Butter a 23 cm/9 in diameter springform tin. Dust with crumbs. Put two-thirds of potato purée into this to make a shell, spooning it across the base and up the sides. Put vegetable mixture into the centre and then the cheeses. Cover with potato, smooth over. Dot with butter or melt butter and spread it over the top then dust with extra crumbs. It can be left at this stage for 12 hours.

Preheat oven to 180°C/350°F. Bake for 20 minutes. Turn oven up to hot, 200°C/400°F and bake for a further 15–20 minutes or until golden. Stand for 5 minutes before carefully removing the springform sides. Serve with almond parsley pesto.

For pesto, put the almonds, parsley, garlic, cheese, lemon, cayenne into a processor. Grind and add oil, mix again and season to taste. Refrigerate for up to 1 week, freeze for up to 1 month.

Serves 6–8

1.5 kg/3 lb floury or all-purpose potatoes, peeled

60 g/2 oz butter

½ cup/4 fl oz warm milk

2 eggs and 1 egg yolk

⅓ cup/1½ oz grated Parmesan cheese

salt and pepper

2 onions, finely chopped

1 red capsicum/bell pepper, finely chopped

250 g/8 oz spinach, blanched in water until soft and well drained

⅓ cup/1 oz breadcrumbs, made from stale bread

½ cup/2 oz diced mozzarella cheese

½ cup/2 oz diced Jarlsburg cheese

extra 45 g/1½ oz butter

some extra breadcrumbs

some extra grated Parmesan cheese

Almond Parsley Pesto

60 g/2 oz almonds, skin on and toasted in the oven for 10 minutes

2 cups/2 oz parsley sprigs

2 cloves garlic, finely chopped

⅓ cup/1 oz grated Parmesan cheese

1 tablespoon lemon juice

dash of cayenne pepper

½ cup/4 fl oz light olive oil

salt and pepper to taste

vegetable samosas

Indians eat samosas at any time of day as a snack. They are popular vendor food but are also great items for the dinner table for casual eating. If made without too much spice children love this kind of food – they always seem more interested in food that is wrapped and eaten with their fingers rather than food eaten with a knife and fork. If you are unable to cope with making the traditional flaky crust, you can cheat and use some commercial puff pastry. Serves with a bowl of chutney or some kind of a mango relish.

For crust, sift flour with salt into a bowl and put into a food processor, add butter, process to make fine crumbs. Add the water a tablespoon at a time until pastry holds together. Remove. Knead well for about 5 minutes. Wrap in plastic and refrigerate, for up to 24 hours.

For stuffing, heat the oil and fry the onion until soft and golden, add ginger, chilli, garlic and fry for a minute, then mix in the spices. Remove to a bowl and add lemon juice. Cut the potatoes into small dice and mix into the spices with the peas. Add coriander/cilantro. Allow to cool completely.

Remove pastry from the refrigerator and knead for a minute. Divide into about 18 little balls. Put each onto a floured board, roll out to a thin circle. Cut circle into halves. Form one half into a cone and overlap the edges slightly. Dip your fingers into water and seal the seam. Put some of the filling into this cone, but not right up to the top. Fold over the cone's edges to make a triangular shape and seal top with water once again. You can leave on a tray in the refrigerator up to 24 hours. Continue to fill cones

To serve, fry in a frying pan in oil. Oil should be hot but not as hot as for chips/fries. When samosas are golden brown turn them over and cook the second side. Drain on paper towel. You can reheat them in the oven if you wish.

Makes about 36

Crust

1½ cups/6 oz plain flour

½ teaspoon salt

60 g/2 oz butter,
cut into small pieces

about ½ cup/4 fl oz warm water

Stuffing

3 tablespoons oil

1 onion, finely chopped

about 1 tablespoon
finely chopped ginger

1 chilli, finely chopped

3 cloves garlic, finely chopped

1 teaspoon salt

1 teaspoon ground coriander

¼ teaspoon ground cumin

1 tablespoon lemon juice

500 g/1 lb waxy potatoes,
cooked and cooled

¼ cup/1½ oz peas, cooked

¼ cup/½ oz chopped
coriander/cilantro

easy ideas *Crispy Malaysian Potato Cakes*

Cook about 4 peeled, medium-sized potatoes in salted water until tender and drain very well. Mash in a bowl just using a fork or potato masher – not a food processor. Finely chopped 6 spring onions/scallions and mix into the potato with a good pinch of cayenne pepper and a little more salt. Using damp hands form into about 10–12 little round patties and flatten slightly. Beat 2 eggs in a shallow soup bowl and dunk the patties into this. Heat a generous amount of oil in a frying pan – enough to cover the base – and carefully slide the potato patties into the oil. The egg will form a crispy little case. Cook about 2 minutes each side until browned and don't crowd the pan or you will have trouble turning them over. You can keep patties warm in the oven if you can't cook them all in one batch. These go with just about anything or you can eat them on their own.

potato salad

easy ideas

*Grated
Potato Cakes*

Grate into a bowl about 4 floury baking potatoes and then squeeze to get rid of some of the liquid. Mix in I teaspoon salt, some pepper and a lightly beaten egg. Have a large pan with sufficient oil to cover the base and put spoonfuls of the potato mixture into this, flattening it out by using the prongs of a fork. Cook until set and is golden on one side, turn over and cook on the second side. Cakes can be kept warm for a short time in a low oven but are best of all eaten almost as soon as they are made. Try them for a special brunch with a poached egg on top.

A traditional potato salad which has some mint added to lend a fresh taste. I usually allow plenty, as potato salad always seems to be a dish everyone comes back to for seconds.

Cook the potatoes in a pot of lightly salted water until they are tender when pierced with a knife. Remove and drain. Allow to cool for about 15 minutes and then peel if you wish, depending on whether the skins are fine and papery. Cut the potatoes into chunky pieces or, if tiny, into halves.

Mix the parsley with mint and lemon rind. Whisk the lemon juice with olive oil and vinegar. Begin making layers in a bowl, put in potato first, season well with salt and pepper, scatter on some herb and lemon mixture and then trickle on a little dressing. Continue until all the potato has been used. Toss gently.

Put the bacon into a dry frying pan and cook until crisp, turning it over. Drain well on kitchen paper towel. Cut into fine strips and chop the egg roughly.

Before serving, gently toss the potato again to ensure it is well mixed. Spoon mayonnaise on top at random and scatter the egg and bacon over the top, adding more parsley if you wish. Serve within an hour once garnished or the egg will dry.

Serves 4

750 g/1 ½ lb waxy potatoes

½ cup/1 oz finely chopped parsley

2 tablespoons finely chopped mint

2 teaspoons finely chopped lemon rind

2 tablespoons lemon juice

⅓ cup/3 fl oz olive oil

2 tablespoons white wine vinegar

salt and freshly cracked black pepper

3 rashers bacon

2 eggs, hard-boiled

½ cup/4 fl oz mayonnaise

sweet potato chips

Sweet potatoes can be cut into slices and fried in the same manner you would if making potato chips. In this dish, they are tossed in a spicy mixture until lightly coated. They are interesting with chicken, at a barbecue, as a snack, or as a pre-dinner appetizer. A suggestion in an American book I have is to cook equal quantities of plain and sweet potato chips and mix. This makes an interesting combination, but they need to be fried separately: the timing for sweet potatoes is different to plain potatoes.

Peel the potatoes and cut them across into very thin circles. Put in a bowl, cover with water and add half a dozen ice cubes. Refrigerate for at least 4 hours. You can leave them all day if you wish.

Remove them, drain and pat dry on kitchen paper towel. Preheat oven to 180°C/350°F. Heat oil in a saucepan: it should sizzle as soon as one of the circles of sweet potato is added. Don't crowd the oil, so fry chips in batches until golden and crisp. Remove carefully with a strainer. When a batch of the potatoes is ready, spread out on a baking tray on paper towel and keep warm in oven while frying the remainder.

Mix the salt with curry powder. Before serving, scatter this over the top and toss quickly so chips are lightly coated. Pile into a bowl or basket lined with a napkin and serve immediately.

3 sweet potatoes

iced water

peanut oil or light olive oil

I teaspoon salt

½ teaspoon curry powder

fish cakes

If you have always believed that fish cakes are a dish reserved for cheap family meal you may be surprised to know that in London some of the really posh establishments have these back on the menu as a star turn. People just love them and pay high prices for old-fashioned nostalgic food such as this. There are, however, fish cakes that are good and ones which are quite horrid, made of large amounts of heavy potato and with bland flavourings. The best fish cakes are quite light to eat, have at least as much fish as potato and are only bound with egg yolk so they hold together but are not too solid. The outside will be golden and crusty. This recipe makes them with canned salmon but any leftover fish could also be used in the cakes. The quantity here makes 8 fish cakes and can easily be doubled. I like to serve them with Fresh Relish but lemon wedges and tartare sauce are good also.

Melt the butter in a small saucepan and cook the onion until it is soft and golden. Flake the salmon and remove the bones, mix with the onion, potato, egg yolk and season well. Stir in the parsley and lemon rind and mix everything very well with a fork. Divide the mixture into 8 portions. Form with damp hands into balls and then flatten to make patties and smooth the edges. Dip them into flour, then into egg and finally into crumbs. Coating must be well sealed with no gaps. Chill for up to 8 hours (this makes the cakes easier to handle, but you can cook them earlier if you need to).

Put the extra butter and about 4 tablespoons oil into a frying pan. When the butter has melted and it is quite hot and sizzling, add the fish cakes. Turn the heat down so they cook over a moderate heat, the outside must be golden brown and the inside hot through. Turn once and serve with some relish.

To make relish, cook everything in a covered saucepan for about 10 minutes or until the vegetables have just softened, stirring once or twice. Cool and store for up to 4 days refrigerated.

Serves 8 as a first course, 4 as a main course

30 g/1 oz butter

1 small onion, finely diced

1 x 210 g/7 oz can red salmon or ½–¾ cup/6–8 oz flaked cooked fish)

½ cup/3 oz cold floury potato, mashed with a fork

1 egg yolk

plenty of salt and pepper

2 tablespoons finely chopped parsley

½ teaspoon grated lemon rind

plain/all-purpose flour

1 egg beaten with 2 teaspoons water

breadcrumbs, made from stale white or brown bread

extra 30 g/1 oz butter, to cook the fish cakes

4 tablespoons oil

Fresh Relish

1 onion, peeled and diced

1 ripe tomato, peeled and diced

1 small apple, peeled, cored and diced

½ red capsicum/bell pepper, deseeded and diced

2 cloves garlic

1 tablespoon sugar

1 tablespoon white vinegar

salt and pepper

hints

To speed up cooking in the oven spear the potato with a metal skewer. Instead of putting potatoes in their skin on a baking tray, put them directly onto the rack so the heat circulates around them. The skin will become especially crisp.

potatoes stuffed with onion and cheese

hint

When cooking potatoes, start by cooking them in cold, salted water without a lid. Then cover once they come to a boil and cook over a very, very low heat so the water is just bubbling slightly at the edges. Drain and leave in the strainer to cool.

These potato cakes have a little, soft savoury surprise in the centre. You could vary it, using herbs with the onion and cheese, or some red capsicum pepper with onion. Whatever you add needs to be cooked. I like to serve these potato cakes with a tomato sauce, made by cooking about 4–5 diced ripe tomatoes with a spoonful of butter, some salt and pepper, and simmering for about 20 minutes. I then put this through a moulin or sieve, and flavour with a little basil or parsley. These cakes can make this a meal with salad, or are be lovely served with some simple roasted chicken.

Peel and cook the potatoes until tender, drain well. Mash or put through a moulin and add the milk. Leave to cool and add self-raising flour. The mixture should not be wet. If it is, add a little more flour. Leave in the refrigerator for about an hour to become firm.

Melt the butter and add onion, cook until softened. Turn up the heat and cook until it has some golden specks. Remove to a bowl, cool slightly and then mix in cheese, salt and pepper.

Form the potato into round balls; you may need to use damp hands if they stick. Flatten out between your hands. Put a little of the filling on one potato patty. Put another one on top to enclose the filling. Pinch the edges together and put on a plate in the refrigerator until firm. Leave to chill for about 30 minutes.

Put some flour on a piece of waxed or greaseproof paper. Beat the eggs with oil and put crumbs on another piece of paper. Dip the patties into flour, then egg and finally crumbs, patting them on gently but firmly. Chill until it is time to cook. You can leave them overnight at this stage if you wish.

To cook, heat a little oil in a frying pan and add the potatoes. Brown one side, turn over and cook until brown on the second side. Drain on some kitchen paper towel.

Note
To make self-raising flour, add 1½ teaspoons baking powder and ½ teaspoon salt to 1 cup/4 oz of plain/all-purpose flour. For 2 tablespoons flour use a pinch of baking powder and a tiny pinch of salt.

Makes about 12 cakes

4 medium-sized all-purpose potatoes

1 tablespoon milk

2 tablespoons self-raising flour (see Note)

45 g/1½ oz butter

1 large onion, finely diced

½ cup/2 oz grated Jarlsburg or Swiss-style cheese

salt and pepper

plain flour

2 eggs mixed with 1 tablespoon light olive oil

breadcrumbs, made from stale bread

a little olive oil

potatoes cooked with mustard seeds

easy ideas

*Potato and
Mushrooms*

Dice 4 medium-
sized potatoes
quite small and
slice about a
dozen mush-
rooms and fry
both in a frying
pan in plenty
of oil until the
mushrooms are
soft. Season well
and add a couple
of cloves of finely
chopped garlic.
Cover and cook
about 10 minutes
over a low heat
until the potatoes
are softened. You
will have some
juices around
them from the
mushrooms.
Scatter on a bit
more pepper and
serve with steaks
or for breakfast
with bacon.

*A grilled steak, some roasted portions of chicken, crispy lamb chops … these
are all types of meat which beg for an interesting potato dish sitting alongside them. Crunchy with mustard seeds and tart from a last-minute yoghurt
coating, this particular hot dish has a lovely golden colour and lots of texture
and flavour. If you prefer a creamier taste and don't care a lot about diet,
instead of the yoghurt you can coat potatoes with a little sour cream.*

If the potatoes are not small, cut them into halves. Heat the oil in a wide
saucepan, add turmeric and mustard seeds and fry until the seeds are
beginning to pop. Add the garlic and potatoes and stir gently so the potatoes get a golden coating. Season, add water and Tabasco or chilli. Cover
and cook until tender, 15–20 minutes. You should find that there is barely
any liquid remaining. If there is quite a bit you can cook without the lid for
a few minutes. Remove the pan from the heat. Add the yoghurt and shake
to coat the potatoes. This must be done at the last minute, off the heat,
or the yoghurt will separate around the potatoes. Add parsley or coriander
and shake gently again.

Serves 6

1 kg/2 lb small waxy
potatoes, peeled

3 tablespoons light olive oil

1 teaspoon ground turmeric

1 tablespoon yellow or
brown mustard seeds

3 cloves garlic, finely chopped

salt and pepper

$1/2$ cup/4 fl oz water

dash of Tabasco or
chilli sauce to taste

$1/2$ cup/4 fl oz natural yoghurt

about $1/4$ cup/$1/2$ oz finely
chopped parsley or
coriander/cilantro

aromatic potatoes

*These potatoes make the house smell with the perfume of rosemary, garlic
and oil. They are crunchy, golden and taste wonderful with poultry or
lamb – or in fact with just about anything.*

Wash the potatoes. You can peel them, although there is really no need.
Cut each one into halves, warm the butter with oil and add the bay leaf
and rosemary. Put the potatoes into a basin, add the butter and garlic and
stir until potatoes are coated with butter. Transfer them to a baking dish,
preferably a metal one that gives a better heat for baking to a crunchy
coating. Season with a little salt and pepper and cook in a moderate oven,
180–190°C/350–375°F, for about 45–60 minutes. Turn potatoes over as they
are cooking so they will colour more evenly. Remove the garlic and bits of
rosemary, which will have become brittle, and drain away any excess oil
or butter from potatoes before serving.

Serves 6

9 medium-sized floury or
all-purpose potatoes

15 g/$1/2$ oz butter

2 tablespoons virgin olive oil

1 bay leaf, crumpled

2 sprigs rosemary

2 large cloves garlic

salt and pepper

baked potatoes

A version of baked potato that gives a crusty base and nice texture.

Wash the potatoes but leave on the skin and cut each one into two. Melt the butter and mix with the oil and dip the cut side into this mixture. Put into a metal baking tin, cut side downwards. Scatter the top with a little salt. Bake in a moderately hot oven, 200°C/400°F, for about 1 hour. The cut side will be a deep golden to brown colour and very crisp. Sprinkle a little pepper over, loosen carefully from the tin in case any of the potato has stuck, and serve immediately.

Serves 6

9 medium-sized floury
or all-purpose potatoes

30 g/1 oz butter

1 tablespoon vegetable
or light olive oil

salt and pepper

french potato and beef salad

I am sure that originally the French would have created this wonderful salad known as Beef Salad Parisienne as a way to use up leftover beef from another meal, perhaps from their traditional beef simmered in red wine until meltingly tender. It has everything you need in the one platter and looks very grand for a group in the centre of the table, with its topping of herbs, eggs and tomato.

It is important that the beef be very moist. You can buy ready cooked beef but check it is very pink in the centre. Better still, cook your own the day before, wrap in foil and refrigerate overnight. Don't stint on meat quality. You don't need much per person so use a top quality cut such as fillet.

The quantities can easily be doubled or trebled.

Put the onion into a bowl of iced water for an hour so it will crisp and become lighter in flavour. Drain well. Cook the potatoes in lightly salted water until tender. Drain and when cool enough, peel (if you wish) and cut into thick slices. Cut the beef into very thin slices and then across so you have some strips about 5 cm/2 in wide. Make up the dressing by putting all ingredients into a jar and shaking until thickened. Mix half the dressing into the beef, potato and onion and toss.

Put the lettuce on an oval platter. Spread the beef and potato mix on this, leaving the lettuce showing at the edges. Cut eggs into quarters and arrange on top, along with tomatoes. Trickle over rest of dressing and top with parsley, dill cucumber and chives, and a grinding of fresh black pepper. You can cover with plastic wrap and refrigerate for an hour but it is best served immediately. The beef and potato mixture, however, can marinate for several hours.

Serves 4

1 large red onion, halved
and sliced wafer-thin

750 g/1½ lb small waxy potatoes

500 g/1 lb cooked rare
roast beef

mignonette or
butter lettuce

4 hard-boiled eggs

4 small ripe tomatoes

¼ cup/½ oz finely
chopped parsley

½ cup/1 oz roughly chopped
or sliced dill cucumber

2 tablespoons finely
chopped chives

freshly ground black pepper

Dressing

¾ cup/6 fl oz olive oil

¼ cup/2 fl oz white wine vinegar

salt and pepper

1 tablespoon French mustard

2 teaspoons dry English mustard

¼ cup/2 fl oz mayonnaise

1 teaspoon brown sugar

easy ideas

Quick Baked Potatoes

Cut some floury large potatoes into very thick slices lengthwise. Put a sheet of baking paper onto an oven tray. Melt about 60 g/2 oz butter and dunk each piece of potato into this, placing them on the tray. Season with salt and pepper, scatter on a bit of paprika or curry powder and bake in a moderately hot oven (200°C/400°F) for about 20 minutes, until crisp and tender. If you don't have time to cook anything else you can scatter a bit of cheese on for the last 5 minutes so they have a melted layer over the top and you have substantial snack or meal.

potato rolls

easy ideas

Potato Wedges

Included because
they are easy and
so popular with
kids. Cut potatoes
with skins left on
into wedges and
toss them in a
basin with plenty
of olive oil and
a tablespoon of
melted butter.
Put into a tray
lined with non-
stick baking paper/
parchment and
bake in a hot
oven (200°C/
400°F) for about
20 minutes, turn-
ing over once so
they colour evenly,
seasoning with
salt and pepper
as you turn them.
Use as a dip or
serve with any
kind of meal.

*This may appear a little more complicated than a plain potato dish
but the flavour of these stuffed rolls of potato is wonderful. It holds up
well if prepared a day beforehand and then reheated when ready to serve.*

Cook the potatoes and mash them with the salt, pepper, butter and egg
yolks, then cool until the mixture is firm enough to spread out on to a
sheet of plastic wrap, making an oblong shape.

To make the filling cook the onion and capsicum until soft in the oil and
add lemon rind and juice and coriander/cilantro. Cool a bit and spread
over the potato. Carefully roll potato over, using the plastic film as a lever.
Chill the roll until it is quite firm. Butter a shallow china dish very generously.
Using a very sharp knife cut the roll into thick slices and place on to the
buttered dish. Melt more butter and trickle it generously on top and then
scatter on cheese if you decide to use it. At this point you can leave,
refrigerated and covered, for up to 24 hours.

To serve, preheat oven to 180°C/350°F and bake for about 25–30 minutes,
until the potato is bubbling hot and topping golden. For a very crusty top
it can be placed under the griller/broiler for a few minutes.

Serves 4–6

1 kg/2 lb floury potatoes

1 teaspoon salt

some pepper

45 g/1 $\frac{1}{2}$ oz butter, cut
into small pieces

2 egg yolks

some extra butter

a little Parmesan cheese
(optional)

Filling

2 tablespoons olive oil

1 large onion, finely diced

1 large red capsicum/bell
pepper, finely diced

1 teaspoon lemon rind

1 tablespoon lemon juice

$\frac{1}{4}$ cup/$\frac{1}{2}$ oz chopped
coriander/cilantro or parsley

potatoes in a creamy chicken sauce

*The dish has a lovely but simple sauce of onion, red capsicum pepper and
chicken stock that is used to coat the potatoes after they have been cooked.
It is important to only use red pepper as the green comes through with too
strong a flavour in the dish. This can also be varied by adding a teaspoon
of finely chopped rosemary and is then wonderful with lamb. Although it is
better to cook the potatoes to be ready at meal time, the sauce can be made
the day before and reheated. It also is a dish that is quite forgiving and
can be kept warm for some time without spoiling.*

Place the potatoes in a saucepan, cover with cold water and season. Cook
gently until tender. You can either leave the skins on or peel them. Heat
the butter and oil in a saucepan and add the onion and red capsicum/bell
pepper. Cook gently until limp, giving it an occasional stir. Add flour and
fry for a few minutes, stirring. Add stock and bring to the boil, stirring
occasionally. Leave to simmer gently for a couple of minutes and then add
cream and parsley.

To serve, if sauce has been made beforehand, reheat gently and then add
potatoes. If potatoes have become cool, warm them through in the sauce,
with the saucepan lid on. The sauce won't coat the potatoes: when serving
you need to spoon some over the top so it can be eaten with each mouthful.

Serves 4 very generously, or 6 small eaters

750 g/1 $\frac{1}{2}$ lb small new potatoes

30 g/1 oz butter

1 tablespoon vegetable oil

1 large onion, finely diced

1 red capsicum/bell pepper,
deseeded and finely diced

1 scant tablespoon flour

1 cup/8 fl oz chicken stock

2 tablespoons cream

salt and pepper to taste

2 tablespoons finely
chopped parsley

italian potato cake

You can eat this for a meal with some mixed salad, it is nourishing, substantial and quite delicious. It is called gatto *in Italian and is usually made with a layer of mozzarella cheese and then one of a smoked cheese in the centre of two layers of potato. I change this a little as I don't find mozzarella flavoursome enough in the potato and don't care so much for smoked cheese, so instead bring in a nutty flavour by using a Swiss-style Emmental or Jarlsburg. The most important thing to ensure the gatto is light is never to put the potato into a food processor, as it then becomes gluey and heavy. Purée it by putting through a moulin or else into a basin and mashing as smoothly as you can with a potato masher.*

Cook the potatoes until tender, drain well, cool slightly and peel them. Mash thoroughly.

Preheat oven to 180°C/350°F. Mix in the Parmesan cheese, eggs, milk and season with salt and pepper. If using ham or salami dice it small and add; if using proscuitto add it plain or fry quickly in a pan for a couple of minutes and then add along with any rendered fat. Grease a shallow ovenproof dish with butter. Shake crumbs into the dish and turn so the butter is coated. Tip out any excess crumbs. Spoon in half the potato and smooth the top. Layer slices of melting cheese to cover the potato and then dab the remaining potato over the cheese so as not to disturb it. Smooth again. Cover with more crumbs. Cut the butter into tiny pieces and dot all over the top. Bake in oven for about 30 minutes or until the top is brown and the potato is quite puffy and set.

Serves 6

1 kg/2 lb floury potatoes

2 tablespoons grated Parmesan cheese

4 large eggs

¾ cup/6 fl oz milk

salt and pepper

125 g/4 oz ham, prosciutto or salami

breadcrumbs, made from stale bread

200 g/7 oz Emmental or Jarlsburg cheese, or a similar nutty melting cheese

125 g/4 oz butter

tomato and yoghurt-topped potatoes

The coating on top of each potato flavours them and also gives an interesting pinkish tinge.

Peel the potatoes and cut each one into halves. Line a flat tray with baking paper/parchment and grease with a little oil. Mix the yoghurt with tomato, pepper and salt. Put the potatoes; cut side downward, on the tray and spoon sufficient of the coating over each to coat. A little will run on to the dish; try not to have so much that you have an excess on the baking tray as this will tend to darken and burn as the potatoes cook. Bake in a moderate oven, 180°C/350°F for about 45 minutes or until the potatoes are tender.

Serves 6

9 medium-sized floury or all-purpose potatoes

a little oil

⅓ cup/3 fl oz natural yoghurt

3 teaspoons tomato paste

generous pinch of cayenne pepper

¼ teaspoon salt

horseradish potato

easy ideas

Potatoes Braised in Wine

Wash a dozen tiny potatoes and cook in a frying pan in a little oil until they are lightly coloured, shaking the pan occasionally. Scatter in some salt and pepper and add 1 cup/ 8 fl oz white or red wine and pinch of sugar and bring to a boil, cover and cook gently until they are tender. To serve, mix in plenty of chopped parsley and toss them so they are coated with green. If there is a lot of liquid left the parsley will just float in it, but you can just spoon some of the wine juices over the potatoes when serving them, or quickly boil liquid to reduce.

Great with roast beef – or any kind of meat or fish that you feel has an affinity with the flavour of horseradish.

Cook the potatoes in a saucepan with salted water and when quite soft, drain. Warm the butter and milk in a saucepan. When they are almost boiling begin adding to the potatoes, use a whisk or fork to mix through. Season to taste. Add the horseradish, also to taste – you should add enough to give a bite.

Serves 6

750 g/1½ lb floury potatoes, peeled and cut into big pieces

60 g/2 oz butter, cut into small pieces

¾ cup/6 fl oz milk

salt and pepper

2 tablespoons freshly grated horseradish

mediterranean potato and tomato salad

This potato salad, flavoured with tomatoes, olives and caper berries or plain capers, makes a nice accompaniment to slices of ham or beef or a meat terrine. Although the salad can be prepared in advance, it is best served at room temperature on the day it is made, as chilling dulls the flavour.

Cook the potatoes in a pot of lightly salted water until tender. Drain and let cool until tepid, then peel if you wish or, if the skins are very fine, leave them on. While the potatoes are cooking, cut the tomatoes into tiny pieces, removing some of the seeds. Mix in a bowl with garlic, onion, and olives. Leave the caper berries aside as a garnish for the top of the salad.

Make up the dressing by mixing everything together and whisking well. Put a ¼ cup/2 fl oz of the dressing over the tomatoes and let them stand for about 30 minutes. While the potatoes are still tepid, mix them with the remaining dressing. Several hours before serving toss the potato gently with the tomato mixture so it makes a very moist potato salad. Colours will bleed a little as it stands so you have a slightly pink look to the potatoes. Scatter with caper berries before serving.

Note
Caper berries (large, golden-brown pickled berries from the caper plant) can be bought at good delicatessens in tiny containers rather than in jars. They are not in liquid, but will keep for a few weeks refrigerated. If you want to store them longer, put into a jar and cover with oil. Instead of caper berries you could use some capers from a jar. Rinse them first, as they are pickled in vinegar, which is very strong.

Serves 4–6

1 kg/2 lb tiny new waxy potatoes

500 g/1 lb tomatoes, peeled

2 cloves garlic, crushed

1 red onion, finely diced

¼ cup/1 oz green or black olives, cut into strips

4 tablespoons caper berries

Dressing

¾ cup/6 fl oz olive oil

2 tablespoons white wine vinegar

2 teaspoons balsamic vinegar

salt and pepper

sweet potato scones

This is the kind of dish you might find if you dined in the American South, where hospitality and heat go hand in hand along the Mississippi. The scones would, of course, be called a 'biscuit' and might accompany a dish of chicken and thick gravy. I was served these once made up as tiny little scones, each one just a mouthful. They had been dabbed in the centre split with a spicy mustard and filled with a thick piece of cured southern ham. They were then piled onto a white cloth in a silver basket and served with strong coffee for afternoon tea.

They are quite sweet, like pumpkin scones, but this seems to be the style for this part of the United States. If you prefer, you can eat them simply buttered.

Butter a flat baking tray and preheat oven to 200°C/400°F.

Put the flour into a bowl and add butter. Cut into tiny pieces or crumble with your fingers. Add the sugar and salt. Make a well in the centre and add the sweet potato and a couple of tablespoons of sour cream or buttermilk. Work to form a very soft and sticky dough; you will need more cream or buttermilk. I find the amount you have to add can vary considerably, depending on how sticky or moist the sweet potato is. Try to mix without kneading or working the dough too much.

Tip out dough onto a floured bench and roll out quickly until about 1.5 cm/½ in thick. Cut into circles with a scone cutter and place them close together on the tray. Bake for about 15 minutes in oven. The tops should be lightly browned. Turn out on to a cloth and wrap once tepid.

You can reheat these: they need just a few seconds in a microwave if heating individually, or you can warm the batch again in the oven. Like any scones, however, they are nicest of all eaten very fresh.

Notes

To make 1 cup/4 oz self-raising flour, add 1½ teaspoons baking powder and ½ teaspoon salt to 1 cup/4 oz plain/all-purpose flour.

Buttermilk produces a very light scone, sour cream a deliciously 'short' buttery scone. If you don't want to use sour cream or buttermilk, plain milk can be substituted.

1 cup/4 oz self-raising flour (see Notes)

30 g/1 oz butter

2 teaspoons sugar

½ teaspoon salt

1 cup/7 oz cooked, mashed sweet potato

⅓ cup/3 fl oz sour cream or buttermilk

pumpkin

Cucurbita maxima; C. moschata; C. pepo

Pumpkin was once mainly known as the accompaniment, along with potatoes and parsnip, to the Sunday roast, being baked in big golden chunks and popular only in countries where this type of meal was traditional. For years pumpkin had an old-fashioned image – mashed pumpkin, pumpkin soup, pumpkin scones were great dishes but we took them for granted. Any vegetable that was used as a coach to transport Cinderella, or has funny little wedges cut out for eyes and a slit for a mouth and then a candle inserted into its innards at Halloween, has difficulty in maintaining any dignity. Perhaps the new awareness of vegetarian diets may have changed the social acceptability of pumpkin, along with an interest in international foods, for it is certainly easier to become excited about dishes like pumpkin ravioli, Sicilian pumpkin antipasto, pumpkin salad and pumpkin lasagne or risotto. I adore pumpkin soup – in fact almost anything that is made with pumpkin.

In this chapter I am referring to the rich, orange, sweet-fleshed variety of the squash family. It is of course a squash and in fact has quite a lengthy and confusing number of relations. Although it may not be technically correct, to most of us bright orange pumpkin is the rich-tasting one, pale coloured squash the insipid member of the family.

planting

Don't consider pumpkin unless you have plenty of space, they trail everywhere and although the leaves provide groundcover they are no respecter of other plants' needs. Small bush-type pumpkin varieties are best for home gardens and you can persuade them to grow along a low fence or trellis.

They grow really easily from seeds and I find masses each year come through from my compost, although this makes growing them like a lucky dip. When I have a particularly good pumpkin I usually dry a few seeds on some newspaper and just plant these. You can buy pumpkin seedlings or packets of seeds but often won't need anywhere near the number you will be given.

Plant them in small inverted hills, well fertilized, in full sun or partial shade, be sure to leave several metres – or yards – between each hill. Sow about 6 seeds in each mound and once there are about 6 leaves branching out, leave in the single strongest one. Cut away carefully so as not to pull out the lot. Give them a feed again after a couple of months and water generously, they like to have plenty so they keep growing steadily, but mostly they just look after themselves quite well.

Temperature Zone	Sow or plant
Tropical	All year round but not good in humid weather
Subtropical	Spring–summer
Temperate	Spring–early summer
Cool	Spring–early summer
First picking	Depending on variety, from 4–5½ months

varieties

Bush varieties

• Butternut – with a sweet flavour
• Golden Nugget – good for stuffing but has lots of seeds and is a bit bland.

Small to medium-sized varieties

• Baby Blue – a good baking pumpkin
• Turk's Cap – with a wonderful colour and butternut again
• Delicata – mini, sometimes known as sweet potato squash
• Rouge Vif d'Etampes - a very bright reddish orange variety.

Large varieties

• Queensland Blue – keeps very well and has bright flesh
• Trombone
• Australian Butter
• Iron Bark - another good dry pumpkin.

diseases and pests

Plant disease-resistant varieties and watch for mildew or bacterial wilt. Try not to handle pumpkin vines when they have just been watered. If you see a wilting vine you should take it out before any disease spreads. Squash vine borers can attack them and the plant will then appear to wilt. Catch them and remove or spray, for once they get inside the plant chemicals are not much good.

harvesting

About 3½–4½ months from planting, depending on the warmth and the variety.

Pumpkins can be eaten once well grown but for the best flavour wait until the stem turns brittle, dries and begins to change colour. Pick the pumpkins before there are too many frosty nights as they are spoilt if they freeze. Be sure to leave on some stem, as if you pull or cut this away it allows insects to get into the pumpkin. After picking you should 'cure' pumpkins in the sun or a dark airy warm spot for a couple of weeks; this toughens the skin. The pumpkins will then keep for months in a cool, airy place but check every so often and if you see any soft spots developing, use quickly as they will rot.

buying and storage

If you buy whole pumpkin in the shops just check the skin is not broken. It is a small gamble to buy a whole one as you can't see the colour or texture of the flesh. Most shops sell pumpkin cut into sections and these cut pumpkin pieces should be moist. Any loose, fibrous-looking parts in the flesh indicate it will be coarse or watery so pass these pumpkins up. Colour is a good indicator of flavour: the deeper the orange and the tighter the texture, the richer will be the flavour, while pale pieces are generally a bit watery and light in taste.

Once you have cut into a pumpkin it has a short life and needs refrigerating with the seeds removed. Try to use the remainder fairly quickly. Uncut pumpkins will keep in a cool airy place for months but you need to check them regularly for any soft patches.

nutrition

As the pumpkin varieties vary so does the nutrition, the brightest orange ones have the highest amount of beta-carotene, which converts to Vitamin A in the body, and most varieties contain Vitamin C.

cooking

To peel or not to peel, that is a personal preference, but also depends on what you are doing with the pumpkin and how tough the skin has become. If you just can't be bothered you can cook it with the skin on and then cut this away later. Roasting is often best done with the skin left on anyway, whereas for soup you should peel it. Just be very careful when cutting up pumpkin as the knife can slide away. This is the time for a great big solid heavy knife. If you are cutting open a large new pumpkin stick the knife right into the centre and then slowly pull down towards the board so you cut through one of the grooves. Cut into wedges and put flat side down onto a board and never, ever, cut towards yourself or your hands. I just cut the skin down on one side towards the board, turn the chunk over and cut on the other side, so even if the knife does slip it lands harmlessly on the board.

For the best flavour roast pieces: cut into chunks about the size of a golf ball and put them into a basin, trickling on some olive oil; toss so all the outside is lightly coated and transfer to a baking tray on some non-stick baking paper and cook in a moderately hot oven (190–200°C/375–400°F). Roast pumpkin is ready when the flesh is soft and there are bits of brown on all the edges, showing that it has a good sugar content and will be sweet. Usually cooking time is 45–60 minutes.

Pumpkin can get a bit watery when boiled so cut into chunks, use only a small amount of water and have a tight-fitting lid on the saucepan so it is actually cooking in steam.

pumpkin vegetable soup

Pumpkin soup never loses popularity as a winter starter as it is very flavoursome, reheats well and is not expensive to make. It is important to use a really good, deep-coloured pumpkin, the type used for baking – a butternut or blue-skinned variety – for the soup. Pale colours and soft flesh make watery soup.

Put onion and leek into a saucepan with the ¼ cup/2 fl oz water and put the lid on top. Cook gently for about 5 minutes or until slightly wilted and then cook without a lid until it has become dry and is picking up a little colour. (If you prefer you can fry them in a tablespoon of oil or 30 g/1 oz butter.) Add the curry and stir for a few seconds in the pan to toast the spices and bring out flavour. Add the remaining ingredients except the cream or milk. Cover and simmer very gently until the vegetables are soft and then purée. You can either purée the entire pot of soup in a food processor or blender, or only do three-quarters, leaving the remaining pieces of vegetable for texture. The consistency of the soup will vary according to the pumpkin, so judge for yourself when it is finished or whether it needs a little more liquid, either stock or water.

Refrigerate covered if not using within a couple of hours and reheat gently, then top with some cream or thin in the pot with a little milk. If you want a garnish, use some finely chopped parsley, a few sunflower seeds or, for a change, try some finely chopped toasted almonds.

Serves 6

I large onion, roughly diced

I large leek, sliced

¼ cup/2 fl oz water

I teaspoon curry powder

I medium-sized carrot, finely diced

I medium-sized potato, peeled and diced

750 g/1½ lb pumpkin, peeled and cut into chunks

3 cups/1½ pints water

3 cups/1½ pints chicken stock

salt and pepper to taste

a little cream to garnish the soup or a little milk to thin it (optional)

spicy pumpkin puff

This is a really fluffy, light dish which seems to go well with most meats. The pumpkin base can be prepared in advance, but it is best to add the egg whites that lighten it close to cooking time, so the whites don't deflate. If the pumpkin base has been prepared beforehand, warm it slightly before adding whites, so that it isn't too firm. The whites will then fold through it more easily.

Put the onion, potato and pumpkin in a medium-sized saucepan and cover with water. Season and cook covered until the vegetables are soft but not breaking up. Drain. Purée the vegetables in a food processor and, while warm, add butter, curry powder, cumin seeds and parsley. Allow to cool slightly but don't cover the bowl or condensation will create water on top. Separate the eggs. Add the yolks to the pumpkin, one at a time. Up to this stage the recipe can be prepared hours in advance.

Preheat oven to 180°C/350°F. If reheating do so gently over a low heat, as you don't want to cook the yolks. A good idea is to put the basin over a pan of hot water for 5 minutes. Beat the whites until they are stiff. Fold one third at a time into the pumpkin, turning the bowl and making big sweeping movements with a spatula. Have a buttered ovenproof dish ready, one which holds about 5 cups/2½ pints of mixture. Tip the pumpkin gently into this. Scatter the top with crumbs and cheese. Bake in oven for about 20 minutes or until puffed and just firm to touch in the centre. Don't overcook. It doesn't matter if the pumpkin is more on the creamy side than firm. Any leftovers can be reheated, in the oven or in a microwave, although won't be quite as light.

Serves 6

1 medium-sized onion, roughly chopped

125 g/4 oz (1 small) potato, peeled and diced

750 g/1½ lb yellow, baking-style pumpkin, peeled and diced

1 teaspoon salt and some pepper

30 g/1 oz butter

1 teaspoon curry powder

1 teaspoon cumin seeds, crushed with a wooden spoon

¼ cup/½ oz finely chopped parsley

3 eggs

3 tablespoons breadcrumbs, made from stale wholemeal bread

¼ cup/1 oz grated Parmesan cheese

easy ideas

Pumpkin Patties

Grate pumpkin until you have 1 cup/8 fl oz, mix into 250 g/8 oz minced chicken or pork, add plenty of salt and pepper, an egg and a tablespoon of satay sauce. Stir through some coriander/cilantro leaves and form into 4 flat patties. Fry gently in some oil until browned on both sides and cooked through and serve on some green salad leaves.

baked pumpkin cubes with sesame seeds

This dish needs to be made from a dry baking pumpkin. It is very easy and quick to prepare and delicious with most roast meats, chicken or plain grilled meats.

Preheat oven to 180°C/350°F. Peel the pumpkin and remove seeds. Cut it into small, neat cubes. Place in a shallow ovenproof dish in which the cubes will fit in one layer. Trickle the oil over the top and dot with butter, then season with salt and pepper. Bake for about 15–20 minutes, turning the cubes over several times. Scatter the sesame seeds over the top and continue cooking for another 10 minutes, or until the pumpkin is tender.

Serves 4

1 kg/2 lb pumpkin

1 tablespoon peanut or light olive oil

30 g/1 oz butter

salt and pepper

2 tablespoons sesame seeds

mascarpone and pumpkin tarts

The filling of mascarpone is very creamy and rich and binds chunks of caramelised pumpkin in a layer in the tarts. I usually cook the pumpkin well in advance so it doesn't seem such a bother and the tarts can be assembled the next day. You need some small tart cases for this recipe – or buy larger individual ones with removable bases, which are well worth having if you like making tarts.

Preheat oven to 200°C/400°F. Peel pumpkin and cut into chunks about 3 cm/1½ in across. Roll in oil and bake in oven until soft.

Cut out circles of puff pastry to fit cases and press into case so pastry comes well up the sides. Prick lightly with a fork. Line with buttered foil and press it down on the base and up the sides. Bake for about 15 minutes or until set, carefully take out the foil and continue to bake until pastry is golden. If they puff, gently prick to allow the hot air to escape. These tart cases can be made days in advance and stored, refrigerated, in a covered container.

To make tarts, preheat oven to 180°C/350°F. Heat butter and oil in a pan, cook the onion until softened. Mix mascarpone with eggs, season well. Arrange some onion, then pumpkin pieces in each pastry shell and spoon around enough mascarpone to hold in place. Scatter with pine nuts and bake in oven until set, about 15 minutes.

Makes 6–8 individual tarts

1 kg/2 lb pumpkin

olive oil

some butter puff pastry

30 g/1 oz butter

1 tablespoon oil

1 red onion, finely chopped

125 g/4 oz mascarpone

2 eggs

salt and pepper

some pine nuts

roasted pumpkin soup

hint

Croutons are a good topping for any soup. Make them more interesting by cutting into heart shapes, triangles or rounds and gently fry in a little butter until golden and crisp. While warm roll the edges in parsley and let cool.

A more intensely flavoured pumpkin soup is made when the pumpkin is first roasted in the oven. It is important to cook it so there are plenty of brown edges on the pieces, these give a rich, caramel flavour.

Preheat oven to 180°C/350°F. Put some thyme onto a baking tray lined with a piece of non-stick baking paper/parchment. Mix the pumpkin with some olive oil – the easiest way to do this is in a basin, turning it over with oil so it has a thin layer on all sides. Tip onto the tray and season. Bake for about an hour or until the pumpkin is really soft and has a bit of caramel brown on the edges. Discard the thyme, remove pumpkin and cool until you can handle it and cut off the skin.

While the pumpkin is cooking gently soften the onion and leek in a little oil in a large pot. Put the pumpkin on top along with the stock and bring to a boil. Simmer, covered, for about 15 minutes and then purée the mixture. Spoon into soup bowls and scatter on some chives.

Serves 4

lots of sprigs of fresh thyme

750 g/1½ lb pumpkin, cut into chunks

olive oil

salt and pepper

1 large onion, finely chopped

1 leek, thinly sliced

3 cups/1½ pints vegetable or chicken stock

some fresh chives

vegetable and cheese galette with poppyseed pastry

pumpkin goes with

butter

oil

garlic

leeks

onion

potatoes

orange

lemon

nutmeg

curry

cumin

cream

cheeses

mascarpone

ricotta

coriander/ cilantro

parsley

rosemary

sage

bacon

sausages

chicken

lamb

beef

pasta

rice

almonds

pine nuts

A great vegetarian meal, this is a round pastry case enclosing a ricotta and pumpkin filling and has a rustic appearance as the centre is not covered, so you can see the brightly coloured vegetable filling. It reheats well so can be made in advance. Just serve some green salad alongside.

Process poppy seeds, flour, butter, sugar and salt until fine crumbs form. Add water and process until it holds together. Remove and flatten and wrap, leave to rest for 30 minutes. Roll out between waxed paper to make a big circle. Put this onto a buttered tray.

Preheat oven to 200°C/400°F. For filling, cook the onion, capsicum and garlic in the oil. Add the carrot, pumpkin and a couple of tablespoons of water. Cover and cook until soft. Drain. Process or whisk the ricotta and mozzarella cheeses together and add the Parmesan, cream, salt, pepper, egg, herbs and vegetables. Put this onto the crust, leaving an edge. Then fold the sides of the pastry up a little over the filling and press down gently. The filling should be exposed in the centre. Bake for 20 minutes, then turn heat down to moderate (180°C/350°F) and cook until set on top. Leave to rest for 5 minutes before moving from the tray. To serve cut into wedges like a cake.

Serves 6–8

1/4 cup/1 oz poppy seeds

1 1/2 cups/6 oz plain/ all-purpose flour

125 g/4 oz butter, cut into small pieces

1 tablespoon brown sugar

1 teaspoon salt

4 tablespoons cold water

Filling

2 tablespoons olive oil

1 large onion, finely chopped

1 red capsicum/bell pepper, cut into small pieces

3 cloves garlic

1 carrot, diced

500 g/1 lb pumpkin, diced small

185 g/6 oz ricotta cheese

90 g/3 oz mozzarella cheese, grated

1/3 cup/1 1/2 oz grated Parmesan cheese

1/4 cup/2 fl oz cream

salt and pepper

1 egg

3 tablespoons mixed fresh herbs

spicy sweet pumpkin muffins

These have a very moist, light texture. You can freeze any leftover ones and microwave or reheat in the oven as you need them.

Preheat oven to 200°C/400°F. Sift flour and cinnamon together. Add sultanas. Combine remaining ingredients and stir into flour, mixing well. Place spoonfuls into buttered muffin pans and bake for about 15 minutes or until well-risen and firm to touch. Turn out onto a rack to cool and serve with some butter.

Note
To make self-raising flour, add 1 1/2 teaspoons baking powder plus 1/2 teaspoon salt to 1 cup plain/all-purpose flour.

Makes 12

2 cups/8 oz self-raising flour (see Note)

1 teaspoon cinnamon

1/2 cup/3 oz sultanas

1/4 cup/2 fl oz oil

2 eggs

3 tablespoons golden syrup

2 tablespoons milk

1 cup/8 oz cold mashed pumpkin

pumpkin timbales for the dieter

I do not usually bother with diet foods, rather with having a good balance of fresh foods, but for anyone who doesn't think low fat has much flavour this is worth trying. The timbale makes a lovely first course, either plain or when served with a salad. Be sure to use a well-flavoured, richly coloured pumpkin.

Preheat oven to 190°C/375°F. Heat a small pan lightly brushed with olive oil, or a non-stick pan, and cook the onion until soft. Put the onion and all other ingredients into a blender and mix well. Spoon into 6 very small or 3 slightly larger moulds which have been lightly brushed with olive oil. Place the dishes in a tray about a quarter filled with warm water and bake in the oven about 15 minutes or until set. Timbales can be served either hot or cold.

Serves 3–6, depending on size of moulds

½ small onion, finely chopped

1 cup/8 oz mashed cooked pumpkin

½ cup/2 oz grated low-fat cheese or freshly grated Parmesan

2 egg whites

pinch of nutmeg

freshly ground pepper

easy ideas

Pumpkin Chips

Cut pumpkin into chip-sized strips and deep fry in fresh oil until golden and tender. Drain well. Season generously with salt and toss while warm with plenty of Parmesan cheese mixed with a small pinch of cayenne pepper.

rum sultana pumpkin pudding

An unusual dish, it is like an exotic bread and butter pudding with an interesting pale orange colour. You can slice and eat warm or cool.

Butter a 20 cm/8 in cake tin, line the base with a circle of non-stick baking paper/parchment and butter this as well. Marinate the sultanas in rum for about 30 minutes or leave overnight if easier.

Preheat oven to 180°C/350°F. Heat the milk and, when bubbling on the edges, pour over the bread in a mixing bowl. Let it stand for about 5 minutes or until the bread has softened, mix well using a wooden spoon or, even better, your hands so you have a thick mixture. Separate the eggs. Beat the yolks with sugar until thick, add the orange rind, the pumpkin purée and sultanas, which should have absorbed the rum by now. Stir into the bread. Beat the whites until they hold stiff peaks and fold gently into the mixture. Pour this into the buttered tin and bake for about 45 minutes or until firm to touch. It will puff on top and become quite brown. This pudding needs to be left for about 10 minutes before inverting on to a plate and, like many of these bread-based desserts, is really nicer eaten tepid or cold when all the flavours can be tasted, rather than piping hot.

Serves 6–8

1 cup/6 oz sultanas

¼ cup/2 fl oz dark rum

2 cups/1 pint milk

250 g/8 oz wholegrain bread, crusts removed and cut into cubes of about 1.25 cm/½ in

3 large eggs

½ cup/4 oz sugar

grated rind of 1 orange

1 cup/8 fl oz puréed cooked pumpkin

pumpkin in cashew nut dressing on rocket salad

uses

Indians in North America used to make an emulsion from a mixture of pumpkin and watermelon seeds and use this to heal wounds.

Exotic enough to be a course on its own, or you could serve it alongside a simple dish like a roast chicken.

Cut the pumpkin into chunks and peel. Season and oil the outside lightly and put into a baking tin on some non-stick baking paper/parchment. Bake at 190°C/375°F until soft and speckled with brown (about 45–60 minutes).

To make the dressing grind the nuts with lemon juice, rice vinegar, sugar and ginger juice then add oil. This dressing is usually too thick so add a little boiling water to lighten the mixture.

Put some rocket onto a plate. Pile pumpkin in the centre and spoon on the nut dressing.

Note
To make ginger juice grate some fresh ginger and then squeeze in your hand until you have some milky liquid. Discard the pulp.

Serves 6

1.5 kg/3 lb pumpkin

salt and pepper

oil

Dressing

125 g/4 oz cashew nuts

2 tablespoons lemon juice

2 tablespoons Chinese rice vinegar

1 teaspoon sugar

1 tablespoon ginger juice (see Note)

2 tablespoons light oil

some rocket

grated pumpkin loaf

Americans tend to call this style of cake a 'bread'. In reality it is a teacake, one that keeps well, is lovely buttered or can be toasted. Pumpkin is not usually associated with cakes, but of course it is no different to using zucchini or carrot to give a moist texture. You can make one teacake with the quantities below, about 20 cm/8 in square or two smaller ones. One can then be eaten and the other frozen, as it keeps really well for about a month in the freezer.

The pumpkin can be grated in a food processor. As the cake is made with oil, you don't have any creaming to do so it is quite quick to assemble. The cake will crack on top and dome slightly, but this is natural for teacakes.

Preheat oven to 170°C/325°F. Put the sultanas and nuts into a small bowl and add orange juice. Leave to stand for about 20 minutes to soften the fruit. Beat the eggs with sugar until fluffy. Add oil, pumpkin and mix well. Sift remaining dry ingredients over the top. Mix, beating by hand, for 30 seconds.

If there is any orange juice left in the sultanas, drain it away. Mix the fruit and nuts into the teacake batter and add vanilla essence. Butter the base and sides of the cake tin or tins, line the base with a little non-stick baking paper/parchment and lightly butter. Pour the pumpkin mixture into the prepared tin and bake in oven for about 1–1¼ hours or until set in the centre (a toothpick when inserted should come out clean). Let the cake rest in the tin for 15 minutes, then turn out on to a cake rack.

1 cup/6 oz sultanas

¼ cup/1 oz chopped pecan nuts

¼ cup/2 fl oz orange juice

3 eggs

¾ cup/3 oz castor/superfine sugar

1 cup/8 fl oz peanut or light olive oil

2½ cups/10 oz coarsely grated pumpkin

2¾ cups/11 oz flour

2 teaspoons cinnamon

½ teaspoon salt

1 teaspoon baking powder

1 teaspoon bicarbonate of soda/baking soda

1 teaspoon vanilla essence

Raphanus sativus – spring radish;
R. sativus var. longipinnatus – winter radish

Radishes are great for kids to plant as they are an almost instant success, with little green tops breaking through the ground and ready to pull in about 3 weeks, depending on the variety. Plucking out baby radishes not only thins them but these sweet young ones can be kept chilled in the fridge for an instant snack. A little posy of young radishes makes an unusual gift, too; you can also seed some pots and when they have a good crop coming through give these away as presents. Experts disagree on their origins, some claim they are native to Eastern Europe and their wild form is still growing near the Caspian Sea, while others believe they came from China. The original variety had dark skins and were a good vegetable during cold winters as they stored well. The little round ones we know, with skins of different colours, are later varieties; most have white flesh now, occasionally tinged with pink.

Look beyond the radish root and pick the tiny leaves for a delicious tang in salads, while the radish sprouts are equally delicious. Although you may just be used to eating radish raw, it can be cooked.

Radishes loosen the soil like potatoes so if you forget them don't feel badly, as when you finally pull them the soil will be nice and friable and the greens can be used as compost.

planting

Just about anywhere is OK for radish, either partial shade or full sun, but it should be in well-forked soil which is very fertile. Make sure there are no odd lumps in the ground or you will have strange-shaped radish. Plant seeds 1 cm/$\frac{1}{2}$ in deep in rows and thin out when you see they are too packed. Spring crops grow much faster than winter ones. Be sure to keep them well watered, for dry radishes can taste bitter.

Temperature Zone	Sow
	Almost everywhere all year around, except that in very cold areas seeds may not germinate in the middle of winter
First picking	*Depending on the season and size you like, about 4–8 weeks*

varieties

Spring varieties are generally round and small, winter ones larger, more oval and can grow quite large.

- French Breakfast – a lovely little oblong radish
- Round Red – the most popular market type
- Easter Egg – a colour kaleidoscope of pink, red, purple and white oval roots
- Long Scarlet, Long White - bigger long roots

Large radish for planting in all seasons

- Japanese – also known as daikon
- Black Spanish
- China Rose
- Green Chinese.

diseases and pests

Pests hardly get time to find them if you grow lots, but if left to go to seed root maggots can attack them.

harvesting

It can take just a few weeks for baby French radish to be ready to harvest, up to 70 days for the larger Japanese radish or green Chinese radish. Harvest whenever you have radish the size that suits you, but the longer you leave them the hotter and coarser they become.

buying and storage

Pick out radishes with crisp-looking, fresh green tops and no split ends. They keep a week, refrigerated, in a vegetable bag in the crisper.

nutrition

Great for Vitamin C, and they also contain iron, dietary fibre and folate. As they are closely related to cabbages they also contain a compound known as isothiocyanates which is now recognized as having anti-cancer action within the body. Radish leaves are also a good source of Vitamin C and beta-carotene.

cooking

Peeling a radish reduces its heat, but this is impossible if you have plucked out baby ones as you won't have anything left – and, besides, the heat is what I find the most interesting. Wash them well and scrub away any dirt, trimming off leaves and the tiny root. Use large ones for cooking, peel them and steam until tender or boil in a little salted water and drain well. They are quite delicate and can be tossed in a little butter or served with some hollandaise sauce on top.

radish and cucumber mint salad

Refreshing with any meat dish, I have used this as a filling inside pita bread with success and under a layer of cooked prawns to make a quick salad.

Trim the radish and dice finely, this bit takes the most time. Cut the cucumber into strips, discarding the seeds and dice into similar size to the radish and mix together. Season well with salt, pepper, and add lemon juice, mint and parsley and stir through the mayonnaise. Chill for 20 minutes. Once you have added mayonnaise serve within the hour or the dish will leak moisture.

Serves 3–4

1 bunch radishes
1/2 small cucumber
salt and pepper
1 tablespoon lemon juice
2 tablespoons mint leaves
2 tablespoons finely chopped parsley
2 tablespoons mayonnaise

radish goes with

bread
butter
fennel
ginger
garlic
cream cheese
cucumber

pickled radish salad

Try this with some chicken or duck in a sandwich, or tossed in lettuce or mixed greens as a salad.

Trim the radishes and cut into thin slices (you can use a food processor). Put into a bowl, add the salt, sugar and vinegar and toss well. Leave to stand for about 2 hours or until there is some liquid around them. Drain the radish. Squeeze with your hands to get rid of the excess liquid. Once done you can refrigerate, covered, for a day.

Serves 4

1 bunch radishes
1 tablespoon salt
1 tablespoon sugar
1 tablespoon vinegar

radishes with bread

The freshest, crisp-chilled radishes are popular as a first course in France. This is such a simple dish but can be very good as a sharply spicy starter before dinner. Each ingredient must be in perfect condition to achieve the point of this simple hors d'oeuvre or it won't be at all interesting.

Wash the radishes. Trim, leaving a small handle of leaves. Serve with little dishes of top quality butter, warm, crusty, freshly baked French breadstick and coarse sea salt. Alternatively, you can slice the radishes thinly and arrange on little rounds of buttered French bread, then sprinkle lightly with salt.

Serves 4

1 bunch small fresh radishes
60 g/2 oz unsalted or low-salt butter
1 French breadstick/baguette
some coarse sea salt

rhubarb

Rheum rhaponticum

Rhubarb once accompanied gluey rice puddings or lumpy custard, and was relegated to the disgusting kind of dessert for most kids that grew up in the Forties or Fifties, especially if they went to boarding school. The taste was too tart, the texture too stringy, and I can't remember anyone who said they liked – or much less loved – rhubarb. Everyone had a big rhubarb patch in their backyard which would just grow happily away with little maintenance and frugal cooks served it constantly to their resigned families. Suddenly what happened is we began to learn how to cook it properly. A few of the great chefs began making delicious dishes like rhubarb tarts, mixing it with soft apple and summer berries, spices like cinnamon and ginger, crunchy nuts or creamy yoghurt, and it became a different thing altogether.

It is a native of Russia, coming from Siberia, where it needed to be hardy to survive. Until the eighteenth century it was only used for medicinal purposes: its roots were given for purging. Botanically it is a vegetable although we regard it more as a fruit and treat it as one, mainly reserving rhubarb for the dessert section of the meal.

planting

Rhubarb is a perennial plant, and one that will only grow well in cool conditions. Buy a division of rhubarb and plant in rich, well-worked soil, either in the sun or partial shade. I find my shaded rhubarb does far better. If you are planting more than one put them about a metre (yard) apart and keep the growing tip slightly beneath the surface of the soil. Keep moist and fertilize. You should leave for the first year so it becomes stronger, then pick after that. You need to pick the stalks, as leaving them to continue growing can result in some rotting if the plant becomes too big. You can divide your own plants in spring when the ground is warm after it has been growing about 3 years. Don't let rhubarb flower, to ensure the leaf stalks keep growing strongly, and keep weeds and grass away as rhubarb resents competition.

Temperature Zone	Plant
Tropical, subtropical	Not suitable
Temperate	Winter
Cool	Winter

varieties

- Prince Albert
- Sydney Crimson
- Victoria
- Stone's Early Albert
- Stone's Early Ruby
- Cherryripe
- Wandin Winter   doesn't die back in winter.

diseases and pests

It is pretty much trouble-free.

harvesting

Aim to take only a third of the stalks in a year, definitely no more than half, to keep the plant strong. To harvest, gently twist off the stalk at the soil line. Take off the leaves, they are poisonous.

buying and storage

Green rhubarb stalks cook to a paler shade and don't look quite as interesting as the red; the red, which is more readily available in winter, is a bit sweeter. Rhubarb wilts quickly after picking, and bunches should be crisp and standing firm. If any leaves remain cut these off, wrap the stalks in some plastic and keep in a covered container in the crisper of the refrigerator, where it will keep for a week.

nutrition

Rhubarb contains only small amounts of vitamins and minerals, plus some dietary fibre.

cooking

Cut away the flat brown part from the bottom of the rhubarb stalk and chop into pieces about 4 cm/1½ in long. The stalks don't often need stringing but you can pull away any hard pieces if they feel tough. Don't take all the strings off or the rhubarb just cooks straight to a mushy sauce, for the strings hold the pieces together.

Cook with just a little water to come level with the stalks, plus a generous scatter of sugar over this, according to how tart you like it, then cover and leave on a gentle heat for anything from 5 to 8 minutes. The younger and thinner the stalk, the faster it becomes tender. I find home-grown cooks faster than bought rhubarb.

orange and rhubarb pie

**rhubarb
goes with**

butter

apples

oranges

ginger

berries

yoghurt

cinnamon

vanilla

honey

all kinds
of sugars

lamb

nuts

Baked in a piecrust the intensity of rhubarb is softened and yet it has a rich flavour, which goes well with buttery biscuit textures. I like to cook the rhubarb before putting into the pie, as it shrinks a lot in the cooking so leaves a gap if you put an uncooked layer under the crust. This is a softer crust than usual, almost a bit cakey, which is perfect with a juicy filling.

The spiced rhubarb can be made a day in advance – and in fact is better put very cold into the pastry. The old trick of brushing a crust with cream and then coating with sugar gives a wonderful texture and taste to a pie with any tart filling. Serve with plenty of runny or lightly whipped cream and or a dish of vanilla ice cream.

Put rhubarb, orange and juice, cinnamon and sugar into a shallow baking dish, cover tightly and cook for about 20 minutes in a moderate oven (180°C/350°F) until softened. (If you can't be bothered putting the oven on, cook gently in a saucepan until tender.) There should just a little juice around. Chill.

For crust, cream butter and sugar together or process until mixed. Add hot water. Mix in both kinds of flour and salt and either blend well with your hands or process until it holds together. Wrap in some plastic wrap and chill for about 20 minutes. Cut into two pieces, a third for the top, two-thirds for the base. Roll out the largest piece and put into a pie plate about 18 cm/7 in diameter, pressing down. Spoon the rhubarb onto this. Roll out the smaller piece and put on top and pinch the edges firmly.

Preheat oven to 180°C/350°F. Brush the crust with cream and scatter on sugar and make a couple of slashes in the top. Bake for about 35 minutes or until browned and crisp. Allow it to cool for at least 10 minutes before cutting, so the juices settle.

Note
To make 1 cup/4 oz self-raising flour, to every 1 cup/4 oz of plain/all-purpose flour add 1½ teaspoons baking powder and ½ teaspoon salt.

Serves 6

500 g/1 lb rhubarb, cut into small sticks about 5 cm/2 in long

1 orange, rind and pith removed

½ cup/4 fl oz orange juice

piece of cinnamon stick

½ cup/4 oz brown sugar

2 tablespoons cream

plenty of sugar

Soft Biscuit Crust
125 g/4 oz butter

¼ cup/1 oz sugar

1 tablespoon hot water

1 cup/4 oz flour

½ cup/2 oz self-raising flour (see Note)

pinch of salt

braised lamb with rhubarb

The idea of combining acid or sweet fruit with a slightly fatty meat such as lamb is typical of many areas of old Russia, Morocco and Persia. The best cut for a dish such as this is a forequarter, or shoulder, which will cook to a succulent soft texture without stringiness and reheat superbly.

These sorts of dishes should be made well in advance so you can chill them and remove the excess fat. Serve with a lovely aromatic rice such as basmati, which makes a good foil for the generous amount of gravy. A smallish amount is usually enough for most people and this should be ample for six to eight, depending on their appetites.

Cut the lamb into 3 cm/$1\frac{1}{4}$ in dice, leaving most of the fat on. Heat the butter with oil and fry the onions quickly for 5 minutes, then add the meat. Scatter with cinnamon and sugar, then add water, stock and seasonings. Bring to a boil, cover, and cook over the lowest possible heat for $1\frac{1}{2}$–2 hours, or until the meat is tender. Add the rhubarb to the pan and cook for a further 30 minutes.

Refrigerate overnight and the following day remove any fat from the top. Take out the pieces of meat, which may have set in a jelly, and put them aside. Boil the sauce, reducing a little to about $1\frac{1}{2}$ cups/12 fl oz. Taste, and if it is too sharp, add a little more sugar. If it is not fresh tasting, add a tablespoon of lemon juice. Mix in the mint, return the lamb to the pan and gently heat through.

Serves 6–8

1.75 kg/4 lb boned forequarter/ shoulder of lamb

30 g/1 oz butter

2 tablespoons olive oil

2 large onions, roughly chopped

$\frac{1}{2}$ teaspoon cinnamon

2 teaspoons sugar

1 cup/8 fl oz water

1 cup/8 fl oz chicken stock

1 teaspoon salt and plenty of pepper

4 stalks rhubarb, cut into 3 cm/$1\frac{1}{4}$ in lengths

1 tablespoon mint leaves

---

easy ideas

Lemon Rhubarb Sauce

Chop 3 or 4 stalks rhubarb into tiny pieces and put into a china bowl with the juice of 2 lemons, $\frac{3}{4}$ cup/ 6 fl oz water and 1 cup/8 oz sugar. Stir and leave for a few hours and then cook gently, stirring every so often, until thickish. Add a big knob of butter and mix through off the heat. Sieve through a food mill (moulin) and use warm over ice cream, with cake, or chill and use as a cold sauce over stewed apple or pear. Add more sugar if you need it sweeter.

---

easy ideas *Rhubarb Layered Delight*

Cook rhubarb as for Easy Stewed Rhubarb (see page 292) and carefully strain off the juice. Boil this rapidly until about $\frac{1}{2}$ cup/4 fl oz remains, mix this back into rhubarb. Don't worry if they break a bit for this dish. Chill. Mix 1 cup/8 fl oz whipped cream with the same amount of thick plain yoghurt. Put a little rhubarb in the bottom of some tall glasses, then a spoonful of the yoghurt–cream mix, then some brown sugar; continue layering in this way. The top layer should be cream. Serves about 2–3, but this depends on the size of the glasses — smaller wine glasses will result in more serving.

strawberries with rhubarb

easy ideas

Easy Stewed Rhubarb

Warm 1 cup/ 8 fl oz orange juice with 1 cup/ 8 fl oz water in a large frying pan. While this is heating cut about 6 stalks (500– 750g/1–1 1/2 lb) rhubarb stalks into pieces about 2.5 cm/1 in long; remove any tough strings. Toss into liquid, shake pan every so often so juice covers fruit and simmer a few minutes, gently, until rhubarb is just tender. Mix 1/2 cup/4 oz sugar with 1 tea- spoon cinnamon and scatter on top, stir gently or shake pan until sugar has dissolved. (Adding sugar in this way ensures rhubarb keeps its shape, as does cooking in a frying pan instead of a saucepan.) To serve, spoon rhubarb around ice cream or chill and eat with cream or yoghurt.

Search for some young rhubarb stalks and make this fresh tasting, rather tart combination of fruits, which goes well after any rich main course. It is a wonderful mix of pink and reds and you can cook the rhubarb base a day or so beforehand. Add the berries a couple of hours before serving and chill so it is quite cold. The rhubarb base should be a bit runny so you have plenty of lovely juice to spoon around the berries.

Cut the rhubarb into pieces about 3 cm/1 1/4 in long. As you cut, pull away any stringy pieces from the stalks. Put the rhubarb into a saucepan with orange juice, water, orange rind, cinnamon stick and sugar. Bring to a boil, gently, and then cover and cook over the lowest possible heat for about 5 minutes. Check for tenderness. Keep cooking if not soft but do not let the rhubarb become a stringy mass. Remove to a bowl, cool and remove the cinnamon stick. Refrigerate for at least 6 hours so it will thicken.

If berries are large cut them into thick slices or halve. An hour or so before serving, mix the berries with the rhubarb.

Serves 6

250 g/8 oz rhubarb

1/2 cup/4 fl oz orange juice

1/2 cup/4 fl oz water

grated rind of 1 orange

1 piece cinnamon stick, about 2.5 cm/1 in long

1/2 cup/4 oz sugar

2 punnets (500 g/1 lb) strawberries, hulled

orange rhubarb cake

This light, buttery upside-down cake is made with a layer of rhubarb pieces on top, which cook to a soft fruity topping. Very good for dessert but also nice as a teacake. It does keep for a few days but is really best if eaten the day it is made. Serve with a big generous bowl of lightly whipped cream or some good vanilla ice cream.

Preheat oven to 180°C/350°F. Cut the rhubarb into 2.5 cm/1 in lengths, removing any large strings. Rub the bottom and sides of a 20 cm/8 in diameter cake tin with the 30 g/1 oz butter. Scatter both kinds of sugar over the top. Put rhubarb on to this, packing firmly as it will shrink quite a bit during the cooking. Cream the butter with the 1/2 cup/4 oz sugar until light and fluffy. Add orange rind and egg, beating well. Sift half the flour over the top and add buttermilk, then the remaining flour. Put small spoonfuls of cake batter on top of the rhubarb so as not to disturb it. Spread evenly. Bake for about 50 minutes, or until the cake is firm to touch on top and rhubarb juices are bubbling on the edges. Let the cake rest for 5 minutes so the juices settle and then run a knife around the edge. Carefully invert on to a plate. Should any pieces of rhubarb stick, just remove them with a knife and replace on top of the cake.

Note
To make 1 cup/4 oz self-raising flour, to every 1 cup/4 oz of plain/all purpose flour add 1 1/2 teaspoons baking powder and 1/2 teaspoon salt.

250 g/8 oz rhubarb

30 g/1 oz butter

2 tablespoons brown sugar

1 tablespoon white sugar

90 g/3 oz butter

1/2 cup/4 oz sugar

1 teaspoon grated orange rind

1 egg

1 1/4 cups/5 oz self-raising flour (see Note)

2/3 cup/6 fl oz buttermilk

rosemary

Rosmarinus officinalis

Rosemary for its aroma, rosemary for remembrance ... it is a herb even more surrounded by legends and tradition than most and has become the symbol of remembrance, friendship and fidelity. It was mentioned as far back as the eleventh century for its use in keeping moths away from clothes and the pungent scent was believed to fight infection, so it was carried to funerals, church festivals, weddings and burnt when incense was scarce. It is a wonderful herb in the garden, for not only does it scent the air but it creeps along the ground and keeps away weeds, then has tiny flowers which are a bright summery blue or snowy white. It flourishes all year and the needle-like leaves are quite attractive, with a deep green to silver colour.

planting

Rosemary, a perennial bush, doesn't like having wet feet but otherwise will grow anywhere except in the coldest positions, and copes well with drought or stony soil. You need to plant it where the ground is well drained. It needs very little fertilizing; indeed, too much feeding and it can become diseased. Best to buy a plant or put one in from cuttings. Just take a piece from a low shoot which has a 'heel' of old wood, attached. Most people are glad to give you a cutting as rosemary bushes need plenty of trimming or they become quite woody. A good time is late summer to late autumn but you can plant from spring onwards. Push your cutting into some sandy soil and keep it moist. Alternatively, put a low-growing branch onto the ground, peg it down and heap some soil over this. In about 5 months you will have a good root system.

As rosemary came from the Mediterranean and grew in the salt sea spray, it still seems to do better in salt winds than many other herbs. Its Latin name means 'dew of the sea'. It likes the sun but will survive frosts and cold.

varieties

Bush rosemary is a tall quite large bush while prostrate rosemary (*Rosmarinus officinalis* var. *protratus*) has similar growing habits, scent and uses but it creeps along the ground.

harvesting

Just pick when the plant is large enough and be sure the sprigs are dry if you are keeping them, or they will become mouldy and rot. Dry by hanging up some branches with string, don't have too many together, allow the air to circulate.

buying and storage

Buy fresh rosemary which smells rich and fragrant and check it is not soggy where the stalk may have been stored in water in the shop. Keep in a plastic bag in the refrigerator, or if you love the smell enjoy it in a small container of water in the kitchen. The leaves will begin to fall after a few days but the aroma in dishes will not be affected. I don't care for bought dried rosemary, which has nowhere near the flavour of the fresh, or even home-grown rosemary you dry yourself.

cooking

It originated in the Mediterranean and the cooks from this region use it so well – and use so much of it in dishes. Rosemary will be studded inside a leg of lamb, while in Tuscany large branches are stuffed inside baby pigs then roasted, and a mixture of the fat, lean meat and crisp skin are pushed, dripping with juices, into some unsalted crusty bread. Rosemary – along with garlic – is the perfect herb for roasting or adding to sautéed potatoes, but the very aroma which makes it so sought

after also can be too strong, so it is usually better to put it under or alongside things that are cooking rather than actually eating it, except in tiny amounts. Branches of rosemary under the leg of lamb, alongside the potatoes, strewn over a pan in which a big piece of pork is to be cooked so its aroma melts into the juices that drip down, are more than enough to flavour food. Throw prunings onto a barbecue, they will scent the air and add a little aroma to the meat and if older kids love to help, give them the task of brushing your barbecuing meat or fish with a long rosemary branch dipped in some oil as it sizzles away outdoors. Somehow it makes fish less 'fishy' smelling, and its links with the cooking of Italy, Spain and southern France make it ideal to give a depth of flavour to simmered casseroles flavoured with wine and garlic. Apart from its fragrance with savoury dishes, you can put a little into biscuits and jams, use with fruits and in pies, but act with caution rather than with too much enthusiasm.

potatoes baked on a bed of herbs

uses

Students in Greece used garlands of rosemary to improve their memory during exam time as the herb does seem to clear the head. Rosemary has properties which expand the tissues, so it increases the blood supply to that area and this has a stimulating effect. It can be used as a tonic for the skin and as a rinse for the growth of new hair.

This dish smells wonderful when the foil package is opened, increasing the aroma of herbs and garlic. Open it at the table when everybody is gathered around, as much of the charm is in the fragrant scent of the dish as much as the flavour. It needs masses – a bed of herbs for the base of the potatoes and a second layer of herbs on top. Allow at least four small potatoes per person and don't peel them. The skin adds to the rustic quality and earthy flavours. The quantity is flexible as the recipe need never be precise.

plenty of branches of fresh rosemary or thyme

4 potatoes per person

rock or sea salt and plenty of black pepper

1 clove garlic per person

some virgin olive oil

Place a big piece of foil on your bench, and on top of this spread out a layer of rosemary. Place the potatoes on top in one layer: a single layer holds about 24; any more becomes too hard to seal and cook, so you may need to make several packages. Season well with salt and pepper, tuck the garlic between the potatoes and sprinkle with virgin olive oil here and there. Put a second layer of herbs on top of the potatoes so that you can barely see them. Place another large sheet of foil on top and pinch the edges all the way round so it is well sealed.

Place in the oven, preheated to 180°C/350°F, or on the barbecue and cook for about 45 minutes–1 hour, depending on the size of the potatoes. It doesn't hurt to leave them a little longer. Once cooked, the potatoes can safely be left in the package where they will keep warm for some time. To serve, put the package on to a tray or serving dish, open and pull away the herbs from the top so the potatoes can be lifted out. However, leave them sitting on the herb base.

easy ideas *Orange and Rosemary Lamb Fillets*

Trim 8 little fillets of lamb (2 per person) of any sinew and cook in a frying pan in a little oil until they are brown on the outside. Remove, season well and pour in ½ cup/ 4 fl oz orange juice and the same amount of chicken stock or seasoned water; scrape up any brown bits from the pan as it boils. Add 1 tablespoon red currant jelly and 1 teaspoon finely chopped rosemary leaves. Return the fillets, turning them over so they are coated with sauce and let them cook a couple of minutes, gently. Slice each one diagonally into three and serve with a bit of sauce which should have cooked down to a small amount by now – if not boil madly.

Rosemary Ricotta

Heat ⅓ cup/3 fl oz oil with several big sprigs rosemary and a clove of finely chopped garlic. When very hot remove to a bowl and leave to cool. Mash about 250 g/8 oz ricotta and strain in the oil. Season with plenty of salt and pepper, a squeeze of lemon juice and mix well. Serve with hot toast as a snack or hollow out fat, juicy, ripe tomatoes and spoon some into the cavity. For colour you can mix in a little finely chopped parsley when adding lemon, but make sure the rosemary flavour is the major taste.

mushroom ragoût

rosemary goes with

most meats, *especially*:

rabbit
lamb
pork
veal
chicken
fish
bread
pizza dough
garlic
onion
olive oil
oregano
thyme
savoury

Pronounced 'ragoo' and prepared with an old traditional method, this style of thick and almost black mushroom dish would have formed part of the large breakfast served in an English household, alongside dishes such as kidneys, kippers and creamy scrambled eggs. It would have been a seasonal dish, made with dark field mushrooms cooked up to an intense flavour. Buy big open mushrooms, which have a wide cap with dark gills underneath. If you can't find these, buy some Swiss browns or use fleshy pine mushrooms. They will make a different dish but one that is just as effective. As a main meal it will serve two people, and as an accompaniment to a thick piece of steak, for example, it will be enough for four.

Melt the butter in a large saucepan and add the onion. Cook gently until it is well coloured and soft. Cut the mushrooms either into thick slices or quarters and add to the pan. Stir for a couple of minutes until they begin to soften and then scatter the flour over the top. Stir. Add the wine and stock; scatter on the rosemary and garlic and season well with salt and pepper. Let the dish simmer over a low heat for about 10 minutes, or until it is thick and richly coloured. For pine mushrooms, you could even leave a little longer. Have the hot toast ready and spoon the mushrooms on to the plate or on top of the toast so the juices seep into it, and serve immediately.

Serves 2–4

60 g/2 oz butter

1 medium-sized onion, finely chopped

250 g/8 oz mushrooms

3 teaspoons flour

$1/2$ cup/4 fl oz red wine

$1/2$ cup/4 fl oz chicken stock

1 teaspoon finely chopped rosemary

1 clove garlic, crushed

salt and pepper

hot toast

rosemary scented fillet steak on a purée

Fillet steak is very tender but has little flavour so lends itself well to a marinade, and rosemary makes an interesting accompaniment to beef. Both parts of the dish are linked as the same herb is also included in the accompanying purée.

Put steaks into a bowl with the oil, lemon, pepper and rosemary and leave to marinate, refrigerated, for several hours.

Cook the vegetables with the sprig of rosemary in a pot of salted boiling water and drain well, discard the rosemary. Process, season and add the butter, then transfer to a bowl. Heat the milk and whisk in enough to make the mixture light. Keep warm or reheat in a microwave.

Leave the oil on the steaks but scrape off any rosemary and cook in a pan over a high heat until they are browned on the outside, pink on the inside and season again. To serve, spoon some purée onto hot plates and top with a steak and any juices from the pan.

Serves 4

4 fillet steaks, trimmed

$1/4$ cup/2 fl oz virgin olive oil

2 strips lemon rind

some ground black pepper

1 tablespoon chopped rosemary leaves

Vegetable Purée

4 medium-sized potatoes, peeled and roughly diced

1 large carrot, peeled and sliced

1 sweet potato, peeled and sliced

1 big sprig rosemary

salt and pepper

45 g/1 $1/2$ oz butter

about $1/2$ cup/4 fl oz milk or cream

chicken with balsamic vinegar

In Modena, a roasting chicken is cooked with a coating of garlic and sprigs of rosemary. Before being brought to the table, it is anointed with some of the family balsamic vinegar that has mellowed through being stored in the cellar for generations. The older the vinegar, the better the finished flavours. I love this simple dish served with some sautéed potatoes, cooked until they form a brown crust and a green spinach salad made with baby leaves. Use any good commercial balsamic vinegar, the addition of brown sugar will balance any acidity.

Rinse the chicken and pat dry. Put a little garlic into the centre cavity and three-quarters of the rosemary. Rub the outside of the chicken with the remaining garlic, chop the rest of the rosemary and rub this over the top. Season with salt and pepper and cover tightly with plastic wrap. Leave in the refrigerator for about 8 hours.

Heat the oven to 190°C/375°F and dab the olive oil over the breast of the chicken, being careful not to disturb the garlic and rosemary coating. Put the chicken into a lightly oiled baking tin, breast side up, and cook for about 45 minutes or until golden, basting every 15 minutes. Turn over and cook again for a further 20 minutes, then turn it again and cook until it is tender. Altogether it will probably take about 90 minutes to cook.

Remove to a board and cut directly through the breast and backbone so that chicken is in halves. Place these on to a warmed platter. Have the balsamic mixed with sugar and trickle this over the top. Leave covered for a couple of minutes in a warm place so that the juices mingle with the vinegar. Cut each portion into halves again for serving.

Note
Taste the balsamic before using. If it is very sharp, you can dilute with a spoonful of water.

Serves 4

1 chicken, about 2 kg/4½ lb
3 cloves garlic, finely chopped
6 fresh rosemary sprigs
salt and plenty of ground black pepper
1 tablespoon virgin olive oil
2 tablespoons balsamic vinegar
½ teaspoon brown sugar

uses

Rosemary oil is said to get rid of a headache if rubbed on your temples and a thick hedge of rosemary will create a shelter for small nesting birds, bring bees into the garden and as a hedge will keep out small animals as it feels prickly.

potato and smothered onion soup with rosemary

This country-style Italian soup is warming and substantial winter fare. I have adapted it from a Marcella Hazan recipe. It's perfect for an easy lunch on the weekend and goes well with some crusty bread. In one of Hazan's books I was interested to note that she uses vegetable oil for some of her soups instead of the more flavoursome olive oil. I prefer to use olive oil in this kind of soup for, like most simple, peasant-inspired soups, olive oil adds a roundness of flavour to the water or stock, which balances the whole.

Peel the potatoes, cut them into 2.5 cm/1 in cubes, rinse in cold water and set aside. Put the butter, oil, onion and a healthy pinch of salt into a soup pot. Turn the heat to medium. Do not cover the pot. Cook the onion at a slow pace, stirring occasionally, until it has wilted and become pale brown. Add the garlic and stir through. Add the diced potatoes, turn up the heat to high and sauté the potatoes briskly, turning them in the onions to coat them well. They tend to stick so you need to watch them. Pour in the stock, add the rosemary, cover the pot and adjust the heat so that the soup comes to a slow steady boil. When the potatoes are very tender, crush most of them by mashing them against the side of the pot with a wooden spoon. It's best to remove the rosemary first or the soup will be too strong. Stir the mixture thoroughly and cook for another 8–10 minutes. If you find the soup becoming too thick, just add more stock or, if you have run out of stock, water can be used instead. Check for seasoning – it needs to be quite peppery and well salted.

Before serving, turn off the heat, swirl in the grated Parmesan and chopped parsley then taste again. Serve with additional grated cheese on the side.

Serves 6

1 kg/2 lb boiling potatoes

45 g/1½ oz butter

3 tablespoons virgin olive oil

750 g/1½ lb onions, sliced very thinly

salt

2 cloves garlic, finely chopped

3 cups/12 fl oz chicken stock

small branch of rosemary

pepper

grated Parmesan cheese

2 tablespoons chopped parsley

bean soup in a tuscan manner

The beans are cooked so they become like a soft, light cream and tiny shells of pasta make this a satisfying soup, which reheats well. I have eaten this kind of soup often in Tuscany and find there is nothing more homely and warming on a cool day than a big bowl of Tuscan bean soup and a basket of crusty bread followed by some pieces of very fresh Parmesan cheese and pears. However, it needs to be well seasoned, with plenty of the spicy pepper taste and, if you like it, a dash of virgin olive oil at the finish will give a rich, fruity oil flavour.

Place the beans into a large bowl, cover with water and let them soak overnight, drain and rinse well. Place in a pot and add 6 cups/3 pints of fresh water. Add the kaiserfleish or piece of bacon, garlic and about 2 teaspoons salt. Add more salt later if needed. Cook gently for about 1½–2 hours or until the beans are very soft. Drain the beans, saving the liquid and removing the kaiserfleish or bacon. Process beans, adding a little liquid in each batch. Cut the bacon into tiny pieces and add to the soup.

Return to the pot and heat, it should resemble a light cream. I find if I make the soup in advance and leave overnight in the refrigerator it thickens more. Next day when reheating you can add a little extra stock or water. When you are ready to serve the soup heat the oil in a frying pan, cut each piece of bread into about half, depending on the size, and add to the pan. Cook on both sides until golden. Add a bit more oil if necessary. Take out the bread and drain on some kitchen paper towel. Scatter the rosemary leaves into the pan and fry gently for half a minute then tip them into the soup along with any remaining oil in the pan. If there are bits of crumbs in the pan don't fuss about these, they will soften in the liquid. Season soup. Cook the pasta in salted water for about 5 minutes, drain and then transfer to the bean mixture and continue to cook until the pasta is tender. To serve, place a piece of bread in the base of a deep soup bowl, pour the bean soup over the top.

Serves 4–6

1¼ cups/10 oz dried cannellini beans

45 g/1½ oz piece of kaiserfleish or bacon

2 cloves garlic

salt

¼ cup/2 fl oz virgin olive oil

salt and pepper

2–3 thick slices of country-style bread

2 teaspoons finely chopped fresh rosemary

freshly ground pepper to taste

90 g/3 oz small pasta shells

lamb rosemary skewers

A dish to make when you have pruned some strong and woody rosemary stems. The skewers impart a light fragrance to the meat and they look rustic and interesting. They can be barbecued but you need to soak the rosemary in water for hours before threading meat on them, or they will just burn up before the meat is cooked. If you do barbecue them make sure the tufty ends of the herb are away from the direct fire.

Remove any sinew from the fillets. Cut vertically into long thin slices: you will be able to get three long slices as a rule from each fillet. Place in a shallow dish. Mix the garlic, salt, cumin, oil, vinegar, lemon, Tabasco and pepper and pour over the lamb, turning meat over with your hands so it is well coated. Leave to marinate for at least 4 hours, preferably overnight.

Remove some of the rosemary tufts from the stalks but trim the other end so you have a pointy skewer. Soak for an hour or so in water. Preheat oven to 190°C/375°F.

Thread the lamb strips onto rosemary skewers, gently pushing meat up towards the rosemary tuft. When ready to cook them, have a baking dish hot in the oven. Place the skewers on this and bake for about 10 minutes. Serve with a light, fresh tomato sauce on the side or pile them on a bed of ratatouille.

Serves 6

6 lamb fillets
2 cloves garlic
$\frac{1}{2}$ teaspoon salt
$\frac{1}{2}$ teaspoon ground cumin
$\frac{1}{3}$ cup/3 fl oz olive oil
2 teaspoons balsamic vinegar
1 tablespoon lemon juice
dash of Tabasco
some cracked black pepper
approx. 12 twigs of rosemary

Salvia officinalis

Sage loves basking in the sun and birds adore it, so it will entice nectar-feeding birds into your garden. There are hundreds of species of *Salvia*, but the one known as '*officinalis*' is the most important for culinary purposes and it is often called true sage. It is a pretty plant, a perennial with green to silvery-grey leaves that have a fragrance when you touch them and, depending on the variety, it can have white, pink or blue flowers. Other species of sage often found in gardens include bog sage, or marsh sage, (*S.uliginosa*). This is a plant with a misleading name, as it is quite happy in dry as well as damp areas and has wonderful, startling, bright blue flowers in summer growing along the long spikes. Pineapple sage (*S. rutilans*) does smell and taste a bit like pineapple and birds love the long flower spikes of bright red. It dies down in winter, comes up again in spring but very cold winters or heavy frost may kill it so it should be grown in a sheltered area.

True sage has been regarded as an important health-giving herb and was once reputed to help with things as diverse as fixing snake bites to a remedy for epilepsy, but most important of all, it was supposed to prevent ageing and prolong youth.

This is a plant which can be spread throughout the garden and its rewards are many, from the scent it lends the beds, the height it gives and the colourful flowers. Some varieties do die back in winter after heavy frost but mostly it is quite hardy.

In England bread stuffing for fatty poultry such as duck was traditionally made with lots of sage in the belief that the herb helped digestion, but sometimes the English dishes appear heavy handed in their use of the herb. In Italy it is handled well; Italians roll tender white veal with a leaf of sage inside, fry or sauté sage leaves until they are crisp and dip sweet and big sage leaves into a batter. Sage tea is sometimes served in little cafés in Greece and in the Dalmatian region of Yugoslavia.

The flavour of sage is a mix of pungency, slight bitterness, warmth and a hint of camphor; fresh it has a gentle taste in comparison to dried but it is one of the herbs that keeps its fragrance when dry and should just be stored in a jar in a cool place. It is powerful dried, so be cautious rather than adding too much to dishes.

planting

True sage is frost- and heat-tolerant and very hardy. You can grow it from seed but a small seedling or plant is easier to handle and sage propagates well by layering. Put a branch onto the soil, heap on some fresh soil and leave for a few months, keeping the soil moist until a root system has formed. Cut away the branch, carefully dig it up and plant so you don't disturb the new root system. Plant seeds or plants from spring to early autumn.

harvesting

Pick sage when the plant is big enough and the leaves are the size you want.

buying and storage

If you have a choice buy a bunch of sage with small leaves as they will have a more delicate taste than older strong leaves. Either keep in the kitchen in a small container in water for a few days or in a plastic bag in the refrigerator, where it should keep about 3 days.

chicken and sage skewers

Pieces of fragrant sage are inserted between chunky cubes of marinated chicken to give a rich herb flavour. If the sage is very large cut the leaves into half, or they may be too strong. Small squares of ham could also be put next to the sage, as a variation on this theme.

Cut chicken into cubes of about 4 cm/1½ in and marinate in the oil, citrus juices and rind for an hour. Skewer chunks of chicken interspersed with small whole or halved sage leaves, putting a leaf at the beginning and end of each skewer. Scatter generously with salt and even more generously with pepper. Grill or barbecue, turning over and brushing several times with melted butter and marinade as they cook. These need watching, as the chicken must be cooked through but it is important it does not dry out.

Serves 4

4 chicken breasts, boned and skinned

3 tablespoons extra virgin oil

3 tablespoons orange juice

2 tablespoons lemon juice

½ teaspoon grated orange rind

lots of sage leaves

salt and pepper

60 g/2 oz butter, melted

pupton

Pupton is a wonderful old English dish made with game that is layered with a tasty mixture of bacon, onion and breadcrumbs and a selection of vegetables aromatic with sage. No doubt it would have been used with very rich, high-tasting game caught on a country shoot. Buy any kind of well-flavoured commercial poultry instead. I like to use squab for this, which is available fresh in many shops that sell game birds, or frozen at all times of the year. You could use chicken but it becomes a different, lighter-flavoured dish.

The squab cooks at the same time as the layers of vegetables and crumbs. The top should be brown and crisp; underneath, the meat should be tender and the vegetables soft. If the top is not crunchy you can finish it off under the griller.

I suspect that in the original versions the bacon would have been very fatty and given more moisture to the dish than is possible now with the lean bacon we find in shops. Moisture can be added by using a tablespoon of oil when sautéing the onion and bacon, or later adding some stock, as I have suggested. Pupton really doesn't need anything much on the plate to accompany it, but a purée of spinach goes nicely alongside if you think that the dish looks a bit too plain.

This is not a dish to reheat because the squab becomes dry, as do the vegetables and crumbs, but it can be assembled hours beforehand, ready for baking.

Cut each squab in half down the backbone, and then into quarters. Put the bacon into a frying pan with the onion and cook gently until the onion has softened and the bacon is cooked. If the pan is dry – and this will depend on the fat in the bacon – moisten with a little oil or butter. Mix onion and bacon with the crumbs, lemon rind, nutmeg and herbs and stir gently to combine.

Preheat oven to 180°C/350°F. Butter a casserole with a tight-fitting lid, one that holds about 5 cups/2½ pints. On the base put about one third of the crumbs mixture. Scatter half the carrot, leek and mushroom over this and season lightly. Arrange squab in the centre of the dish and cover with the remaining vegetables, season again and then top with the remainder of the crumbs and dot with butter. Put a lid on the casserole and bake for 1 hour or until the squab is tender.

Should the dish appear dry, add some chicken stock halfway through the cooking, trickling it down the sides a little at a time. This will moisten and create steam. Do not pour stock over the top or it will just make the crumbs soggy. When squab is cooked remove the lid and either return to the oven for another 10 minutes to crisp the crumbs or put the dish under a griller/broiler for a few minutes. When you serve it, spoon out the crumbs first to one side of the plate, then some vegetable and squab, dividing the portions evenly.

Serves 8

4 squab/pigeon

3 rashers bacon, sliced in small pieces

1 large onion, cut into half and sliced

125 g/4 oz breadcrumbs, made from stale white or brown bread

grated rind of 1 lemon

¼ teaspoon grated nutmeg

2 tablespoons finely chopped parsley

6 baby leaves of fresh sage

2 medium-sized carrots, finely chopped

2 medium-sized leeks, finely sliced

125 g/4 oz mushrooms, cut into quarters

salt and pepper

some butter

about ½ cup/4 fl oz chicken stock (optional)

uses

Drunk as a tea, it is a tonic for the nerves and blood and, if used as a lotion, improves the condition of hair and skin. It helps keep teeth white in a mouthwash. Red sage tea is an old remedy for sore throats.

sage and garlic butter

sage goes with

poultry, particularly duck and goose

lamb

veal

onions

peas

dried beans of all kinds

cheese

mixed herbs

olive oil

An easy butter to spoon over pieces of veal, chicken or pork or onto some ravioli or filled vegetable pasta. You need quite big sage leaves for this as the little ones are a bit difficult to serve and divide between the portions.

Put the garlic into a frying pan with half the butter and let it cook gently until pale gold and softened. You need to keep the heat low so the butter doesn't burn. Remove garlic from the pan, add the rest of the butter and turn up the heat a little. When foaming add the sage leaves and cook until they are crisp. Cool immediately by plunging the pan into some cold water or the butter will overheat and brown. Return the garlic, scatter on pepper and spoon over the meat.

Enough for 4

8 cloves garlic, halved

90 g/3 oz butter, cut into small pieces

8 sage leaves

black pepper

old-fashioned sage and onion stuffing

This has the rich flavour of onions, bacon and sage, resulting in a very aromatic stuffing, reminiscent of the old-fashioned ones once used in almost every kind of poultry from chicken to duck. You can prepare the stuffing the day before you need it, but don't stuff the turkey or goose until the day you are cooking. For a chicken stuffing, just make about a third or even a quarter of the amount, depending on whether you have a large or small bird.

Melt butter in a saucepan and add onions and bacon and leave to cook gently until they are soft and tinged with gold. Add the apple and cook until beginning to soften. Remove everything to a bowl and mix in the remaining ingredients. Stir until well blended. Spoon into the cavity of a turkey or a goose, packing in lightly.

60 g/2 oz butter

3 large onions, roughly diced

3 rashers bacon, chopped into strips

2 large apples, peeled, cored and finely diced

4 cups/12 oz breadcrumbs, made from white or brown bread

1/4 cup/1/2 oz finely chopped parsley

grated rind of 1 large lemon

1 tablespoon chopped sage

1 teaspoon salt

lots of cracked black pepper

1 large egg and 1 egg white

extra 60 g/2 oz butter, cut into tiny pieces

Sanguisorba minor

I am frequently asked the name of my salad burnet plant, which would indicate that it is a herb not commonly grown, and it does seem to have been overlooked in modern herb gardens. Perhaps its particular flavour is not strong or dominant enough. It is a very delicate looking little herb, whose fragile appearance is quite misleading for salad burnet is hardy and strong. It originally came from Mediterranean countries and since the sixteenth century has been grown in England, where it grows wild on the chalk hills. The very pretty foliage, with fine-toothed edges, of this low-growing plant makes it ideal as a garnish for all kinds of food and a couple of sprigs or sprays on a plate almost immediately add a delicate tone. The flavour is slightly like cucumber, but a little nutty, and you just pull off the

▲ salad burnet and cheese spread (recipe page 309)

leaves from the stalk. Great for salads and you can be generous with this herb. Although not invasive once you have planted some and let a couple of the flower stems seed it will come in small clumps around the original plant forever after unless you pull everything out. The flowers are not used so much in cooking but are quite a pretty, round globular shape.

Salad burnet is a perennial and makes a very pretty border; it is quite neat and round and is very good either for a formal garden or for growing among paving stones. It is equally happy in sun or under partial shade.

planting

Salad burnet is not at all fussy, although is prefers slightly chalky or limey soil. Although you can plant seeds I think it is best to put in a small seedling and keep cutting it back as soon as a flower shoot appears, so you then immediately get a supply of new baby leaves. Big leaves are not quite as tender for a salad but fine for drinks so keep a mix of different leaves on the one plant. It can be grown indoors or outdoors in a pot and doesn't mind frost or even light snow – in fact, it survives most weather conditions. Seedlings can be planted from spring to late summer, while seeds should be sown in spring.

buying

I have never found it available in the shops fresh so this is one herb that you need to grow yourself.

salad of grilled lamb, cucumber and salad burnet

The lamb I use in this recipe is known as a 'trim lamb' cut and is called lamb strap, or rib-eye: it is just the boned-out meat of the middle loin of lamb. If you can't get this cut just buy a middle loin of about 12 chops yourself and remove the succulent meat between the bone and fat. As you want the meat an even thickness pound it gently between some plastic wrap using a meat mallet until you have a very even and thin sheet. Always brush the meat with olive oil and season with salt and pepper before cooking. Pick masses of young salad burnet stalks and then just run your hands down the stems to remove the leaves gently. You need lots to give the salad a distinct taste of the herb.

Cut cucumber lengthwise in long strips away from the seeds and discard seeds. Then cut cucumber into fine sticks, season with plenty of salt and stand for an hour.

Brush meat with olive oil and season. Cook for about a minute each side in a frying pan over high heat – exact timing depends on thickness. Remove from pan, spread quickly with mustard on one side, wrap tightly in foil and leave to rest for 20 minutes. The lamb need only be tepid for this salad but needs to be used fresh, as chilling with harden and spoil the meat.

Heat ¼ cup/2 fl oz of the oil, add tomatoes, garlic and chilli if using, cook a couple of minutes until soft and remove to a bowl, add sugar, vinegar and remainder of oil, or enough to give it the sharpness you like. Season.

Drain and squeeze out juices from cucumber, mix with dressing and most of the salad burnet leaves and check seasoning. Cut meat into strips and arrange on 4 plates, pile some cucumber and tomato salad in the centre of the meat and trickle any juices from the foil over the top. Garnish with remaining salad burnet.

Serves 4

1 long, continental cucumber, peeled

plenty of salt

1 boned lamb strap, flattened

olive oil

salt and pepper

2 teaspoons French mustard

¾ cup/6 fl oz olive oil

2 ripe tomatoes, peeled and roughly chopped

2 cloves garlic, finely chopped

1 chilli, deseeded and finely chopped (optional)

2 teaspoons sugar

2 tablespoons white or red wine vinegar

1 cup/2 oz salad burnet leaves

salad burnet and cheese spread

There are times when something on toast is just the very thing you feel like – food that is comforting and tasty and makes a quick easy snack or an almost instant dish for when a friend calls in. This spread can be made in a minute. Instead of salad burnet you could try other herbs such as parsley or use some mixed fresh herbs. If you want to store it, the cheese spread keeps well for a day. To use just spread a thick layer on some toast and put under the griller until it is bubbling and a crusty golden brown.

Mash the garlic with pepper and salt and mix in the remaining ingredients, mashing everything well. It should be moist, if not add a tablespoon of milk or cream. Keep refrigerated and cover well or it smells very strong in the refrigerator and won't improve the flavour of any delicate food being stored.

Makes enough for 4 slices of toast

2 cloves garlic, crushed

$1/2$ teaspoon salt and some pepper

$1/4$ cup/$1/2$ oz chopped salad burnet leaves

1 cup/4 oz grated tasty/ cheddar cheese

$1/4$ cup/2 fl oz mayonnaise

uses

Burnet tea has a pleasant flavour and it is a diuretic. Salad burnet improves the complexion if added to a facial steam, and can help the digestion if sprinkled over rich foods.

salad burnet lemon juice

Brush over fish while it is cooking or spoon a little onto the top of cooked fish or chicken. I once found it very good added to fish soup, which needed a refreshing note.

Chop the rind small and put into a jug with salad burnet leaves. Warm the lemon juice with water and honey until it has come to a boil. Pour over the top of the rind and herb and cover. Leave at room temperature for about 4 hours and then strain. Keep refrigerated for up to a couple of days.

6 strips lemon rind

a good handful of roughly chopped salad burnet leaves

4 tablespoons lemon juice

1 tablespoon water

2 teaspoons honey

salad burnet goes with

other kinds of leaves in a salad

parsley and mint

rosemary and tarragon

fish

herb and cream cheese mix

yoghurt drinks

Beta vulgaris var. cicla

I am always puzzled why anyone would grow plain green and white silverbeet when it is just as easy to put in the colourful rainbow chard variety which gives the most tender leaves along with juicy golden, red or cream stems. The flavour is the same as the green and white variety, too. This is one of the best of all greens to grow, incredibly giving, for as soon as you cut the leaves away silverbeet produces baby shoots again within a few days. Silverbeet is closely related to beetroot. It originated in Switzerland, where the leaves continued to grow when the root shrivelled in the freezing winter soil. The colourful tops were mistaken for those of the thistlelike cardoon, the *chardon*, and silverbeet thus became known as Swiss chard, a name that has stuck ever since around the world. In Australia we call it silverbeet but the names silverbeet and spinach are sometimes used interchangeable, which causes confusion. The vegetables are quite different, and it is a shame that silverbeet has become known as the poor relation to spinach.

In the same way that children were encouraged to eat spinach, they were told to eat up their silverbeet because of the iron in it. However, the high amount of oxalic acid also present in silverbeet prevents the iron being absorbed by the body.

If left to become large and coarse any leafy green tastes strong and unpleasant when cooked, so pick them young. I personally think the very large leaves of silverbeet sold in bunches in the shops are mostly too big and the stalks are too coarse. Always pick leaves when they are quite small with tender stalks, and for salads harvest baby leaves – they are best mixed with a variety of other greens rather than used on their own. It is curious that when we are so enthusiastic about harvesting baby turnips and carrots, baby beans and peas, and adore baby spinach, consumers have not yet demanded baby silverbeet except for the few leaves found in mixed salad greens.

Think of growing it in the garden as a border or put a row at the back of some low-growing flowers. Those multi-coloured stems with their crinkly rosettes of green leaves look really interesting and a family could have a meal of silverbeet every week from just one plant ... no doubt something that might cause children to draw in their breath in horror. One meal of coarse silverbeet boiled and left watery is enough to destroy any desire to eat it again, which is a great shame. Perhaps poor cooking is the reason it has fallen out of favour, yet it holds its shape well

in cooking, can be the base for many dishes and the stalks on their own are an interesting vegetable.

Silverbeet makes a good wrapping for food as it can be blanched so it rolls up easily, but won't tear like spinach. You can line a terrine or loaf tin with it before filling with a minced meat, or wrap little chunks of fish inside blanched silverbeet leaves and then steam them, or roll leaves around a spiced rice and meat filling. Silverbeet makes very good soup in the same way that spinach does, and in fact teams well with similar ingredients. Some cream can be added to a purée of silverbeet greens, while cooked silverbeet can be mixed with a white sauce on hot toast and a poached egg on top; a very nice frittata can be made using silverbeet, cooked onion, a few currants for sweetness and, of course, eggs.

planting

Silverbeet doesn't mind a little shade but likes to be in well-fertilized and well-drained soil. Loosen the ground first so it is quite free and light. Plant seeds or seedlings: I find both successful. Put seeds down into the soil about 2 cm/¾ in deep and 15 cm/6 in apart, as plants don't mind being fairly close together. Keep well watered, especially when you begin picking, so the plant will quickly grow more leaves.

Temperature Zone	Plant or Sow
Tropical	No suitable
Subtropical	Autumn–winter
Temperate	Spring–early autumn
Cool	Spring–early autumn
First picking	*2–3 months*

varieties

- Fordhook – white stems and deep green leaves
- Rainbow Chard, or Ruby Chard
- Seeds sold under 'Five Colour Mix' have a range of orange, cream, white and yellow stems, and leaves ranging from pale green to a very dark green with a red streak.

diseases and pests

Silverbeet is a hardy plant; aphids like it but you can hose them off or pick away the affected leaf. Do the same if you have leaf miners in the garden: these will lay rows of pearl-white eggs down the leaf, cut away this leaf and don't put it into the compost.

harvesting

About 2½–3 months from planting seed and 2–2½ months from seedlings. Outer leaves can become spotty if left too long, but you should have ample silverbeet so choose just the best leaves and don't let them get bigger than 20 cm/8 in long. For salads pick them at about 5 cm/2 in. Pull away individual leaves with a firm downwards motion or cut the whole top of the plant down low and let it grow back. Any flower stems should be cut off or the plant can become unproductive.

Although silverbeet is usually grown as an annual and at its best in the first year I have one plant of rainbow chard that was forgotten at the side of the garden. This has formed the shape of a baby tree, with five separate, brightly coloured red branches and in its third year is producing the sweetest, freshest crop from every branch.

nutrition

Silverbeet has lots of dietary fibre, more than most vegetables, is a good source of vitamins C and K plus folate; it also provides beta-carotene which the body converts to Vitamin A.

buying and storage

Choose the youngest and smallest available and be sure there is not too much insect damage on the leaves. Avoid floppy leaves and check the stalks are firm and straight. Rainbow chard will be thinner-stalked than green silverbeet but is harder to find in the shops. Keep in the crisper section of the refrigerator in a vegetable storage bag for about 2 days. If the bunches are large and long it is sensible to chop off the stalks first.

cooking

Wash it well, as all those little crinkles in the leaves harbour dirt, and trim the stems. If stems are large pull away the strings from the outside, cut into thin slices; shred the leaves coarsely. If you are cooking both, give the stalks a head start as they take much longer and the leaves only need a few minutes. Stalks take from 5–10 minutes in salted water or steamed, depending on their size; when they are almost tender add the silverbeet leaves. If cooking only leaves, cook them with just the rinsing water that clings to the leaves, in a covered saucepan, until tender. They discolour if overcooked, changing from bright green to a dull colour. However you cook them be sure to drain well as water clings to the leaves.

stir-fried silverbeet, vietnamese style

This is not such a nice dish if the silverbeet has large stalks, in which case remove some of the thick ends, or else cut into strips lengthwise and then across. I find it goes best with rice and chicken.

Cut the stalks finely and the green leaves into thin strips. Heat the oil in a wok and add the stalks, cook for a minute or two, add the garlic and cook for another 30 seconds. Add the green leaves and cook, tossing until wilted. Mix sugar with fish sauce and water, add the liquid to the chard and keep tossing until it is cooked through. Season generously with pepper and serve immediately so that it doesn't overcook.

Serves 4 as a side dish

1 bunch silverbeet (about 12–15 medium-sized stalks)

2 tablespoons oil

2 large cloves garlic, finely chopped

1 teaspoon sugar

1 tablespoon fish sauce

1/4 cup/2 fl oz water

pepper

silverbeet and pork pie

I like using a mix of some wholemeal and white flour for this pie pastry. If you just can't bring yourself to make pastry, use some buttery bought puff instead. The silverbeet gives the pie lots of texture and the pork filling is quite sweet and light. When baked it resembles a big pastie. It should be ample for four people with a bowl of salad.

Cut the stalks into tiny pieces. Cut the leaves across so they are finely shredded. Melt the butter in a frying pan, add the chard stalks first and cook 5 minutes, and then add the leaves. Mix in garlic and shallots and cook until softened. Remove to a bowl. Add the pork to the same pan. There is no need to add any more butter, there should be enough left. Stir to break up the pork so that it doesn't form any lumpy pieces and when it has browned add the cornflour mixed with stock or water. Cook until it has thickened lightly, then add the herbs. Mix with the silverbeet and add the egg when it has cooled a bit. Leave to become quite cold before placing in the pastry. You can prepare the filling a day before you intend to serve the dish.

Preheat oven to 180°C/350°F.

To make pastry, sift the flours together and return the wholemeal husks to the bowl. Cut the butter into small pieces and work into the flour by hand, or put it into a food processor. Mix in the egg and sufficient lemon juice, wine or water to bind the mixture, and knead gently for 30 seconds. Wrap in some plastic, and leave rest for 20 minutes. Roll out into a circle. It is best rolled between waxed paper. Now put pastry on a buttered baking tray (it is awkward to move once filled).

Put the filling on one side of the pastry circle, fold over the other side, and pinch the edges together well. You can moisten with a little water or beaten egg, if you wish. Brush the top of the pastry with a little cream, milk or beaten egg. Make a couple of slits in the top and bake for 30 minutes, or until the pastry is brown and the juices are beginning to bubble through the slits. Leave to rest for 5 minutes before removing to a platter to serve. You can eat this plain or accompany it with a relish or some pickled cucumbers.

Serves 4

about 12 baby silverbeet leaves, or 6 if larger

45 g/1½ oz butter

2 cloves garlic, crushed

2 tablespoons chopped shallots

250 g/8 oz minced pork

2 teaspoons cornflour/cornstarch

¼ cup/2 fl oz cold stock or water

1 teaspoon chopped fresh thyme

1 tablespoon finely chopped parsley

1 egg

Pastry

¾ cup/4½ oz wholemeal/wholewheat flour

¾ cup/3 oz plain/all-purpose flour

100 g/3 oz butter

1 egg

lemon juice, some white wine or water

silverbeet goes with

butter

olive oil

eggs

cream

cheese

ricotta

garlic

ginger

onions

lemon

currants

salmon

bacon

ham

sesame seeds

nuts

soy sauce

nutmeg

easy ideas *Silverbeet Soup*

Cook 1 chopped onion in 45 g/1½ oz butter until softened and add a large potato, finely diced, 4 cups/2 pints chicken or vegetable stock and cook about 10 minutes. Add the shredded green tops of 250 g/8 oz silverbeet, cook until tender and purée the mixture. When serving trickle in a little cream and scatter on some nutmeg. Serves 4.

a gratin of silverbeet

easy ideas

*Stir-fried
Silverbeet Stalks*

Cut about
10 silverbeet
stalks up finely.
Fry 1 chilli,
1 clove chop-
ped garlic and
1 tablespoon
shredded ginger
in some oil. Add
the stalks and
toss, then pour
some water or
stock around
the edges and
toss until the
stalks are crisp
but tender. Mix
1 tablespoon
satay sauce with
¼ cup/2 fl oz
water and pour
into the pan. Toss
again until the
stalks are coated
with sauce. Serve
with chicken
or rice.

I like to make this with coloured chard but whether you use that or white-stalked silverbeet, use small stalks and tender leaves. If the stalks are large, split them lengthwise and then cut into strips. This recipe goes beautifully with some sliced ham and country-style bread as a light dish for lunch.

Remove the leaves from the stalks and cut stalks into thin pieces. Bring a pot of water to the boil and salt it, add the leaves and cook for about 3–5 minutes or until tender. Remove with a slotted spoon and drain in a colander. Put the stalks into the water and cook for about 2–3 minutes, or until barely tender. Drain. Chop the leaves and drain. Heat the oil, add the leaves and garlic, and fry until aromatic.

Next, make the sauce. Melt the butter, add the flour, and cook, stirring until the flour has fried. Don't let it brown. Add the milk and stir constantly until the mixture thickens, and is boiling. Cook over the lowest heat for a couple of minutes, then season with salt, pepper and nutmeg. Mix the stalks and leaves into the cream sauce and put into a 5-cup/2-pint shallow casserole. Scatter with breadcrumbs and then cheese. You can prepare the dish up to this stage about 8 hours in advance. When ready to cook preheat oven to 180°C/350°F. Bake for about 15–20 minutes if freshly prepared, 25–30 minutes if dish has been chilled in the refrigerator, until it is golden and bubbling hot.

Serves 4

1 bunch silverbeet
(about 12–15 medium-sized
stalks, about 500 g/1 lb)

2 tablespoons light olive oil

1 large clove garlic, finely chopped

45 g/1½ oz butter

2 tablespoons plain/
all-purpose flour

2 cups/1 pint milk

salt, pepper and pinch of nutmeg

½ cup/1½ oz breadcrumbs,
made from stale bread

⅓ cup/1½ oz grated
Parmesan cheese

Rumex acetosa

The first time I tasted sorrel was at the three-star Michelin restaurant run by the Troisgros brothers. Their local restaurant opposite the station had become famous, with travellers making the long trip to Roanne to dine with the exuberant brothers and order 'Escalope de saumon a l'oseille Troisgros' created for Paul Bocuse's Legion d'Honneur lunch for Giscard d'Estaing. The bed of sorrel was an elegant but dull subtle green, on top rested pale pink salmon fillets, with a creamy buttery crème fraiche sauce lightly coating both of them. I can still remember the tastes, the acidity of sorrel balanced the richness of salmon and the herbs in the sauce. No other green would have been quite as perfect. However sorrel does not seem to be used much.

Perhaps the colour is off putting, lacking the sparkle of spinach or other greens, or maybe it is because it can taste a bit acid if not treated carefully and will be strong in a salad unless picked young. Its bright green leaves change almost instantly to a very dull colour once cooked, almost like muddy water, so you have to use it for the flavour it gives and forget the appearance.

Sorrel grows easily and is most attractive in the garden. Once you have a clump it requires little work to maintain and even if you just use sorrel in a mixed salad you will become quite charmed by the very fresh quality it lends to mixed greens, especially if they are an accompaniment to fish. The sharp, tangy taste comes from the high content of oxalic acid and Vitamin C. I have read that the stems of sorrel, crushed with some leaves, can be used to curdle milk and make junket.

Sorrel is a member of the dock family and there are two varieties. One is known as garden or wild sorrel but the French sorrel is the one you should look for and buy, as it is less acid and a finer-tasting herb. If it is not labelled you should recognize it by the broad, round leaves shaped like a shield – garden sorrel has long slender leaves.

Romans and Egyptians ate sorrel to counteract the richness of food served in their banquets and it was introduced to Britain in the late 1500s. Sorrel grows wild in meadows and along the roads – indeed, in ditches – in Europe and Asia, and most countries which have a temperate climate.

planting

It is a perennial, lives for years and is undemanding, although occasionally some fertilizer will increase its vigour. Propagate by division of the roots in spring or autumn and plant in a sunny or slightly shaded spot in rich soil. Cut back the flowers so the plants don't go to seed. After about four years you will need to take out the woody bits and replant.

You can plant seeds, but they take months before you can pick them. Potted plants can be put in anytime except the heart of a cold winter.

harvesting

Once there are some tiny leaves begin picking: the spring leaves or tiny ones are the best for salads, the older leaves can be used in cooking. It will die down in winter unless covered but as soon as the ground warms will shoot again. It is best used with a mix of other green in salads as on its own the flavour is too strong.

buying

I have not been able to find sorrel sold in many shops as it is one of the more unusual herbs, so you will have to ask around for a supply if you don't grow your own. It does grow in a pot quite well and, shielded in a warm place, can last most of the winter.

hints

This herb must not be cooked in iron or aluminum. Use stainless steel, enamel or china as the acidity in the sorrel will react with the pan, making the dish grey and bitter and developing a metallic taste.

chicken cakes with a sorrel sauce

uses

Sorrel tea
is diuretic and
can help treat
kidney, liver
and blood
disorders and
fevers. It also
can be used to
treat mouth
ulcers, sores,
and other
skin wounds.

The sorrel theme is continued throughout this dish, with some in the chicken and more in the sauce. The sorrel sauce can also be used with some poached fish and, as with the chicken cakes, has the effect of lending a fresh, slightly acid taste and tang. If you don't want to be bothered with the sauce, the chicken cakes are good on their own, the sorrel adding a sharp, lemon flavour. The same dish could be made using tarragon in both the chicken and in the sauce.

Remove any skin from the chicken, chop into a few pieces and process until minced. Cook the onion and garlic gently in butter in a stainless steel or enamel pan until soft. Add the sorrel, stir and remove immediately from the heat. Let the mixture cool and mix into the chicken with lemon juice, crumbs, parsley, mayonnaise and cream. Season well and form either into 4 round cakes or small oblong cakes, patting them to get a nice shape. You can refrigerate cakes for some hours, covered.

Heat a big pan and melt a big knob of butter in enough olive oil to cover the base with a thin layer. Cook cakes, turning once, until they are golden on both sides and the juices run clear when pierced with a fine skewer. Just be careful not to overcook, as chicken can become dry.

To make sauce, heat the cream with mustard and nutmeg. Leave it reduce by about a third. In a separate enamel or stainless steel pan heat the butter, add sorrel and cook only until wilted – this means just seconds. Add the shreds of sorrel to the cream sauce and mix through, seasoning well. If you want a thinner sauce just add the chicken stock, this gives a lighter flavour. Serve a spoon of sauce over the top of each chicken cake.

The same sauce can be served with fish which has been grilled, lightly poached or sautéed. It can be made in advance and reheated, the sorrel becomes darker as it is cooked but retains its fresh, sharp flavour.

Serves 4

**sorrel
goes with**

fish of all kinds

eggs, in an
omelette or
frittata

spinach

leeks

lettuce

lamb and
beef stews

salads

500 g/1 lb chicken breast

1 large onion, finely diced

1 clove garlic, chopped

30 g/1 oz butter

½ cup/½ oz sorrel shreds

1 tablespoon lemon juice

⅓ cup/1 oz breadcrumbs, made from stale bread

1 tablespoon chopped parsley

2 tablespoons mayonnaise

2 tablespoons cream

1 teaspoon salt and some pepper

extra butter

olive oil

Sorrel Sauce

1 cup/8 fl oz cream

1 tablespoon French mustard

pinch of nutmeg

30 g/1 oz butter

1½ cups/1½ oz sorrel shreds

salt and pepper

¼ cup/2 fl oz chicken stock (optional, if the sauce should become too thick)

Spinacia oleracea

Spinach is related to silverbeet and the two can be confused. In some areas, silverbeet is erroneously called spinach, so occasionally true spinach is called English spinach to distinguish it. A taste for spinach is usually a sign of a maturing palate, for most children dislike it, only recognizing later in life how many things it complements. It can be by turn crisp and fresh, velvety, soft and gentle or strong and strident. Some time in the sixth century the Persians are believed to have domesticated spinach and, unlike some other vegetables which were regarded with suspicion, it spread widely and once introduced to England quickly became popular. In America it took a cartoon character named Popeye to double the popularity of spinach, in the belief that it was energy food which made it possible to attempt great feats. This is not far wrong, because it is one of the most nutritious vegetables you can eat.

New Zealand spinach (*Tetragonia expansa*) which is mainly available to gardeners in seed packets at specialist outlets, is not really spinach at all, despite its name. However, it is similar in taste to plain spinach – in fact you can't really tell the difference once cooked. Its big advantage is that it is more heat-tolerant than spinach. It has weak spreading stems and deep green leaves, which are a bit fuzzy.

planting

This is not the easiest thing to grow. I find it allows itself to be mastered by the vagaries of the weather: too hot and it bolts to seed, too cool and it wilts, and it doesn't like frost. However, it is worth growing if only for the tiny leaves, which can be used for salads or decoration and looks pretty in borders. Bright and green with little pointed leaves; it requires some sun but tolerates partial shade and needs plenty of water. You can grow it in containers too; they should be about 40 cm/15 in across and the same depth.

Spinach dislikes acid soil so work in a well-balanced fertilizer before sowing. Sow 1 cm/½ in deep and about 5 cm/2 in apart. Spinach seeds are small clusters that each produce several seedlings so you need to thin them. When they are through the ground, take out the smaller seedlings, leaving in the strongest, cutting them off at ground level.

New Zealand spinach has similar cultivation needs to spinach. Plant at the same depth but 30 cm/1 ft apart, to allow for spreading. Seedlings are easier to plant than seeds but listen to the weather as if it is too hot when you put them in they will go to seed quickly. Keep weeds away, spinach hates them.

special handling

Put some fine mulch, such as fine lucerne or fine straw, around plants so the dirt won't splash up when you are watering them. They are wretched to wash, as grit nestles comfortably wherever it can find a cavity in the leaves.

Temperature Zone	Plant or sow
Tropical	Not suitable
Subtropical	Autumn
Temperate	Autumn–early spring
Cool	Autumn–late spring
First picking	About 6–8 weeks

varieties

- English Hybrid
- Bloomsdale Long Standing – crumply leaves and can stand quite hot weather.

diseases and pests

Most varieties sold are rust resistant, as spinach is susceptible to rust. If you do get any signs of rust take out the plant immediately and don't put into the compost. New Zealand spinach has no disease problems.

harvesting

Spinach: 40–60 days; New Zealand spinach: 60–80 days.

Either pick little leaves from the plants as you want to use them or pull up plants one at a time. New Zealand spinach needs just the tips cut from the stems and loves to be picked, producing new growth all the time.

buying and storage

Fresh, bright, lively bunches that are not too large. Watch out how they are tied for rubber bands around the stems can cause bunches to sweat and become slimy, while tying too tight does the same. Even with care some outer leaves can be broken, as long as there are not many of these a bunch will be fine as they tear easily when very fresh. Loosen the bunch when you get home but don't wash until near to using, as spinach deteriorates quickly. You can pack into a vegetable bag and store refrigerated for a couple of days.

nutrition

A good source of Vitamin C, folate, beta-carotene, Vitamin E and fibre. The newer varieties have less oxalic acid, which reduces the strong, rather bitter taste which made spinach so unpopular, particularly with children. These new types of spinach with less acid allow the body to absorb more readily the iron it contains.

cooking

You need to wash and wash. I first fill a sink with lots of water so the dirt floats to the bottom and then pick up the leaves and shake them gently, letting the water run out, and then repeat this. Don't empty the sink until you have taken out the leaves or you allow them to rest on the grit on the base. Washed spinach can be bought; it is a bit more expensive but if you are busy a sensible choice.

Take the leaf off the stem. This requires some patience but if you have big spinach you really need to remove the central stem (don't bother with baby leaves, these have tender stems).

Just hold up the leaf and fold in half, pull away the stem with the other hand and drop it into a bowl and wash again. Discard stem. There is masses of wastage and it can vary according to the bunches. If I state '500 g/1 lb spinach' in the recipes, you only need to buy that amount as I have calculated that you will end up with about 300 g/10 oz.

Once spinach is washed roll in a tea towel if you are not using it immediately. This will keep it from going slimy. Store refrigerated, but use that day.

I used to follow the school that said just cook spinach with the water left on the leaves but found you need to keep turning it over. Now I often put a cup – or perhaps 2 cups, depending on the size of the pot – of water in a large shallow pot, add the well-washed spinach and let it cook fast, turning over just once. It only takes a couple of minutes to cook to a soft texture. Drain well. Press down on top with the back of a large wooden spoon to get rid of more moisture as water tends to stay in the leaves, or press down with the side of a small plate or saucer.

spinach salad with top hat eggs

These little rounds of croutons which have an egg sitting in the centre are supposed to resemble a hat. I have also heard them called 'one-eyed Susans'. As a rule they are made with large pieces of bread and big eggs but for this salad an elegant presentation is produced with baby croutons and quail eggs. They are quite easy to make and you can have the dressing and salad prepared ready to assemble. This dish could be the start of a special dinner, or use it for a light-hearted lunch.

Make dressing: put all ingredients into a jar and shake well. You can make this hours ahead. Just give it a shake again before using.

Put the onion in water in the refrigerator for an hour to make it quite cold. Drain well and keep refrigerated. Put the spinach into a bowl and chill. Cut circles about 5 cm/2 in diameter from the bread, then cut out another circle in the centres, about 2.5 cm/1 in diameter, which will fit the poached egg. Heat a knob of butter in a frying pan. Cook the rings of bread for a minute until golden brown and then turn over. Crack open a quail egg and slide it into the centre. Cook over a medium–low heat until the egg is just cooked through. If you have a problem with the egg setting you can carefully flip the little circles over.

Put some dressing on the spinach and toss. Put a little pile onto plates, top with some onion, shavings of Parmesan and then an egg in a top hat.

Note
Leaving onion in chilled water for a short time makes it crisp and crunchy and less strident in dishes when eaten raw.

Serves 4 as a first course, 2 for lunch

½ small red onion, cut into wafer thin slices

about 24 baby spinach leaves, stalks trimmed away

4 slices white or brown bread

butter

4 quail eggs

4 tablespoons fine Parmesan shavings

Dressing

6 tablespoons olive oil

1 tablespoon wine vinegar

1 tablespoon balsamic vinegar

1 teaspoon French mustard

¼ teaspoon brown sugar

salt and pepper

oysters with spinach

One of the most famous dishes in New Orleans is Oysters Rockefeller, so named because they are as rich in flavour as Rockefeller was with dollars. It is a dish rarely seen outside this state in America now and is time-consuming to prepare. Additionally, many think the topping totally over-whelms the oyster. This is a simple variation and makes a lovely first course for a special dinner. You can make up the spinach topping in advance and put over the oysters near dinnertime.

Cook the onion in the butter in a saucepan until it is softened and pale gold. Put into a bowl along with the butter juices. Chop the spinach quite finely and make sure it is squeezed dry. Mix into the buttery onion and stir well. Add salt, pepper and cream and chill.

Preheat oven to 200°C/400°F. Put oysters out on a bench and top with a little of the spinach mixture. Scatter on a few crumbs and put them onto a baking tray which has a bit of rock salt or some crumpled foil on the bottom to balance the oysters so they won't fall over. Bake for about 5 minutes until the whole shell and topping is quite hot.

Serves 6

1 small onion, finely chopped

60 g/2 oz butter

1 bunch (about 500 g/1 lb) spinach, washed and cooked

salt and pepper

3 tablespoons cream

3 dozen oysters

1/2 cup/1 1/2 oz breadcrumbs, made from stale bread

spinach soup

A good use for large or older spinach leaves, which may have been overlooked in the garden, or the leaves left over if you have used baby ones in a salad. Trim them a bit, taking away any tough or stringy stalks. To make the soup more interesting I usually make up some little cheese omelettes and cut these into strips, scattering them on the soup as a garnish, but this is optional. For a substantial meal you can poach a small egg for each person and slide one carefully into the bowl of soup.

Cook the onion in oil until softened, add potato and spinach and cook for a few minutes, then pour on stock and cook until the vegetables are tender. Process, season and add cream. This reheats very well if made a day in advance.

For omelettes, beat the eggs and cheese together. Lightly grease a small frying pan, add just enough of the mixture to coat the base and cook until set on one side, then flip over and cook for a few seconds only on the second side. Transfer to a board and let it cool and then roll up and cut into strips. Repeat until all mixture used. Do this in advance if you like because you will find the omelette heats through quite well in the soup.

Serves 4

1 onion, finely chopped

2 tablespoons olive oil

500 g/1 lb spinach, well washed

1 large potato, peeled and diced

4 cups/2 pints vegetable or chicken stock

salt and pepper

1/2 cup/4 fl oz cream

Cheese Omelettes

2 eggs

1/4 cup/1/2 oz grated Parmesan cheese

salt and pepper

pan-seared fish in ginger and spinach broth

This is a combination of fish stew and soup, the base being a lovely mix of vegetables and spinach topped with a crusty, coated fillet of fish. It is a dish that needs to be done at the last minute, but if everything is ready diced or sliced it only takes a short time to cook. Use a white-fleshed fish with a medium texture.

Mix the cornflour/cornstarch and curry and rub lightly into both sides of the fish.

Heat the oil in a saucepan and fry the carrot and garlic until wilted. Add the ginger and fry for a minute. Add the spinach, sugar, water and stock and bring to a boil. Cook for a minute, then leave aside and keep warm while cooking the fish.

Heat a little additional oil, enough to cover the base of a pan. When very hot fry the fish quickly on both sides, then remove pan from the heat and put a lid on top. Leave to stand for a minute.

Divide the broth and vegetables between 4 shallow bowls. Scatter with coriander and spring onion/scallion and rest a piece of fish on top. If the fish is too large for the bowls cut them into halves.

Serves 4

4 fish fillets, about 100g/3½ oz each

1 teaspoon cornflour/cornstarch

1 teaspoon curry powder

2 tablespoons light olive oil

1 carrot, cut into matchstick pieces

1 clove garlic, finely chopped

1 piece fresh ginger, about 2 cm/¾ in long, peeled and cut into fine strips

a generous handful of baby spinach leaves for each serving

1 teaspoon sugar

1 cup/8 fl oz water

1 cup/8 fl oz fish stock or light chicken stock

a little additional olive oil

2 tablespoons coriander/ cilantro sprigs

2 tablespoons finely chopped spring onion/scallion

frittata with the flavours of nice

Spinach, pine nuts and tiny currants are served in cafés in the south of France in the form of light, flat omelettes. In this frittata with a similar theme, the spinach has a strong flavour but the tiny burst of sweetness from the currants is a surprising and good contrast. It is essential to use fresh spinach as it has more texture than the frozen variety, which cooks to a very mushy purée.

Place the spinach in a large saucepan with only the water left on the leaves after washing, and cook, turning it over until wilted. Remove and drain very well. Chop finely with a sharp knife (it is best left in small pieces, not puréed).

Heat a little oil and, when hot, add the pine nuts. Cook until they are golden; drain on some kitchen paper towel. Add a little extra oil and fry the spinach quickly for a couple of minutes. Place in a bowl; add currants and pine nuts.

Beat eggs with cream and add to the bowl of spinach. Season well. Heat a little oil in a heavy-based frying pan, and when very hot add the frittata mixture. Turn down the heat and cook slowly until it is set on the base and cooked halfway through. Transfer the pan to the griller/broiler and cook until the top has set. Rest a couple of minutes before serving.

Serves 4

1 bunch (about 500 g/1 lb) spinach, well washed and any tough stalks removed

some light olive oil or virgin olive oil

3 tablespoons pine nuts

3 tablespoons currants

4 eggs

2 tablespoons cream

salt and pepper

spinach salad with potato and bacon

easy ideas

*Mushrooms Stuffed
with Spinach*

Take the stalks
from 4–8 big
mushrooms and
chop these finely.
Oil base of mush-
rooms. Cook stalks
in a little oil in a
pan. Add 250 g/
8 oz washed
spinach with the
water that is still
on its leaves and
cook until tender.
Drain well; chop
finely. Stir in a
clove of finely
chopped garlic
and a little lemon
juice and fill the
mushroom cups
with this mixture.
Top with ¼ cup/
2 oz chopped
macadamia nuts
mixed with 1 table-
spoon desiccated
coconut and
½ teaspoon curry
powder. Bake on
tray in oven for
about 20–25 min-
utes at 180°C/350°F.

Use your own baby spinach leaves from the garden for this recipe, or buy delicate baby spinach leaves which are generally sold loose at markets, or some shops. Otherwise buy a bunch of spinach and select the tiny leaves, using the big ones for another dish. You need enough leaves to cover the base of a dinner plate. This makes a wonderful lunch or brunch dish.

It is easiest if you make the dressing first. That way, there will be no delay when the salad is ready. Mix the oils with mustard and vinegar or lemon juice, taste and adjust proportions if necessary. It should not be too sharp; neither should it be too oily.

Wash the spinach leaves well, dry them and put into a plastic bag and refrigerate. Peel the potato and dice very small. Heat sufficient oil (1 cm/ ½ in deep) in the pan and add the potato. Cook gently, turning over until the dice are golden brown. Remove and drain. Season lightly with salt, and generously with some cracked black pepper and keep warm in a low oven. While the potato is cooking, fry the bacon in a dry frying pan until it is crisp. Drain on some kitchen paper towel. Keep warm in the oven.

Have a pan of simmering water ready. When the potatoes are done, break the eggs on to a saucer and slide them gently into the pan. Let them cook, spooning some boiling water gently over the top to seal the yolks, but keep them on the very soft side. Remove carefully with an egg slice. Trim the edges if they are very ragged.

Have the spinach ready on 2 dinner plates. Trickle a little dressing on top, and then place an egg in the centre of the spinach. Scatter potato around this, put the bacon on top and serve immediately.

Serves 2

baby spinach leaves

1 large potato

light olive oil or peanut oil

salt and pepper

3 rashers bacon, cut into strips

2 large eggs

Dressing

3 tablespoons light olive oil

1 tablespoon virgin olive oil

1 teaspoon Dijon mustard

3 teaspoons white wine vinegar or lemon juice

chicken with spinach and water chestnuts

An easy and quick stir fry, which has an interesting crunchy taste from the addition of water chestnuts. Those addicted to spicy food can add some finely chopped chilli to the dish, or a dash of chilli sauce. If you stir through some finely cooked hot egg noodles at the finish, it would easily serve six people.

Cut the chicken breasts into strips and put them into a bowl with the soy, sugar, sake or mirin and ginger, stir so the chicken is lightly coated. There won't seem to be much mixture around chicken but the idea is not to overpower the lightness of the poultry. If you like strong flavours, double quantities of this marinade. Let it stand for about 30 minutes.

Wash the spinach well, remove any tough stalks and shred coarsely. Wash the leek well and slice thinly. Heat half the oil in a wok or large frying pan and add the leek and cook for a few minutes until slightly softened. Add spinach and stir fry for about 30 seconds. Remove both the vegetables to a bowl. Add the remaining tablespoon of oil to the pan and when very hot add the chicken, tossing until it has changed colour on the outside. Put a lid over the top, turn the heat to very low and let it cook gently for about 3–4 minutes.

Increase the heat, add the spinach, leek and water chestnuts. Add water and cook a further 2 minutes or until the mixture is hot. It usually doesn't need salt and pepper for my taste but add if you wish.

Serves 4

3 large or 4 small chicken breasts

3 teaspoons soy sauce

1 teaspoon sugar

1 tablespoon sake or mirin

2 teaspoons grated fresh ginger

$^1/_2$ bunch spinach

1 large leek or 2 small ones

2 tablespoons vegetable oil

$^1/_2$ cup/3 oz drained sliced water chestnuts

1 tablespoon water

salt and pepper, to taste

hint

Ricotta has a special affinity with spinach in tarts and baked dishes. It should have a gentle flavour with a hint of sweetness. If it smells cheesy or has a creamy rather than white colour, it is not fresh enough so don't buy it. Once home use as soon as possible. The good news is that ricotta is low in fat.

easy ideas *Easy Spinach and Cheese Toasts*

Cook 1 bunch spinach (about 500 g/1 lb) in salted water until tender then drain very well. Chop finely, season and add a clove of finely chopped garlic. Hard boil 4 eggs and cut into quarters. Toast 4 pieces of country-style, crusty bread. Spread toast with spinach, arrange egg quarters on top, with yolk down. Cover generously with grated melting cheese such as Jarlsburg, Emmenthaler or Gruyère on top. Grill/broil until the cheese has melted. Serve immediately –

these can only be assembled and cooked at the last minute or the spinach will make the toast soggy. This is less likely to happen if you put a slice of ham on to the toast first, before the spinach layer. This recipe should make enough for 6 pieces, but of course depends on the size of the toast; if you add the ham layer it becomes quite a substantial snack for 4 people.

spinach gnocchi

hint

One of the best sauces for spinach gnocchi can be made by melting 90 g/3 oz butter with a dozen sage leaves until it is beginning to smell nutty and become slightly brown – but not too dark. Pour over gnocchi, top with grated Parmesan and serve immediately.

Italian gnocchi can be heavy and seriously solid, not a dish I order in a restaurant unless I know the reputation of the kitchen. Yet good home-made gnocchi which are light, melting and yet at the same time have enough texture to comfort the palate, make you understand why they are so loved in Italy. These are very good gnocchi with a cheesy taste, speckled green with spinach. The final heating is done by coating them with cream, nothing else is really successful to create the right sauce, which soaks into these gnocchi – so don't try and skip this part. If you feel guilty about using cream, best to do another sort of dish instead.

Purée the ricotta, add the spinach and process. Transfer to a bowl and mix in the remaining ingredients except for cream and stir well. Cover and refrigerate for at least an hour.

Preheat oven to 200°C/400°F. Have a big pot of water boiling and season with salt. Form little spoonfuls of the mixture into rough round balls, drop into the water and cook in batches of about 8–10 at a time until each one rises to the surface of the water. Take out with a slotted spoon and drain a moment then put into a shallow ovenproof dish. Repeat until all are cooked. Warm the cream and pour over the top of the gnocchi and then top with a fine dusting of Parmesan. Bake for about 12 minutes or until the top is bubbling and the cheese a lovely crusty gold.

To prepare this in advance: cook the gnocchi and put onto a dish, covering tightly with plastic wrap and refrigerate. Heat the cream rather than just warm – and you may need a little extra cream if the gnocchi are very cold. Cover the casserole with foil and bake for 10 minutes, then take off the foil and cook another 10 minutes until golden.

375 g/12 oz ricotta

250 g/8 oz spinach leaves, no stalks

2 eggs

½ cup/2 oz plain/all-purpose flour

1 teaspoon salt

⅓ cup/1 oz grated Parmesan cheese plus a little extra

¾ cup/6 oz cream

green rice

Australian author Alexandra Michell wrote a marvellous book some years ago called Particular Picnics, *containing recipes for all manner of picnics with special themes. This recipe comes from a section titled 'Evening in the Park' and was served with a piece of beef that had an unusual sauce of bananas and tamarind alongside. You can serve the green rice with chicken or beef, even just alongside thick slices of ripe, flavoursome tomato and hard-boiled eggs.*

Preheat oven to 200°C/400°F. Put the spinach, herbs, chilli and garlic into a food processor and purée. Heat the oil in an ovenproof dish and stir in the rice, add the green purée, chicken stock which has been heated until it is boiling and season with salt and pepper. Cover and cook in oven for about 18 minutes. Remove and let rice cool before stirring with a fork so the herbs are evenly distributed.

Serves 6

a small handful of spinach leaves

6 sprigs parsley

6 sprigs coriander/cilantro

1 small chilli, deseeded and chopped

1 clove garlic, crushed

2 tablespoons oil

200 g/7 oz long grain rice

2 cups/1 pint chicken stock (or vegetable stock, if using as a vegetarian dish)

salt and freshly ground pepper

soup with baby meatballs, noodles and spinach

A Chinese-style soup which, I was told, is part of the authentic cuisine of northern China. The original was served to me minus the noodles that I like to include. Instead it had a cup of bean sprouts added with the spinach. Either version is good, but the noodles make it more of a meal. Use either a flat or a round noodle or dried pasta. I like it very much made with the thick, udon noodles from Japan. You can buy these in Asian stores, particularly those which sell Japanese foods. They are often sold frozen but need only 20 minutes to thaw sufficiently so they can be cooked. Whatever type of noodle you use, be sure to cook it separately or else it will make the stock starchy.

If you are good at using chopsticks, the noodles, meat and spinach can be picked out and the soup drunk directly from the bowl, provided of course it is a small deep one. Otherwise it is a help to provide a spoon and fork to make the noodles easier to eat.

Put the meat into a bowl with the soy, rice wine, sesame and cornflour and mix in salt, ginger and spring onion. Stir well with your hand in one direction only – this ensures the meat will not only be well blended but lighter.

Heat the stock with pepper. Form the meat into tiny balls – easy if you wet your hands first. Drop the balls into the stock and leave to simmer very gently for about 8 minutes. Remove any scum.

Separately heat a large pot of water, add the noodles and cook until just tender. Taste to check: you don't want firm noodles in a dish such as this but remember they will probably be heated again. Drain well. Mix the noodles into the stock with the meatballs. Add spinach and push it under the liquid. Cover and cook for a couple of minutes or until it has wilted. Taste now for seasonings and, lastly, add the few drops of sesame oil.

Note

If using Japanese udon noodles, never add salt to the water when cooking them. Cook them in boiling water and remove when tender. Then add a teaspoon of salt to the water, return the noodles and let them sit for 3 minutes before draining. Run cold water through the noodles and let drain again. They are then reheated in the soup.

Serves 6

250 g/8 oz finely minced lean beef

1 tablespoon soy sauce

1 tablespoon rice wine

2 teaspoons cornflour/cornstarch

1 teaspoon sesame oil

$1/4$ teaspoon salt

1 teaspoon finely grated fresh ginger

2 tablespoons finely chopped spring onion/scallion

5 cups/2$1/2$ pints chicken stock

a little pepper

125 g/4 oz fresh white noodles

250 g/8 oz fresh spinach leaves, well washed

few drops of sesame oil

easy ideas *White Bean and Spinach Soup*

Drain a 450 g/1 lb can of white beans such as cannellini and rinse. Put into a saucepan with 3 cups/12 fl oz chicken or vege-table stock along with 3 whole, peeled cloves garlic. Simmer for 10 minutes, covered, then purée. Add more stock if it is too thick. Return purée to pan and add a couple of handfuls of washed young spinach leaves, a pinch of cumin and a squeeze of lemon juice. Cook 5 minutes, or until spinach is tender. Serves 4, approximately.

a slice of greens

The main ingredient in this dish is spinach, but several other greens are used to create a slice which looks like a marbled savoury cake. It can be eaten warm but is very good cold and makes an interesting and easy-to-carry picnic dish – just cut it into wedges or squares for serving.

Preheat oven to 180°C/350°F. Cook the onion in oil until softened, grate the zucchini/courgette and add, cooking for a few minutes until tender. Put into a large bowl with peas. Cook the spinach in a pot until softened and drain well. Chop roughly. Mix with zucchini and all remaining ingredients. Lightly butter a shallow dish about 20 cm/8 in diameter and put in the mixture, level the top. Bake in oven for about 25 minutes or until it is set and the top is golden. Remove from the oven; put a cloth lightly over the top – or a baking tin – so a little steam forms and keeps the top moist. Leave 10 minutes before cutting into wedges for serving or allow to cool completely and store refrigerated.

Serves 6–8

1 large onion, finely chopped

3 tablespoons olive oil

2 medium-sized zucchini/cougettes

½ cup/2½ oz peas, cooked until tender

1 big bunch (500 g/1 lb) spinach, well washed

½ cup/2 oz grated melting cheese or 100 g/3 oz goat's cheese, broken into small pieces

½ cup/2 oz grated Parmesan cheese

6 eggs

½ cup/1½ oz breadcrumbs, made from stale bread

salt and pepper

Artemisia dracunculus

tarragon

Don't bother with anything but French tarragon, _Artemisia dracunculus_, as the related Russian tarragon – _Artemisia dracunculoides_ – has hardly any flavour at all and what it does have is coarse. The disadvantage is that French tarragon is a little more temperamental to grow. It dies down in winter but will usually reappear next summer and can be likened to a delicate child in the way it loves to be nurtured. The taste is wonderful – both sweet and pungent at the same time with a tang of anise – and worth any bother, for tarragon is a luxury herb. If you see a plant, which is thriving and spreading everywhere it is more likely to be Russian than French. The best test before buying a plant is to have a taste, as you really want to be sure it is a good plant and chewing a fresh leaf should make your tongue go numb. Not something most nurseries encourage,

tarragon vinegar (recipe page 332) ▶

but the only real way to ensure you are buying the best species because they are not always labelled correctly. Russian tarragon doesn't have much taste at all; neither does it have an aroma when you crush a leaf.

Tarragon is the base for many exquisite French dishes, for instance chicken in a creamy tarragon sauce, and it is the most important ingredient for sauce béarnaise and for a sauce tartare. Tarragon vinegar is one of the best of all flavours for salad or to freshen up a dressing and can be sprinkled over sliced tomatoes for a change from basil. The French tuck sprigs of tarragon into plump chickens and roast them, and in fact consider these two ingredients to have an affinity for each other in the same way the Italians do tomatoes and basil. Tarragon is a major ingredient in herb mixes for mayonnaise for pickles or marinades.

planting

Buy a runner or get a root from a friend and plant in the sun in spring to early summer. It likes rich soil but dislikes a wet spot. In winter it will appear to die away but it is a perennial and should come back in spring as soon as the ground warms. After a couple of years you can take more runners from your tarragon and replant again in the garden. It can be grown in a pot indoors but needs to be placed in full light near a window and watered sparingly.

harvesting

Pick tarragon when the plant is big enough to cope with losing a few leaves. It does benefit from being harvested regularly and if it looks straggly in a hot summer prune back to encourage new growth.

buying

If buying fresh be sure that you apply the same rules you do when buying a plant. Have a good sniff and be sure it doesn't just smell of greens, rather of anise. Black stems are waterlogged and don't buy the bunch, nor should you be bothered with it if the herb looks limp and wilted. Store it unwashed in a plastic bag lined with kitchen paper towel in the refrigerator. Tarragon is not much good dried, the flavour changes too much, so instead keep some tarragon vinegar in the cupboard and some tarragon butter in the freezer so you will have a continuous supply of the herb during winter.

tarragon vinegar

Pick or buy about 4 sprigs of fresh tarragon and push into a clean bottle or jar. Fill with white wine vinegar and cork tightly. Leave in the kitchen or a warm place for about 2 weeks and then have a taste. If you think it is strong enough strain and discard this tarragon. If not leave another week. Add a fresh sprig and bottle again, storing in a dark, cool place. It should keep until next season.

tarragon

white wine vinegar

easy ideas *Tarragon Stuffed Chicken*

Lift the skin gently up from 4 chicken breasts, leaving attached on one side so you have a pocket. Mash about 90 g/3 oz butter with 1 tablespoon chopped tarragon leaves, 1 egg yolk and ½ cup/1½ oz breadcrumbs and push a little of this over the chicken flesh inside the skin, then pull skin over to cover. Brush chicken skin with oil, season generously and put in a shallow ovenproof dish. Pour some chicken stock around to come a third of the way up breasts and cook in oven at 180°C/350°F for about 20 minutes or until cooked. The buttery, tarragon-scented juices should be spooned over the top of each serving.

tarragon butter

Make up a big batch of this, then roll into small sections in foil, label each one well and store in the freezer. Use tarragon butter inside chicken or over the skin, cut little pieces and toss over the top of steamed vegetables so it just melts as you are serving them, mix into tiny boiled potatoes which will go with chicken or put a big knob onto the top of grilled fish.

Tiny cloves of crushed garlic could be added to the butter, or some chopped parsley and chives if you wish, but I prefer to make it plain and add the other ingredients later.

Process the butter until creamy. Transfer to a bowl and keep working through the tarragon with a fork until it is well blended in. Add the lemon and mix again and divide the butter into 6 pieces. Use damp hands to make little sausage shapes and wrap in some baking paper. Then roll each one in a little package of foil and screw up the ends up like a bon bon and freeze.

250 g/8 oz butter, cut into small pieces

1 cup/2 oz chopped tarragon leaves

2 tablespoons lemon juice

tarragon goes with

creamy sauces

vinegar

chicken

veal

potatoes

steamed vegetables

vinegar

mayonnaise

eggs

shallots

tarragon rice

A few sprigs of tarragon are cooked in with the rice, then some tarragon butter added at the finish so it melts and coats each grain. Try as a bed under chicken or poultry, as an accompaniment to fish or you could spoon an assortment of tiny steamed or sautéed young vegetables on top of the rice.

Heat the oil in a heavy-based saucepan and cook the onion gently until golden. Add the rice and stir until the grains begin to turn opaque, about 3 minutes. Pour over the stock, it will come to a boil in a minute, add the balsamic vinegar and push the tarragon into the rice. Cover and cook on the lowest heat for 20 minutes. Take off the heat but don't lift the lid for 10 minutes. Cut the butter into a few pieces and mix through the rice using two forks so it is fluffed up lightly. Take out the tarragon before serving.

Serves 4

3 tablespoons oil

1 onion, finely chopped

1 cup/7 oz long grain rice

2 cups/1 pint well-seasoned chicken or vegetable stock

2 teaspoons balsamic vinegar

2 sprigs tarragon

60 g/2 oz tarragon butter

uses

The French name 'estragon' also means little dragon, and it was once believed that tarragon could cure the bits and stings of venomous animals, but its main use now is culinary.

thyme

*Thymus vulgaris; T. citriodorus;
T. vulgaris var. westmoreland*

There is a large number of varieties in this family but, put simply, there are two main types, one which grows into a tiny shrubby plant, the other which spreads out like a creeping mat between paving stones, in cracks or through rockeries. The creeping one is best left in your garden as a decoration; the little upright thyme has the flavour for the kitchen. This is usually referred to as garden thyme and has a rich aroma and taste in dishes and a pink flower. Lemon thyme, a low bush thyme with pink flowers, is an interesting one to consider too, for as the name suggests it does have a light lemon flavour that goes well in chicken casseroles or with vegetables. There is a golden leaf variety you can buy which not only has the same flavour but is even prettier. Westmoreland thyme can be called Turkey thyme and is very fragrant, with pinky purple flowers that look wonderful in spring and summer. This is a richly flavoured thyme for dishes and I use it along my borders in the garden.

Wherever you plant thyme you will have bees buzzing around it, they love the fragrance of both the flowers and the leaves. I have masses of thyme in the garden; more than I could ever use, but love to walk along thyme-lined paths and tuck a plant between every crack and cranny that I can. Everyone can enjoy the scent as they wander through the garden. It is also discourages weeds, for which I am always grateful.

I have read there are over 100 species and they are all developed from the wild thyme, known as the 'mother of thyme'. It is a volatile oil, thymol, which gives the herb its particular aroma and flavour, and story has it that the name came from the Greek word 'thymon' which means to fumigate. Thyme was often used instead of incense in temples. It became a very popular herb, ladies of the court in medieval England painstakingly embroidered thyme on tokens for their knights, for it was associated with courage and valour.

Thyme is a strong, vigorous herb and you need to remember that when adding it to dishes as it can easily overpower a delicate flavour, so team it with robust food. Be cautious using dried thyme as it is very strong, but it is one of the most successful herbs to dry yourself as it retains so much aroma and flavour. Just cut some branches, tie with string and hang in an airy place until dried. You can keep them in an airtight container or pull the leaves from the stalks and keep them in a jar in a cool dark cupboard. You can also dry thyme by spreading it out onto paper in the dark somewhere, then rubbing off the leaves. If you can harvest for drying when there are flowers this results in an even truer taste.

planting

Thyme is a perennial and very hardy. It likes the sun. Buy seeds, a plant or get a small root from a friend as it transplants quite easily. Cuttings should be from old wood and don't plant in winter as they will rot, this needs to be done in late spring onwards – preferably not when the plant is in the middle of

flowering. Then to encourage new plants later you can put some of the woody branches down on the ground, heap a little soil on top and leave and it will 'layer' itself, growing new roots from the stems.

It rather likes a lime soil, can be left in quite a dry position and every 3 years you should divide or replant as the plants can lose some aroma when they get really straggly. Cut back in winter to prevent it becoming too endy and you should be able to keep thyme plants for the kitchen for the whole year.

harvesting

Just pick, as often as you like as soon as the plant is established and has a number of small branches.

cocktail cheese slices

A slice which has spicy sausage mingled with an onion and garlic layer and creamy cheese. I usually cut them into strips for serving as a nibble with drinks, but they are a great light lunch cut into generous-sized squares with some mixed green salad alongside.

Heat the oil and fry the onion until it is soft and golden. Add the garlic and cured pork and cook until the pork fat has run a little. Remove to a bowl and mix in the eggs, cheeses, cream and season well.

Preheat oven to 200°C/400°F. Line the base of a shallow container, such as a lamington tin, with the puff pastry. Press a sheet of lightly buttered foil on top and bake for 10 minutes. Remove the foil and continue cooking until the pastry is golden – about 5–8 more minutes. Leave to cool for 5 minutes then spread the mixture on top and shake gently to level it. Spread slices out evenly, you will only have a thin layer. Reduce oven to 180°C/350°F and bake for about 12 minutes or until the top is set.

Remove and cut into pieces while slightly warm. Loosen from the tray when cold. Reheat, if required, in a moderate oven for about 6 minutes – or 5 minutes longer if reheating it whole. Do not use the microwave to reheat or the pastry will become soggy.

2 tablespoons olive oil

1 onion, finely chopped

2 cloves garlic, finely chopped

100 g sliced meat such as a prosciutto, salami or calabrese

4 eggs

1/4 cup/1 oz grated Jarlsburg or Swiss-type cheese

1/3 cup/1 1/2 oz grated Parmesan cheese

1/4 cup/2 fl oz cream

a tiny amount of salt and plenty of cracked black pepper

puff pastry

2 teaspoons thyme leaves

thyme goes with

sausages

liver

all kinds of stews

long-cooked dishes with a wine sauce

stuffings for poultry

a bed for grilled or roasted food

bouquet garni

parsley

rosemary

marjoram

bay

celery

onion

orange

lemon

easy ideas *Gratin of Thyme and Potatoes*

Heat 2 cups/1 pint chicken stock with 2 sprigs thyme and when boiling remove from heat. Slice 1 kg/2 lb baking potatoes thinly and put a layer in a shallow, buttered, ovenproof dish. Season potato, then pour some stock through sieve over potato; continue layering with potatoes, seasoning and stock until all potato has been used. Stock should be level with top of potatoes; if not, heat some more and add. Brush top layer generously with melted butter, scatter on a few fresh thyme leaves, cover with foil and bake in oven at 180°C/350°F for 1 hour, or until cooked. Remove foil and return to oven until top has browned and become crisp – or put under grill/broiler.

calves liver with apples, mustard and thyme

general herb hint

There are times when it is not possible to find fresh herbs and you must use dried. As these are stronger than fresh, use only a third of the amount specified in the recipe for fresh herbs. Add early in the cooking, so the heat releases their essential oils and aromas.

A most delicious combination is made by coating liver with a flour and thyme mixture and serving it with a tart apple sauce.

Peel, core and thinly slice the apples. Cook them in a saucepan with the butter, wine, sugar and pepper until they are soft. Cover if the apples are becoming dry. Stir well with a wooden spoon so that the apple is broken into a kind of rough purée. Keep warm on the side or reheat if you wish. Mash the mustard into the soft butter with lemon juice and pepper and set aside.

Dip the liver into flour which is mixed with thyme and press down so you have a light layer sticking to the liver. Heat the oil and add the liver. Cook, turning it over until it is brown on the outside and just barely done. It takes only a few minutes. Put on to a warmed plate and wipe out the pan.

Pour the stock into the pan in which you cooked the liver and bring to a boil. To serve, put a little warmed apple purée on to the plates and top with liver. Put a teaspoon or two of the liquid from the pan on top and in the centre of the liver a dab of the mustard and lemon butter. Decorate with a few sprigs of fresh thyme.

Serves 4

500 g/1 lb Granny Smith or other cooking apple

30 g/1 oz butter

2 tablespoons dry white wine

1 teaspoon sugar

1/4 teaspoon coarsely ground black pepper

1 teaspoon dry English mustard

45 g/1 1/2 oz soft butter

1 teaspoon lemon juice

1/2 teaspoon coarsely cracked black pepper

500 g/1 lb calves liver, thinly sliced

plain/all-purpose flour

2 teaspoons finely chopped thyme leaves

1 tablespoon olive oil

1/4 cup chicken stock

some fresh thyme for garnishing

lamb with thyme stuffing

There is a growing custom of buying joints that have been boned but they never quite have the succulence of a large portion of meat with the bone left in to add sweetness. I usually trim away the fat on a leg where it is very thick but otherwise leave a thin layer which will melt over the meat as it cooks and keep the stuffing moist, as the lamb becomes aromatic with the fragrance of fresh thyme.

Cut some deep slashes into the lamb. Cook onion in oil, stirring every so often, until soft and mix in remaining ingredients. Let this cool. Push bits of stuffing into the slashes until you have used it all up. The lamb can be left for 24 hours, refrigerated, at this stage.

Preheat oven to 180°C/350°F. Season the outside of lamb well and bake in oven for about 1 1/2 hours, basting with its own juices and fat occasionally. Remove from oven and wrap tightly in 2 sheets of foil and throw a towel over the top. Let lamb rest for 20 minutes before carving on a diagonal down to the bone, so you can see the layers of thyme-scented stuffing.

Serves 6

1 leg of lamb, about 1.5 kg/3 lb

1 large onion, finely chopped

3 tablespoons oil

1 tablespoon fresh thyme leaves

1/2 cup/1 1/2 oz breadcrumbs made from stale white bread

1 egg yolk

2 tablespoons finely chopped parsley

1 clove garlic, finely chopped

'say cheese' sandwich spread

This is an old-fashioned spread I can remember from childhood. For some strange reason it was called 'Mock Chicken', yet it does not taste of chicken. Perhaps the herbs make it taste like chicken stuffing ...? In hard times, however, it was tasty and economical, could be used on sandwiches, is delicious on biscuits or bread and, packed in a small crock, is an ideal picnic dish. It needs to be refrigerated at all times.

Any tasty or cheddar cheese can be used, even small leftover portions – as long as they are not too dry and have a rich cheese taste.

Melt the butter in a small saucepan, add the onion, and cook with the lid on until softened. Peel the tomato after softening the skin with boiling water, and dice finely. Add the tomato to the onion and herbs, and cook without a lid until the mixture is fairly thick. Beat the egg in a bowl; add the hot tomato and onion mixture and stir. Return to the pan and cook slowly on low heat until it thickens, being careful not to turn it into scrambled egg. Remove from the heat and add the cheese. The warmth of the pan will melt the cheese quickly. Let it cool and then add salt and pepper – amount of seasoning will depend on the cheese. Pack into a crock and cover the top with some foil or store in a container with a lid.

30 g/1 oz butter

1 medium-sized onion, finely diced

1 large ripe tomato

generous pinch of dried thyme and dried marjoram or some fresh herbs, finely chopped

1 egg

1 cup/4 oz grated tasty/ cheddar cheese

salt and pepper

uses

Thyme aids the digestion of rich food, which is why it is so good in stuffings inside poultry such as duck. If taken in a tea, sweetened with honey, thyme makes an excellent cough mixture. Lemon thyme is used in pot pourris, perfumes and soap and is sometimes an ingredient in toothpaste or powder.

tomato

Lycopersicon esculentum

The tomato is one of the most perfect little packages created by nature, sweet and full of flavour ... and all this richness is contained inside a skin. It is difficult to imagine life without them – how dull cooking would be. It was first discovered growing wild among the maize fields of the early Incas and they cultivated the seeds, giving it the name of 'tomatl' and believing that its sweet, soft fruit was a good sign from the gods. It was brought to Europe by early Spanish explorers but unlike the Incas, who loved it, Europeans regarded it with suspicion, as it was a cousin to deadly nightshade, tobacco and the potato. Just as serious was the belief that tomato was a powerful aphrodisiac and even a spoonful of tomato could cause moral decay in a person. Remember that all those early tomatoes were yellow and the name 'golden apple' or 'love apple'

was given to it as it became treasured in the late sixteenth century.

Italian cooking would be a poor thing in comparison to the vibrant colours and flavours it exhibits now without tomato.

planting

Either begin from seed if you want heirloom varieties or plant seedlings of those you decide to grow if they are available. To help the gardener, most seedlings are named and it is easy to find out their background. Sow seeds about 1 cm/¾ in deep in rows about 60 cm/2 ft apart, although I prefer to begin them in small containers where I can put them in a warm place and check they are kept moist. The soil must be warm or you are wasting your time as the seeds won't germinate, but in most places spring to early summer is fine.

When planting seedlings slip the little plants in gently and plant in soil up to the first leaves. If the stem is spindly put it on a slight slant so only the leaves are above the ground and more roots will grow from the stem, so you have a sturdier plant.

I have a tendency to plant too many, not because I can't use them but until they grow I forget they need to have plenty of space. An average plant will give about 5 kg/12 lb of tomatoes, very successful prolific plants far more, depending on how much you feed them and the variety.

Sometimes reading about tomato growing makes it seem complicated: tall varieties, ground varieties which sprawl and spread over the garden, tomatoes classified by the size and shape of their fruit and tomatoes which have all manner of different uses. I keep it simple. All my tomatoes are staked or grown in cages made

from stalks and twine or I find they get walked upon on the paths and I get more bugs if I leave them lying on the ground. Occasionally I leave a branch or two to sprawl as they will grow new roots wherever the stems touch and add vigour to the main plant. If you do stake you should grow them on one straight stem and prune away the suckers which come below the first fruiting cluster, leaving more energy for the tomato to grow fruit. But you need to allow plenty of leaf to provide shade and I don't trim away my stems to produce only one long straight stalk that is trained up a stake. The main reason is that it leaves them more unprotected for the bird population, who like to feast constantly on the open bushes, and you can end up with almost no tomatoes for yourself.

Basil is planted with abandon around every bush and in every spot near the tomatoes. It helps them thrive. I fertilize the tomatoes and water generously, mulch and feed again. They need a good amount of feeding to keep reproducing. Unless you have acres of garden you will have to be selective and I suggest grow some red and a few unusual coloured tomatoes for fun.

Then every year it is like a lucky dip as the ground in the garden keeps sprouting with dozens of tomato seedlings, from last year's lot. The very vigorous ones I usually transplant somewhere fresh, even if it is a pot. Tomatoes grow well in pots, plant one tomato for each pot and a couple of basil plants around it and be sure to keep the pot well watered; fertilize every 14 days.

Young tomato plants are more disease-resistant than ones left too long so it is a good idea to plant a second crop

8 weeks after the first so you have fresh tomatoes to carry you through into late autumn.

In a hot summer the leaves may look soft and wilted during the day but this is their way of protecting themselves, the only time this should concern you is if they are wilted first thing in the morning – make sure you give them a good drink.

Temperature Zone	Plant or Sow
Tropical	All year round
Subtropical	All year round, except where there may be occasional frost
Temperate	Spring–early or mid summer
Cool	Mid spring–early summer

Cherry tomatoes can be planted a little earlier than standard varieties, and will continue cropping for longer in cool weather than large tomatoes.

varieties

A list of tomato varieties you can buy would fill a book. There are so many, in such a range of colours that it is always difficult to choose what to buy and what to grow. I choose a few different varieties each year and keep names of the ones I love the most, discarding those which don't grow well in my garden.

If you are serious about growing a number of varieties I suggest you get a catalogue from a top seed merchant, such as Diggers Club or Kings Seeds, and go through all the varieties. It can be quite addictive to plant tomatoes; the range is so extensive it makes the choice hard.

Tomatoes can be roughly divided into the following categories.

- Cherry, for nibbling
- Beef tomatoes, for slicing into salads, grilling, sautéing or dicing
- Plum or egg tomatoes, for baking, semi-drying or for sauces
- Hollow flattish big tomatoes, for stuffing, as the hollow compartment gives lots of space, or use for slicing
- Round tomatoes, often ground-grown sprawling ones, for just about everything from cooking to salads.

Below are some of the ones which I suggest and some that I have grown over the past few years.

- Tommy Toe – rated by judging panels of chefs as tops for taste of all the tomatoes
- New Grosse Lisse – large smooth fruit
- Mixed Beefsteak – lovely big juicy, fruity tomatoes in mixed colours, for slicing or cooking
- Verna Orange – doesn't go mushy in sandwiches even when made hours in advance
- Shimmeig Greg – bred by Tom Wagner, a meaty pink-streaked yellow tomato, very beautiful-looking and it has a great flavour
- Burke's Backyard – for a good flavour and quite prolific
- Tigerella – huge yield and produces apricot fruit with a yellow fleck
- Black Krim – from southern Russia, a medium-sized tomato with black, red and green skin, low in acid and it confuses the birds as to when it is ripe
- Yellow Delicious – like the true love

apple with unblemished skin and an exquisite rich flavour
- Brandywine Pink – yellow or black, large tomatoes with different colours but great flavours; they look stunning in a mix on a salad
- Aunt Ruby's German Green – from Tennessee, with lime green and gold centres; each tomato grows up to 500 g/1 lb and has great flavour
- Amish Pasta – an oxheart for making paste, baking or bottling, with few seeds.

Cherry tomatoes

- Yellow Currant – tiny sweet fruit kids can eat like baby grapes
- Pink Cherry and Red Cherry – just because they are great for salads and nibbling.

diseases and pests

Tomatoes are susceptible to a few pests and you need to watch or these can destroy the tomatoes without you even noticing. Aphids, tomato caterpillars, fruit fly and whitefly or cutworms can attack them. Where you can plant disease-resistant varieties. Most of all be sure to have a healthy garden, the greatest bonus of all.

I have read that smokers should not handle the plants without thoroughly washing their hands as they can spread tobacco mosaic virus to them.

harvesting

Whenever you see they are ripe, red or – in the case of the end of the season –

when the plants are beginning to wither. Don't leave the last of the green tomatoes on the vine, take them inside where they will continue to ripen, or you can make all manner of pickles, chutneys or soups with green tomatoes.

Many tomatoes may be lumpy or a little uneven; this never matters, as growing your own is about flavour.

buying and storage

Red is the first rule; the second one is to stop bothering whether they look perfect. Individual tomatoes with uneven sides are generally the best in flavour and we need to push for flavoursome tomatoes from growers rather than looking at trays of perfect, tasteless shapes. Many shop tomatoes have tough skins and you can get around this by peeling them away but you can't overcome a lack of taste in a tomato. Choose a few that are perfectly ripe, then some which still have a little green at the shoulders so you can gently allow them to ripen at home.

Refrigeration dulls tomato flavour so best to buy just as many as you need. Once they are ripe it is better than to cook them and use in a sauce or some other way than to refrigerate them. It is a good idea to get a few extra and then as they ripen become creative with dishes for lunch or dinner. If you have too many of your own home-grown ones and do have to refrigerate them take out several hours before you need to use them so they are not cold and include in cooked dishes rather than eating raw.

nutrition

Cherry tomatoes have more Vitamin C than other tomatoes but all tomatoes are an excellent source of Vitamin C. They also provide beta-carotene, potassium and Vitamin E and are a rich source of lycopene. This is being studied as being a protective agent against prostate cancer and some eye disorders suffered by the elderly. The redder the tomato the higher the content of beta-carotene and lycopene. Yellow and other coloured tomatoes of course will have a different set of carotenoids.

cooking

Tomatoes are generally eaten raw and cooked during summer in equal amounts, but more are cooked in winter. If you are making a sauce or including them in a dish it is a good idea to skin them as tomato skin rolls into long strips and tastes quite unpleasant. The best way to do this is to cut a small cross in the base, put them into a basin and pour over a jug of boiling water so they are completely covered. Leave for about 15 seconds and drain. The skin can easily be peeled away from the cuts. Seeds of tomato are bitter if processed so if you have cooked them you can't process to make a sauce. The pulp needs to be pushed through a sieve or put through a moulin. Timewise it won't make much difference and the flavour of the sieved sauce is better. Otherwise skin and then cut the raw tomato into quarters and flick out the seeds, cook and you can process them.

tomatoes with olive stuffing

This stuffing will spark up even uninteresting tomatoes, although the better the flavour of the tomato, the better the dish. It is particularly good with lamb, but I rather like it as a small course on its own.

Cut the tomatoes into halves and scoop out the flesh, leaving a casing.

Heat 2 tablespoons of oil and fry the onion until it is golden and quite soft, add the garlic and tomato flesh from the centre and cook until thick. Put into a bowl with the crumbs, chilli, basil, seasonings and olives. Spoon the stuffing into the tomatoes and level the top. They can be completed to this stage hours in advance.

Preheat oven to 180°C/350°F. Lightly grease the base of a shallow dish and arrange the tomatoes in this. Bake in a moderate oven for 15 minutes or until the tomatoes are quite soft, but not breaking up – timing it really depends very much on the type of tomato. While the tomatoes are cooking, fry the pine nuts in 1 tablespoon oil, stirring with a fork so they don't burn. Before serving, scatter the pine nuts on top of each tomato.

Serves 4

4 medium-sized tomatoes

3 tablespoons olive oil

I small onion, finely chopped

I clove garlic, finely chopped

⅓ cup/1½ oz breadcrumbs, made from stale bread

dash of chilli sauce

12 basil leaves, cut into small shreds

salt and pepper

½ teaspoon sugar

¼ cup/2 oz chopped black olives

¼ cup/½ oz pine nuts

summer tomato soup

The Spanish rely heavily on gazpacho, icy-cold tomato soup onto which they scatter a mix of salad vegetables, as something cooling on a shimmering hot summer's day. It is the acid and sweetness in tomato which produce this refreshing quality. Tomato soup is a marvellous summer dish that can be left plain, topped with a garnish of diced ham or some pieces of prawn, some cucumber and yoghurt or sour cream, a little mix of fresh herbs or whatever you fancy that has an affinity with tomato. I make this when there are plenty of well-flavoured sun-ripened tomatoes around so the soup is sweet rather than acid.

Chop the tomatoes roughly and process them for half a minute until pulpy but not for long or you will break up the tomato seeds and the soup will be bitter. Then push through a moulin or a sieve to get rid of the skins and pips. (If you want to blend or process the mixture totally, skin the tomatoes and cut into quarters, removing seeds before processing.) Add the salt. Grate the onion and add its juice to the mixture, along with lemon juice, sugar and stock. Stir well and refrigerate for several hours until it is icy cold.

Put the soup into bowls and trickle a couple of teaspoons of cream into the centre of each bowl. Stir with a fork so that you have a pretty pink and cream marbled effect. Scatter with a few chopped green chives. Serve immediately.

Ample for 4 people

750 g/1½ lb ripe tomatoes

½ teaspoon salt

½ onion

juice of small lemon

3 teaspoons sugar

3 cups/1½ pints fat-free chicken stock

3 tablespoons runny/single cream

1 tablespoon finely chopped chives

easy ideas *Tomato and Olive Spread*

Purée 1 cup/8 oz stoned black olives with 2 cloves finely chopped garlic and 3 tablespoons oil. Transfer to a bowl and mix in about 4 tablespoons chopped spring onion/ scallion, 2 tablespoons of chopped parsley and 2 small, ripe, very finely chopped tomatoes. Season with pepper (the olives will provide plenty of salt). Serve with toast fingers, put a dollop on top of a bowl of vegetable soup or spoon a little on top of pasta.

tomato soup with green tomatoes

easy ideas

Sautéed Cherries

Toss some cherry tomatoes in a little butter in a small saucepan. When the skins are beginning to burst season with salt, pepper and a generous pinch of sugar, trickle on a tablespoon of cream and add a few shredded basil leaves and gently shake the pan so you have a sauce. Serve with meat or over hot toast.

Make this when you know the last of the tomatoes on the bushes are never going to ripen and you are tired of making pantry goods like pickles. The flavour of the soup will vary according to how green the tomatoes are and it can range from very sharp and a little acidic if they are hard and green to mild and fresh flavoured if the tomatoes are green on the outside but changing to a light pink inside. You can adjust the acidity easily with an additional teaspoon of sugar. It is a soup that has a most refreshing flavour and is particularly good if served before a rich course, such as hot ham, pork, game or duck.

This soup keeps for several days refrigerated.

Cut the tomatoes into rough pieces. Heat the oil with butter, add onions and fry until they are wilted and light golden on the edges. Add the garlic and tomatoes and cook for about 10 minutes or until the tomatoes have begun to soften. Mix in sugar, bay leaf, tomato paste and bring to a boil. Cover and cook over gentle heat for 10 minutes. Add the stock and continue cooking for a further 20 minutes or until the tomatoes have totally softened. Don't blend as it will break up the seeds. Rather put through a moulin or a coarse sieve, as you don't want any bitterness from the seeds to spoil the flavour. Return to the pot and check the seasoning. Just before serving, shred the basil leaves and scatter on top.

Serves 4, generously

1 kg/2 lb green or unripe tomatoes

2 tablespoons light olive oil

30 g/1 oz butter

2 large white onions, finely diced

2 cloves garlic, roughly chopped

3 teaspoons sugar

1 bay leaf

1 tablespoon tomato paste

3 cups/1 1/2 pints chicken stock

about 6 basil leaves

stuffed cherry tomatoes

Handy for serving with drinks or just to put out on a rustic platter when you have people around.

Pour boiling water over the cherry tomatoes, leave until you count to 10 and drain. Carefully peel away the skin. Cut the top third away from the tomato and scoop out the centre carefully using a tiny coffee spoon. Turn them upside down to drain.

Mash the remaining ingredients in a bowl. Fill the tomatoes with the mixture, heaping it up a little, and then refrigerate until ready to serve. It is a good idea to take them from the refrigerator about an hour before serving so the cheese filling won't be too hard.

Makes 18

18 cherry tomatoes

60 g/2 oz soft cheese such as brie, camembert, goat's cheese, or whatever you fancy

2 tablespoons pine nuts, browned in oil and finely chopped

1 teaspoon finely chopped parsley

2 teaspoons finely chopped basil

1 tablespoon finely chopped semi-dried tomatoes

tomato tart

A big square or round thin tart is one of the best dishes to use when you have a crowd coming or just want a lunch for a couple of people that seems very summery. Cut it into big pieces or use for snack food, cutting into small strips you can pick up in your fingers. The combination of buttery, crisp brown crust with sharply sweet garlic-scented tomatoes on top of a bit of runny cheese makes it so good. Like any puff-pastry tart it is best made at the last moment but I find it reheats fine, in the oven on a tray until crisp again – approximately 12 minutes.

Preheat oven to 200°C/400°F. Cut 3 tomatoes into rough pieces and cook in a small saucepan for about 5 minutes or until you have some juice. Push through a sieve so you have a bit of thick sauce. Mix with garlic, a bit of oil and season with salt, pepper and sugar and add basil.

Cut the rest of the tomatoes into medium-thick slices and let them rest on a piece of paper towel so they are not too wet. Have a piece of pastry about 20 cm/8 in diameter and score a border about 2 cm/³⁄₄ in from the edge, then prick with a fork all over the pastry. Spread the tomato sauce close up to the scored edge and scatter the cheese over it, then lay the slices of tomato on top in a single layer. You may not need them all and it is important not to be too generous by overlapping them or they will give out too much liquid and you end up with a soggy mess. Season them well and brush the edge of the pastry with a bit of oil. Bake in oven until the pastry is golden and puffed and the tomatoes soft – about 25 minutes. Let it sit for a few minutes before cutting.

Serves 4

7 medium-sized ripe tomatoes

2 cloves garlic, crushed

dash of olive oil

salt, pepper and 1 teaspoon sugar

12 basil leaves, roughly torn

½ cup/2 oz grated cheese, such as Jarlsburg, or chopped mozzarella

1 piece puff pastry, preferably made with butter

green tomato and mint chutney

This has a sharp, clean flavour, neither too cloying nor sweet. It is also a good way to use up any green or unripe tomatoes. If you don't have any green tomatoes buy some very firm, unripe tomatoes to make this. Be sure they are not red or the chutney will be too sweet. Serve with any meats or curry, in sandwiches or add a dash to mince for a meatloaf. It is very good with hamburgers as a change from tomato sauce.

Put all the ingredients except for mint into a large saucepan or preserving pan and bring the mixture to a simmer over medium to low heat. Leave to simmer uncovered for about an hour, stirring occasionally with a wooden spoon, taking care not to crush or break up the vegetables or to let the mixture bubble too fiercely. Stir in the mint and simmer a further 15 minutes or until the vegetables are tender but not too soft.

Pack the chutney into hot, sterilized jars. Leave to cool and then seal and store in a cool, dark place to mature for about a month before using.

Makes about 6-7 cups/ 3 pints

1.5 kg/3 lb green tomatoes, finely diced

3 brown onions, finely chopped

400 g/13 oz demerara sugar

1 cup/8 fl oz cider vinegar

2 tablespoons peeled and finely sliced fresh ginger

1 teaspoon cayenne pepper

½ teaspoon salt

60 g/2 oz coarsely chopped fresh mint leaves

tomatoes go with

just about everything from pasta to pizza

polenta

breads

oil

butter

in salad combinations

onions

chilli

cucumber

garlic

capsicum/ bell pepper

eggplant/ aubergine

lettuce

most herbs but especially basil

cheese of all kinds

fish

chicken

beef

lamb

pork

ham

balsamic vinegar

wine vinegar

green tomato pie

easy ideas

Tomatoes and Bocconcini

Peel ripe tomatoes and cut into cubes. Add sea salt, pepper and 2 tablespoons virgin olive oil with 2 teaspoons wine vinegar. Stand 5 minutes until juices have formed around the mixture. Add some baby bocconcini, a crushed clove of garlic and small whole basil leaves and serve with crusty bread as a first course.

A sweet dessert pie which is unusual but very good and made with a really rustic country look by just folding the crust casually over the lemon and green tomato filling with some little folds in it. I have made it successfully with green, hard tomatoes and with tomatoes that have a faint tinge of pink in them. The main difference is in the cooking time. Hard tomatoes take a little longer, so check with a skewer before removing from the oven. The tomatoes become glazed and sweet, with a deep caramel colour on the edges, and the juices seep into the crust slightly. I make this pie in a deep pie dish (about 20 cm/8 in diameter) and heap it up.

Although you can reheat the pie, the crust will soften as the syrup that forms soaks slightly into the pie crust. If you can, make it close to dinner time – it retains its heat well and doesn't need to be served piping hot. If you do have to make it as long as a day in advance, it would be better to make it with the tomato base and only put a crust on the top.

For crust, put flour, salt and sugar in a basin or food processor. Add the butter and mix until it is in crumbs. Add iced water and mix to a dough. Wrap in plastic and rest for 20 minutes or so while you prepare the tomato. Chill if the kitchen is warm.

Lightly grease the pie dish and preheat oven to 200°C/400°F.

Cut both ends from the tomatoes and discard these pieces, then slice the rest of the tomato very thinly. Put tomato slices into a bowl with the lemon rind, juice and sultanas. Stir to coat them well. Mix flour and sugar in a separate bowl.

Roll out the pastry between two sheets of plastic wrap or waxed greaseproof paper. Put it into the pie dish, letting pastry overlap the edge. Put about a third of the flour and sugar mixture on the base. Add half the tomatoes and press down gently so that the layer is even. Add more of the flour and sugar, the rest of the tomatoes, then the rest of the flour and sugar. Dot with butter. Fold the pastry over the top of the tomato, it will have some folds on the curves. The edges won't meet in the centre so some tomato will show through. It is meant to look very rustic so don't fuss if it is uneven. Place in hot oven for 15 minutes, then turn the oven down to 170°C/325°F for a further 45–50 minutes or until the pastry is brown and the tomato is soft when you pierce the centre with a skewer. By this time the syrup should be ample and there will be a bit of deep brown caramel edge on the crust. Leave for 10–15 minutes at least before cutting, as pie will be bubbling and very juicy when it first comes from the oven. As it rests, the juices thicken into a glazed sauce.

I like to serve it with some clotted cream if I can get it, or else some thick pure cream spooned over each portion.

Serves 8

Pie crust

2 cups/8 oz plain/all-purpose flour

½ teaspoon salt

1 tablespoon sugar

200 g/6½ oz butter, cut into small pieces

⅓–½ cup/3–4 fl oz iced water

Tomato filling

6 medium-sized green tomatoes

grated rind of 1 large lemon

⅓ cup/3 fl oz lemon juice

½ cup/3 oz sultanas

⅓ cup/1½ oz plain/all-purpose flour

½ cup/4 oz sugar

1 teaspoon cinnamon

30 g/1 oz butter, cut into small pieces

bruschetta with tomatoes

easy ideas

*Quick Summer
Tomato Sauce*

Skin 1 kg/2 lb tomatoes. Chop them roughly and put into a saucepan with 1/4 cup/ 2 fl oz virgin olive oil, plenty of pepper and salt, and a teaspoon of sugar. Let mixture cook gently, uncovered, for about 15 minutes or until you have a thick, rich sauce. It will have some texture and for this particular sauce there is no need to cook for hours – as you often do for an Italian sauce – as you want a fresh, light, true tomato mixture. For a spicier sauce just add a chopped small chilli, and if you like garlic add a finely chopped clove at the start of cooking.

I have included this as there are many disappointing recipes around for bruschetta, which do little justice to the dish. It is mainly served in central and southern Italy where wonderful fruity olive oils are made and the dish should be kept quite simple. Some crusty bread is rubbed with fresh garlic, then anointed with oil and thick slices of very ripe tomato put on top. It is meant to be eaten as a snack on a summer's day, the bread being toasted on a wood fire or grill while everyone sits in the garden watching and consumed outdoors with a glass of new wine. Traditionally the bread used is unsalted but as this is not easy to always buy just make sure you buy some really crusty, coarse white bread. Fine bread will just break up in the oil so it is of no use in this dish.

Toast the bread and while it is hot rub on both sides with the cut clove of garlic. Put a layer of basil leaves onto a platter and put the bread on top. Warm the oil until tepid and trickle over the bread so you have a bit on each slice. Cut the tomatoes into slices and arrange on the bread so it is almost covered and serve immediately. Each person can pick up some of the basil underneath their slice of bread and eat this alongside or on top.

Serves 6

12 slices crusty Italian-style bread

2 fat cloves garlic, peeled and halved

12–18 large basil leaves

1/3 cup/3 fl oz virgin olive oil

salt and plenty of ground black pepper

2 large very ripe tomatoes

portuguese tomato rice

Instinct makes me want to reach for a wedge of fresh Parmesan and grate a little on top of this rice. But, of course, that would give it Italian flavours rather than those of Portugal where it is a great favourite as a side dish for meats, the rice being used to mop up the juices of casseroles or stewed meat.

Portuguese tomatoes are very flavoursome as a result of the intense summer sun. I add a little tomato paste in winter to give an additional red hue and intensify the tomato paste, as our winter tomatoes are both colourless and often flavourless.

Heat the olive oil and fat in a heavy-based saucepan and add the onions and garlic. Cook them slowly until they are soft and golden, giving them an occasional stir. Add the tomatoes, cover and cook gently for about 15 minutes until you have lots of juice. Mix in the stock, bring to a boil and add the rice and seasonings. Bring back to a boil, cover and cook very gently for 20 minutes or until the rice has absorbed all the liquid and is tender. Pull off the heat and let it sit in the pot for a couple of minutes without lifting the lid so it will steam through. Fluff it up with two forks to keep it light.

Serves 4 as a side dish

3 tablespoons olive oil

1 tablespoon bacon or pork fat

2 large onions, roughly chopped

2 cloves garlic, finely chopped

2 large ripe tomatoes, peeled and roughly chopped

1 1/2 cups/12 fl oz chicken or beef stock

1 cup long grain rice

salt, to taste

1/2 teaspoon ground black pepper

tomato sauce from emilia romagna

A simple, basic sauce from the Italian region of Emilia Romagna that you can toss through pasta, adding some leaves of fresh basil. Fold it through a risotto or use it as a layer in lasagne. In summer it will be even sweeter of course than in winter but it is a good recipe for when you do need some tomato sauce but there are no fresh tomatoes so you have to rely on firm and often tasteless shop tomatoes. The recipe can easily be doubled and I stock up the freezer in summer with little cartons as it freezes very well. The sauce can be made up to 4 days before serving. After preparing it, cool, cover and store in the refrigerator. You can freeze the sauce for up to 4 months.

Heat the oil over a medium heat in a large, heavy-based saucepan. Drop in the finely diced vegetables and parsley. Sauté, stirring often, for 10 minutes or until golden brown. Add the garlic and herbs and cook for only 30 seconds. Add the tomato paste and tomatoes, crushing the tomatoes as they go into the pot. Bring the sauce to a lively bubble and keep it uncovered as you cook over medium heat for 8 minutes or until thickened. Taste before seasoning. Toss with pasta and serve immediately with freshly grated Parmesan cheese.

Makes sufficient sauce for 500 g/1 lb dried pasta

3 tablespoons extra-virgin olive oil

1 medium-sized onion, very finely diced

1 small carrot, very finely diced

1 small stalk celery with leaves, very finely diced

3 tablespoons very finely chopped flat-leaf parsley

1 large clove garlic, very finely diced

3 tablespoons chopped fresh basil leaves or 2 fresh sage leaves and a 1.5 cm/½ in sprig fresh rosemary

1 tablespoon tomato paste

1 kg/2 lb peeled and chopped fresh tomatoes

pinch of sugar (optional)

salt and freshly ground pepper to taste

tomato and fresh mozzarella tart

Roma tomatoes make a great topping for a tart. They will keep a good shape, not leak too much juice, and yet give the tart a rich flavour. This tart is meant to be a meal, enjoyed with a green or mixed salad alongside. The base of onion and mozzarella prevents the tomato juices from soaking into the pastry. You can put the filling into any plain, cooked shortcrust pastry case or, if you are short on time, cook up a flat sheet of some commercial butter puff pastry and use it as the base.

Heat the oil in a saucepan and cook the onions until they are golden and very soft. Don't hurry, as the slower they are cooked the sweeter they will be. Season well with salt, pepper and sugar and fry gently again to soften the sugar. Remove and cool, then spread the onions in a layer on top of the pastry. Cut the bocconcini into slices and layer over the onion, then scatter on the Parmesan. Cut the tomatoes into slices and arrange on the top, totally covering the cheese. Season the tomatoes with more salt and pepper and brush with olive oil.

Preheat oven to 180°C/350°F. Bake tart for about 20 minutes or until the cheese has formed a runny layer and the tomatoes are softened. Leave for about 10 minutes before serving, as it is nicer warm rather than piping hot.

Makes enough filling for a tart about 22 cm/9 in diameter

1 pastry case, baked blind (see side column)

Filling

2 large onions, roughly diced

3 tablespoons olive oil

salt and pepper

1 teaspoon sugar

4 fresh bocconcini (mozzarella balls)

2 tablespoons finely grated fresh Parmesan cheese

8 Roma tomatoes, or enough to cover the top of the tart

a little extra olive oil

some basil or sliced black olives, to garnish

hint

Baking Blind

'Baking blind' is cooking a pastry case without a filling, so it will be crisp when baked again with filling. Press your pastry into a lightly buttered tin so it sits firmly against the sides. Prick lightly in a couple of places but not through to the tin and line with a sheet of non-stick baking paper/parchment, which comes above the sides of the pastry. Fill with some dried beans or weights. Push them against and up the sides so the pastry won't shrink. Bake in a moderately hot oven (200°C/400°F) for about 15–20 minutes to set the crust, then carefully take out the paper and beans or weights and continue cooking until case is a pale golden colour and crisp to touch. Don't let it brown too much if you are baking it again with a filling but if using as a base and not cooking again you should bake it until browned.

spicy questa

easy ideas

*Tomato and
Burghul*

Mix ½ cup/3 oz
burghul (cracked
wheat/bulgar)
with ½ cup/
4 fl oz water
until the water is
absorbed. Chop
4 ripe, medium-
sized tomatoes
into tiny pieces.
Mix ½ cup/2 fl oz
oil, ¼ cup/2 fl oz
lemon juice, 1 cup/
2 oz chopped
parsley, ¼ cup/
½ oz chopped
mint and lots of
salt and pepper.
Let this stand for
about 10 minutes
and then mix into
the burghul gently.
Very good in pita
bread or with
lamb fillets, as a
side dish.

Particularly flavoursome and very brightly coloured, this is an ideal relish – more interesting than many tomato relishes and very easy to make. Great for any meats and only needs a few days maturing before it can be used. It keeps well for a year, and even if you don't have gorgeous red, rich, summery tomatoes it still has a good flavour. You can cheat in winter and add a tablespoon of tomato paste to give more colour and a stronger tomato taste. Try using it mixed with some mayonnaise as a dip, serve with meats, add a spoonful to a meatloaf or spread over meat near to the finish of cooking to give a spicy flavour.

Cut the tomatoes into rough pieces and place into a large saucepan with the sugar, sultanas, ginger, garlic, chilli, salt and 1 cup vinegar. Bring slowly to a boil and cook for about 30 minutes or until fairly thick. Mix the flour with the remaining vinegar, add to the pan and stir so it thickens it. Cook a couple of minutes and then spoon into sterilized bottles, sealing with non-metal lids.

Makes about 5 cups/2½ pints

1.5 kg/3 lb tomatoes, peeled

1½ cups/12 oz sugar

½ cup/3 oz sultanas

1 piece fresh ginger, 2.5 cm/1 in long, finely shredded

6 cloves garlic, roughly chopped

3 hot chillies, roughly chopped (more if you wish)

1 tablespoon salt

1¼ cups/10 fl oz white vinegar

1 tablespoon plain/ all-purpose flour

spicy pickled green tomato slices

This is a simple pickled tomato dish, which can be eaten after 48 hours and keeps well in a cool cupboard for about 12 months. The curry powder and mustard make it spicy, but it is not throat-searingly hot. The tomatoes stay in slices, which makes it looks quite different to the usual chopped green pickle. Great in meat sandwiches and with cold meats.

Halve the green tomatoes and then slice thinly. Do the same to the onions. Put both into a basin, cover with the water and salt, stir to mix and leave to stand overnight, or about 8–10 hours at least.

Next day, bring the tomato and onion to a boil in a saucepan, together with the liquid in which they were soaked. Drain immediately and discard the liquid. Heat the vinegar, mixed spice and sugar in the pan and when it has just come to the boil, add the tomato and onion mixture. Bring to a boil and cook gently for about 5 minutes. Be careful not to let all the liquid cook away. You can place a lid on top, a little to one side of the pan, so the steam can escape.

Mix the curry powder with turmeric, mustard and flour and add sufficient additional vinegar to makes this a thinnish paste. Add to the boiling mixture, stirring constantly. Bring to a boil again, cook for 1 minute and remove from the heat. Pour into hot, dry, sterilized jars and seal.

Makes about 4½–5 cups/2–2½ pints

500 g/1 lb green tomatoes

500 g/1 lb white onions

4 cups/2 pints water

45 g/1½ oz salt

3 cups/1½ pints white wine vinegar

¼ teaspoon mixed spice

1 cup/8 oz sugar

1 tablespoon curry powder

1 teaspoon ground turmeric

1 tablespoon dry English mustard

1½ tablespoons flour

a little extra vinegar

panzanella

This is a typical Italian summer dish that would be served as an appetizer or the main course for a light casual lunch. It is a bread salad, which may not sound very exciting but the flavour can be wonderful if everything is very fresh, the tomatoes are ripe and the bread is good. In Umbria they use a greater variety of vegetables than in Tuscany, where it is mainly made of tomato. I prefer this Tuscan version which I use when I have some juicy, sunny, plump and very red tomatoes, otherwise I don't think it is worth bothering to make it.

Dice the bread neatly. Fry in oil, turning over until golden. Drain on kitchen paper towel and set aside. Cut the tomato into small dice. Don't refrigerate either of these or they won't taste as fresh, so prepare them at the most only a few hours in advance.

Mix cucumber with onion and capsicum/bell pepper. Refrigerate this. Mix the dressing ingredients together in a bowl, stirring briskly with a fork. Just before serving mix the tomato into the bread. Add cucumber mix and remaining ingredients except olives. Whisk all dressing ingredients together and pour over the top. Toss very well but not so as to break up the bread and decorate with some olives.

Eat within an hour while the bread has still got some texture, although it is still delicious even if the bread becomes soft.

Serves 4

2–3 thick slices country-style bread, crusts removed

olive oil

4 large ripe tomatoes, peeled

1 small or ½ continental cucumber, peeled and cut into small dice

1 small red onion, quartered and thinly sliced

1 capsicum/bell pepper, grilled and cut into strips

1 chilli, finely chopped

a few olives, to garnish

Dressing

4 cloves garlic, crushed

8 tablespoons olive oil

2 tablespoons wine vinegar

1 tablespoon lemon juice

10 basil leaves, shredded

salt and pepper

1 teaspoon sugar

6 anchovy fillets, finely chopped – fewer if large

mum's tomato sauce

The apple and onion lighten the sauce a little in both colour and flavour, and you could add some chilli if you want a spicier flavour. Very good with cold meats or sausages. Do not use a food processor as it grinds the seeds and skin making a bitter taste.

Wash the tomatoes and chop roughly, there is no need to skin or remove the seeds. Put into a saucepan with the apple and onion. Cook gently until the apples and onions are tender and the mixture has very slightly thickened. Put through a sieve or moulin and return to the saucepan. Add the remaining ingredients. Cook the mixture over a gentle heat, uncovered, until it is a rich, red sauce. It should take only a few minutes. Pour into sterilized jars or bottles while warm. Be sure to heat the containers too, to ensure they will not crack.

Makes about 4–5 cups/2 pints

1 kg/2 lb ripe tomatoes

1 large Granny Smith apple, peeled, cored and roughly diced

2 large onions, roughly diced

1 teaspoon salt

1 teaspoon white or black pepper

generous pinch of cloves

¼ teaspoon nutmeg

1 cup/8 fl oz white vinegar

1 cup/8 oz white sugar

tomatoes stuffed with minced pork

I used to love making a Vietnamese-influenced dish of tomatoes stuffed with bean curd. An Asian friend told me that this kind of dish is often made with minced meats instead and served with rice as a main dish. Here is a version of that dish, tasty and quite easy to prepare as you can do the minced meat in advance, but it does need richly flavoured tomato to give the pork filling the perfect balance.

Heat the oil and fry the ginger, chilli, half the spring onions/scallions and all the garlic until aromatic. Add the minced pork and stir fry until it has changed colour, add the sugar and stock, fish sauce and simmer gently, covered, for 10 minutes. Add water chestnuts. Thicken lightly by mixing cornflour/cornstarch paste and stirring until a light sauce. Keep cooking gently until it is the thickness you want. (You can refrigerate for up to 24 hours at this point if you wish.)

Preheat oven to 180°C/350°F. Cut the tomatoes into halves. Scoop out the centre to leave a thick shell. Fill with the pork mixture and bake for about 15–20 minutes depending on the ripeness of the tomatoes. Before serving scatter the top generously with spring onions.

Variations

Other things you can do with this particular pork sauce:

- Mix with noodles (don't have the pork sauce too thick).

- Spoon over pieces of firm tofu that have been fried in a little oil until golden on the outside, top with spring onions/scallions and coriander/cilantro.

- Cook the sauce until it is quite thick. Cool. Mix with 4 eggs and pour into a shallow dish lined on the base with non-stick baking paper/parchment. Bake in a moderate oven (180°C/350°F) until set; cut into squares for serving.

Serves 4

4 tablespoons oil

2 teaspoons finely chopped fresh ginger

1 small chilli, deseeded and finely chopped

8 spring onions/scallions, finely chopped

2 cloves garlic, finely chopped

250 g/8 oz finely minced pork

2 teaspoons sugar

1 cup/8 fl oz chicken stock

1 tablespoon fish sauce

¼ cup/1½ oz drained, rinsed and chopped water chestnuts

2 teaspoons cornflour/cornstarch mixed with 2 tablespoons cold water

4 large or 6 medium-sized tomatoes

extra spring onions/scallions, chopped, to garnish

baked tomatoes with toppings

easy ideas

*Tomato and
Potato Curry*

Boil about 750 g/
1½ lb baby potatoes
and while they are
cooking fry a large
chopped onion in
plenty of oil with a
couple of chopped
cloves of garlic.
When onion and
garlic are soft add
a tablespoon of
curry powder and 5
peeled, diced, ripe,
medium-sized tom-
atoes. Let mixture
simmer for about
10 minutes. Drain
cooked potatoes,
cut into halves and
add to the tomato
sauce, stirring so
they are coated.
Scatter the top
with some mustard
seeds and sprigs
of coriander.

*For this dish, use big fat round varieties of tomato, which will sit flat and
have a good surface for covering with a tasty topping. I usually cut the
tomatoes in half across and make several small slashes in the top, then
season them lightly with salt, more generously with pepper and press on the
topping. As a rule, the tomatoes should take about 15–20 minutes, depending
on their size, to become just a little squashy and soft, yet not breaking up,
and the topping firm and lightly coloured.*

*Baked tomatoes with herb topping could accompany almost any meat dish,
or they make a good light meal with some toast or bread alongside. If you
make the anchovy topping you will find it pungent and heavily scented and
this tomato should be eaten on its own, rather than as an accompaniment.*

*If I think the skins are tough I cook the tomatoes and before serving just slide
the skin away with your fingers, it will come apart from the flesh very easily.*

Halve tomatoes. For herb topping, mix everything except the olive oil in a
bowl. Once the crumbs and herbs have been well mixed, add enough oil to
moisten. Press firmly on to the tomato halves and bake at 180°C/350°F for
15–20 minutes.

For anchovy topping, mix everything (you can add some parsley if you wish
to give lightness and a good colour). Cook as above.

Serves 4 as a side dish, 2 as a light meal

4 large tomatoes

Herb Topping

1 clove garlic, crushed

½ cup/2 oz breadcrumbs,
made from stale white bread

¼ cup/½ oz finely chopped basil

2 tablespoons finely
chopped parsley

1 teaspoon finely chopped
fresh rosemary

2 teaspoons finely chopped
fresh thyme

2 teaspoons finely chopped
fresh marjoram

salt and pepper

virgin olive oil

Anchovy Topping

2 cloves garlic, crushed

½ cup/2 oz breadcrumbs

4 anchovy fillets, chopped,
or to taste

2 tablespoons grated
Parmesan cheese

enough oil to moisten

baked tomatoes

*Best to do a bit extra of these as if you have any over they can be kept for
5 days and they are one of the most useful things to have on hand. Serve them
with any kind of antipasto as a first course, dice and mix into cooked pasta
or just put a thick layer between slices of bread for a rich tomato sandwich.
You need to do this at the last minute as the tomato is a bit squashy.*

Cut the tomatoes into halves lengthwise; season with salt, pepper, sugar and
brush with oil. Put a tiny bit of chilli sauce on top and arrange a garlic clove
on this. Put on some baking paper in a barely moderate oven, 160°C/325°F,
and leave for about 1½ hours or until well cooked and the tomato is almost
dry on the outside. But don't cook so they become a sun-dried tomato, they
are meant to have juice in the centre.

10 roma or egg-shaped tomatoes

salt and pepper

dash of sugar

a little oil

some Thai sweet chilli sauce

cloves of garlic, cut into shallow
slices lengthwise (optional)

tomatoes au gratin

Use ripe large tomatoes, allowing one per person. This dish is mild in flavour, despite the anchovy and garlic. The recipe comes from a cookbook that I love from that old Hemingway haunt – Harry's Bar in Venice. It needs to be made with a light-textured bread from a bakery, preferably a couple of days old. The quantity of bread will depend on what kind of bread you use, as coarse country bread like a sourdough absorbs more moisture. Whatever you do don't make it with soft fresh supermarket bread, which produces a tacky, soft topping without any texture. I like some finely grated fresh Parmesan cheese dusted on top when it is cooked, but this depends on what you may be serving with the tomato.

Preheat the oven to 180°C/350°F. Core the tomatoes and slice off the top, about 1½ cm/½ in down from top. Scoop out the seeds with your fingers and carefully squeeze out any remaining seeds and juice without breaking the sides of the tomatoes. Combine the oil, anchovy, onion and garlic in a small saucepan and cook over medium–low heat for 4–5 minutes or until the onion is translucent but not brown. Remove the pan from the heat and stir in the breadcrumbs, parsley, oregano and some salt and pepper. It will look quite a wet mixture. Fill the tomatoes with this, put them in an oiled ovenproof dish and bake for 20 minutes. The top should be a good golden-brown colour. If not, you can pop them under a griller/broiler for a few minutes to finish.

Serves 6

6 medium-sized tomatoes

¼ cup/2 fl oz olive oil

1–2 anchovy fillets, chopped

1 tablespoon finely chopped onion

1 garlic clove, chopped

1 cup/2 oz breadcrumbs, made from stale bread

2 tablespoons chopped flat-leaf parsley

1 tablespoon chopped fresh oregano or ¼ teaspoon dried

salt and ground pepper

grandmother's tomato relish

This has been a favourite ever since I can remember, a quite sweet, yet tart, relish which is chunky and different to tomato sauce as an accompaniment to meat pies, sausages. Use it in sandwiches or with any grilled or barbecued meat. It keeps really well from one tomato season to the next.

Put the tomatoes, onion and garlic into a big bowl and scatter salt on top. Let them stand for about 30–60 minutes and then strain and discard the liquid which has formed around them. If they are very ripe 30 minutes should be enough time, with firm tomatoes you can leave them for an hour. Put into a big saucepan with the sugar, allspice, cayenne, both kinds of vinegar and cook on a moderate heat until the tomato is soft and the mixture reduced by about half. It takes about 45 minutes but rely on the look rather than the timing. Mix the curry with mustard and cornflour. Add a bit of vinegar so you have a very thin paste and mix this into the tomato, stirring briskly. It will thicken quickly, just cook for a few more minutes and bottle straight away in hot, sterilized jars. Leave it for a few days before opening.

Makes about 4–5 cups/2 pints

1 kg/2 lb ripe tomatoes, peeled and cut into small pieces

1 large onion, diced small

3 cloves garlic, finely chopped

2 tablespoons kitchen salt

375 g/12 oz sugar

1 teaspoon allspice

¼ teaspoon cayenne pepper

1 cup/8 fl oz brown malt vinegar

1 cup/8 fl oz white wine vinegar

1 tablespoon curry powder

1 tablespoon cornflour/cornstarch

sufficient vinegar to make a thin paste

a french chicken curry

It may seem an unlikely dish from France but I first ate this in a wonderful little restaurant set close to the forest in the artist's town of Barbizon, just outside of Paris. It is very delicate, the base being made with rich summery tomatoes. You can use this lovely light curry base with other meats such as pieces of lamb or beef. It is aromatic but not too spicy.

Heat the oil and butter in a frying pan with a lid. Season the chicken pieces and cook gently on all sides until golden. Add about ½ cup/4 fl oz water, cover the pan and cook until tender. Remove the chicken and reserve the liquid.

To make the curry sauce, heat some oil and fry the onion until soft and golden. Add the tomatoes with the garlic and curry powder and fry until aromatic. Add the liquid from the chicken and cover the pan. Let it cook gently for 15 minutes then add the apple and cook again for a further 15–20 minutes or until everything is very soft. Purée the sauce in a food processor or, even better, put through a moulin. Return to the pan and add the cream, season and bring back to a boil, then add the chicken, spooning lots of juices over the top to coat each portion. You can then leave it at this stage for reheating. Refrigerate covered for anything up to 24 hours.

Reheat either in the oven or in a saucepan and serve with the top scattered with herbs and almonds. When reheating, if you feel the sauce has become too thick, add a few spoonfuls of stock or water. Some rice, a little mango chutney and pappadams can be served alongside.

Serves 4

3 tablespoons olive oil

30 g/1 oz butter

8 chicken portions, such as legs and thighs

salt and pepper

water

Curry Sauce

2 large onions, finely chopped

oil

3 large ripe tomatoes, peeled and chopped

3 cloves garlic, finely chopped

2 tablespoons mild curry powder

½ cup/4 fl oz chicken stock (from above)

1 large Granny Smith apple, peeled and diced

⅓ cup/3 fl oz thick/double cream

salt and pepper

finely chopped parsley, coriander/cilantro or basil, to garnish

some browned blanched almonds, to garnish

tomato and basil mayonnaise

The addition of tomato to a mayonnaise makes it more summery and interesting for a chicken salad, or you could spoon this over some halves of hard-boiled eggs laid flat on a platter so they are coated with a filmy pink layer. Any left over can be kept and spread on bread for salad sandwiches. Although this will keep well for several days, the basil will darken. I don't mind that because the flavour is often enhanced, but it is not so pretty.

If the skin of the tomato is firm, peel it. Cut the tomato into quarters and remove the seeds. Purée the tomato and mix into the mayonnaise, adding the pepper and basil. Stir and taste for seasonings and then refrigerate.

Enough to coat 1 small chicken or an egg salad for 4

1 large ripe tomato

½ cup/4 fl oz mayonnaise

dash of pepper

1 tablespoon finely chopped basil

easy ideas

Quick Winter Tomato Sauce

To make at times of the year when there are really no good tomatoes around but you still yearn for a tomato sauce for pasta or to accompany meat. This sauce has a good colour and very good flavour. Cook a chopped onion in ¼ cup/ 2 fl oz olive oil until softened, add 2 chopped cloves garlic. Mix in a 450 g/1 lb can of plum-style tomatoes, roughly breaking them up in the pan, and cook gently for 10 minutes. Take the skin from 1 kg/2 lb of fresh tomatoes, chop roughly and put into the sauce- pan with the cooked tomato mix, season and simmer another 10 minutes until thick and rich.

spicy tomato sauce

A simple but very good tomato sauce to bottle and keep for serving with sausages in the winter or meat pies. I often add more chilli than in this recipe but I rather like it very spicy. It is easy to sieve it if you have a moulin, otherwise you need to have a little patience and put it through a coarse sieve. You cannot use a food processor for this because it grinds up the seeds and skin and the flavour will then be bitter.

Wash the tomatoes and chop roughly. No need to skin or seed for tomato sauce. Put into a saucepan with the onion and garlic and cook over a gentle heat until slightly thickened. Pour the mixture through a sieve or moulin, then return to the saucepan and add the remaining ingredients. Cook a bit more until the consistency of a thickish sauce is reached. Pour while warm into equally warm sterilized bottles or jars.

Hint
It is easier to put through a sieve or a moulin if you don't let it become too thick first. It is quite easy then to simmer more until the right texture, remembering of course that it will be thicker when cold than when hot.

Makes about 4–5 cups/2 pints

1 kg/2 lb ripe tomatoes

1 large onion, roughly chopped

1 large clove garlic, chopped

1 hot chilli, roughly chopped

1 teaspoon paprika

1 cup/4 oz brown sugar

1 tablespoon lemon juice

1 cup/8 fl oz white malt
  or wine vinegar

1 teaspoon salt

generous pinch of cayenne pepper

sliced tomatoes with cheese topping

Baked in individual gratin dishes, this is great for lunch with toast or you can bake it as one big shallow ovenproof dish of tomatoes and serve it with plain meats. Almost any kind of melting cheese is suitable except ones that are very soft, although creamy cheese such as brie or camembert-style cook to an oily stage. It is not a dish for every day, with the lashings of cream and cheese, but tastes quite fresh because of the tomato base. I allow a large tomato for each person as a brunch or lunch dish, with some hot strips of buttered toast to mop up the juices, and serve them in little individual white gratin dishes.

Preheat oven to 180ºC/350ºF. Cut the tomatoes into thick slices and divide between 4 buttered shallow gratin dishes, or put all into a casserole dish. Dribble the sherry over the top of the tomato. Scatter with basil and bake for about 10 minutes or until the tomato is looking soft and juicy. Scatter cream over each one, using about 2 tablespoons per gratin dish. Then scatter the cheese so that the tops are evenly covered. Return to the oven and cook a further 10–15 minutes or until you have a creamy, crusty, magically scented golden seal on top. Decorate with a little parsley if you like some green on top of creamy things.

Serves 4

4 large ripe tomatoes

salt and pepper

1 tablespoon dry sherry

half a dozen basil leaves,
cut into shreds

½ cup/4 fl oz cream

90 g/3 oz grated cheese,
such as tasty/cheddar

a little chopped parsley

tomato tart tatin

Two impoverished gentlewomen from Lamotte-Beuvron in Sologne were forced to earn their living by baking apple pies with a caramel topping, turning them upside down. This became the famous Tarte Des Demoiselles Tatin and it became one of the most famous apple pies in the world. Following this all manner of variations evolved from their recipe, most picking up the name to indicate an upside-down tart. I have eaten peach tatin, pear tatin and now there is a tomato tatin. The principle is similar to the apple in that it has a well-flavoured, slightly sweet base of tomato with a crusty savoury biscuit topping that is inverted so you have an open tart to slice. The secret is to have a firm enough crust that is doesn't become soggy with juices that seep from the tomatoes, and light enough so it melts in your mouth. It is not really a bother to make, especially if you bake the roma tomatoes well in advance. I use a non-stick shallow cake tin and find it better than a glass or china container. Serve it for lunch or for a first course; leave it as the star as it has enough rich flavours not to take kindly to competition, except from a crisp and refreshing green salad.

6 roma tomatoes

salt and pepper

2 teaspoons sugar

some olive oil

2 onions, halved and thinly sliced

45 g/1 ½ oz butter

1 tablespoon sugar

1 tablespoon balsamic vinegar

basil leaves, to garnish

Pastry

1 cup/4 oz plain/all-purpose flour

pinch of salt

75 g/2½ oz butter, cut into small pieces

1 egg, beaten

a few teaspoons iced water, if needed

Cut tomatoes into halves, lengthwise, season with salt, pepper and plenty of sugar and dab a bit of oil on top. Bake in a barely moderate oven (160°C/325°F) for about 2 hours or until very soft. Let cool. Cook the onions with butter until very soft and golden; don't hurry this, as you want them to be quite sweet. Add the sugar and balsamic vinegar and cook again until well coloured. You can prepare both tomatoes and onions hours in advance.

Preheat oven to 200°C/400°F. Make the pastry by putting flour, salt and butter into a processor and process until crumbly. Add the egg and process again until it holds together, adding water if necessary. Put the tomatoes cut side down into a metal cake tin which has been generously smeared with butter. Top them with the onions. Roll out the pastry and put on top, cutting around the edges to fit and pressing down to give a good edge. Press down gently and bake in oven for about 25 minutes or until the pastry is cooked through. Run a knife around the edge carefully to loosen the pastry from the edge and leave for at least 10 minutes so the tomato juices settle, then invert onto a plate and garnish with small basil leaves.

Serves 6 as a first course, 4 as a lunch dish

tomato and vegetable chutney

easy ideas

*Tomato and
Salmon Salad*

Cut 500 g/1 lb
salmon into very
tiny dice and mix
with ½ cup/4 fl oz
lemon juice and a
teaspoon of salt.
Let fish stand for
30 minutes,
refrigerated and
covered. While it
is marinating mix
together a small
diced red onion,
3 finely diced ripe
tomatoes, a small
chilli with the
seeds discarded
and 3 tablespoons
oil. Strain the fish –
you don't want to
use the lemon juice
– mix into the
tomato and onion;
add some parsley
or coriander and
another fresh
squeeze of lemon
if the mixture is
not fresh tasting.
Serve as a first
course with some
crusty bread.

When cooked the vegetables blend into a tasty and lightly textured chutney, although the dominating colour and flavour are still those of tomato. This particular recipe improves with age, so leave for several weeks before opening any of the jars.

Put the capsicum/bell pepper, celery, onions and vinegar into a large saucepan and cook very gently until the vegetables are tender. It is best to put a lid on the pan once it has come to boil or the vinegar tends to boil away before the ingredients are softened sufficiently. While this is cooking, peel the tomatoes. Once peeled, chop the tomatoes, there is no need to remove the seeds. Put the tomatoes into the softened vegetables and vinegar. Add the cloves, salt, sugar and garlic. Simmer, uncovered, until thick. Depending on how juicy the tomatoes are – some varieties do have quite a bit of liquid – the cooking can take as long as 45–60 minutes. Leave to cool a little before bottling.

Makes 6–7 cups/3 pints

2 red capsicum/bell peppers, deseeded and flesh cut into small dice

2 stalks celery, finely sliced

3 large onions, finely diced

1 cup/8 fl oz brown vinegar

1.5 kg/3 lb ripe tomatoes

6 cloves

2 teaspoons salt

1 cup/8 oz sugar

2 large cloves garlic, chopped roughly

green tomato chutney

Use the green tomatoes on your bushes which you know will never have a chance to ripen or make it when you have so many ripe tomatoes that you need to think of something different with the rest of the crop. It is in the style of old country chutneys that, thick and slightly sweet, were served with all manner of cold meats or spread in sandwiches. It is best kept for a week before opening and will store for 12 months but, if you are keeping it that long, seal the top with a layer of paraffin wax first to prevent it drying out.

Put all ingredients into a saucepan and stir well. Cook over a medium heat, with a lid just slightly to one side of the pan until it is thickish and the colour has deepened. Give it an occasional stir but don't let it lose too much moisture. It usually takes 1½ hours to cook, but that will depend on the liquid in the tomatoes and the type of pan. Fill into hot, dry, sterilized jars and seal with a layer of paraffin wax and then a lid. If not keeping for long, a lid is sufficient.

Makes about 4 cups/2 pints (depending on how far you reduce mixture)

500 g/1 lb green tomatoes, cut into very small pieces

250 g/1/2 lb peeled, cored apples, finely diced

½ cup/3 oz sultanas

1 medium-sized onion, finely chopped

1 teaspoon salt

185 g/6 oz sugar

1½ cups/12 fl oz white wine vinegar

1 teaspoon ground pimento (all spice)

tomato chocolate cake

This may sound a strange cake, tomato and chocolate, but you would never know that the cake included tomatoes when eating it, just that this sticky chocolate cake is soft in texture with a rich pink chocolate colour. The quantity here makes 2 small cakes, which can be layered with cream between them, or freeze one for another time. I like 'gilding the lily': first a cream filling and then usually I spread a layer of fudge icing on top and let it trickle down the sides.

Butter two 20cm/8 in diameter cake tins. Line the bases with non-stick baking paper/parchment and lightly butter. Preheat oven to 180°C/350°F.

Peel the tomatoes and remove seeds, blend until smooth – you need 1¼ cups/10 fl oz of purée. In a basin over hot water, add the chocolate to the brown sugar, milk and 1 egg yolk and leave to cook until the chocolate has melted and the mixture is smooth and slightly thickened. Leave aside. Sift the flour with bicarbonate of soda and salt.

Cream the butter until light. Slowly beat in the sugar and add the remaining egg yolks, one at a time. Add the tomato pulp and vanilla essence and then slowly stir in the chocolate mixture. Add the flour and mix well. Beat the egg whites until stiff and fold into the batter, half at a time. Put the mixture into the cake tins, and bake in oven for about 25–30 minutes or until a toothpick inserted in the centre comes out clean.

Let cakes cool slightly before turning out of tins. The cake will be very moist, so it will be best to have a piece of non-stick paper on the cake rack. Fill with cream if desired.

For frosting, in a saucepan warm cocoa, butter and brown sugar, bring to a boil, add cream and cook until lightly thickened. Pour over the cake, smoothing it to the edges. It sets quickly.

500 g/1 lb ripe tomatoes

125 g/4 oz dark chocolate

1 cup/8 oz brown sugar

¼ cup/2 fl oz milk

3 egg yolks

2 cups/8 oz flour

1 teaspoon bicarbonate of soda/baking soda

pinch of salt

125 g/4 oz butter

1 cup/8 oz sugar

1 teaspoon vanilla essence

2 egg whites

Fudge Frosting

3 tablespoons sifted cocoa

60 g/2 oz unsalted butter

½ cup/4 oz brown sugar

⅓ cup/3 fl oz cream

turnip

Brassica rapa

Turnips are usually grown for their root, which is not really a root but rather a big swelling at the end of the stem, yet the green tops picked very young are spicy and delicious in soups and baby leaves can be tucked into salads or added to a stir fry. They are often considered to be rather a boring, low-class vegetable – at the very least one that can taste strong and coarse – but sadly this is so often because they are let grow too large and then they can be unpleasant. Luckily you can buy bunches of baby turnips. These are quite expensive and appear in top restaurants, alongside game, chicken or included in long-simmered casseroles. These little ones seem to have elevated the image of the turnip and baby turnips are prized in Europe. You can pickle turnips, glaze them so they are sticky and sweet, steam baby ones, cook the tops separately and then toss both together and serve with a casserole. If they are tiny enough they can be scrubbed and nibbled like radishes or used with dips.

They originated in eastern Afghanistan and parts of Pakistan. Much of their popularity in Europe is no doubt because they can be grown so easily despite cold European winters and have long-keeping qualities. They have an affinity with the dishes that go best in chilly weather: richly braised meats, lashings of butter and cream and pastries.

Swede are grown in a similar manner. These are a 'new' vegetable, having been created less than 200 years ago by crossing a turnip with a cabbage. Swede take up much more room than turnips in the garden and unless you love them and have lots of gaps in the vegetable bed it is probably best just to buy them. Swedes keep for a long time – for months in a cool place – and they are cooked in the same ways as large turnips, being especially good mashed with lashings of butter and some cream.

planting

Turnips do best in moist, well-drained soil. You don't need too much nitrogen or you get more tops, less turnip root. I find them really easy to grow once the weather is cool. I just scatter rows of seeds along my borders and then I lightly throw some soil on top. They are always far too close but as they come through, I thin them and these little thinnings of the baby green tops are quite special included in salads.

Temperature Zone	Sow
Tropical	Not suitable
Subtropical	Autumn–winter
Temperate	Autumn–early spring
Cool	Autumn-early spring
First picking	*3–4½ months*

varieties

Turnips

- White Globe
- White Stone
- Tokyo White Cross – a tiny turnip
- Gilfeather – an heirloom, even smaller with a mild sweet flavour.

Swede

- Royal Rose
- Champion Purple Top.

diseases and pests

Aphids like them; hose them off the plants or, if a really bad infestation, you can spray but mostly hosing works well.

harvesting

30 days, for green tops, to 60 days for turnips. Thin out the babies and use these tops, then continue taking them out as you wish. You may prefer to use them when the swollen root is tiny or allow some to become larger.

buying and storage

Turnips vary lots in shape and size. They are at their best in the shops once we have a spell of cold weather. Tops should look very fresh and the turnips should be heavy and firm. Rather than buying one large turnip, which is more likely to taste strong, it is better to choose several smaller ones for cooking. Swede should also look taut and firm and skip the monsters, they are more likely to be stringy.

Remove the leaves but don't wash, just put into the crisper in a vegetable bag and they should keep well for about 5 days. The tops have a short life and will wilt quickly so use within a day.

nutrition

Vitamin C, a sprinkling of other vitamins and some dietary fibre. The tops also have vitamins C and E, beta-carotene that is converted to Vitamin A in the body plus iron and are a good source of folate.

cooking

Very baby ones, especially if you have grown them yourself, may not need peeling but most others do as the skin can be bitter. Peel carefully and if large cut into small cubes or segments and boil in salted water in a covered pot until tender. Large turnips are not exciting boiled unless you jazz them up, glaze them, cover with a big knob of butter or use them in with other vegetables. They can be processed as they do not go gluey like potatoes and, with some cream, butter and plenty of pepper added, make a light, delicate dish. Tiny ones can be rolled generously in olive oil and baked in the oven just like small baked potatoes. Turnips can be pickled in the same way as carrots can (see p. 92).

If cooking turnip tops, the inner leaves are the best, sometimes a few of the outside leaves need to be discarded. Wash them well and cook in lightly salted water or stock; they take 4–6 minutes, depending on size.

turnip, vegetable and turmeric pasties

turnip goes with

butter

oil

lemon

orange

onions

carrots and other root vegetables

garlic

honey

leeks

beetroot

ginger

sausages

bacon

ham

duck

game

chicken

pork

rich casseroles

cheese

vinegar

pasta

An old-fashioned favourite, pasties can be made with meat in the filling as they were in Cornwall, but for many people they make a substantial vegetarian dish. The turmeric in this recipe gives a golden tinge to the turnips. It is important to cut the vegetables into very tiny dice so that everything will cook through in the centre of the pasties.

Peel the turnips, carrots and potato and cut into tiny dice. Put into a basin with the garlic, onion, salt, pepper and herbs. Chop the almonds roughly and mix through. Put a sheet of puff pastry on to the bench. If you want a thin crust you can roll it out a little.

Cut out a circle using a plate as a guide. Butter a flat tray and put the pastry to one side, as it is difficult to move once filled. Put a quarter of the turnip and carrot mixture on one side, fold the other side over and pinch the edges, rolling over slightly. Brush with egg on the edges and on top. Repeat – you will need 2 trays at least for the pasties.

Prick each pasty in the centre to release steam. You can leave them at this stage for up to 2 hours, refrigerated.

Preheat oven to 200°C/400°F and bake pasties for 10 minutes, and then turn the oven down to moderate (180°C/350°F) and cook for a further 20 minutes or until the vegetable juices are beginning to bubble through the top of each pasty. Let them rest for 5 minutes before serving.

Of course, these can be reheated if you want to make them in advance.

Serves 4

4 smallish or 2 medium-sized turnips

2 medium-sized carrots

1 large potato

2 cloves garlic, finely chopped

1 onion, finely diced

1 teaspoon salt

2 teaspoons ground turmeric

1/2 teaspoon ground pepper

2 tablespoons finely chopped parsley

2 teaspoons finely chopped fresh thyme

2 teaspoons finely chopped fresh sage

2 teaspoons finely chopped fresh marjoram

1/3 cup/1 1/2 oz blanched almonds, toasted

4 sheets butter puff pastry

1 egg beaten with 2 teaspoons milk

creamy mashed turnips or swede

An excellent purée to serve with any kind of winter casserole or crisp, grilled sausages. The addition of potato both lends a gentler flavour and helps to give some body to the turnip or swede, as they make a very sloppy purée on their own.

Cook turnips or swede together with potato in salted water until soft. Drain well. Purée in a food processor, adding butter and cream and season with some pepper. This will be a light, soft purée. Warm again before serving as it should be piping hot.

Serves 4

500 g/1 lb turnips or swede, peeled and cubed

1 medium-sized potato, peeled and cubed

salt and pepper

60 g/2 oz butter, cut into small pieces

1/4 cup/2 fl oz cream

turnip crunchies

Eat these as an interesting side dish to meat or game, or serve them as a nibble with drinks for something different. The turnip flavour is quite delicate as they are blanched first before they are fried with a crumb coating, which gives them a crunchy brown crust. I don't find these crunchies keep warm very successfully in the oven - they don't stay lovely and crisp.

Trim the ends from the turnip and cook in salted water for about 10 minutes or until barely tender. Drain and cool. Cut into thickish slices (sometimes I discard the small bits on the ends, which are difficult and too fiddling to crumb). Mix breadcrumbs with flour and spices and beat the egg with a fork. Pat the turnip rounds dry. Dip each round first into egg and then into the crumb mixture, pressing on lightly so it forms a coating on both sides. Leave on some kitchen paper towel in the refrigerator if preparing in advance but don't leave them longer than a few hours or the crumbs may go soft.

Deep fry in oil until golden and crisp and take them out with a slotted spoon, leaving them to drain on some crumpled paper. They should only take a few minutes to cook. Scatter a little sea salt and ground pepper on top.

Serves 6 as a side dish

3 medium-sized turnips

¾ cup/3 oz breadcrumbs, made from stale white bread

2 tablespoons plain/ all-purpose flour

½ teaspoon curry powder

good pinch of cayenne pepper

1 egg

sea salt and ground black pepper

easy ideas

Honey Turnip Cubes

Peel several smallish turnips and cut into cubes, cook quickly in plenty of salted water until tender and drain. Add a tablespoon of honey to the pot along with a big knob of butter, toss the cubes in this until glazed and tinged with gold. Season with some fresh pepper at the finish.

easy ideas *Turnips in Stock*

Cut 3–4 small peeled turnips into thin slices. Put into a saucepan with a small knob of butter, whole clove of peeled garlic and ½ cup/4 fl oz chicken stock. Cover and cook until tender, take off the lid and boil until the liquid is syrupy, add a generous pinch of brown sugar, a tablespoon of freshly chopped mixed herbs and a teaspoon of balsamic vinegar, toss and serve.

zucchini (courgette) and pattypan squash

Cucurbita sp.

Zucchini and pattypan squash both belong to the cucumber family, which has members in all manner of shapes and sizes. In gardening books they are referred to as summer squash. Most people who cook would only ask for them in the shops by their better-known name of zucchini, while punnets in nurseries are labelled zucchini whether they be yellow or green, custard or scalloped, button or pattypan squash, the name for the little round golden squash. Zucchini is one of the most rewarding plants to put into any garden because they are so easy to grow and give so generously. In the Australian sunshine zucchini have a wonderful flavour. You don't need many plants unless you intend to feed the whole street, along with your friends and family too. Zucchini are so prolific that a couple of plants is enough for a family of four to have a meal every day; half a dozen and it is difficult to use all the zucchini you will get. On my first attempt I planted too many and within a short time had no access to the paths as they sprawled casually across to the next garden, swallowing up the parsley in their wake as the vegetable garden turned into one giant zucchini monster.

planting

Like greedy new babies they are heavy feeders so plant in well-worked soil with good drainage, soil that has been well fertilized with compost dug in. It is usual to make a little hill and plant seeds or seedlings in this. I plant seedlings, mainly because a packet of seeds gives so many that most are wasted. If you do plant seeds place three seeds to form the corners of a triangle, each side about 6 cm/4 in long. This allows for the removal of the weaker two seeds when they come through the ground. Don't however just pull them out, cut the roots of the unwanted ones just below the surface so as not to disturb the strong plant.

Leave lots of space around them so they can sprawl out, spacing is important because zucchini and squash need plenty of air. They need lots of water too and on hot days the leaves can look wilted. This is of no concern unless it is first thing in the morning, indicating the roots are dry. If this happens water immediately. As soon as they are established and the weather is becoming warm I mulch around each plant very generously with lucerne or straw.

Temperature Zone	Plant
Tropical	All year, but not in the wet season
Subtropical	Early winter–mid summer
Temperate	Spring–mid summer
Cool	Mid spring–early summer
First picking	*8 weeks*

varieties

- Black Beauty – excellent, but mostly available only from seed and you can sow it earlier than Black Jack
- Black Jack – the most common
- Crookneck – a golden swan-necked plant
- Golden Zucchini – a popular hybrid
- There is a pale green, slightly striped one, is sold as white zucchini or occasionally Lebanese zucchini.

harvesting

The secret is to pick and pick them. Small they are exquisite and sweet and can be used in almost any dish, but large zucchini are quite coarse and watery and need to be limited to grating in dishes or being baked with stuffing. Medium-sized are good for grating, in cakes or pickling. Picking also helps the plant; as big zucchini left on suppress flowering and reduce the crop. Cut carefully with a small paring knife so you have a little bit of stalk. The knife should be wiped clean in case there is any disease, which you could spread to other plants.

The male blossom of all the squash family has a long stem, it provides pollen but no fruit, while the female can be identified by the swelling at the base which turns into the zucchini. Either of the blossoms can be picked and stuffed, used in salads, soups or for garnishing. It is optional whether you just use the flower or also pick the baby zucchini it is attached to.

Pattypan squash hang down from tiny branches and are at their most exquisite when quite tiny, with a buttery, melting taste. Care must be taken when picking as it is quite difficult to get under the big leaves of the plant so you need to lift the leaves gently and carefully cut away the squash or snip them through at the stalk with your fingernails. They snap off quite easily, as they are brittle.

diseases and pests

The main ones are squash bugs, borers or cucumber beetles, but they don't show up as a rule unless the plants are well developed with plenty of vegetables. I find mildew more of a problem and bacterial wilt. Ideally you should not water from the top, but this is not practical in my garden. I find it helps to make sure the garden is very healthy. Any plants that become infected should be removed straight away so disease doesn't spread. Don't put them into your compost, discard them completely. A good idea is to plant in spring, then again in mid summer for a second crop, as new plants are less liable to get powdery mildew.

buying and storage

Zucchini must be fresh and any soft bits indicate bitterness so don't buy them, the skin should be glossy, taut but not tough to touch. Refrigerate in a vegetable bag and use within a couple of days.

Pattypan squash vary a lot in the shops and the best are small; the older ones can have a tinge of bitterness if not very fresh. They don't keep well, the fresher the sweeter, and store in a vegetable bag in the refrigerator for again no more than a couple of days.

nutrition

Diets that are very high in squash – that includes zucchini – have been linked to lower rates of stomach cancer.

cooking

Don't peel zucchini unless you have picked a monster which will have tough, inedible skin. Zucchini only need a bit of the stalk end cut away and cooking in butter or oil, or they can be steamed. Boiling can make them a bit watery and they lose their delicate fresh flavour so it should be the last option.

It is best not to mess around with tiny pattypan squash, it would be a shame not to just leave them alone. They only need steaming or quickly boiling until just tender when pierced with a fine skewer. Drain and return them to the pan with a tiny knob of butter or a dash of good olive oil. If they are a little larger you can cook them until tender, drain and allow cooling a bit and cutting the squash into thick slices. Return it to the pan with some butter, salt and pepper and a little chopped parsley and shake it around over the heat until buttery juices surround the squash.

zucchini with chermoula

Chermoula is a highly flavoured Moroccan seasoning that is used with vegetables, poultry and fish. It is a combination of garlic and onion, coriander/cilantro and flat-leafed continental parsley, spiked with hot pepper or chilli. In this dish, chermoula is used with zucchini to give a great spicy taste to a vegetable, which can be bland. Serve on its own as a light lunch with some rice or use as an accompaniment to a grilled chicken or meat dish. Don't be tempted to throw the lot into a food processor, this will bruise the mixture and the flavours are not as good, additionally the juices that form develop a strong, slightly bitter taste. Chop very finely by hand to get the best texture and flavour.

Chop the onion finely. Crush the garlic and mix with chilli, pepper, cumin, cinnamon, salt and stir in the olive oil. Add the water and mix well. Wash the zucchini/courgette, top and tail them and cut each into halves lengthwise then put into a large frying pan (use two if necessary, as unless your pan is large you won't be able to fit them all in and they must sit in a single layer). Pour the chermoula over the top and move the zucchini/courgette aside a little so the liquid runs down into the pan. Cook over medium heat until boiling, turn the heat down and cook gently until the zucchini/courgette is tender, turning over once. It will take 12–15 minutes, depending on their size. If the pan is drying out too much add a few more spoonfuls of water. Scatter coriander/cilantro on top and squeeze a bit of lemon juice over at the finish.

Serves 6

1 small white onion

2 large cloves garlic

1 small chilli, deseeded and finely chopped

1/4 teaspoon ground black pepper

1/2 teaspoon ground cumin

pinch of cinnamon

1/2 teaspoon salt

6 tablespoons light olive oil

6 tablespoons water

12 baby zucchini/courgettes

1/4 cup/1/4 oz coriander/cilantro leaves

lemon juice

stuffed zucchini flowers

Cooked rice mixed with finely diced vegetables makes a lovely stuffing for zucchini flowers. A mix of cooked mushrooms bound with a spoonful of very thick cream sauce is another good stuffing, or you can cook one zucchini, dice finely, add it to some crumbs with cheese and tuck this into the flower.

This is a richer filling, made with ricotta cheese, and it is more suitable for a first course rather than an accompaniment. I admit it is a bit of a bother to make but an exquisite dish to share with special friends.

Gently open up the flower and remove the stamen. Check that there are no insects inside, but don't wash unless they are dirty. Heat the oil and fry the onion gently until quite soft. Add the sugar and fry for 30 seconds, then remove to a bowl. Purée ricotta in a food processor and add the egg. Mix into the onion and season well with salt and pepper. Add the spring onion/scallion or chives and cheese. Chill the filling so that it firms, or you will find it difficult to handle. Open out the flower and, using a spoon, fill with the stuffing. Carefully fold the petals over, they stick quite easily. You can do this in advance and put them on a dinner plate in the refrigerator.

When ready to cook, have a frying pan with enough oil to come about a third of the way up the sides and put the flour on to a plate. Beat the eggs in a bowl. Dip each flower into flour, shaking it over the top with a spoon if you find it messy, then quickly dip into egg, drain a little and immediately transfer to the pan. Let them cook gently so they sizzle, turning them over so they become golden on all sides and the filling sets. Drain well on kitchen paper towel and serve immediately. If you want an accompaniment, a fresh, light tomato sauce is best.

Serves 6

18 baby zucchini/courgette flowers

1 tablespoon oil

1 small onion, finely chopped

good pinch of sugar

¾ cup/3 oz ricotta cheese

1 egg

salt and pepper

3 tablespoons finely chopped spring onion/scallion or chives

2 tablespoons grated Parmesan cheese

plain/all-purpose flour

2 eggs, beaten with ½ teaspoon salt

a little oil

easy ideas *Zucchini Crumbed Chips*

One way to get children who hate zucchini to try this vegetable. You can use slightly larger zucchini for these. Cut into big fat sticks, just like chips. Dust with flour, then dip into some egg and finally breadcrumbs made from stale bread, patting them on. Chill on a plate for up to 6 hours. Cook in hot oil until crispy, remove and dust with a little salt or scatter with some cheese and grill a plate of the sticks until the cheese has melted on top.

savoury vegetable pudding

zucchini and
pattypan
squash go with

butter

olive oil

garlic

onions

lemon

pine nuts

walnuts

tomato

mint

coriander/
cilantro

basil

parsley

cheese

cream

anchovies

capsicum/
bell pepper

eggplant/
aubergine

This is like a savoury bread and butter pudding in which the bread is steeped in a mixture of milk and eggs, then combined with cooked vegetables and a generous amount of cheese. It makes a tasty, easy and economical dish that is very comforting to eat, like a childhood pudding. It can be prepared ahead, then cooked until it is lightly puffed, just set and the cheese has melted. A fresh tomato sauce can accompany it although the dish is quite moist on its own.

Put all the vegetables in a saucepan with the oil and water and let them stew gently for about 15 minutes, then cover and cook until very tender. Season well. Put the eggs and milk in a large basin, beat with a fork until combined. Cut the bread into small cubes, including the crusts for more texture. Add to the egg and milk; stir gently, then tip in the cooked vegetables, along with any juices and both cheeses. Leave to stand for an hour.

Butter an ovenproof casserole well. It is best to use a deep one such as a soufflé dish with a 5 cup/2½ pint capacity, so the dish does not cook too quickly. Preheat oven to 180°C/350°F. Put mixture into casserole and bake for 15 minutes, then turn the oven down to barely moderate (160°C/325°F) and continue baking for 15–20 minutes or until it is set to touch. Remove and let it sit for 5 minutes before serving in big spoonfuls or squares.

Serves 6

2 medium-sized onions, finely chopped

1 red capsicum/bell pepper, finely diced

2 cloves garlic, finely chopped

125 g/4 oz zucchini/courgette, cut into small pieces

1 medium-sized carrot, finely diced

kernels from 1 corn cob

2 tablespoons light olive oil

2 tablespoons water

1 teaspoon salt and some pepper

4 eggs

2 cups/1 pint milk

4 slices white, brown or wholemeal bread

1 cup/4 oz grated tasty/cheddar cheese

¼ cup/1 oz grated Parmesan cheese

zucchini salsa

Salsa really means a sauce and when making one everything should be cut up very small to be effective. Usually there is something hot in a salsa, something fresh and tart – some herbs and one or two main fresh ingredients. As it is eaten like a relish, it needs to be quite highly flavoured to be effective. You can make tomato salsa, mango salsa, pineapple salsa, chilli salsa, avocado salsa ... and you can buy several varieties in jars, however, these bear little resemblance to the taste of a freshly made one. Serve this particular salsa with grilled scallops or grilled or sautéed fish; it is also good on top of baked chicken.

Put the lemon juice, chilli, salt, pepper, oil and garlic in a basin.

Cut the zucchini/courgette into thin slices and again to make thin strips. Stack the strips and dice them. Mix the zucchini/courgette, tomato and onion into the dressing in the basin, stir and leave to marinate for about an hour, but not longer than 4 hours as both the zucchini/courgette and the tomato give out liquid. Drain a little if very wet before you serve it.

Serves about 4

1 tablespoon lemon juice

1 small red chilli, deseeded and chopped

¼ teaspoon salt

generous grind of black pepper

4 tablespoons vegetable or peanut oil

1 clove garlic, crushed

2 small zucchini/courgettes (in all weighing about 125 g/4 oz)

1 large tomato, peeled and diced

3 tablespoons finely diced red onion or mild white onion

2 tablespoons coriander/cilantro sprigs

zucchini and macaroni salad

Based on Italian salads which use a diced mixture of fresh tomato, basil, garlic, all well seasoned and left to stand so the tomato gives out highly flavoursome juice, this is an understated dish that is really far more delicious than it may sound. It is much lighter than the usual macaroni salad, which tends to be thick and heavy with creamy mayonnaise. As this is meant to be a zucchini dish rather than macaroni one, I use more zucchini than macaroni. It's essential, of course, to use really flavoursome tomatoes and good olive oil.

Marinate tomatoes in a bowl with the salt, sugar, chilli, garlic and basil and let stand while you finish the dish. There will be plenty of tomato juices by the time the macaroni is cooked. Put on a pot with plenty of boiling water and salt, add the macaroni and cook until just tender. Drain.

While the macaroni is cooking, cut zucchini/courgette lengthwise, then into strips and medium-sized dice. Heat the oil and fry the diced zucchini/courgette until it has brown bits on the edges and is just tender. Stir frequently so it colours evenly. Take off the heat and stir through balsamic vinegar.

Put the macaroni and zucchini into the tomato base with any garlic-flavoured oil from the pan, stir everything together and let the salad cool. Eat it straight away if you like or leave overnight refrigerated, more liquid then forms but this juice has a lovely flavour. Give it a good stir next day before serving.

Serves 4

4 ripe tomatoes, peeled and diced

1 teaspoon salt

1 teaspoon sugar

1 small chilli, deseeded and finely chopped

2 cloves garlic, crushed

12 basil leaves, torn in tiny pieces

250 g/8 oz small macaroni

6 small zucchini/courgettes (weighing about 600 g/ 1 1/4 lb in all)

1/3 cup/3 fl oz extra-virgin olive oil

1 tablespoon balsamic vinegar

easy ideas

Grated Zucchini

Grate on a coarse grater and gently squeeze out some of the liquid, but not until it is dry, as some juice is part of the charm of this dish. Heat a knob of butter; add a dash of virgin olive oil and cook, stirring until softened. It takes about 3 minutes. Mix in a clove of crushed garlic, salt and pepper and serve. It will be quite sauce-like.

zucchini purée

I first made this when I had a surplus of zucchini but discovered it was no good with large ones, which made a watery dish, as against small or even medium-sized zucchini with a full fresh flavour. I mainly use it as a side dish or a base for grilled meats or with fish.

Cook whole zucchini/courgette in a covered pan in plenty of boiling salted water until quite tender, it is important that the vegetable softens right through. Drain in a colander. Using a knife chop into the zucchini/courgette, cutting through into sections so you break it up, this allows more liquid to come away. Let it drain for at least 10 minutes more in the colander.

Heat the oil in a wide saucepan or frying pan, add the garlic and cook a few seconds, add zucchini/courgette and turn over until it is well flavoured with garlic oil and season. Transfer to a food processor and purée, adding basil halfway through. It reheats well in a pan or microwave and can be kept overnight in the refrigerator. Check seasoning, it should be a little spicy with pepper.

Serves 4

750 g/1 1/2 lb small zucchini/courgettes

salt

3 tablespoons extra-virgin olive oil

2 cloves garlic, finely chopped

salt and pepper

12 large basil leaves

green pie

The main ingredient is zucchini but several other greens are used at the same time to create a 'pie' which does not have a crust but rather the appearance of a savoury cake. It can be eaten warm but is very good cold and makes an interesting and easy-to-carry picnic dish, just cut it into wedges for serving.

Slice zucchini/courgette thinly and put into a colander with salt, turn over and leave to stand for 30 minutes, then rinse and drain well. Squeeze with your hands so you soften the slices. Mix with peas. Cook the spinach for a few minutes in water until softened, drain well and add to the other greens along with cheeses. Beat the eggs with a fork and add with crumbs, salt and pepper to the vegetables.

Heat oven to 180°C/350°F. Lightly butter a cake tin about 23 cm/9 in diameter and line the base with some non-stick baking paper/parchment. Put in the greens, pressing down firmly with the back of a spoon. Bake in oven for about 30 minutes or until it is set and the top is golden, the zucchini/courgette cooked through. Remove from the oven; put a plate over the tin and leave to rest for 15 minutes before inverting. Cut into wedges for serving.

Hint
To reduce the huge amount of liquid found in very large zucchini, grate and put onto a plate with a little table salt over the layers. Leave for 30 minutes, then squeeze out the excess liquid. A small trace of saltiness will remain so don't salt the dish and don't use this grated zucchini/courgette in sweet dishes such as a cake.

Serves 6–8

250 g/8 oz zucchini/courgette (about 3 smallish ones)

1 teaspoon salt

½ cup/2 oz peas, cooked until tender

½ bunch (250 g/8 oz) spinach, well washed and roughly shredded

125 g/4 oz goat's cheese, broken into small pieces

½ cup/2 oz grated Parmesan cheese

6 eggs

¼ cup/1 oz breadcrumbs, made from stale bread

salt and pepper

zucchini and rice casserole

This is rather similar in flavour to a pilaf, the rice is cooked in stock and becomes flavoured with zucchini and tomato. A great family dish as you can put it into the oven and then forget about it for a while until dinner time. I don't usually serve anything with it as the dish is quite substantial.

Heat oil and add rice and onions and cook until golden brown, stirring frequently. Add stock and bring to boil. Cover the pan and simmer for 10 minutes, stirring occasionally.

Place half the rice mixture in a buttered ovenproof dish and layer with half the zucchini/courgette slices. Pour over half the tomato sauce. Top with remaining rice, zucchini slices and tomato sauce. Sprinkle the top with cheese.

Preheat oven to 180°C/350°F. Cover casserole and bake for 30 minutes. For the last 10 minutes remove the cover and allow the cheese topping to brown.

Serves 4

2 tablespoons olive oil

1 cup/6½ oz long grain rice

2 onions, sliced

2 cups/1 pint chicken stock

4 zucchini/courgette, thinly sliced

2 cups/1 pint fresh tomato sauce (see 'easy ideas' on page 350 or 358)

1 cup/4 oz grated tasty/ cheddar cheese

stuffed pattypan squash

Use any larger ones for stuffing and as they are in season at the same time as corn is full of juice and sweetness, the combination of the two is a magic mix. It is not easy to judge the amount of stuffing as the squash can vary so much in size so you will just have to work that out a bit yourself when you buy them.

Boil the squash for about 5 minutes or until partly softened. You don't want them too hard or you won't be able to take out the centre easily. Grate the corn into a bowl; mix in the remaining ingredients except for crumbs. As soon as you can handle the squash take out the centre seedy part, leaving a cavity. Heap the ricotta and corn filling into this. Put into a lightly oiled baking dish and scatter on crumbs. Cover with foil and bake in a moderate oven (180°C/350°F) for about 20 minutes, then uncover and continue cooking for a further 20 minutes or until the squash is quite soft and the topping golden. They stay hot for some time in the centre so exercise a little caution and hold back before putting a big spoonful into your mouth.

Serves 4

8–12 pattypan squash, depending on size

2 corn cobs

1/4 cup/2 oz ricotta cheese

4 spring onions/scallions, finely chopped

salt and pepper

1/2 cup/2 oz grated tasty/ cheddar cheese

1 egg yolk

1/2 cup/2 oz breadcrumbs, made from stale bread

creamed zucchini

Julia Child, American icon of food, gave me this recipe and I love it because it is one dish that is good with zucchini which is not yet turned into a giant but is a little bigger than usual. The flavour of zucchini combined with a melting nutty cheese becomes quite sweet. It has been useful on many occasions when I need a side dish or base for some roasted meat that would be best served with a soft accompaniment.

Cook the onion in the oil in a frying pan until it is softened. Add garlic and zucchini/courgette and stir until it has softened. Melt the butter in a saucepan, add flour and cook, stirring for a few minutes, add zucchini/courgette and milk and stir it around until you have a thickened mixture. Take off the heat; mix in the cheese and season and transfer to a shallow ovenproof dish. You can complete the dish to this stage in the morning, cover and refrigerate.

Preheat oven to 200°C/400°F. Top casserole with crumbs and bake for about 25 minutes until the top is nicely browned and the dish is very hot.

Serves 4

1 onion, finely chopped

3 tablespoons olive oil

1 clove garlic, finely chopped

500 g/1 lb zucchini/ courgette, peeled and grated

45 g/1 1/2 oz butter

2 tablespoons flour

1/2 cup/4 fl oz milk

salt and pepper and dash of cayenne pepper

1/3 cup/1 1/2 oz grated melting-type cheese

1/4 cup/1 oz breadcrumbs, made from stale bread

easy ideas

Zucchini and Cheese Sauce for Pasta

Cook about 200 g/ 6 1/2 oz small mac-aroni and drain. While it is cooking soften 1 cup/4 oz roughly chopped spring onion/ scallion In a frying pan in some oil – it will only take a couple of minutes – and then add a couple of grated medium-sized zucc-hini/courgette, lots of salt and pepper and stir gently until they are soft and juicy. Add 1/4 cup/ 2 fl oz cream and heat. The sauce should be very moist. Stir through some grated Par-mesan, mix into the macaroni and then top each por-tion with a little more, preferably in fine shavings to give a different texture and richer cheese flavour. This makes enough for a meal for 2 people but can easily be doubled.

chocolate zucchini cake

Impossible to taste any zucchini in this cake. It has quite a crisp crust and a very moist, sticky centre, almost like a pudding and, of course, like most vegetable and yoghurt-based cakes, will keep for a week.

Preheat oven to 190°C/375°F. Cream the butter with sugar and citrus rinds. Beat the eggs with a fork and gradually beat into the creamed base. Mix in zucchini/courgette. Sift the flour with cocoa over the top and then mix through, adding buttermilk. Stir in the nuts last. Butter and line the base of a 23 cm/9 in diameter cake tin with some non-stick baking paper, put in the cake mixture and bake for about 45 minutes or until firm to touch. Leave for 5 minutes before inverting onto a rack.

To make icing, warm the butter with brown sugar until the sugar is melted. Sift the cocoa into the saucepan and stir over the heat, and then add cream. Boil for a minute, cool just a minute or two but don't leave it thicken too much and pour over the top of the cake, allowing it to trickle down the sides. Scatter extra nuts on top, if desired.

Note
To make 1 cup/4 oz self-raising flour, to each 1 cup/4 oz plain/all-purpose flour add 1½ teaspoons baking powder and ½ teaspoon salt.

185 g/6 oz butter, cut into small pieces

1 cup/8 oz light brown sugar

1 teaspoon grated orange rind

1 teaspoon grated lemon rind

2 large eggs

1½ cups/6 oz grated zucchini/courgette, squeezed as dry as possible

1½ cups/6 oz self-raising flour (see Note)

2 tablespoons cocoa

¾ cup/6 fl oz buttermilk

⅓ cup/2½ oz roughly chopped pistachio or pecan nuts

Icing
45 g/1½ oz unsalted butter

¼ cup/1 oz brown sugar

¼ cup/1 oz cocoa

¼ cup/2 fl oz cream

pistachio or pecan nuts, to decorate

zucchini bread

This is rather more like a cake than bread but is one of the most useful and moist breads. The recipe was first published in the United States. Like many of these recipes it has a base of oil rather than butter, good if you are on a low-fat diet, and makes an inexpensive bread as zucchini is so reasonably priced in summer. It freezes very well.

Butter a loaf tin 20 x 10 cm (8 x 4 in), and line the base with some non-stick baking paper/parchment. Preheat oven to 180°C/350°F.

Beat the eggs with sugar and vanilla until thick. Grate the zucchini/courgette. You should have a good, firmly packed cup. Add to the egg and mix in oil. Sift the dry ingredients over the top and stir with a wooden spoon for 30 seconds, add the nuts and stir again for another 30 seconds and pour into the prepared tin.

Bake for about 45 minutes or until golden brown on top and firm to touch. Leave to cool in the tin for 10 minutes, then turn out on to a cake rack to cool completely. This is so moist it will taste a little doughy if you try to eat it warm so give it about 4 hours to become quite cold before cutting with a sharp, serrated knife.

2 large eggs

1 cup/8 oz castor/superfine sugar

a little vanilla essence

200 g/6½ oz zucchini/courgette

⅓ cup/3 fl oz light olive oil or peanut oil

1½ cups/6 oz plain/all-purpose flour

½ teaspoon bicarbonate of soda/baking soda

½ teaspoon baking powder

½ teaspoon cinnamon

⅓ cup/1½ oz roughly chopped walnuts

chocolate zucchini cake ▶

zucchini pickles

Bread and butter pickles were always made with cucumber and big jars of them were kept in country kitchens. Sometimes they were known as Same Day Pickles because you can eat them just a few hours after they are made. They are a very easy and quick pickle. This version uses zucchini and I like it even more than when made with cucumber. It goes very well with cheese, meats or in sandwiches. Choose firm, medium-sized zucchini and if you find some which have played hide and seek with you and managed to evade being cut from the bush you can use these – unless they have tough skin.

Put the onions into a large bowl. Slice the zucchini/courgette thinly, a little on the diagonal rather than straight so you have a large surface. Cover with cold water, add salt and put a plate on top to weight them down. Leave stand for 2 hours and drain.

Put all the remaining ingredients into a large saucepan and bring slowly to a boil until the sugar has dissolved. Tip the onion and zucchini into this and stir, pushing the mixture under the liquid, as there won't seem to be enough. Heat for 1 minute, then tip into the basin and let cool completely. Bottle in sterilized jars and leave for a few hours before using. It is best eaten within 3 months and, when you open a jar, store the rest it in the refrigerator.

Makes about 6 cups/3 pints

3 medium-sized white onions, finely sliced

1 kg/2 lb zucchini/courgettes

1/3 cup/2 oz kitchen salt

2 cups/1 pint white wine vinegar

250 g/8 oz white sugar

1 tablespoon yellow mustard seeds

2 teaspoons ground turmeric

generous pinch of cayenne pepper

zucchini pancakes

An easy way to get kids to eat zucchini. You can also serve them as a stack with grated cheese between each pancake, or spread with some finely diced tomato mixed with a little basil and sour cream or yoghurt. I quite like them cold next day topped with a dollop of mayonnaise. They are very moist and quite fragile so when you are turning them flip over gently.

Cook the onion in butter or oil until softened. Put into a bowl and grate zucchini/courgette over the top. Mix eggs with all the remaining ingredients except oil and when thoroughly blended add to the vegetable. Once you have mixed batter the pancakes should be cooked within an hour as the zucchini/courgette leaks liquid into the base. Have a little oil in a frying pan, add a big spoonful of the batter and spread out thinly so the grated zucchini/courgette will cook through. Once golden turn over and cook on the second side. Don't have the heat too high or the pancakes brown too much before the mixture is properly cooked. Transfer to some kitchen paper towel and keep warm in a low oven while you cook the rest.

Note
To make self-raising flour, to each cup/4 oz plain/all-purpose flour add 1½ teaspoons baking powder and ½ teaspoon salt.

Makes about 16 small pancakes

1 onion, finely chopped

45 g/1½ oz butter or 2 tablespoons olive oil

500 g/1 lb zucchini/courgette

2 eggs

½ cup/2 oz breadcrumbs, made from stale bread

¼ cup/1 oz self-raising flour (see Note)

salt and pepper

pinch of cayenne pepper

1/3 cup/1½ oz grated melting cheese such as Jarlsburg

some oil to cook the pancakes

bibliography

Magic and Medicine of Plants. Reader's Digest, Sydney. 1994.

Alexander, Stephanie. *The Cook's Companion.* Viking, Ringwood, Vic. 1996.

Barron, Rosemary. *Flavours of Greece.* William Morrow & Co., NY; Ebury Press, London. 1991.

Boxer, Arabella and Traeger, Tessa. *A Visual Feast – The Year in Food.* Random Century Ltd, London. 1991.

Brown, Kathy. *The Edible Flower Garden.* Lorenz Books, London. 1999.

Budwig, Robert. *The Vegetable Market Cookbook.* Angus & Robertson, Pymble, NSW. 1993.

Bugialli, Giuliano. *Giuliano Bugialli's Foods of Italy.* Stewart, Tabori & Chang, N.Y. 1984.

Carrier, Robert. *A Taste of Morocco.* Boxtree Ltd, London. 1997.

Child, Julia. *The Way to Cook.* Alfred A. Knopf Inc., NY. 1989.

Cipriani, Arrigo. *The Harry's Bar Cookbook.* Smith Gryphon Ltd, London. 1991.

Duff, Gail. *The Countryside Cook Book.* Sphere, London. 1982.

Duff, Gail & Mick. *Food from the Country.* Macmillan, London. 1981.

French, Jackie. *The Best of Jackie French.* Harper Collins, Pymble, NSW. 2000

Green, Bert. *Greene on Greens.* Workman, NY. 1984.

Grigson, Jane. *Jane Grigson's Vegetable Book.* Michael Joseph, London. 1978.

Hughes, Phyllis. *Pueblo Indian Cookbook.* Museum of New Mexico Press, Santa Fe, NM. 1977.

Jaffrey, Madhur. *Eastern Vegetarian Cooking.* Jonathan Cape, London. 1983.

Larkcom, Joy. *Creative Vegetable Gardening.* Mitchell Beazley, London. 1997.

Lee-Richards, Michael. *Cook!.* Reed Books, Auckland. 1995.

Lo San Ross, Rosa. *Beyond Bok Choy.* Artisan, NY. 1996.

Loewenfeld, Claire and Back, Philippa. *The Complete Book of Herbs and Spices.* David & Charles, Newton Abbott, UK. 1974.

Levy, Faye. *Fresh from France: Vegetable Creations.* E. P. Dutton, NY. 1987.

Sahni, Julie. *Indian Heritage Cooking.* Walker Books, London. 1988.

Slater, Nigel. *Real Good Food.* Fourth Estate, London. 1995.

Spieler, Marlena. *The Flavour of California.* Angus & Robertson, Pymble, NSW 1992.

Stanton, Rosemary. *Vegetables.* Allen & Unwin, Sydney, NSW. 2000.

Trotter, Charlie. *Charlie Trotter's Vegetables.* Ten Speed Press, Berkeley, CA. 1996.

Tropp, Barbara. *The Modern Art of Chinese Cooking.* William Morrow & Co. Inc., NY. 1982.

index